DATE DUE

DEMCO 38-296

CAMBRIDGE STUDIES IN ENGLISH LEGAL HISTORY

THE EARLY HISTORY OF THE LAW OF BILLS AND NOTES

CAMBRIDGE STUDIES
IN ENGLISH LEGAL HISTORY

Edited by

J. H. BAKER

Fellow of St Catharine's College, Cambridge

Recent series titles include

The law of treason in England in the later Middle Ages
J. G. BELLAMY

William Sheppard, Cromwell's law reformer
NANCY L. MATTHEWS

The English judiciary in the age of Glanvill and Bracton *c.* 1176–1239
RALPH V. TURNER

Pettyfoggers and vipers of the Commonwealth
The 'lower branch' of the legal profession in early modern England
CHRISTOPHER W. BROOKS

Sir William Scott, Lord Stowell
Judge of the High Court of Admiralty, 1798–1828
HENRY J. BOURGUIGNON

Sir Henry Maine
A study in Victorian jurisprudence
R. C. J. COCKS

Roman canon law in Reformation England
R. H. HELMHOLZ

Fundamental authority in late Medieval English law
NORMAN DOE

Law, Politics and the Church of England
The Career of Stephen Lushington 1782–1873
S. M. WADDAMS

The early history of the law of bills and notes
A study of the origins of Anglo-American commercial law
JAMES STEVEN ROGERS

THE EARLY HISTORY
OF THE
LAW OF BILLS
AND NOTES

A STUDY OF THE ORIGINS
OF ANGLO-AMERICAN COMMERCIAL
LAW

JAMES STEVEN ROGERS

Boston College Law School

CAMBRIDGE
UNIVERSITY PRESS

the University of Cambridge
treet, Cambridge CB2 1RP
, NY 10011–4211, USA
elbourne 3166, Australia

© Cambridge University Press 1995

First published 1995
Reprinted 1996

Printed in Great Britain by Athenæum Press Ltd, Gateshead, Tyne & Wear

A catalogue record for this book is available from the British Library

Library of Congress cataloguing in publication data

Rogers, James Steven, 1951–
The early history of the law of bills and notes: a study of the
origins of Anglo-American commercial law / by James Steven Rogers.
      p.   cm. – (Cambridge studies in English legal history)
Includes bibliographical references.
ISBN 0 521 44212 5
1. Negotiable instruments – Great Britain – History. 2. Bills of
exchange – Great Britain – History. I. Title. II. Series.
KD1695.R64 1995
346.41'096 – dc20
[344.10696]   94–15928   CIP

ISBN 0 521 44212 5 hardback

TO
DOROTHY AND EMMA

CONTENTS

Preface   *page* xi
Table of cases and precedents   xv
Note on citation   xxv

Introduction   1

1   The central courts, commercial law, and the law
      merchant   12
      Commercial cases in the central courts   12
      The law merchant and the mercantile courts   20
      The law merchant in the central courts   27

2   Early exchange transactions: commercial practice   32
      Exchange transactions as means of funds transfer   32
      Exchange transactions as finance   36
      The dual functions of exchange   41

3   Early exchange transactions: private law   44
      Exchange contracts in the mercantile courts   44
      Exchange contracts in the Admiralty Court   51
      Exchange contracts in the common law courts   54

4   Early exchange transactions: public law and policy   69
      The debate over usury in exchange   70
      The exchange controversy in England   75
      The significance of the public controversy over
      exchange   88

5   From exchange transactions to bills of exchange:
      the transformation of commercial practice   94
      The era of exchange transactions and the era of bills of
      exchange   94
      The middleman economy and the development of
      inland bills   100

The economic functions of bills in the seventeenth
and eighteenth centuries   108

6 The custom of merchants and the development of
   the law of bills   125
   Actions on bills versus actions on exchange contracts   125
   Development of pleadings for actions on bills   127
   The significance of the changes in pleading   131
   The role of the custom of merchants   137

7 The civilians and the law of bills in the seventeenth
   century   151
   Civilian literature on the law merchant and exchange   151
   The political context of the seventeenth-century
   English literature on the law merchant   153
   A genuine but unsuccessful effort to incorporate
   civilian law   160
   The impossibility of incorporation   164

8 Transferability and negotiability   170
   Transferability   170
   The promissory notes cases: drawing the boundary
   between the law of bills and the general law of
   obligations   177
   Rights of bona fide holders   186

9 The law of bills and notes in the eighteenth century   194
   Acceptance   195
   Delay in presentment and notice of dishonour   202
   Lord Mansfield and the law of bills   210

10 The problem of accommodation bills   223
   The Livesey bankruptcy and accommodation bills   223
   The economic context of the accommodation bills
   cases   228
   The judicial response to accommodation bills   232
   The accommodation bills controversy as an illustration
   of the role of law in economic controversies   246

   Conclusion   250

   Bibliography   253
   Index   265

PREFACE

The research and study that resulted in this book was prompted not by an interest in legal history as such, but by a concern with the state of modern commercial law. Some years ago, in the process of teaching American law school courses in commercial law, I came to the realization that something was amiss with the law of negotiable instruments as embodied in Articles 3 and 4 of the American Uniform Commercial Code, which serves as the basis for much of the law governing payments by cheque. Standard sources on modern law included enough historical background to make it clear, even to one unschooled in legal history, that the transactions involved in the eighteenth-century English cases in which what we now know as negotiable instruments law developed bore little if any resemblance to modern payment and credit transactions. The basic rules and conceptual structure of the law, however, seem to have remained unchanged. I could not help but suspect that many of the problems in current law might be attributable to the profession's failure to give serious consideration to whether the basic concepts of negotiable instruments law remained a sound basis for modern law. That concern was heightened by the realization that we were rapidly moving toward a payment system in which the pieces of paper that form the basis of negotiable instruments law would be replaced by electronic media. Ironically, the concern for the future of commercial law led me to examine its past. Much of the literature on the emerging law of electronic payment systems seemed to proceed from the assumption that present law is well adapted to the technology and practice of the cheque system, and that the problem is to determine what changes are made necessary by new technology. By contrast, I had come to believe that the basic conceptual structure of twentieth-century law was itself a relic of the past and fundamentally ill-suited even to the paper-based cheque system. Prompted by these concerns, I set out on what I thought would be a relatively brief foray into the history of negotiable instruments law which would serve as the basis for further work on problems of the commercial law of the present and future.

What I initially envisioned as a project involving nothing more than tracing American law of bills and notes from the early nineteenth century to the present quickly grew to encompass not only law but business and economic history, not only the Anglo-American experience but that of many cultures, and not only the recent past but many centuries. Along the way, I became fascinated with legal history in its own right, and nearly gave up any thought of returning to work on modern law. The original impetus has, however, had a significant impact on the scope and approach of the project, and it may be appropriate to elaborate in order to assist the reader in assessing this work.

As I began examining early-nineteenth-century American cases involving bills and notes, I found that I could not understand the history of negotiable instruments law without a better understanding of the history of commercial practice. Accordingly I turned to the literature on business and economic history, starting with accounts of nineteenth-century American practice. I found, however, that I could not understand American practice in isolation, both because of the extent to which the American economy was linked to the English economy and because American commercial practice and law was largely based on earlier English experience. I turned to an examination of English practice and law, but found that since the English drew much of their commercial technique from the Dutch, I had to examine the practice of merchants of the Low Countries in the sixteenth and seventeenth centuries, and since the merchants of the Low Countries drew much of their commercial technique from the Italian merchants who had established outposts in Bruges and elsewhere in northern Europe, my path led back to the affairs of the merchants and bankers of Renaissance Italy. No doubt early Italian commercial techniques were influenced by the practices of the medieval Arabic merchants with whom they traded on the eastern shores of the Mediterranean, but I concluded that enough was enough.

Armed with some sense of the history of commercial practice, I turned to the examination of strictly legal sources. Again I encountered the problem of a constantly expanding universe of fruitful lines of inquiry. Initially, I thought that since my study was focused on the specifics of law and practice concerning negotiable instruments, there was neither need nor occasion for me to devote much attention to broader questions about the development of commercial law generally nor to enter into the long-standing debates about the jurisprudential nature of the 'law merchant'. I found, though, that in the Anglo-American tradition the subject of bills and notes has occupied such a prominent place in theories of the development of commercial law and accounts of the relationship between the law merchant and the common law, that it was not possible to separate the narrower from the broader inquiry. Indeed, the inquiry into the meaning of the law merchant seemed to move irresistibly from the background to centre stage, and the history of the law of bills became less the subject itself than the vehicle for examination of larger issues about the relationship between commercial law and commercial practice and the role of social and economic conflict in the evolution of private law rules.

One consequence of my inability to maintain firm control over the definition of the subject is that this work may well be open to the criticism of dilettantism. I am convinced that allowing the scope to expand has enabled me to produce a richer account of the history of the law of bills than that found in the standard works on Anglo-American legal history or modern commercial law, yet I realize that I have covered far more material than I could hope to master completely and have undoubtedly overlooked many bodies of literature that would have contributed to a more complete and accurate understanding of various aspects of the topics that I have touched upon. In particular, I have made only the most limited use of the rich literature of continental legal history that might provide a valuable comparative perspective on, and might indeed be directly relevant to, the story of the development of Anglo-American commercial law.

The rather circuitous path that this work has taken also explains, though may not entirely justify, the ambiguity about whether this is strictly a work on legal history or a work on the historical foundations of modern law, and whether it is a work on English law, American law, or both. Measured by the events, ideas, and legal doctrines described, this is unquestionably a work on English legal history. Yet inasmuch as the work began as, and remains in part, an effort by an American commercial law professor to understand the historical origins of his subject, it can be described as a work on the origins of Anglo-American commercial law. Fortunately, for the period covered, it seems fair to speak of English and American law as a single system. As in so many other fields, American law of bills and notes was in large measure based on English sources, and throughout the late eighteenth and early nineteenth centuries each system freely drew upon authorities from the other. By the middle of the nineteenth century, the differences in practice and in particular substantive legal rules had probably become sufficiently significant that a comprehensive history of doctrine and practice would require separate treatment of the two systems. This work, however, carries the story only up to the beginning of the nineteenth century, so treating the subject as Anglo-American seems appropriate. Since the assumptions about the historical foundations of negotiability described herein are common to both systems, where reference to modern law or practice is required in order to illustrate the assumptions that underlie the traditional accounts of the early history of the law of bills, I have drawn freely upon my own familiarity with modern American law and practice rather than seeking out parallel examples in modern English law and practice.

I am indebted to many persons for comments and encouragement on this project, or parts of it, at various stages. In particular, I wish to thank John Baker, Daniel Coquillette, Charles Donahue, Domenico Maffei, James Oldham, and Vito Piergiovanni. The staffs of the Boston College Law School Library and Harvard Law School Library provided great assistance.

Earlier versions of parts of this book have been published in article form as 'The Myth of Negotiability', *Boston College Law Review* 31 (1990): 265–334, and 'The Problem of Accommodation Bills: Banking Theory and The Law of Bills and Notes in the Early Nineteenth Century', in *The Growth of the Bank as Institution and the Development of Money-Business Law*, edited by Vito Piergiovanni, 119–55, Comparative Studies in Continental and Anglo-American Legal History, band 12, Berlin: Duncker & Humblot, 1993.

TABLE OF CASES AND PRECEDENTS

Abingdon v. *Martin* (1293), 23 SS 65   *page* 173, 174

Aboas v. *Raworth* (1666), Vidian, *Exact Pleader*, 30   128, 171

Ancher v. *Bank of England* (1781), 2 Doug. 637   212

Anon. (*c.* 1560s), Rastell, *Entrees*, 10r   57, 132, 133

Anon. (1647), Style 31   15

Anon. (1652), Style 366   146

Anon. (1693), Holt 115, Skin. 343, query s.c. *Williams* v.
    Field (1693), 3 Salk. 68   172–73

Anon. (1697), 1 Com. 43   189, 220

Anon. (1698), 1 Ld Raym. 738, 1 Salk. 126, 3 Salk. 71   187

Anon. (1698), 2 Salk. 669   167

Anon. (1698), Holt 296, 12 Mod. 345   198

Anon. (1700), Holt 298, 12 Mod. 408   203

Anon. (1701), 12 Mod. 447   196

Anon. v. *Elborough* (1677), 3 Keb. 765   182

Appleby v. *Biddle* (1717), cited in *Morice* v. *Lee* (1725), 8
    Mod. 362   185

Appleton v. *Sweetapple* (1782), 3 Doug. 137   205, 212, 221

Ashurst v. *Thomas* (1666), Vidian, *Exact Pleader*, 33   128

Aswel v. *Osborn* (1627), Vidian, *Exact Pleader*, 67   128

Aubrey v. *Flory* (1321), Y.B. 14 Edw. II, Eyre of London,
    86 SS 235   14, 24, 30

Austen v. *Castelyn* (1541), *Select Pleas Admiralty*, 6 SS 106   52

Bagshaw v. *Playn* (1596), Cro. Eliz. 536, Moore 704   56

Banbury v. *Lisset* (1744), 2 Str. 1211   213–14, 220

Bandon's Case, Y.B. 6 & 7 Edw. II, Eyre of Kent, 27 SS
    48, s.c. *Seclect Cases Law Merchant*, 46 SS lxxxi; s.c.
    sub nom. *Compton* v. *Anon.*, *Select Cases Law Merchant*,
    46 SS lxxxii; s.c. sub nom. *Comberton* v. *Comberton*,
    Select Cases Law Merchant, 46 SS lxxxiv   30–31

Bank of England v. *Newman* (1698), 12 Mod. 241, 1 Ld
  Raym. 442, 1 Com. 57   146–47
Bank of Ireland v. *Archer & Daly* (1843), 11 M. & W. 383   201
Barnaby v. *Rigalt* (1632), Cro. Car. 301   128, 136, 140
Barnesley v. *Baldwyn* (1741), 7 Mod. 417   185
Bate's Case (1606), 2 Howell's State Trials 371   157
Beaulieu v. *Finglam* (1401), Y.B. 2 Hen. IV, f. 18, pl. 6   142
Bellasis v. *Hester* (1697), 1 Ld Raym. 280   222
Beresford v. *Bacon* (1604), 2 Lutw. 1317   139
Bickerdike v. *Bollman* (1786), 1 T.R. 405 172, 208–9, 240, 243–44
Bilson v. *Hill* (1734), 7 Mod. 198   216
Blackhan v. *Doren* (1810), 2 Camp. 503   209
Blanke v. *Spinula* (1520), K.B. 27/1036, m. 75   6
Blesard v. *Hirst* (1770), 5 Burr. 2670   153, 219
Bolay v. *Whitring* (1320), *Court Baron*, 4 SS 131   25
Bomley v. *Frazier* (1721), 1 Str. 441   188, 215, 217, 220
Boyer v. *Bampton* (1741), 7 Mod. 334, 2 Str. 1155   190
Bromwich v. *Loyd* (1697), 2 Lutw. 1582   140, 182
Brown v. *Harraden* (1791), 4 T.R. 148   210
Brown v. *Robinson* (1634), Mich. 9 Car. I, cited in Viner's
  Abridgment, Account 019   18
Browne v. *London* (1670), 1 Mod. 285   165
Brun de St. Michel v. *Troner* (1275), 2 SS 152   173
Buckley v. *Cambell* (1706), 11 Mod. 92, 1 Salk. 131   222
Bucknam v. *Carr* (n.d.), Vidian, *Exact Pleader*, 17   128
Buller v. *Crips* (1703), 6 Mod. 29   101, 141, 177–86, 218
Burman v. *Buckle* (1686), Comb. 9   183
Burton v. *Davy* (1437), *Select Cases Law Merchant*, 49 SS
  117   45–51, 174
C. W. v. *J. B.* (1595), Rastell, *Entrees*, 3rd edn 338r   58–59,
                                                63–67, 129, 132, 135
Camby v. *Sardouch* (1364), *Calendar of London Plea and
  Memoranda Rolls*, 2: 10   48–49
Carrier's Case (1473), Y.B. 13 Edw. IV, 64 SS 30, 32   22
Carter v. *Downish* (1688), 1 Show. 127, Carth. 83, 3 Mod.
  226   142–43, 165
Carter v. *Palmer* (1700), 12 Mod. 380   141, 173
Carvick v. *Vickery* (1783), 2 Doug. 653   213
Case de Tanistry (1608), Davis 28   139
Chantflower v. *Priestly* (1603), Cro. Eliz. 914   14

Charles v. *Marsden* (1808), 1 Taunt. 224   237
Chievly v. *Bond* (1691), 4 Mod. 105, Carth. 226, 1 Show.
341, Holt 427   167
Clarke v. *Cock* (1803), 4 East 57   201
Clarke v. *Robinson* (1662), Vidian, *Exact Pleader*, 34   171
Clavey v. *Dolbin* (1736), Cas. t. Hard. 278   198
Claxton v. *Swift* (1686), 2 Show. 441, 494, Comb. 4,
3 Mod. 86, 1 Lutw. 878, Skin. 255   146, 171, 173, 188
Clegg v. *Cotton* (1802), 3 Bos. & Pul. 239   209
Clerke v. *Martin* (1702), 2 Ld Raym. 757, 1 Salk. 129   177–86,
218
Colehan v. *Cooke* (1743), Willes 393, 2 Str. 1217   153, 185
Coleman v. *Marham* (1321), Y.B. 14 Edw. II, Eyre of
London, 86 SS 353   19
Collins v. *Butler* (1738), 2 Str. 1087   216
Collis v. *Emett* (1790), 1 Bl. H. 313   226–27, 234
Collot v. *Haigh* (1812), 3 Camp. 281   238
Colville v. *Cutler* (1666), Vidian, *Exact Pleader*, 31   128, 171
Cooksey v. *Boverie* (1683), 2 Show. 296   176, 203
Coolidge v. *Payson*, (1817), 15 U.S. (2 Wheat.) 66   201
Cooper v. *Le Blanc* (1730), Cas. t. Hard. 295, 2 Str. 1051   216
Core v. *May* (1536), Dyer 20, printed with record entry in
Baker and Milsom, *Sources of English Legal History*, 243   19
Cory v. *Scott* (1820), 3 Barn. & Ald. 619   209, 243–44, 248
Cowley v. *Dunlop* (1798), 7 T.R. 565   241
Cramlington v. *Evans* (1690), Skin. 264, 1 Show. 4, 2 Show.
509, Carth. 5, Holt 108, 2 Vent. 296, 307   143, 144–46
Crawley v. *Crowther* (1702), 2 Freem. Chy. 257   203
Critchlow v. *Parry* (1809), 2 Camp. 182   189
Crook v. *Jadis* (1834), 5 Barn. & Adol. 909   191
Curteis v. *Geoffrey de St Romain* (1287), 23 SS 26   173
Cutting v. *Williams* (1703), 7 Mod. 154   180
Dane v. *Holbein* (1388), Y.B. 11 Rich. II (Ames Ser.) 238   16–17
Darbishire v. *Parker* (1805), 6 East 3   207
Darrach v. *Savage* (1691), 1 Show. 155, Holt 113   175, 203
Dashwood v. *Lee* (1667), 2 Keb. 303   171
Dawkes v. *De Lorane* (1771), 3 Wils. K.B. 207, 2 Bl. W.
782   154
De la Chaumette v. *Bank of England* (1829), 9 Barn. &
Cress. 208   241

Death v. *Serwonters* (1685), 1 Lutw. 885   171
Dederic v. *Abbot of Ramsey* (1315), *Select Cases Law
    Merchant*, 46 SS 86   28, 220
Dehers v. *Harriot* (1691), 1 Show. 163   150, 220
Denaker v. *Mason* (1564), *Select Pleas Admiralty*, 11 SS
    73, 126   51
Dennis v. *Morrice* (1800), 3 Esp. 158   209
Dingwall v. *Dunster* (1779), 1 Doug. 247   238
Disher v. *Disher* (1712), 1 P. Wms. 204   185
Duncan v. *Scott* (1807), 1 Camp. 100   241
Eaglechild's Case (1630), Het. 167   136, 140
Edgar v. *Chut* (1663), 1 Keb. 592, 636   98, 125–26, 140, 182
Edie v. *East India Co.* (1761), 2 Burr. 1216   212, 221
Ex parte Earle (1801), 5 Ves. Jun. 833   241
Ex parte Heath (1813), 2 Ves. & Bea. 240   209
Ex parte Metcalfe (1805), 11 Ves. Jun. 404   241
Ex parte Rawson (1821), Jac. 274   241, 242–43
Ex parte Walker (1798), 4 Ves. Jun. 373   241, 242–43
Fentum v. *Pocock* (1813), 5 Taunt. 192   239
Ford v. *Hopkins* (1700), Holt 119   187
Frederick v. *Cotton* (1678), 2 Show. 8   140
Fry v. *Hill* (1817), 7 Taunt. 397   207
Fuller v. *Thorne* (1533), *Select Pleas Admiralty*, 6 SS
    38–41, 179–81   51–52
Furze v. *Sharwood* (1841), 2 Q.B. 388   210
Garnet v. *Clarke* (1709), 11 Mod. 226   185
Geill v. *Jeremy* (1827), M. & M. 61   208
Gibson v. *Hunter* (1794), 2 Bl. H. 288   226, 227
Gibson v. *Minet* (1791), 1 Bl. H. 569   226, 233–37
Gill v. *Cubitt* (1824), 3 Barn. & Cress. 466   191
Glemerod v. *Brounesford* (1345), *Calendar of London Plea
    and Memoranda Rolls*, 1: 217   50
Glynn v. *Bank of England* (1750), 2 Ves. Sen. 38   177, 187
Gomersall v. *Gomersall* (1586), Godb. 55, 58, 2 Leo. 194,
    196   18
Goodman v. *Harvey* (1836), 4 Ad. & E. 870   191
Gosbert de Bozeis v. *Alexander of Marwell* (1292), 57 SS
    69   29
Goupy v. *Harden* (1816), 7 Taunt. 159   198, 207
Grant v. *Vaughan* (1764), 3 Burr. 1516   177, 188, 191, 212–13

Grene v. *Warde* (c. 1460), Barbour, *History of Contract in*
  Early English Equity, 76   56
H. S. v. *R. W.* (1678), *Brownlow Latine Redivivus*, 74   128
Hackshaw v. *Clerke* (1696), 5 Mod. 314   167
Hamilton v. *Mackrell* (1736), Cas. t. Hard. 322   216
Hampton v. *Calthrope* (1584), Brown, *Vade Mecum*, 23   59,
                         63, 65, 129, 132, 135, 174
Hankey v. *Jones* (1778), Cowp. 745   214
Hankey v. *Trotman* (1746), 1 Bl. W. 1   203
Harrison v. *Courtauld* (1832), 3 Barn. & Adol. 36   239
Harry v. *Perrit* (1710), 1 Salk. 133   216
Haward v. *Bank of England* (1723), 1 Str. 550   203
Hawkins v. *Cardy* (1698), 1 Ld Raym. 360, Carth. 466,
  1 Salk. 65, 12 Mod. 213   146, 148, 222
Haynes v. *Birks* (1804), 3 Bos. & Pul. 599   208
Heath v. *Sansom* (1831), 2 Barn. & Adol. 291   241, 244
Heylyn v. *Adamson* (1758), 2 Burr. 669   146, 188, 215–18
Hill v. *Lewis* (1694), 1 Salk. 132, Holt 116, Skin. 410,
  query s.c. *Tassel* v. *Lewis* (1695), 1 Ld Raym. 743   175,
                                 178, 203
Hilliard v. *Smith* (1686), Comb. 19   167
Hinton's Case (1682), 2 Show. 235   173
Hoar v. *Dacosta* (1732), 2 Str. 910   203
Hodges v. *Steward* (1693), 12 Mod. 36, 1 Salk. 125, 3 Salk.
  68, Skin. 332, 346, Holt 115, Comb. 204   173, 174–75
Holme v. *Barry* (1721), 1 Str. 415   203
Holmton v. *Walworth* (1390), *Calendar of London Plea and*
  Memoranda Rolls, 3: 176   50
Hoppman v. *Richard of Welborne* (1302), 23 SS 86   173
Horton v. *Coggs* (1691), 3 Lev. 296, 299   173, 175, 176
Hussey v. *Jacob* (1696), 1 Ld Raym. 87, Carth. 356, 1 Com.
  4, Holt 328, 5 Mod. 170, 175, 12 Mod. 96, 1 Salk. 344   148,
                                167, 190
J. L. v. *E.* (1594), Rastell, *Entrees*, 3rd edn, 338r   57–58, 61,
                                 132, 133
Jenney v. *Herle* (1724), 2 Ld Raym. 1361, 8 Mod. 265, 11
  Mod. 384, 1 Str. 591   186
John Bate v. *J. Luce* (n.d.), Vidian, *Exact Pleader*, 70   135
John the Spicer v. *Walter of Leicester* (1288), *Select Cases*
  Law Merchant, 46 SS 45   16

Johnson v. *Collings* (1800), 1 East 98   201
Jones v. *Brooke* (1812), 4 Taunt. 464   237
Jordon v. *Barloe* (1700), 3 Salk. 67   173
Josceline v. *Lassere* (1713), Fort. 281, 10 Mod. 294, 316   186
Julian v. *Shobrooke* (1753), 2 Wils. K.B. 9   196, 198
Kerrison v. *Cooke* (1813), 3 Camp. 362   238–39
King v. *Milsom* (1809), 2 Camp. 5   241
Knappe v. *Hedley* (1600), K.B. 27/1359, m. 621   134
Lambert v. *Oakes* (1699), 1 Ld Raym. 443, 12 Mod. 244,
     Holt 117, 118, 1 Salk. 127   146–47, 189, 217
Lawrence v. *Jacob* (1722), 8 Mod. 43, 1 Str. 515   216
Lawson v. *Weston* (1801), 4 Esp. 56   191
Laxton v. *Peat* (1809), 2 Camp. 185   238–39
Le Fort v. *Le Fort* (1599), *Select Pleas Admiralty*, 11 SS 192   51
Lickabarrow v. *Mason* (1787), 2 T.R. 63   215
Lilly v. *Ewer* (1779), 1 Doug. 72   211
Lowe v. *Waller* (1781), 2 Doug. 736   190
Luke v. *Lyde* (1759), 2 Burr. 882   168, 219
Lumley v. *Palmer* (1734), Cas. t. Hard. 74, 7 Mod. 216,
     2 Str. 1000   153, 198–99
Manwaring v. *Harrison* (1722), 1 Str. 508   203
Martin v. *Boure* (1603), Cro. Jac. 6   136
Mason v. *Hunt* (1779), 1 Doug. 297   196
Matthew Reuse v. *Charles H.* (1605), Brownlow, *Declara-
     tions and Pleadings in English*, 1: 267   128, 131–32, 135–36
Maynard v. *Dyce* (1542), K.B. 27/1125, m. 110   60
Mead v. *Caswell* (1723), 9 Mod. 60   203
Medcalf v. *Hall* (1782), 3 Doug. 113   204–5, 206–7, 211,
                                                                    212, 214
Miller v. *Race* (1758), 1 Burr. 452   187–88, 191
Mills v. *Barber* (1836), 1 M. & W. 426   244
Milton's Case (1668), Hardr. 485, reported as *Anon.*,
     identified as *Milton's Case* in *Browne* v. *London* (1670),
     1 Mod. 285   139, 144, 165–66
Minet v. *Gibson* (1789), 3 T.R. 481, aff'd 1 Bl. H. 569
     (1791)   226, 234
Mogadara v. *Holt* (1691), 1 Show. 317, Holt 113, 12 Mod.
     15   131, 141, 148, 152, 165
Moore v. *Warren* (1721), 1 Str. 415   203
More v. *Morecomb* (1601), Cro. Eliz. 864   14

Morgan v. *Richardon* (n.d.), 1 Camp. 40n, 7 East 482n 192
Morris v. *Lee* (1786), cited in J. Bayley, *Law of Bills of Exchange*, 74 190
Mounsey v. *Traves* (1620), Vidian, *Exact Pleader*, 66 128, 174
Nichols v. *Norris* (1831), 3 Barn. & Adol. 41 239
Nicholson v. *Sedgwick* (1697), 1 Ld Raym. 180, s.c. sub nom. *Nicholson* v. *Seldnith*, 3 Salk. 67 173, 174, 175, 176, 177
Oades v. *Potter* (1683), Clift, *Declarations*, 893 129, 131
Oaste v. *Taylor* (1612), Cro. Jac. 306 130, 136, 140
Obbard v. *Betham* (1830), M. & M. 483 192
Odi v. *Aringi* (1321), Y.B. 14 Edw. II, Eyre of London, 86 SS 217 19
Orr v. *Maginnis* (1806), 7 East 359 209
Oshey v. *Hicks* (1610), Cro. Jac. 263 14
Pardo v. *Fuller* (1738), 2 Com. 579 216
Peacock v. *Rhodes* (1781), 2 Doug. 633 188, 189–90, 191, 198, 214–15
Pearson v. *Garrett* (1693), 4 Mod. 242, Skin. 398, Comb. 227 182–83
Peirson v. *Ponuteis* (1608), 1 Brownl. & Golds. 102 56
Percival v. *Frampton* (1835), 2 Cr. M. & R. 180 244
Peter de Prill v. *Philip Barnardi* (1616), Brownlow, *Declarations* 2: 58 128, 131–32, 135–36
Petit v. *Benson* (1697), Comb. 452 197
Phillips v. *Phillips* (1700), 2 Freem. Chy. 247 203
Pierson v. *Dunlop* (1777), 2 Cowp. 571 211
Pillans v. *Van Mierop* (1765), 3 Burr. 1663 200–1, 219, 222
Pinkney v. *Hall* (1697), 1 Ld Raym. 175, 1 Salk. 126 139, 143
Pirton v. *Tumby* (1315), Y.B. 8 Edw. II, 41 SS 59 17
Potter v. *Pearson* (1703), 2 Ld Raym. 759, 1 Salk. 129, Holt 33 180
Powell v. *Monnier* (1737), 1 Atk. 611 198
Price v. *Edmunds* (1830), 10 Barn. & Cress. 578 239
Pylat v. *Reginald* (1308), *Select Cases Law Merchant*, 46 SS 78 16
R. G. v. *J. T.* (1636), Brown, *Vade Mecum*, 22 128–30, 136
Randolf v. *Abbot of Hayles* (1311), Y.B. 4 Edw. II, 42 SS 19, s.c. Y.B. 6 & 7 Edw. II, Eyre of Kent, 27 SS 32 14
Rands v. *Peck* (1621), Cro. Jac. 618 56

Rann v. *Hughes* (1778), 4 Bro. P.C. 27, 7 T.R. 350   200
Renew v. *Axton* (1687), Carth. 3   167
Roberts v. *Peake* (1757), 1 Burr. 323   185
Rogers v. *Stephens* (1788), 2 T.R. 713   209
Rowe v. *Young* (1820), 2 Br. & B. 165   238
Rucker v. *Hiller* (1812), 16 East 43   209
Russel v. *Wiggin* (1839), 21 F. Cas. 68 (C.C.D. Ma.) (No. 12,165)   201
S. v. *J. W.* (n.d.), *Brownlow Latine Redivivus*, 77   128
Salomons v. *Staveley* (1783), 3 Doug. 298   154, 219
Salvaigus v. *Grill* (1462), *Calendar of London Plea and Memoranda Rolls*, 6: 21   48
Sarsfield v. *Witherly* (1689), 1 Show. 125, 2 Vent. 292, Holt 112, Carth. 82, Comb. 45, 152   97, 140, 143, 146, 182
Scottow v. *Birkeleghe* (1312), Y.B. 5 Edw. II, 33 SS 205   16
Selby v. *Palfrayman* (1389), Y.B. 13 Rich. II (Ames Ser.) 79   19
Septvaux v. *Marchaunt* (1385), Y.B. 8–10 Rich. II (Ames Ser.) 187   19
Shelden v. *Hentley* (1681), 2 Show. 160   173
Sheppard v. *Beecher* (1600), K.B. 27/1361, m. 507d, Brown, *Vade Mecum*, 29   132–33
Ship Money Case (1637), 3 Howell's State Trials 825   157
Simmonds v. *Parminter* (1747), 1 Wils. K.B. 185   153, 237
Simpson v. *Clarke* (1835), 2 Cr. M. & R. 342   241, 244–45
Slade's Case (1602), 4 Co. Rep. 92   64, 136
Smith v. *Abbott* (1741), 2 Str. 1152, 7 Mod. 426   196–97, 220
Smith v. *Chester* (1787), 1 T.R. 654   188, 233
Smith v. *Haytwell* (1747), Amb. 66, 3 Atk. 566   189
Smith v. *Knox* (1799), 3 Esp. 47   237
Smith v. *Mullett* (1809), 2 Camp. 208   208
Snelling v. *Briggs* (1741), Buller, *Nisi Prius*, 274   190
Soper v. *Dible* (1697), 1 Ld Raym. 175   131
Southcote's Case (1601), 4 Co. Rep. 83b   18
Speye v. *Ledet* (1310), Y.B. 4 Edw. II, 26 SS 8   14
Sproat v. *Matthews* (1786), 1 T.R. 182   196, 198, 199
Staples v. *Okines* (1795), 1 Esp. 332   209
Stone v. *Freeland* (1769), reported in a note to *Collis* v. *Emett* (1790), 1 Bl. H. at 313   226

Stone v. *Rawlinson* (1745), Willes 559, Barnes 164, 2 Str.
1260, 3 Wils. K.B. 1   220
Stowey v. *Prior of Bruton* (1378), Y.B. 2 Rich. II (Ames
Ser.) 11   14, 15
Syderbottom v. *Smith* (1725), 1 Str. 649   216
Tassel v. *Lewis* (1695), 1 Ld Raym. 743, query s.c. *Hill* v.
Lewis (1694), 1 Salk. 132, Holt 116, Skin. 410   150, 203, 220
Tatlock v. *Harris* (1789), 3 T.R. 174   234
Tercese v. *Geray* (1677), Finch 301   171, 187
Thackray v. *Blackett* (1812), 3 Camp. 164   209
Thomas v. *Bishop* (1733), 7 Mod. 180, Cas. t. Hard. 1,
2 Str. 955, 2 Barn. K.B. 320, 335   190
Thomas v. *Newton* (1827), 2 Car. & P. 606   241
Thorne v. *Vincent* (1541), *Select Pleas Admiralty*, 6 SS 92   52
Thorold v. *Smith* (1706), Holt 462, 463, 11 Mod. 71, 87   153
Tindal v. *Brown* (1786), 1 T.R. 167   206, 210, 222
Toft v. *Garraway* (1613), Brown, *Vade Mecum*, 27   58, 132, 133
Tonkin v. *Fuller* (1783), 3 Doug. 300   215
Turner v. *Mead*, (1720), 1 Str. 416   203
Tye v. *Gwynne* (1810), 2 Camp. 346   192
Vanheath v. *Turner* (1621), Winch 24   136, 148, 152
Vernon v. *Boverie* (1683), 2 Show. 296   203
W. S. v. *R. H.* (n.d., 1570s/1580s), Herne, *Pleader*, 136   135, 174
Walker v. *Atwood* (1708), 11 Mod. 190   197
Walker v. *Myddylton* (1542), K.B. 27/1122, m. 105d   55
Walmsley v. *Child* (1749), 1 Ves. Sen. 341   177, 187
Walwyn v. *St Quintin* (1797), 1 Bos. & Pul. 652   209, 240,
                                                                                      243–44
Ward v. *Evans* (1703), 2 Ld Raym. 928, 1 Com. 138, 6
Mod. 36, 12 Mod. 521, Holt 120, 2 Salk. 442, 3 Salk. 118   153,
                                                                                  176, 202–3
Ward v. *Kedsgrove* (1625), Latch. 4, W. Jones 69   56
Wegersloffe v. *Keene* (1719), 1 Str. 214   153, 197
White v. *Ledwick* (1785), 4 Doug. 247   154, 214
Whitmore v. *Hunt* (n.d., *c.* 1620–40), Brownlow, *Declara-*
tion, 1: 269   128, 174
Wildes v. *Savage*, (1839), 29 F. Cas. 1226 (C.C.D. Ma.)
(No. 17,653)   201
Williams v. *Field* (1693), 3 Salk. 68, query s.c. *Anon.*
(1693), Holt 115, Skin. 343   172–73

Williams v. *Smith* (1819), 2 Barn. & Ald. 496　　　　208, 210

Williams v. *Williams* (1693), Carth. 269.　　　　　　131

Williamson v. *Harrison* (1690), Carth. 160, Holt 359, Salk.
197　　　　　　　　　　　　　　144, 146, 148, 167

Williamson v. *Holiday* (1611), Brown, *Vade Mecum*, 26　59–60,
63, 129, 132, 135, 174

Woodford v. *Wyatt* (1626), ms. report printed in Baker
and Milsom, *Sources of English Legal History*, 458　　　136

Woodward v. *Rowe* (1666), 2 Keb. 105, 132　　　139, 140–41

Woolvil v. *Young* (1697), 5 Mod. 367　　　　　　　183

Y.B. 21 & 22 Edw. I (1293), (Rolls Ser.) 74　　　　　30

Y.B. 34 & 35 Edw. I (1306), (Rolls Ser.) 294　　　　　16

Y.B. 2 & 3 Edw. II (1308), 19 SS 34　　　　　　　　17

Y.B. 14 Edw. III (1340), (Rolls Ser.) lxviii　　　　　19

Y.B. Hil. 5 Hen. V, f. 4, pl. 10 (1413)　　　　　　　45

Y.B. Mich. 35 Hen. VI, f. 25, pl. 33 (1456)　　　　　138

Y.B. Mich. 8 Edw. IV, f. 18, pl. 30 (1465)　　　　　137

Y.B. 10 Edw. IV, 49 Hen. VI (1470), 47 SS 118　　　15

Y.B. Pasch. 21 Edw. IV, f. 28, pl. 23 (1482)　　　　137

Y.B. Pasch. 22 Edw. IV, f. 8, pl. 24 (1483)　　　　　137

Yates Case (1655), Style 477, 2 Rolle 471　　　　　139

Yeoman v. *Bradshaw* (1696), Carth. 373, Comb. 392, Holt
42, 12 Mod. 107, 3 Salk. 70, 164　　　　　　　167

Young v. *Hockley* (1772), 3 Wils. 346　　　　　　237

NOTE ON CITATION

Reported decisions from the seventeenth to the nineteenth centuries are cited by the common abbreviation of named report, e.g. 2 Burr. 669, and may be found in reprint in the *English Reports* (1900–30). Yearbook cases are cited to the modern editions (Rolls series, Selden Society, and Ames Foundation) if included therein, otherwise to the 'black letter' editions of 1678–80. Excerpts from court rolls printed in publications of the Selden Society are cited in the fashion of reported decisions, by volume number and page of the Selden Society publication, e.g., 49 SS 117. Cases from the London Mayor's Court are cited to the *Calendar of Early Mayor's Court Rolls* (1924) and *Calendar of Plea and Memoranda Rolls* (1926–61). Pleadings included in seventeenth-century form books are cited in the fashion of reported decisions; the form books so used are listed in the bibliography. For an overview of forms of legal literature in the period covered in this book, see Baker, *Introduction to English Legal History*, 200–22, and sources there cited.

INTRODUCTION

English commercial law is commonly said to have developed by a process of incorporation of the law merchant.[1] In rough form, the conventional theory is that before the seventeenth century commercial cases were not heard in the regular common law courts but in specialized mercantile tribunals associated with fairs and principal cities and towns. Cases brought in these courts were decided not by the regular judges but by the merchants themselves. The substantive law applied was not the common law but the law merchant, a specialized body of transnational customary law based on commercial practice and uncluttered by the technicalities of the common law. By the sixteenth and seventeenth centuries, however, the mercantile courts of the fairs and towns went into decline, and merchants were forced to bring their cases in the common law courts. Initially the judges of the common law courts were unfamiliar with and even hostile toward the law merchant. At most, the common law courts would treat the principles of the law merchant as customary rules that required specific proof in each case. In time, the antagonism of the common law judges was overcome, and the courts began to treat the rules of the law merchant as authentic principles of law, binding of their own force

---

[1] The incorporation theory of the history of commercial law in general can be found in various sources, including Holdsworth, *History of English Law*, 5: 102–54; Macdonell, Introduction to Smith's *Compendium of Mercantile Law*, lxiii–lxxxiii; Plucknett, *History of the Common Law*, 657–70; and Scrutton, *Elements of Mercantile Law*, 1–39. With specific reference to the law of bills, see Beutel, 'Development of Negotiable Instruments'; Fifoot, 'Development of the Law of Negotiable Instruments'; Holden, *History of Negotiable Instruments*; Jenks, 'Early History of Negotiable Instruments'; Street, *Foundations of Legal Liability*, 2: 323–428. For criticism of the incorporation theory see Baker, 'Law Merchant and Common Law'; Coquillette, *Civilian Writers of Doctors' Commons*, 149–58, 215–55; Ewart, 'What is the Law Merchant?'; Sutherland, 'Law Merchant in England'.

1

without special proof as custom. By the end of the seventeenth century, the courts began to recognize explicitly that the law merchant was part of the common law. In the eighteenth century, particularly during the tenure of Lord Mansfield as Chief Justice of the King's Bench from 1756 to 1788, the process of incorporation was largely completed.

The general thesis of this book is that the traditional incorporation theory is inaccurate, at least with respect to the law of bills and notes. The judges of the English common law courts did not borrow the rules of the law of bills from sources external to the common law system. Rather, the English law of bills developed within the common law system itself, in response to developments in commercial and financial practice. Though this book considers only the law of bills and notes, the conclusions drawn have broader relevance. Assumptions about the early history of the law of bills of exchange have played a major role in the formulation of the incorporation theory of the origins of English commercial law in general. The fact that the incorporation theory is inaccurate with respect to bills casts considerable doubt on its soundness as applied to other areas.

Most accounts of the history of the law of bills and notes are based on the assumption that the main focus of this body of law has always been the concept of negotiability, in the sense of the rules that permit a bona fide holder to take an instrument free from all claims to it and free from most defences that the parties obligated on it might have had in the underlying transaction for which the instrument was given. The pre-eminent place of the concept of negotiability in modern law is apparent in virtually any modern book on the law of bills and notes. The books typically begin with an introductory chapter or passage explaining how the concept of negotiability differs from the general rules of assignment applicable to other forms of property and why this special concept is essential to commercial transactions.[2] The chapter or chapters

---

[2] The following passage from Bigelow, *Law of Bills, Notes, and Cheques*, 2–3, is illustrative:

> Negotiability is the property by which certain choses in action, that is, undertakings to pay, pass from hand to hand like money. The common law knew nothing of that; or rather the common law repudiated entirely the notion that a promise by A to B could be treated as a promise extending also to C. The utmost which the law allowed was assignment; and that only after long debate and serious misgiving. Assignment merely works the appoint-

devoted to the holder in due course will be the major parts of the books, and all other chapters will emphasize the relationship between the matters under discussion and the holder in due course doctrine. The discussion of the formal requirements of negotiable instruments will typically explain that the point of the definitional rules is to specify the requirements that an instrument must meet if a purchaser is to qualify as a holder in due course; the treatment of transfer rules will explain that unless the transfer takes the proper form the transferee will not be a holder who can qualify as a holder in due course; and the discussion of defences will consist primarily of a differentiation of the 'personal' defences which cannot be asserted against a holder in due course from the 'real' defences which can.[3]

Given this sense of modern law, it is not surprising that legal historians have taken it as their agenda to describe the process by which the concept of negotiability developed. Holdsworth, for example, began his treatment of the topic by noting that 'the characteristic features of negotiability in our modern law ... are three in number: (i) Negotiable instruments are transferable by delivery if made payable to bearer, or by indorsement and delivery if made payable to order; and the transferee to whom they have been thus delivered can sue upon them in his own name. (ii) Consideration is presumed. (iii) A transferee, who takes one of these instruments in good faith and for value, acquires a good title, even though his transferor had a defective title, or no title at all.'[4] He then stated that 'the questions which I must try to answer are, first, what were the germs from which instruments having these qualities were developed; and, secondly, what were the technical processes by which this development took place?'[5]

The focus on the concept of negotiability is very much related to the idea that the origins of English commercial law are to be found

ment of another as beneficiary of the assignor's rights; the assignee 'takes the shoes' of the assignor. That would never have served the purpose of circulating paper; that purpose required a denial of the maxim Nemo dat quod non habet. The new taker of a bill of exchange must have a perfect right, if his purchase of it was in due course, a right in no way to be affected by the rights of him from whom he bought it.

[3] The principal mid-twentieth-century American book on the subject stated explicitly that the holder in due course 'principle, with its ramifications, is, by far, the most important principle in the whole law of bills and notes'. Britton, *Law of Bills and Notes*, 25.

[4] Holdsworth, *History of English Law* 8: 113–14.   [5] Ibid., 114.

in the struggle between the law merchant and the common law. Bills of exchange seem to present the clearest case of a conflict between the rules of the law merchant and those of the common law. It is generally assumed that one of the main functions of bills of exchange has always been to serve as freely transferable evidences of indebtedness that could be used as currency substitutes. The holder in due course rules seem to be essential if debt instruments are to be used as currency substitutes.[6] It is commonly asserted that the principles of negotiability were developed as part of the law merchant as early as the Middle Ages, but the merchants faced formidable difficulties in their effort to have English law recognize the economically essential concept of negotiability. Thus, most accounts of the early history of the English law of bills have focused on explaining how the concept of negotiability developed and how it was introduced into the common law. The following passage, from an early-twentieth-century American treatise on the law of bills, is typical of the story that has become familiar to generations of lawyers:

Originally all instruments, including bills of exchange, promissory notes and bank checks were non-negotiable – in the sense that the maker could, when asked for payment, deduct from the amount due on the instrument any just claim that he had against the original owner. Such a claim was termed a counter-claim, or set-off. In the revival of commerce in Italy, in the eleventh century, merchants and traders, feeling the need of a commercial instrument, similar to a bank bill that could be used in their barter and trade and commercial transactions, and realizing that no such instrument could be passed from hand to hand or sold readily, no matter how good the financial standing of the maker was, if he, the maker, could always insist on adjusting accounts with the original owner – adopted a custom later known as the law merchant, under which notes, checks, drafts, and bills of exchange, drawn in certain prescribed forms, and in the hands of a *bona fide* purchaser, could be enforced to their full extent against the maker, regardless of certain defences or counter-claims that the maker might have against the original holder. Such instruments were negotiable and such was the origin of negotiability.[7]

---

6 The modern term 'holder in due course' has been used for convenience even though this is somewhat anachronistic. The term 'holder in due course' seems to have been first used in the Bills of Exchange Act of 1882, 45 & 46 Vict., c. 61. Before then the common phrase was 'bona fide holder'. Indeed, Chalmers, the draftsman of the Bills of Exchange Act, had used the conventional 'bona fide' terminology four years earlier in his *Digest of the Law of Bills of Exchange*, which served as the model for the 1882 Act.

7 Ogden, *Law of Negotiable Instruments*, 9–10.

One of the themes of this book is that it is a mistake to treat the concept of negotiability as the centrepiece of the history of the law of bills and notes. Surprising as this may seem to modern lawyers, the holder in due course rules played only a modest role in the law of bills and notes in the era when this body of law developed. One way of demonstrating that point is by an analysis of the issues involved in reported decisions concerning bills and notes. In the period from the beginning of the eighteenth century to the end of Lord Mansfield's tenure as Chief Justice of the King's Bench in 1788, there were over 200 reported cases concerning bills and notes. The issues presented in these cases can be divided roughly as follows:[8]

Issue	Cases	Percentage
Pleading and procedure	39	18%
Diligence (e.g. time of presentment, notice of dishonour, etc.)	30	14%
Bankruptcy cases involving bills	31	14%
Formal requirements of bills and notes	27	13%
Other bills and notes law issues (e.g. form of indorsements, damages in actions on dishonoured bills, liabilities of parties, etc.)	27	13%
Whether taking instrument discharges debt (mostly cases where parties took bank notes for debts and the bank failed before the notes were presented)	17	8%
Acceptance (e.g. what counts as acceptance, parol acceptances, conditional acceptances, etc.)	17	8%

[8] This tabulation is based on the collection in J. Chitty, Jr, *Treatise on Bills of Exchange*, which reprints all of the statutes and reported decisions on bills and notes from the early seventeenth century until 1833. The tabulation is necessarily somewhat imprecise. Cases included in Chitty's collection that only tangentially involve bills have been excluded from the calculation, and no effort has been made to verify whether Chitty included all reported cases from the period covered. The categorization of the cases is also somewhat imprecise, but suffices for the purpose of demonstrating that holder in due course issues were by no means dominant.

Issues other than bills and notes law (e.g. infancy and other capacity issues, illegality of consideration, etc., when raised by immediate parties)	16	7%
Holder in due course – lost or stolen instrument	6	3%
Holder in due course – defences	5	2%
Total	215	100%

Most of these subjects will be analysed in detail in chapters 8 and 9. For present purposes, the important point is that cases involving efforts to assert claims or defences against holders in due course formed only a small part of the corpus of the law of bills and notes.

An examination of treatises on the law of bills published in the late eighteenth and early nineteenth centuries confirms the view that the role of the concept of negotiability has been greatly exaggerated. Although there are a few English law books concerning the subject in the early and mid-eighteenth century, the modern tradition of bills and notes treatises begins with the generation of legal writers who flourished just after the retirement of Lord Mansfield as Chief Justice of the King's Bench in 1788. Four books first published in this era stand out as the pre-eminent works on the law of bills and notes in the late eighteenth and early nineteenth centuries. In order of the appearance of the first editions, they are John Bayley, *A Short Treatise on the Law of Bills of Exchange, Cash Bills, and Promissory Notes* (1789); Stewart Kyd, *A Treatise on the Law of Bills of Exchange and Promissory Notes* (1790); Joseph Chitty, *A Treatise on the Law of Bills of Exchange, Checks on Bankers, Promissory Notes, Bankers' Cash Notes, and Bank-Notes* (1799); and John Byles, *A Practical Compendium of the Law of Bills of Exchange, Promissory Notes, Bankers' Cash-Notes, and Checks* (1829). Each of these went through numerous editions, and together they dominated the field until at least the mid-nineteenth century. One can get a fair picture of the profession's sense of this body of law by looking at the organization and emphasis of the topics in these four works.[9]

---

[9] A more detailed discussion of these and other treatises, and their authors, appears in Rogers, 'The Myth of Negotiability', 272–83. The author, however, cannot

There is a striking difference between the twentieth-century books and the treatises of the late eighteenth and early nineteenth centuries in the way that they describe the distinguishing characteristics of negotiable instruments. The twentieth-century books invariably state that the key definitional characteristic of negotiable instruments is negotiability, in the sense of freedom from claims and defences. By contrast, Byles stated that 'the contracts arising upon a bill of exchange ... differ from other simple contracts in these two particulars: first, that they are assignable; secondly, that consideration will be presumed until the contrary appear'.[10] Kyd, Bayley, and Chitty had similar passages specifying the two peculiar characteristics of bills of exchange as assignability and presumption of consideration.[11] The distinctive characteristic of the modern definitions, negotiability in the sense of freedom from claims and defences, is conspicuously absent. Neither Bayley, nor Kyd, nor Chitty, nor Byles had an introductory passage or chapter explaining the concept of negotiability in the sense of freedom from claims and defences. None of them had a passage contrasting negotiability with mere assignability. None of them had a separate chapter on the rights of bona fide holders.[12]

resist repeating two interesting bits of trivia about the authors of bills and notes treatises. (1) Stewart Kyd probably has the distinction of being the only author of bills treatise ever to have been indicted for treason. In the 1790s he was a member of the Society for Constitutional Information and, along with Thomas Hardy, John Horne Tooke, and ten others, was indicted for high treason in 1794. Hardy and Tooke were tried first and were acquitted, whereupon the charges against Kyd were dropped. *Dictionary of National Biography*, 11: 348. (2) John Barnard Byles was responsible for what may be the only bills and notes joke. He is said to have named his horse 'Bills' so that as he rode up people could say, 'Here comes Byles on Bills'. Simpson, ed., *Biographical Dictionary of the Common Law*, 95.

[10] Byles, 2.

[11] Kyd, 30–32; Bayley, 1; Chitty, 1–2, 7–8. Chitty is the only one of these authors whose statement of the characteristics of bills comes close to mentioning the modern concept of negotiability. He states that bills of exchange 'are instruments by means of which a creditor may assign to a third person, not originally party to a contract, the *legal* as well as equitable interest in a debt raised by it, so as to vest in such assignee a right of action against the original debtor'. Chitty, 1.

[12] It was not until the eighth edition of Byles, published in 1862, that a passage expressly discussing the rights of 'bona fide holders' was added, and this passage amounted to only a few pages in the chapter entitled 'Of the Consideration'.

The early books also differ dramatically from modern works in their treatment of defences to actions on bills and notes. Twentieth-century books on negotiable instruments always include a lengthy section on defences, organized in accordance with the holder in due course rules that distinguish between real and personal defences. The earlier books had no chapter on the holder in due course doctrine, and the coverage of defences was not organized around any such concept. Rather, the matters that would now be placed under the headings of real and personal defences were treated in a variety of places. For example, the defence that some party to the instrument lacked contractual capacity, on grounds of infancy, insanity, or the like, which would be treated in twentieth-century books in the section on the real defences, is often treated in the earlier books in a chapter or chapters entitled something like 'Of the Parties to a Bill of Exchange' along with many other issues of capacity and agency. Similarly, the defences that the twentieth-century authors take to be the primary concern of the law of bills and notes, such as breach of warranty, fraud, or other matters relating to the original payee's failure properly to render the performance for which the instrument was given, are treated in the earlier books in a variety of places, rarely with much prominence. Thus, in both Bayley and Kyd the defences of illegality, want, or failure of consideration were not covered in the principal chapters of the books on the major legal issues concerning bills, but were placed into a final chapter on procedure and evidence in actions on bills.[13] In Chitty, these issues were treated somewhat as an aside in a chapter on the form of bills of exchange in which Chitty gives the typical language of a bill of exchange, appending the discussion of consideration to

Byles, *Law of Bills of Exchange*, 8th edn, 111–12. The first law book on bills and notes to include an entire chapter specifically devoted to the rights of bona fide holders of instruments seems to be Theophilus Parsons' 1863 work, *Law of Promissory Notes and Bills of Exchange*.

[13] In the first edition of Bayley, this chapter was entitled 'Of the Evidence necessary to entitle the Plaintiff to recover upon a Bill or Note, and the Defence which may be set up against him', and comprised eight of the total of seventy pages in the book. The consideration defences got only four pages, most of that being on illegality of consideration. Similarly the first edition of Kyd had a final chapter entitled 'Of the Proof necessary at the Trial, and of the Defence that may be set up there', which accounted for twenty-nine of the total of one hundred and sixty pages in the book. The consideration defences were covered in the last five pages of this chapter.

his mention of the phrase 'for value received' that customarily appeared in bills of exchange.

Even where the defences of failure of consideration and the like are given more prominence, the discussion is far from what one familiar with twentieth-century works would expect. In twentieth-century books, the discussion of these defences focuses on the original obligor's effort to raise defences when sued by a transferee of the instrument. Defences available between the original parties usually receive only brief treatment. In treatises of the late eighteenth and early nineteenth centuries, the emphasis is just the reverse. Byles, for example, had a separate chapter entitled 'Of the Consideration' which covered, among other things, some of the defences that twentieth-century authors discuss under the heading of real and personal defences. Byles began his discussion of consideration by explaining that although there is a presumption of consideration in actions on bills, that presumption can be rebutted in actions between immediate parties to a bill.[14] He then proceeded with a detailed examination of whether particular contentions do or do not give rise to good defences of want, failure, or illegality of consideration. There is nothing of the sense, so prominent in twentieth-century books, that the problem is whether a bona fide purchaser takes subject to defences available against the original holder, nor is there any mention of the argument that such special treatment for bona fide purchasers is necessary in order to promote the use of bills in commerce. Indeed, the phrase 'bona fide holder' does not even appear in the discussion.

Lest the point be misunderstood, I should hasten to add that it is not my contention that the rules that twentieth-century lawyers catalogue under the heading of holder in due course were unknown in earlier times or that they were unimportant. It is clear from any number of cases in the seventeenth and eighteenth centuries that the judges thought that protection of the rights of bona fide holders was an important consideration in the law of bills and notes. So too, though the treatises of that era do not use the holder in due course concept as a central organizing principle, one can find in the treatises statements that are substantively equivalent to the modern holder in due course rules, albeit often expressed in

---

[14] Byles, *Law of Bills of Exchange*, 37–38.

different terms.[15] The point is not that the substantive rules were
different in earlier times. Rather, the point is that a history of the
law of bills and notes written solely or predominantly from the
perspective of an effort to trace the evolution of these particular
rules is bound to be seriously distorted. The holder in due course
rules were important, but they were not the be all and end all of the
law of bills.

The orthodox accounts of the history of the law of bills and notes
push to the level of a priori assumption all of the issues that ought
to be principal subjects of the historical inquiry. If one takes it as
axiomatic that the law of bills and notes evolved in response to a
universal mercantile need for freely transferable debt instruments,
and that the main theme in the history of the English law of bills
was the struggle to get the common law courts to accept the
principles of negotiability, then there is no place or need for
empirical historical inquiry into actual mercantile practice with
bills and notes nor for study of the relationship between changes in
mercantile practice and changes in commercial law. For example, a
large part of Jenks' seminal 1893 article on the early history of
negotiable instruments law consisted of a synopsis of the findings
of continental jurists concerning the presence of language akin to
order and bearer clauses in a miscellany of medieval documents,
including not only early bills of exchange and bonds evidencing
debts, but also real estate conveyances, provisions of wills concerning the designation of guardians, and a writing 'in which a
monk makes over to the church (amongst other things) the right to
avenge his death if he shall be murdered'.[16] Yet the only thing that
links this hodgepodge to the law of bills of exchange is the a priori
assumption that the whole point of the development of the law of
bills was to make possible a system in which debt instruments
could freely be transferred. Without that assumption, there is no
reason to regard instances of transfers of legal documents as part of
the history of mercantile practice or law. Theories about the
development and significance of bearer clauses and order clauses
might be of interest in the history of representation in litigation,
but that would be a part of the history of civil procedure, not
commercial law. What Holdsworth, Jenks, Scrutton, and others

[15] E.g., Byles, *Law of Bills of Exchange*, 37–38.
[16] Jenks, 'Early History of Negotiable Instruments', 61.

have provided is not really an account of the history of the law of bills and notes, but an account of the supposed origins of the legal concept of negotiability. The goal of the present work is to reverse that focus.

1

THE CENTRAL COURTS, COMMERCIAL LAW,
AND THE LAW MERCHANT

Before examining the early history of the law of bills of exchange, one must clear up a common misconception about early English commercial law in general. The starting point of most treatments of the early history of English mercantile law is the assumption that there were essentially no cases concerning commercial matters in the common law courts before the seventeenth or eighteenth centuries. Thomas Scrutton began his influential work on the history of mercantile law by noting that 'if you read the law reports of the seventeenth century you will be struck with one very remarkable fact; either Englishmen of that day did not engage in commerce, or they appear not to have been litigious people in commercial matters, each of which alternatives appears improbable'.[1] In the same vein, a mid-twentieth-century American treatise on the law of bills and notes notes that 'from the 1000's to the 1600's scarcely a case, dealing with commercial paper, was reported in the common law courts of England, though these instruments were in use in England, as well as in Europe, as early as 1300'.[2] A careful examination of the early English sources, however, belies this assumption. As J. H. Baker has shown,[3] the common law courts regularly dealt with commercial matters from the earliest times.

COMMERCIAL CASES IN THE CENTRAL COURTS

The apparent absence of commercial cases from the records of the common law courts is largely an illusion, attributable to the failure

[1] Scrutton, *Elements of Mercantile Law*, 4.
[2] Britton, *Law of Bills and Notes*, 5.
[3] Baker, 'Law Merchant and Common Law'.

to realize fully the implications of the fact that so much of early English law was organized by procedural categories. To be sure, one will come up empty-handed if one looks for words or topics such as 'merchant', 'mercantile', 'commercial', 'sales', 'bills of exchange', or 'insurance', in the table of contents, indices, or headings of early English law books. But to conclude that there are no 'commercial cases' in the books is to confuse the table of contents with the actual contents. If one looks carefully under the headings for the procedural categories through which rights arising out of commercial transactions could have been enforced, such as 'debt', 'covenant', and 'account',[4] one will find all the commercial law one would expect in a society that was still primarily agricultural.

Although the secondary sources on early English law rarely identify the parties to cases with any specificity, the excerpts from the original plea rolls that have been edited and published under the auspices of the Selden Society show that merchants were litigating disputes before the king's justices from the earliest times. For example, published excerpts of thirteenth- and fourteenth-century Exchequer plea rolls show a large number of actions to collect mercantile debts,[5] including cases involving well-known medieval merchant firms such as the Society of the Frescobaldi,[6] and disputes over large amounts, as in a case concerning the sale of wool to a company of Florentine merchants in which the amount in controversy was the enormous sum of £840.[7] In many of the cases, the plea roll entries do not indicate anything about the nature of the debts; the only indication of their mercantile character is the identification of the plaintiff as a merchant. In others, however, it is specifically noted that the debts arose out of sales of cloth or wool.[8] Examples of mercantile debt collection actions can also be found in the yearbooks, although the nature of these reports is

---

[4] For an overview of the early common law procedures for the enforcement of contractual obligations, see Baker, *Introduction to English Legal History*, 360–73.
[5] *Select Cases Exchequer*, 48 SS 67, 78, 86, 89, 90, 97, 162, 203, 210. Because of the importance of Italian merchants as lenders to the crown, they were given the privilege of using proceedings in Exchequer to collect their claims against private debtors. Prestwich, 'Italian Merchants in Late Thirteenth and Early Fourteenth Century England', 90–91.
[6] *Select Cases Law Merchant*, 46 SS 79 (1309).
[7] *Select Cases Exchequer*, 48 SS 93 (1278).
[8] *Select Cases Law Merchant*, 46 SS 79; *Select Cases Exchequer*, 48 SS 86, 94.

such that only the occasional debt cases that happened to present interesting disputes about procedure or pleading would attract the attention of compilers.[9]

From medieval times until at least the eighteenth century, one of the most common legal forms used for agreements of all sorts was the penal bond with a condition that the obligation would be void if some act were performed.[10] Since the action of debt was the standard means for enforcing bonds, a wide variety of complex commercial disputes came before the central courts in actions on conditional bonds. For example, in the Elizabethan case of *More* v. *Morecomb* (1601),[11] an action of debt was brought on a bond the condition of which was that the defendant was to deliver a ship and its equipment, or pay the value thereof. Even where a bond was not used, complex commercial disputes might be brought in actions of debt so long as the plaintiff claimed a liquidated sum. There are, for example, several cases in the Exchequer rolls in the late thirteenth and early fourteenth centuries where English wool producers had entered into long term contracts for the sale of wool to continental merchant firms, performance of which was interrupted by wars or other trade disruptions.[12] The agreements provided for earnest money payments by the merchants at the outset, to be applied to wool bought in the final year of the contract term. Thus, the disputes that arose when the continental merchants were unable to come to England to take the wool could be litigated within the action of debt by having the merchants bring a claim that the wool sellers were wrongfully detaining the earnest money paid.[13]

---

[9] *Speye* v. *Ledet* (1310), Y.B. 4 Edw. II, 26 SS 8 (action of debt on a bond brought by two merchants of Lucca); *Randolf* v. *Abbot of Hayles* (1311), Y.B. 4 Edw. II, 42 SS 19, s.c. Y.B. 6 & 7 Edw. II, Eyre of Kent, 27 SS 32 (£100 debt for wool contracted on behalf of an abbot by one of the monks of the house); *Stowey* v. *Prior of Bruton* (1378), Y.B. 2 Rich. II (Ames Ser.) 11 (debt by prior for price of sheep bought by defendant's bailiff at fair of Bristol). A succinct explanation of the nature of the yearbooks can be found in Baker, *Introduction to English Legal History*, 204–07.

[10] Simpson, *History of the Common Law of Contract*, 88–135.

[11] Cro. Eliz. 864.

[12] *Select Cases Law Merchant*, 46 SS 63, 69.

[13] There are also some cases in the yearbooks and early nominate reports where commercial disputes were litigated in actions of covenant. E.g., *Aubrey* v. *Flory* (1321), Y.B. 14 Edw. II, Eyre of London, 86 SS 235 (agreement to buy merchandise at the fair of Lynn); *Chantflower* v. *Priestly* (1603), Cro. Eliz. 914 (contract for the sale of twenty tons of copper); *Oshey* v. *Hicks* (1610), Cro. Jac.

It seems entirely likely that these occasional reports in the yearbooks and early reports reflect but a fraction of the central courts' involvement with mercantile cases via actions of debt or covenant. Consider the following item from a late-fifteenth-century yearbook:

Note by Littleton, J. that in debt brought by two executors, where one was summoned and severed, and the other and the defendant were at issue, and then the case went without day; that in this case the resummons shall be sued by the executor who was received to sue alone, and not by both etc.[14]

No one would suppose that such an item had any connection with commercial affairs. Indeed, the modern edition of the yearbook notes that the case was digested in Fitzherbert's *Abridgment* under the heading for 'Resummons' rather than 'Debt'[15] However, the corresponding entry from the plea rolls shows that Littleton's remark was made in connection with a debt action brought by the executors of one London mercer against another London mercer on a bill obligatory in the amount of £126 17s. The editor of this yearbook notes that the Common Pleas rolls for the Easter term alone contained approximately 3,800 cases, of which 2,700 were actions of debt, most of them brief notations of the entry of the plea and the defendant's default.[16] One cannot help but suppose that the yearbooks and reports show only the smallest tip of an iceberg of commercial litigation that might be discovered in the actions of debt in the plea rolls of the central courts for the fourteenth to the seventeenth centuries.[17]

The great treasure trove of commercial litigation in the early records of the central courts is not, however, to be found in the actions of debt or covenant, but in the action of account.[18] The

263 (agreement to take a one-half interest in a shipment of corn to be purchased at Danzig and shipped to Leghorn); *Anon.* (1647), Style 31 (agreement to pay the costs of repairing and outfitting a ship).
[14] Y.B. 10 Edw. IV, 49 Hen. VI (1470), 47 SS 118.
[15] 47 SS 182 (concordance with Fitzherbert).
[16] Neilson, Introduction to *Yearbooks of Edward IV*, 47 SS xix.
[17] Baker has noted that 'the rolls of the Common Pleas for the fourteenth and fifteenth centuries, especially those of the London filazers, are full of commercial cases involving city tradesmen and merchants; and the proportion of foreign names there bears witness to the international character of some of the business'. Baker, 'Law Merchant and Common Law', 348–49.
[18] On the history of the action of account, see Ames, 'History of Parol Contracts'; Belsheim, 'Action of Account'; Hening, 'History of the Beneficiary's Action in

action of account was originally designed to provide a remedy for the defalcations of manorial bailiffs, guardians, and the like. During the fourteenth century it became generally available as the means of enforcing the obligations of all manner of agents and fiduciaries to their principals.[19] Accordingly, the writ of account could be used in a variety of commercial disputes, such as actions among partners or cases where merchants sued factors to whom they had entrusted their goods for sale.[20] Whether the surviving records reveal the commercial nature of the underlying disputes is largely fortuitous.

Although there are many cases of account in the yearbook period, the yearbook reports themselves often give no indication whether they arose from mercantile disputes. However, the plea roll entries appended to the reports in the modern editions sometimes do show that the cases arose out of commercial disputes. For example, in *Dane* v. *Holbein* (1388),[21] the yearbook report describes only the argument between counsel about procedure in account actions. The record, however, reveals that case arose out of a dispute between a prominent London merchant and his sales agent over a period of nearly eighteen years, involving large quantities of wool and cloth and sums of money amounting to £1,000. This case is a particularly good illustration of the way that the mercantile character of actions of account might pass into oblivion in the ordinary sources of early English law. Other than leafing through the books page by page, yearbook reports can be found

Assumpsit'; Langdell, 'Brief Survey of Equity Jurisprudence'; Stoljar, "Transformation of Account'; Street, *Foundations of Legal Liability*, 3: 99–113.

[19] Stoljar, 'Transformation of Account', 206–07.
[20] Sample pleadings for such actions can be found in fourteenth-century manuals. *Novae Narrationes*, 80 SS 294; *Early Registers of Writs*, 87 SS 208. There are instances of such actions among partners in the central courts even earlier. *John the Spicer* v. *Walter of Leicester* (1288), *Select Cases Law Merchant*, 46 SS 45; *Pylat* v. *Reginald* (1308), *Select Cases Law Merchant*, 46 SS 78; Y.B. 34 & 35 Edw. I (1306), (Rolls Ser.) 294.
[21] Y.B. 11 Rich. II (Ames Ser.) 238. In *Scottow* v. *Birkeleghe* (1312), Y.B. 5 Edw. II, 33 SS 205, the yearbook notes only that the plaintiff had brought a writ of account against the defendant as receiver of his moneys, but the plea roll entry shows that the defendant sold 'spices and divers merchandises' for the plaintiff for which he was accountable for the large sum of £200. See also *Select Cases Law Merchant*, 46 SS 126–31, 163–68 (auditors' report in account action against factors in Calais of a York wool merchant); *Select Cases Law Merchant*, 46 SS 106, 156–59 (auditors' report in account action against factor in Spain of an Ipswich merchant, whose trade seems to have been primarily the export of cloth and import of iron).

only through the abridgments that digested and indexed the cases. Yet the only entry for *Dane* v. *Holbein* in Statham's *Abridgment* was the laconic note that 'in account it is a good plea to say that he has accounted before the plaintiff himself'.[22]

In some instances, though, the use of account as a remedy for commercial disputes presented the sort of pleading question that would be likely to be recorded in the yearbooks. There was, for example, a lively dispute in the fourteenth century about whether factors to whom goods had been consigned for sale should be treated as bailiffs to whom the goods had been entrusted or receivers of the money collected from the sales. The facts of the underlying dispute would come out in the argument over proper pleading, and hence the commercial nature of the transaction would be noted in the records, as in a 1308 yearbook case against a factor who had sold cloth worth forty marks and failed to turn over the proceeds to his principal.[23] On the other hand, a similar case seven years later[24] shows how much fortuity there is in the content of the records of the common law courts. Counsel for a person sued as bailiff of certain linens and cloths objected that since the dispute involved the money from the sale of the cloth, he should have been sued as receiver of money rather than as bailiff of goods. Chief Justice Bereford was evidently not thinking of the problems of future historians when he hit upon a clever solution to the problem. The yearbook tells us that 'this averment was put on the roll by Bereford, C.J., without any reference to linens or cloths'. The yearbook's modern editor did locate the roll entry for this case, and indeed it makes no mention of the cloth, referring to the defendant only as the plaintiff's bailiff in a certain town. Thus, contrary to the usual pattern of a sketchy yearbook item whose commercial setting is revealed only by the plea rolls, here a plea roll entry that appears to have nothing to do with mercantile affairs is illuminated by the arguments recorded in the yearbook.

Not only did the central courts hear cases involving merchants, they also took account of the special needs of commerce in the development and application of legal rules. For example, there are cases from the fourteenth to the seventeenth centuries dealing with such issues as whether one charged as bailiff of goods was entitled

---

[22] Y.B. 11 Rich. II (Ames Ser.) 238, quoting Statham's *Abridgment*, Accompt, 46.
[23] Y.B. 2 & 3 Edw. II (1308), 19 SS 34.
[24] *Pirton* v. *Tumby* (1315), Y.B. 8 Edw. II, 41 SS 59.

to deduct his expenses and compensation, whether he was chargeable for profits that he made or should have made, and whether he was discharged if the goods were lost by theft or shipwreck.[25] Account actions among partners are a particularly good example of how the central courts deliberately adapted the forms of the common law to the needs of commerce. In ordinary actions of account, one who charged the defendant as receiver of his money rather than as bailiff of lands or goods was required to show by whose hands the defendant had received the money,[26] an obviously difficult task in actions among partners. Moreover, prior to a statute enacted in the early eighteenth century, it was doubtful whether an action of account would lie in a dispute among joint owners, unless one had specifically designated the other as bailiff.[27] These limitations, however, were dispensed with in actions between merchants. Coke notes that 'this was provided by Law in favour of merchants, and for the advancement of trade and traffique'.[28]

The action of account was also used as a remedy for recovery of money invested in others' trading ventures. Until the relaxation of the proscription against usury at the time of the Reformation, one of the principal forms of investment for those having surplus funds was to deliver the money to a merchant to be used in his trade. The investor would receive a share of the profits and be subject to the risk of loss. The modern literature on business history shows that such arrangements, generally referred to as *commenda* in Italian, were commonplace in continental trade in medieval times.[29] A wealthy merchant or nobleman might invest surplus funds with a younger man who was willing to take the risks and hardships of the travel but lacked the capital necessary for the venture, merchants still actively engaged in travelling trade ventures might invest part of their capital in other merchants' ventures as a way of diversify-

25 Viner's *Abridgment*, Account O 1, *citing* 41 Edw. III, 4 (1368); Stoljar, 'Transformation of Account', 207, *citing* Y.B. 46 Edw. III, f. 9, pl. 4 (1372); Viner's *Abridgment*, Account O 20, *citing* 6 Rich. II (1383); *Gomersall* v. *Gomersall* (1586), Godb. 55, 58, 2 Leo. 194, 196; *Southcote's Case* (1601), 4 Co. Rep. 83b; Viner's *Abridgment*, Account O 19, *citing Brown* v. *Robinson* (1634), Mich. 9 Car. I.
26 Belsheim, 'Action of Account', 482.
27 Coke, *First Part of the Institutes of the Laws of England*, 200b; Statute of 4 Anne, c. 16, § 27 (1705).
28 Coke, *First Part of the Institutes of the Laws of England*, 172a.
29 Lopez and Raymond, *Medieval Trade in the Mediterranean World*, 174–84.

ing their risks, and even persons of modest means might invest small amounts in the trading ventures of merchants.

The legal treatment of such arrangements is one of the most revealing phenomena in the early history of English commercial law. In the literature on continental trade and law, one finds extensive discussion of *commenda* contracts and their variants.[30] By contrast, in the literature on English trade and mercantile law, one finds relatively little discussion of the legal forms of investment in trade. At most, one will find occasional remarks that *commenda* arrangements may have been known in England.[31] It would be easy to conclude that such arrangements were unimportant in English law and commerce, at least in comparison to their prominent role on the continent. In fact, however, there are numerous actions of account in the English central courts, as early as the fourteenth century, involving investments in trade of essentially the same sort as the continental *commenda* arrangements. The parties involved in the English cases show the same variety of investors, from widows to wealthy merchants, as in the continental literature.[32]

In the English system, where the surviving legal records are primarily reports of lawsuits, organized by procedural categories, these cases would be digested, if at all, simply as cases of account. It would make no difference whether the transaction had been an advance of money from a passive investor to a merchant in a profit-sharing arrangement, an investment by one merchant in another's trading venture, a partnership or joint venture arrangement among merchants, or a consignment of goods from a merchant to his factor or commission agent. Indeed, these mercantile cases would be grouped together as an undifferentiated mass with the far larger number of account actions involving manorial bail-

---

30 It has been noted that 'perhaps ... no aspect of commercial law has been the subject of so much heated controversy as the origin, legal character, and economic function of the commenda'. Ibid., 174.

31 Holdsworth, *History of English Law*, 8: 195 ('The [*commenda*] contract was very common all over Europe in the Middle Ages, and it was known in England.').

32 *Selby v. Palfrayman* (1389), Y.B. 13 Rich. II (Ames Ser.) 79; *Septvaux v. Marchaunt* (1385), Y.B. 8–10 Rich. II (Ames Ser.) 187; Y.B. 14 Edw. III (1340), (Rolls Ser.) lxviii; *Coleman v. Marham* (1321), Y.B. 14 Edw. II, Eyre of London, 86 SS 353, 354; *Odi v. Aringi* (1321), Y.B. 14 Edw. II, Eyre of London, 86 SS 217. See also *Core v. May* (1536), Dyer 20, printed with record entry in Baker and Milsom, *Sources of English Legal History*, 243 (debt on sealed bill given for money to be invested in a commercial venture).

iffs, guardians in socage, and the like. By contrast, in continental systems, where one of the principal sources is the records of the notaries who prepared legal documents, and where the legal system is organized by substantive categories, a slight difference in the exact terms of an arrangement between merchants or investors might lead to an entirely different legal characterization of the transaction. Thus, the seeming difference between continental and English law may be nothing more than a matter of organization, not content.

THE LAW MERCHANT AND THE MERCANTILE COURTS

The preceding section of this chapter showed that the usual assumption that merchants shunned the common law courts is inaccurate. The remainder of this chapter considers the other side of the traditional account of early English commercial law, the thesis that mercantile disputes were governed by a distinct body of law known as the law merchant, administered in specialized mercantile courts. In the standard accounts of the history of commercial law, the law merchant is usually taken to have been a body of substantive law based on mercantile custom, distinct from the common law applied in the central courts. Although this view has won nearly universal acceptance among writers on commercial law, the evidence shows that it is quite inaccurate.

Some aspects of the traditional view of the law merchant are indisputable. It is clear that by late medieval times many disputes among merchants were heard in the courts associated with fairs and markets and in the municipal courts of the principal commercial cities and towns. Further, it is clear from contemporary sources that medieval lawyers frequently used the term law merchant in speaking of the law followed in these courts and that they understood this as something distinct from the common law. Perhaps the clearest example of this usage is in the Statute of the Staple of 1353, which directs that actions involving merchants coming to the staple 'shall be ruled by the law merchant, of all things touching the staple, and not by the common law of the land, not by the usage of cities, boroughs, or other towns'.[33] It does not,

---

[33] 27 Edw. III, stat. 2, c. 8 (1353), *Statutes of the Realm*, 1: 336.

however, follow that the law merchant was a distinct body of substantive law, nor that the courts of the fairs and markets were exclusively concerned with mercantile matters governed by the law merchant. To the contrary, Baker has argued persuasively that the phrase 'law merchant' as used in early English sources did not refer to a distinct body of substantive law. 'When medieval lawyers distinguished systems of "law" they usually had procedure in mind. . . . The medieval law merchant was not so much a corpus of mercantile practice or commercial law as an expeditious procedure especially adapted for the needs of men who could not tarry for the common law.'[34]

The earliest-known English source on the law merchant, believed to date from about 1280, is a brief Latin treatise titled *Lex Mercatoria* preserved in the municipal records of Bristol as part of the so-called *Little Red Book of Bristol*.[35] The work is a guide to procedure in cases involving merchants, not a code of substantive commercial law. Moreover, even as a system of procedure, the law merchant as described in this treatise was by no means wholly different from the procedure applied in the central courts. Indeed, a passage in the treatise specifically states that there are only three differences: 'The law of the market [place] differs from the common law of the realm in three ways. In the first place it reaches decisions more quickly. Secondly, whoever pledges for anyone to answer to a [plea of] trespass, covenant, debt, or detinue of chattels pledges for the whole debt, damages and expenses sought. . . . And in the third place, it differs in that it does not admit anyone to [wage] law on the negative side; but always in that law it is for the plaintiff and not the defendant to make proof, whether by suit or by deed or otherwise. And as for other [matters] such as prosecutions, defences, essoins, defaults, delays, judgments and executions of judgments, the same procedure is to be observed as in other laws.'[36]

Speedy adjudication is the characteristic of the law merchant most emphasized in the early sources. The *Carta Mercatoria* of 1303, by which Edward I granted various privileges to foreign

---

[34] Baker, 'Law Merchant and Common Law', 346, 347.
[35] *Lex Mercatoria*, printed in Bickley, ed., *Little Red Book of Bristol*. An English translation appears in Teetor, 'England's Earliest Treatise on the Law Merchant'. D. R. Coquillette is presently preparing a new scholarly edition.
[36] Teetor transl., 182–83.

merchants in exchange for customs dues, requires that 'all bailiffs, and ministers of fairs, cities, boroughs, and market-towns, do speedy justice to the merchants aforesaid who complain before them from day to day without delay according to the Law Merchant'.[37] In a well-known yearbook case heard before all of the justices assembled in Exchequer Chamber, the Chancellor is said to have remarked that alien merchants were 'not bound to sue according to the law of the land to await trial by twelve men and other formalities of the law of the land'. Rather, their cases should be determined 'from hour to hour and day to day'.[38] Indeed, Coke suggested that the fair courts came to be called 'piedpowders' because 'there shall be as speedy justice done . . . as the dust can fall from the foot'.[39] The claim of speedy justice was evidently not an idle boast. Early on the morning of Friday, 5 May 1458, a merchant sued another merchant on a £60 debt in the piedpowder court of Colchester. The defendant failed to appear as summoned hourly from nine o'clock until noon, judgment was entered by default, and by four o'clock that afternoon woollen cloths of the defendant had been seized in execution, appraised, and turned over to the plaintiff in satisfaction of the debt.[40]

One must, however, be careful to avoid romanticizing the mercantile courts in light of modern conceptions of the desirability of specialized commercial tribunals or modern abhorrence of medieval legal procedure. The impression conveyed by the discussions of the law merchant and the mercantile courts found in most modern books on commercial law is that medieval merchants were level-headed men of the late nineteenth or early twentieth century who, suffering the misfortune of having been born in the wrong century, did their best to secede from the culture of their contemporaries. As one mid-twentieth-century bills and notes book puts it, 'the rules of procedure in Common Law Courts were stupid and irrational. The forms of pleading were technical and meritorious cases were often thrown out of court because of slight failure to follow technicalities. Moreover there was the ridiculous procedure known as Wager of Law in the Common Law Courts . . .

---

[37] *Carta Mercatoria*, 31 Edw. I, printed in Bland, Brown, and Tawney, eds., *English Economic History: Select Documents*, 211–16.
[38] *The Carrier's Case* (1473), Y.B. 13 Edw. IV, 64 SS 30, 32.
[39] Coke, *Fourth Part of the Institutes of the Laws of England*, 272.
[40] *Select Cases Law Merchant*, 23 SS 122.

Merchants were practical men and they abhorred the crude, slow and irrational methods of trial in the Common Law Courts.'[41]

The actual records of the fair and town courts present a rather different image. The legal culture of the fair courts may not have been all that different from that of the common law courts. For example, although suits could be brought in the fair or town courts without obtaining the appropriate form of writ from the Chancery, the conceptual scheme associated with the writ system is as evident in the fair and town courts as in the central courts. The rolls of the fair and town courts regularly refer to the cases as actions of debt, covenant, detinue, account, and the like. Although the specific rules of pleading in the fair courts may have differed from those of the central courts, the rules seem to have been applied every bit as rigorously. For example the records of the court at the Fair of St Ives in the late thirteenth century contain numerous examples of cases being dismissed on such technical points as insufficient specificity in pleading or misstating a party's name.[42]

Similarly, the methods of proof in the mercantile courts differed from those of the central courts in detail, not in fundamental attitude. To be sure, there were circumstances in which an issue that would have been settled by wager of law[43] in the central courts was determined by inquiry in the fair courts, but that was not because compurgation was unknown in the fair courts. Quite the contrary, there are innumerable instances in the fair and town courts' records where defendants wage law, including cases where wager would not have been allowed in the central courts. To give

---

[41] Whitney, *Outline of Bills and Notes*, 3.

[42] *Select Cases Law Merchant*, 23 SS 17, 46, 57.

[43] Wager of law, or compurgation, was a standard means of defence in actions in debt on informal contracts. The defendant offered to 'wage his law' that the debt was not due. The court set a time for the defendant to appear, along with his oath-helpers, usually eleven, and swear a formal oath denying the debt. If all of the compurgators swore the oath without slipping, the defendant won the lawsuit. Simpson, *History of the Common Law of Contract*, 138–44. In its temporal and cultural context, the procedure was not at all irrational. As Simpson notes, "To a lawyer of the twentieth century, trial by wager of law seems slightly ridiculous; ... modern man, however religiously minded, does not believe in hell in the straightforward and vivid way in which men believed in it in the age of faith. But even today I suppose it would be difficult to collect eleven perjurers in order to resist an action for breach of contract; in the fifteenth century it must have been even more difficult, and the evidence shows that in a very considerable proportion of cases, defendants opted for trial by jury'. Ibid., 138–39.

but one example, in an assault action in 1287 before the fair court at St Ives, the defendant denied the assault and waged his law, but failed when one of his oath helpers slipped up, naming the defendant as Robert instead of Henry.[44] The fair courts and the central courts simply had differing rules on the choice among the various methods of proof, most of which seem irrational to people living more than half a millennium later.

Much of the confusion concerning the law merchant and the mercantile courts may be attributable to the misleading assumption that the courts of the fairs, markets, and towns were specialized commercial courts created by merchants as forums for resolution of their complex mercantile disputes. From the portrayal of these courts in most modern works on commercial law, one gets the impression of a group of cosmopolitan merchants, consulting their equivalents of the Uniform Commercial Code or Code du Commerce in an effort to resolve intricate problems of sales law, insurance, charter-parties, security arrangements, and the like. The best cure for that impression is simply to read through some of the now published records of these courts. To be sure, there are no end of disputes about debts and sales. Yet equally common are cases arising out of brawls between neighbours, prosecutions for maintaining houses of prostitution, complaints of obstructing roads or improper disposal of rubbish, complaints by those duped by con-men, and what must be one of the classics of English legal records – the prosecution of a gang of London tailors for having 'made an assembly, under colour of playing with a football, in order to assault others, occasion disputes, and perpetrate other evil deeds against the peace'.[45] As such items indicate, the term 'mercantile courts' is a misnomer as applied to the courts of the fairs and markets, or the municipal

[44] *Select Cases Law Merchant*, 23 SS 20. Wager survived in the seignorial and town courts in many situations, such as trespasses and even felony, long after it had been excluded in the central courts. Pollock and Maitland, *History of English Law*, 2: 634–35. In *Aubrey* v. *Flory* (1321), Y.B. 14 Edw. II, Eyre of London, 86 SS 235, it was contended that under law merchant procedure the defendant could disprove breach of a covenant by wager of law, even though such an issue would be resolved by a jury at common law. Wager of law was also a very common method of proof in actions in the London Mayor's Court. Thomas, Introduction to *Calendar of London Mayor's Court Rolls*, xxx–xxxix.
[45] See, e.g., *Select Pleas Manorial Courts*, 2 SS 143; *Select Cases Law Merchant*, 23 SS 36, 106; *Calendar of London Plea and Memoranda Rolls* 2: 152 (1373) (the football case).

courts of the major cities and towns. These were not specialized commercial courts, whose jurisdiction depended on the commercial nature of a dispute. Rather, they were simply local courts of general jurisdiction held at places where a great deal of trade took place. The prevalence of commercial disputes in the courts of the fairs, markets, and towns is not a product of the system of law applied by those courts but the entirely unsurprising result of a geographical division of the jurisdiction of the local court systems.

The effort to draw conclusions about medieval English commercial law from comparisons between the mercantile courts and the common law courts is fundamentally misguided. Although it may well be true that procedure was less formal in the fair courts than in the common law courts, it is a non sequitur to attribute this to the prevalence of commercial disputes in the fair courts. The phenomenon might simply be a matter of differences between local courts and the central courts. Inferences about the influence of commercial needs on legal procedure could be drawn only if significant differences were found by a comprehensive comparison between the courts of the fairs and towns and those of the manors or other local courts in less commercially developed areas. That would be a monumental undertaking. Yet even a cursory examination of some of the now published records of medieval manorial courts is instructive.

Although the manorial court proceedings are, not surprisingly, dominated by questions of agricultural organization, mercantile matters are encountered on occasion. For example, in a fourteenth-century manorial court roll there is a record of an action for breach of a covenant concerning money delivered 'to be converted in merchandise',[46] and in a thirteenth-century manuscript treatise on manorial court proceedings there is a precedent for an action by a vintner complaining that another had wrongfully induced a Southampton wine merchant to renege on a contract for the sale of a ton of wine by disparaging the plaintiff's credit.[47] On matters of procedure, the similarities between the manorial courts and the

---

[46] *Bolay* v. *Whitring* (1320), *Court Baron*, 4 SS 131. Apparently Whitring had failed to deliver the full sum agreed, and Bolay recovered damages for that default, while Whitring was held liable for return of the moneys that were received. The case resembles those involving investments in trade that were handled by the central courts in the action of account.

[47] *Court Baron*, 4 SS 40.

mercantile courts are as striking as the differences between either and the central courts. As in the courts of the fairs and towns, most actions in the manorial and other local courts were initiated simply by a verbal or written complaint, without the formality of obtaining a writ from Chancery of the sort needed in the central courts,[48] and many disputes as to fact or customary law were settled by inquest of those attending the court. Indeed, where one does find differences between mercantile and manorial local courts, they do not necessarily show that the merchants were especially averse to 'legalistic' procedure. For example, although professional pleaders were commonly prohibited in manorial courts, they regularly appeared in courts of the fairs.[49]

Even the aspect of procedure that is usually taken to be the pre-eminent attribute of the law merchant – that difficult questions of law should be resolved by a convocation of the merchants themselves – may not be peculiar to the mercantile courts. Consider, for example, two actions on debts, one from a manorial court and one from a fair court. In the manorial court case, the plaintiff sued for the price of a bull sold on credit. The defendant contended that 'he is not bound to answer because [the plaintiff] had not produced suit nor named any certain day as the day for payment'. The issue was resolved as follows:

[T]he parties have prayed that this be inquired by the township. And the township said that he has produced sufficient suit. Afterwards it was testified by the whole [township or by the whole court] that the said Nicholas was bound to the said Bartholomew in the said 5d.[50]

In the fair court case, the plaintiff sued for the price of a horse sold on credit, alleging that God's penny had been given. The defendant denied the allegation and sought to wage his law, whereupon the plaintiff sought the ruling 'of the merchants as to whether the [defendant] by his law can abate' the action. After an adjournment to a day when more were in attendance at court,

it is awarded by the merchants that whereas the contract ... was confirmed with a farthing ... as a God's penny, which God's penny the

[48] Turner, Introduction to *Brevia Placitata*, 66 SS xvi.
[49] Maitland, Introduction to *Select Pleas Manorial Courts*, 2 SS 135–36; Gross, Introduction to *Select Cases Law Merchant*, 23 SS xxxiv–xxxv.
[50] *Select Pleas Manorial Courts*, 2 SS 118 (1295) (Manorial Court of Abbot of Ramsey at King's Ripton).

[defendant] did not mention in his denial, therefore [the defendant] shall remain as one undefended.[51]

Both cases involve what might well be considered the most significant issue in early debtor-creditor law: what counts as sufficient proof or disproof of a debt. In both cases there was a dispute on the issue of law, and in both cases the matter was resolved not by a judge but by consultation of the persons in attendance at the court.

THE LAW MERCHANT IN THE CENTRAL COURTS

Another perspective on early English commercial law is provided by an examination of the role of the law merchant in the central courts. According to the traditional view, that should be a subject easily dismissed – the whole point of the establishment of the mercantile courts is supposed to have been that the common law courts would not recognize the law merchant. In fact, however, the central courts did hear disputes concerning the law merchant and even applied law merchant procedure and rules in mercantile cases.

One way that the central courts might be called upon to determine disputes about the law merchant was through the exercise of their supervisory authority over local court actions. Just as parties dissatisfied with the decisions of manorial or other local courts might, in certain circumstances, be able to have the matter heard by the courts at Westminster, so too cases originating in the courts of the fairs and towns might be brought before the common law courts for review. In that way the central courts might be called upon to decide questions of both the scope and content of the law merchant. For example, there are cases in which defendants sued in fair courts sought relief from the central courts on the grounds that their cases should not have been heard in the fair courts.[52] Even closer to the core of the law merchant are the cases where the contention in the central courts was simply that the fair court erred in its decision on the rules of the law merchant. A good example is

---

[51] *Select Cases Law Merchant*, 23 SS 39 (1291) (Fair Court of St Ives). 'God's penny' was a form of earnest money given to bind a bargain. See Pollock and Maitland, *History of English Law*, 2: 208–09.
[52] *Select Cases Law Merchant*, 46 SS 103, 109.

Dederic v. *Abbot of Ramsey* (1315),[53] a case in the King's Bench for trespass brought by a merchant against the bailiffs of St Ives fair. The merchant had sent cloths by his 'yeoman and servant' to the fair, where they were attached by the bailiffs of the fair court for personal debts of the servant. The merchant contended that according to the law merchant where there was a suggestion that goods seized by a fair court belonged to another, the goods were to be held for one year to give the owner an opportunity to come and prove his ownership. By contrast, the bailiffs claimed that the law merchant rule was that if the owner did not come and prove his claim by the end of the fair, the goods could be sold. Thus, the action in the King's Bench turned entirely on a specific dispute about the rules of the law merchant. It is also worthy of note that the King's Bench resolved the matter by a procedure usually assumed to have been the exclusive province of the mercantile courts – a jury of merchants was summoned to Westminster to resolve the legal issue.[54]

Application of law merchant procedure was not limited to cases arising in the courts of the fairs or towns. In the era before the evolution of the *nisi prius* system, cases that could not conveniently be litigated in the ordinary sessions at Westminster were often tried by justices of the central courts and others acting pursuant to special commissions from the king.[55] Many such commissions explicitly directed that the cases be resolved according to the law merchant.[56] A good example is a late-thirteenth-century case in which a Winchester merchant complained that wool delivered to him was not of the same quality as the sample which had been the basis of the sale. The commissioners were directed by the king 'to inquire in the presence of lawful and discreet merchants and citizens of Winchester, by the oath of good and lawful men of the same city through whom the truth of the matter can best be known in the premises, and for the swift and competent amends to be made according to the law merchant'.[57]

Another such case shows how a court at Westminster, as well as

---

53 *Select Cases Law Merchant*, 46 SS 86.
54 The King's Bench must have thought this a significant issue; four juries of twelve merchants were summoned, from London, Lincoln, Westminster, and Northampton.
55 Holdsworth, *History of English Law*, 1: 49–51, 264–85.
56 Baker, 'Law Merchant and Common Law', 346, 346–47 n. 25.
57 *Select Cases Law Merchant*, 46 SS 28.

the justices appointed by the special commission, might be brought into disputes about the law merchant. A Southampton merchant had sold wool on credit to a Winchester merchant and his wife. The debtors died and their executors refused to pay the debt. On the Southampton merchant's complaint to the king, a special commission was issued for the case to be heard at Winchester, 'and as this should be done rightfully and in accordance with the law merchant, . . . the lord king has instructed the aforesaid justices . . . they should proceed in that suit as quickly as it should be done according to the law merchant'.[58] At the trial in Winchester, the seller produced a tally alleged to have been given as evidence of the debt and offered 'to prove that tally according to the law merchant'.[59] The executors objected that although during the debtors' lives 'proof of that tally ought to have been allowed according to the law merchant, inasmuch as that action is in the persons of the executors, those executors ought to be tried according to common law and not according to law merchant'. The defendants' contention was rejected and judgment was entered against them. The dispute was then brought before the King's Bench at Westminster, the defendants assigning as error that proof by tally should not be allowed against a merchant's executors. Furthermore, the defendants contended that by the time of the suit the plaintiff had withdrawn from trade and thus because he was 'a knight and not a merchant . . . he ought not to have been admitted to prove the aforesaid tally according to law merchant'. Faced with these thorny issues about the details of law merchant procedure, the justices of the King's Bench directed that 'eighteen merchants, expert in merchant law' should be summoned from London, Lincoln, York, and Winchester 'to certify the king on some points concerning the law merchant'.[60]

Application of law merchant rules and procedures in central court cases was not limited to proceedings initiated by special

---

[58] *Gosbert de Bozeis* v. *Alexander of Marwell* (1292), 57 SS 69.
[59] A tally was a wooden stick on which notches were carved to represent the amount of the debt. The stick was then split in two lengthwise, and the debtor and creditor would each receive one half. If the amount of the debt was later disputed, the two pieces could be put together, to see whether they 'tallied'. Salzman, *English Trade in the Middle Ages*, 25–28.
[60] It appears from the record that the matter was not ultimately resolved by a merchant jury; rather, the defendants switched to a defence of an alleged satisfaction and lost on that issue before an ordinary jury.

commission. In at least one type of case, actions of account
between partners, the standard form contained in the register of
writs for initiation of actions in the central courts specifically refers
to the law merchant. The general form of the writ of account states
that the defendant should be required 'to render to [the plaintiff]
his reasonable account for the time when he was his bailiff [or
receiver] . . . if he can reasonably show that he ought to render it'.
By contrast, in the version for an account against one charged as
receiver of monies to the profit of the plaintiff, or to the common
profit of the plaintiff and the defendant, the defendant is to
account if the plaintiff 'can reasonably show *by the law merchant*'
that he ought to render account.[61] There is also some evidence that
writs used in other forms of action were sometimes made out in a
similar form, specifying that the plaintiff is to make his proof
according to the law merchant.[62] Perhaps the most interesting is an
early-fourteenth-century yearbook case, *Bandon's Case*,[63] where a
merchant brought an action of debt against another merchant by a
writ in the usual form save that it ended with the words 'as the
aforesaid John shall reasonably be able to show, according to the
law merchant, that he ought to pay him'. The plaintiff produced a
tally as evidence of the debt, and the defendant sought to wage his
law. When the plaintiff objected that 'we are pleading at the law
merchant which does not suffer any law to be waged in this case',
the defendant answered that 'we are here in the King's court where
we ought to be led by the common law and not by the law

---

[61] *Registrum Brevium*, 4th edn (1687), 135; Fitzherbert, *New Natura Brevium*, 117
(emphasis added). For examples of such actions, see 46 SS 78 (1308), 46 SS 53
(1291). In the latter case, the Barons of the Exchequer had occasion to summon
merchant juries to assist with questions of the law merchant and the interpretation of accounting records written in Italian.
[62] Y.B. 21 & 22 Edw. I (1293) (Rolls Ser.) 7₊ ('Note that, one B brought a writ of
Debt against C; and they pleaded according to the Law Merchant'). In *Aubrey* v.
Flory (1321), Y.B. 14 Edw. II, Eyre of London, 86 SS 235, a merchant brought
an action for breach of covenant concerning the goods to be delivered at the fair
of Lynn. The defendant objected that since the breach was alleged to have
occurred at Lynn, the action could not be tried in London. The plaintiff
responded that in actions among merchants, contract disputes could be tried
wherever the parties were found. Perhaps to bolster that claim, the plaintiff then
obtained a writ directing that the case be heard either by the common law or the
law merchant.
[63] Y.B. 6 & 7 Edw. II, Eyre of Kent, 27 SS 48, s.c. *Select Cases Law Merchant*, 46
SS lxxxi; s.c. sub nom. *Compton* v. *Anon*, *Select Cases Law Merchant*, 46 SS
lxxxii; s.c. sub nom. *Comberton* v. *Comberton*, *Select Cases Law Merchant*, 46 SS
lxxxiv.

merchant'. The plaintiff responded with the contention that 'although we be here at the common law, none the less the justices have power to plead all pleas as well according to the law merchant as according to the common law'.[64] The court agreed and gave judgment for the plaintiff on the grounds that the defendant failed to respond to 'the proof which [the plaintiff] offers in accordance with the Law Merchant and the nature of his writ'.[65] One could hardly imagine a clearer ruling on the point that the law merchant would be applied by the common law courts in cases where it was applicable.[66]

---

[64] 46 SS lxxxiv.   [65] 27 SS 49–50.

[66] The rule that in actions among merchants the defendant may not wage law against a tally is also stated in several medieval treatises dating from the mid- to late thirteenth century. *Brevia Placitata*, 66 SS 28; *Casus Placitorum*, 69 SS 25. Similarly, *Fleta* states that in an action of debt, 'if the plaintiff produces suit, the defendant must defend himself . . . and this he does by [wager of] law. The same procedure will be followed when the plaintiff proffers tallies, unless he be a merchant . . .' *Fleta*, 72 SS 203.

2

EARLY EXCHANGE TRANSACTIONS:
COMMERCIAL PRACTICE

To understand the development of the law of bills, one must begin
by considering how merchants actually used bills in early commerce and what issues of economic and social policy were raised by
the transactions in which bills were used. The key to that inquiry is
to begin not with bills themselves, but with the exchange transactions in which bills were used.

EXCHANGE TRANSACTIONS AS
MEANS OF FUNDS TRANSFER

Accustomed as we now are to highly developed systems of
communications and shipping, and specialized institutions for the
settlement of financial transactions, it is easy to overlook how
different the task of the merchant was in the era preceding all such
developments. The French historian Fernand Braudel has pointed
out that the problem of making returns is inherent in any form of
trade. 'Since exchange by definition means reciprocity, any
journey from A to B must be balanced by a return journey –
however complicated and roundabout – from B to A. The round
trip, once complete, forms a circuit. Trade circuits are like
electrical circuits: they work only when the connection is
unbroken.'[1] In the modern world, the problem of 'making returns'
is a macro-economic phenomenon ordinarily discussed only at the
level of statistical measures of the aggregate flow of trade among
nations or regions. In earlier times, the problem of making returns
was a direct and immediate concern for every individual merchant.

In the earliest form of trade organization, making returns meant
simply carrying back the fruits of one's trading journeys. Mer-

[1] Braudel, *Civilization and Capitalism*, 2: 140.

32

chants bought goods in one place, took them to a foreign market, sold them, bought other goods with the proceeds, and then returned home to sell the goods acquired in the foreign market. Having no representatives in other locations nor any international banking system to assist them in making returns, travelling merchants sought to sell their goods and quickly acquire a return cargo, either by direct barter or by purchasing the return goods with the money proceeds of the sale of their goods.[2]

By the thirteenth century, a new form of trade organization began to develop in which 'sedentary merchants' conducted their affairs through a more complex organizational structure.[3] In the simplest form, the merchant would entrust the goods to an agent or employee who travelled with the goods and arranged for their sale and the purchase of a return cargo. In a more developed form, the merchant had representatives who resided permanently in the foreign market. The merchant could then ship the goods to the foreign market on consignment to an agent who arranged for the sale of the goods and purchase of the returns. As Braudel has noted, 'By the end of the sixteenth century, the commission system ... was tending to become general. All merchants – in Italy or in Amsterdam for instance – worked on commission for other merchants, who did the same for them.'[4]

Bills of exchange had their origins in a new mechanism of making returns that became possible with the transition to the regime of the sedentary merchant and the development of the commission merchant system.[5] Suppose, for example, that an Italian merchant shipped spices from Italy to his representative in Flanders. Once the agent in Flanders had sold the spices, he would have funds in Flanders due to his principal in Italy. Suppose that another merchant in Flanders was in the business of buying English wool and shipping it to Italy. Once the Flemish wool merchant's agent in Italy had sold the goods, he would have funds in Italy due to his principal in Flanders. The problem of making

[2] Gras, *Business and Capitalism*, 39, 43.
[3] Gras, *Business and Capitalism*, 37–44, 67–92; de Roover, 'The Commercial Revolution of the Thirteenth Century'.
[4] Braudel, *Civilization and Capitalism*, 2: 150. See also Willan, 'Factor or Agent in Foreign Trade'; Westerfield, *Middlemen in English Business*, 350–62; Elder, 'The van der Molen', 78–145.
[5] Usher, *Early History of Deposit Banking*, 80–81; de Roover, *Money, Banking and Credit in Mediaeval Bruges*, 49–51.

returns could be solved by having the Italian spice merchant's factor in Flanders pay money to the wool merchant, and the Flemish wool merchant's factor in Italy pay money to the Italian spice merchant. In effect, the Flemish wool merchant's outward cargo would have become the Italian spice merchant's return cargo, and vice versa.

The English economic historian Eileen Power gives a lucid illustration of how such exchange transactions were used by the English Merchants of the Staple, who sold English wool at the markets in Flanders,

The Staplers could transfer their money home ... by bills of exchange drawn upon the London offices of merchants who imported on a large scale, and this was the method they habitually employed; they 'made it over', as the phrase went, usually by means of the mercers, who were importers buying heavily at the Flemish marts. The Staplers had Flemish money in Calais, where they sold, and in the marts, where they collected their debts; they wanted English money in the Cotswolds and London where they bought. The mercers had English money in London, where they sold, and needed Flemish money at the marts, where they bought. So the Stapler on the continent delivered his money to a mercer and received a bill of exchange payable at a future date in London in English money.[6]

An exchange transaction of this form would have involved four parties. In Flanders, the Stapler (A), would deliver money to the mercer (B). B would draw a bill of exchange on his representative in London (C), making it payable to the Stapler's representative in London (D). A would send the bill to D in London, who would present it to C for payment, thereby completing the transaction. In modern terminology, the parties would be described by reference to their role on the bill: B would be called the drawer, C the drawee, and D the payee. A, who would not have been a party to the bill itself, would be referred to as the remitter. The terminology commonly used in early exchange practice was somewhat different, focusing more on the two parties who initiated the exchange transaction than on the bill through which the exchange contract was carried out. Thus, A, the party in Flanders who paid the money, would have been referred to as the deliverer or remitter, and B, the party who received the money, would have been referred to as the taker.[7]

[6] Power, 'Wool Trade in the Fifteenth Century', 68.
[7] de Roover, *Gresham on Foreign Exchange*, 99–100.

Early exchange transactions bear some similarity to some modern forms of funds transmission, such as when someone who needs to send money abroad purchases a draft from a bank, drawn on the bank's foreign correspondent. There are, however, important differences. Modern exchange transactions are conducted through specialized financial institutions, and the users of the funds transmission service rarely, if ever, need to concern themselves with the details of how the service operates. By contrast, in early exchange transactions the parties would frequently not have been financial professionals, but merchants who sought out other merchants whose trade flowed in the opposite direction.[8]

Moreover, there is a sense in which 'funds transmission' is a subtly misleading characterization of the problem faced by a factor or other commission merchant in making returns to his principal. The prototype modern commercial transaction giving rise to the need for a funds transfer system is a sale of goods at a distance, that is, the seller ships the goods to a distant buyer and the buyer arranges to transmit the funds to the seller. By contrast, given the hazards and slowness of both communication and transport in the early commercial world, the prototype commercial transaction of the period was not a sale at a distance, but the shipment of goods by the seller to his foreign commission agent. The buyers purchased the goods from the seller's commission agent and made payment to the selling agent, either immediately or at the agreed credit interval. That stage involved no international payment. The problem of international funds transfers was not a concern of the buyer, but of the commission agent who sold the goods.

Viewed from the perspective of the principal for whose account the goods had been sold, the funds transfer problem is not how to *send money abroad*, but how to *get money back from abroad*. In the era before modern methods of communication and transport, any method of getting funds back from abroad necessarily took time. No merchant, however, would ever want to leave any portion of his capital lying idle for any period of time. Thus, just as a Stapler

---

[8] Supple, *Commercial Crisis and Change in England*, 84. Exchange transactions were commonly handled through brokers. The entry on 'broker' in Postlethwayt's *Dictionary of Trade and Commerce* notes that 'the exchange brokers make it their business to know the alteration of the course of exchange, to inform the merchants how it goes, and to give notice to those who have money to receive or pay beyond the sea, who are the proper persons for negotiating the exchange with'.

made money by investing his capital in wool bought in England and shipping it to Flanders for resale, so too he would have wanted to make productive use of his capital on the return leg of his trade circuit. Thus, the wool merchant's funds transfer problem can be described not simply as *how to get money back from abroad* but as *how to make profitable use of funds abroad.*

EXCHANGE TRANSACTIONS AS FINANCE

One of the ways of making profitable use of funds, in any location, is to lend them to another. Historians of medieval business practice, particularly Raymond de Roover, have shown that finance, rather than simply funds transmission, was a central element of early exchange transactions.[9]

According to de Roover, the antecedents of bills of exchange were the notarial exchange contracts of the era when much of the international trade of Europe was concentrated at the great fairs of Champagne.[10] From the thirteenth century it was common for merchants to take up money in Italian cities in order to finance the purchase of goods which they were to take to the fairs of Champagne, agreeing to repay the money at the next fair in Champagne. These exchange contracts took a somewhat different form than the later-developed bills of exchange. They were formal instruments drawn up by a public notary, and the recipient of the money himself promised to repay it rather than directing another to do so. As European trade and finance developed beyond the stage of travelling merchants exchanging their wares at periodic fairs, the significance of exchange dealings as a financial technique greatly increased. The early form of finance by exchange contracts payable at the fairs was feasible only for merchants who planned to travel to the fairs where they would be in a position to repay the funds. With

---

9 de Roover, *Gresham on Foreign Exchange*, 94–172; de Roover, *Medici Bank*, 108–41; de Roover, *Money, Banking and Credit in Mediaeval Bruges*, 48–75; de Roover, 'What is Dry Exchange?'.

10 de Roover, *Money, Banking and Credit in Mediaeval Bruges*, 49–52. See also Usher, *Early History of Deposit Banking*, 61–72; Blomquist, 'Dawn of Banking in an Italian Commune', 69–75. Translations of several letters dating from the 1260s sent to and from the Champagne fairs by partners of a merchant banker firm in Siena reporting on lending and collection activities and describing market conditions can be found in Lopez and Raymond, *Medieval Trade in the Mediterranean World*, 388–94.

the evolution of the system of sedentary merchants with permanent representatives abroad, this method of finance became feasible for a far broader range of activities. Any merchant who had regular dealings through factors or other representatives could take up funds in his home location, giving a bill of exchange directing his representative in another location to repay the advance to the lender's representative in the other location.

Consider a hypothetical English merchant who has sold goods through his factor in Flanders. Suppose that there is someone else in Flanders who wishes to buy goods for export to England, but lacks sufficient funds. If the prospective buyer could borrow the necessary funds in Flanders, he could ship the goods to London for sale, and then be in a position to repay the loan in London. The needs of the two merchants are perfectly complementary. The English merchant has funds in Flanders and seeks a profitable means of returning them to London. The Flemish merchant seeks a source of finance for a shipment of goods from Flanders to London. The English merchant's factor in Flanders would deliver the money to the Flemish merchant, who would draw a bill of exchange on his factor in London, instructing him to repay the value to the English merchant. Needless to say, one would expect that the amount to be repaid in London would exceed the amount advanced in Flanders, the difference being the interest paid by the Flemish merchant on the loan.[11]

The pricing mechanism of exchange lending was rather complex, as indicated by the explanation given in a memorandum prepared for an English Royal Commission on Exchanges in 1564:

And here we must note that the Exchange is the governor of prices of all wares interchangeably vented between this Realme and the Low Countries, because the greatest quantity of wares transported either outward or inward is bought by money taken up by Exchange, and also because, although the wares be bought with his own money, in selling of his hundred pounds worth of wares he Considered what gains he might have made by Exchange of so much money, and he makes the price of his wares accordingly or to some convenient overplus.

As for Example, one taketh up in Lombard Street 100 pound English for usance at 22 shillings 6 pence flemish. Now transporting English wares bought therewith into Flanders, he needeth make no greater price thereof

---

[11] Numerous examples of such transactions from the records of a family of English wool merchants trading with Flanders are described in Hanham, *The Celys*, 189–202.

but to Answer his Exchange, which Cometh to 112 pound 10 shilling flemish, saving for a Reasonable overplus to bear his Charges and to Answer his Stock.

Again for Example, one taketh up at Antwerp 110 pound 16 shillings 8 pence flemish for usance at 22s 2d flemish, for the Exchange at Antwerp keepeth about 4d flemish under the Exchange in Lombard Street, and transporteth strange wares bought therewith in to England. Now he must need raise his price thereof, both to Answer his Exchange, which is a 100 pound English, and also for some reasonable overplus to beare his Charges and to amend his stock.[12]

The examples given in the Royal Commission memorandum may be explained as follows: The hypothetical English merchant borrowed £100 in London to finance the export of goods to Flanders. He would have drawn a bill of exchange on his factor or correspondent in Antwerp, giving it to the lender in London, who would send it to Antwerp for payment. The exchange rate was 22s 6d Flemish per pound English, so when the bill came due one month later, the English borrower's factor in Antwerp would have been required to repay 100 × 22s 6d, or £112 10s Flemish. Similarly, the hypothetical Flemish merchant borrowed money in Antwerp to finance a shipment of goods to England. The bill of exchange that he would have given to his lender would have taken the same form as the English bill, except that the location of the parties would have been reversed. The merchant in Antwerp took up £110 16s 8d Flemish, at the rate of 22s 2d Flemish per pound English. Thus, when the bill came due, the Flemish merchant's correspondent in London would have been required to repay the loan in English currency, amounting to £110 16s 8d Flemish at 22s 2d to the pound, or £100 English.

The key to understanding the pricing of exchange lending transactions such as these is that the exchange rate would always be different in the two cities. Thus, in the Royal Commission

---

[12] 'Memorandum Prepared for the Royal Commission on the Exchanges, 1564', in *Tudor Economic Documents*, 3: 347–48. The term 'usance' referred to the customary period for which bills of exchange between particular places were made payable. For example, the usance between London and Antwerp was one month, between London and Spain, two months, and between London and Italy, three months. Thus, the bills of exchange in the Royal Commission memorandum example, payable at usance between London and Antwerp, would have called for payment one month after date. Bills might also be drawn at shorter or longer intervals, expressed, for example, as at half usance or double usance.

examples the rate in London was 22s 6d Flemish per pound English while in Antwerp the rate was 22s 2d. The difference between these two exchange rates determined the effective interest rate on the loans. As the Royal Commission memorandum puts it:

> Here is also to be noted that when the Exchange in Lombard street for usance goeth at 22s 6d flemish, and the re-exchange thereof at Antwerp for usance goeth at 22 shillings 2 pence flemish, then thereby the English pound is valued worth just 22 shillings 4 pence flemish, because the 2 pence more than the value for the Exchange in Lombard street is the hire and the interest that the deliverer doth bargain to have for delivering and letting out his English pound a month beforehand, and the 2d less than the value for the Exchange at Antwerp is the hire and Interest cut off by the deliverer for letting out and delivering of his flemish money a month beforehand.

Perhaps the best way of unpacking that explanation is to consider the transaction from the viewpoint of the lender. Suppose that a lender in London lent £100 English at usance at the rate of 22s 6d Flemish per pound English. When the loan was repaid one month later, the lender's correspondent in Antwerp would have collected £112 10s Flemish. Suppose that the lender in London had instructed his correspondent in Antwerp to relend the money by exchange from Antwerp to London. The correspondent in Antwerp would have lent the £112 10s Flemish to someone in Antwerp at usance at the rate of 22s 2d Flemish per pound English, sending the bill of exchange from this second 'rechange' loan to the London banker. When the second bill came due, the London banker would have received English money amounting to £112 10s Flemish at 22s 2d to the pound, or £101 11s 2d. Thus, in the two-month period, the lender's £100 would have earned a return of £1 11s 2d, equivalent to a bit over 9 per cent per annum.

The effective interest rate on exchange lending was determined by the spread between the exchange rates quoted in the two different cities, not the absolute level of the exchange rate.[13] For instance, Malynes' seventeenth-century book on mercantile affairs gives an example of such an exchange transaction where the exchange rates were 34s 6d Flemish per pound in London, and 33s 6d per pound in Amsterdam.[14] Assuming that these figures, as

---

[13] de Roover, *Gresham on Foreign Exchange*, 141–50; de Roover, 'What is Dry Exchange?', 187–94.

[14] Malynes, *Lex Mercatoria*, 269–70.

well as those in the Royal Commission's report, corresponded
roughly to actual rates prevailing at the times they were written,
the change in the rates reflects two different kinds of change in
economic condition. First, the value of the English pound had
risen against the Flemish pound. Secondly, the spread between the
rates as quoted in England and the Low Countries had increased,
from 4 pence in the examples in the Royal Commission's report in
1564 to 1 shilling in the example in Malynes. At the rates in
Malynes' example, a lender would have earned nearly 18 per cent
per annum on exchange lending.

Exchange lending played a key role in the European financial
system at least until the early seventeenth century. For example, in
the passage from the 1564 report of the English Royal Commission
on Exchanges quoted above, it is explicitly stated that most of the
import and export business between England and the Low Countries was financed 'by money taken up by Exchange'. Financing
trade by exchange formed a principal part of the business of the
great banking firms of Renaissance Italy, such as the Medici.[15]
Exchange lending, in the form of exchange and rechange or
'ricorsa' bill transactions, was a major part of the business of the
financiers of the fairs of Lyons and the Antwerp bourse.[16]
Exchange dealings were essential to the financial operation of the
major governments of Europe. The Spanish wars in the Low
Countries were financed in large measure by Genoese bankers who
financed the shipment of Italian cloth and goods which were sold
for distribution throughout northern Europe at the fairs and
markets in the Low Countries. Thus, the Genoese bankers had
funds due to them in Antwerp, which they could lend to the
Spanish crown for the expenses of the wars, receiving payment of
the advances in Spain or Italy from the silver coming to Spain from
the rich mines of South America.[17] The English crown too was a
major borrower in Antwerp. Queen Elizabeth I's most trusted
financial adviser, Sir Thomas Gresham, spent a large part of his
career arranging exchange lending transactions for the crown on
the Antwerp bourse.[18]

[15] de Roover, *Medici Bank*.
[16] Ehrenberg, *Capital & Finance in the Renaissance*, 244–46, 287–88.
[17] Braudel, *Civilization and Capitalism*, 3: 164–69.
[18] de Roover, *Gresham on Foreign Exchange*, 18–30; Ehrenberg, *Capital & Finance in the Renaissance*, 252–55.

THE DUAL FUNCTIONS OF EXCHANGE

Having described exchange transactions as serving the two functions of funds transfer and lending, it may be appropriate to consider briefly the relationship between these two functions and their relative significance. There is certainly ample evidence that, in some situations, the funds transfer aspect of exchange was of primary significance. For example, pilgrims and other travellers often sent funds abroad by purchasing bills of exchange drawn by Italian merchant bankers in London on their correspondents abroad.[19] Merchants too in some situations used exchange solely as a means of funds transmission. A late-sixteenth-century memorandum prepared by a group of Italian merchants residing in London describes a variety of such transactions.[20] For example, Italian merchant bankers in London sold bills of exchange on Bordeaux to English vintners who needed to make payments to Bordeaux merchants for wine imported to England.

The pricing mechanism of exchange transactions in which bankers provided funds transfer services to merchants and others is somewhat puzzling. Given the pattern of exchange rates described above, it would seem that bankers who sold bills of exchange would have lost money on every such transaction, for their agents abroad would have paid out more value in the foreign currency than they had received from the purchasers of the bills. The explanation may be that the early bankers were interested in selling bills of exchange whenever they believed that they could profitably use the funds. The merchant manuals of the time indicate that the bankers were aware of regular seasonal fluctuations in the supply and demand for funds in the various commercial centres of Europe and kept a careful eye on trade conditions, currency regulations, and the like in an effort to anticipate shifts in

---

[19] There are a number of cases in the London Mayor's Court Rolls in the fourteenth and fifteenth centuries involving travellers who bought letters of exchange payable at their intended destinations but failed to complete their journeys because of sickness or death. *Calendar of London Plea and Memoranda Rolls*, 2: 77, 3: 200, 4: 13, 4: 226. The cases seem to have been quite uncomplicated, the only issue being factual disputes about whether the money had already been paid out abroad.

[20] 'Protest by the Italian Merchants of the City against State Control of Exchange Business, 1576', in *Tudor Economic Documents*, 2: 169–73.

the money market.[21] The desire of the bankers to borrow funds to augment their capital or to adjust the state of their balances among the various cities in which they operated would mean that they were often interested in taking up money in one location to be paid out in another. Thus, bankers might have been willing to sell bills to persons who wished to transfer funds to distant locations for essentially the same reason that banks today pay interest on deposits.[22]

Though there is evidence that in some situations the funds transfer aspect of exchange may have been predominant, there is no question that in other situations the lending aspect was the critical function of exchange. It may, though, be misleading to ask whether the funds transfer or finance function of early exchange transactions was more important. In many situations these were not two different practices but simply different descriptions of the same phenomenon. Consider, for example, the exchange transactions in which the Merchants of the Staple who sold English wool in Flanders made return of their funds by buying bills of exchange from merchants in Flanders who shipped goods to London. From one perspective, this can be described as the mechanism by which the Staplers' agents in Flanders transmitted the proceeds of the sales of wool back to their principals in London. Yet someone who took up money in Flanders giving a bill of exchange for it on his correspondent in London would ordinarily be paying a price for the use of the funds between the time the funds were taken up in Flanders and the time that they were paid out in London. Or, looking at the exchange transaction from the other side, someone who delivered money in Flanders in return for a bill of exchange on London was hoping to make a profit on the

---

[21] de Roover, *Money, Banking and Credit in Mediaeval Bruges*, 66–67.

[22] Another possible explanation is provided by Peter Spufford, who has compiled data on exchange rate quotations throughout Europe in the medieval period. Spufford notes that some exchange quotations between different cities do not fit the pattern described by de Roover in which, for example, the exchange rate between English and Flemish currency, stated in terms of Flemish shillings per English pound, would have been higher in London than in Flanders. Spufford notes instances in which the difference is in the opposite direction, so that one buying a bill in one place would effectively receive less value in the other location when the bill came due. From this data Spufford suggests that there may have been 'two sets of rates for bills of exchange, one for ... those who wished to transfer funds, and the other for "exchange", for those who wished to invest funds'. Spufford, *Handbook of Medieval Exchange*, xliii.

use of the funds during the period. When an English wool merchant instructed his factor in Flanders to make returns by buying bills in Flanders drawn on London, rather than by shipping specie or goods, he was making an investment decision as much as a funds transfer decision. Accordingly, the exchange transaction would have been both a form of funds transfer and a form of lending.

3

EARLY EXCHANGE TRANSACTIONS:
PRIVATE LAW

Having examined how early exchange transactions were actually conducted, we can now trace the development of the law of exchange and bills of exchange. This chapter examines the private law of exchange contracts in the period up to the early part of the seventeenth century. Just as the common view that the early common law courts did not handle commercial cases in general proves false, careful examination of the evidence indicates that the common law courts, as well as other courts in England, did entertain actions to enforce the obligations of parties to exchange transactions long before the seventeenth century.

EXCHANGE CONTRACTS IN THE MERCANTILE COURTS

In seeking evidence of how courts treated exchange transactions, one must be careful to avoid being misled by incidental references to bills of exchange in early cases that did not actually involve any dispute concerning the rights and obligations of the parties to the exchange transaction. For example, an entry in the London Mayor's Court Rolls dating from 1300[1] is commonly cited as the earliest action on a bill in the English mercantile courts.[2] The entry, however, merely records that a chaplain complained that his rector had stolen money and delivered it to an Italian merchant in London who gave him a letter of payment addressed to his correspondent in Paris. The Italian merchant said that he had written to his correspondents in various cities asking them not to pay the

---

[1] *Calendar of London Mayor's Court Rolls*, 94.
[2] Beutel, 'Development of Negotiable Instruments', 830, 830 n. 84; Fifoot, 'Development of the Law of Negotiable Instruments', 434; Holden, *History of Negotiable Instruments*, 21, 21 n. 2; Holdsworth, *History of English Law*, 8: 130–31.

money, but he had not yet learned whether it had already been paid. The court simply told the Italian merchant not to repay the money until further information was obtained. The report of this event tells nothing about the legal rights and duties of participants in exchange transactions. It was simply a case where someone who had lost money by theft sought to recover it, the party who had received the money from the thief volunteered to try to assist the owner, and the court left it at that. If one takes an item like this as proof that the London Mayor's Court 'recognized' bills of exchange, then one can make the same proof for the common law courts. There is a similar incidental reference to the exchange dealings in a yearbook case where the defendant in an account action admitted that he had received money on the plaintiff's behalf, but contended that he had done so on the understanding that he was to take the money to a Lombard in London, obtain a letter of exchange for it, and send the letter of exchange to the plaintiff.[3] The yearbook report deals only with a pleading question; it does not indicate what went awry with the letter of exchange, let alone how the common law court would have analysed the legal obligations growing out of the exchange transaction itself. In that respect, this yearbook record is exactly the same as the 1300 entry from the London Mayor's Court. Neither the yearbook case nor the Mayor's Court case can be described as an action to 'enforce' a bill of exchange. Rather, these cases show only that disputes tangentially related to exchange dealings might be heard either by local courts, such as the London Mayor's Court, or, where otherwise appropriate, by the central courts of the common law.

We have seen that the paradigmatic early exchange transaction was one in which someone took up money in one location, engaging that his representative in another location would repay it to the representative of the person who had advanced the funds. Accordingly, to study the legal treatment of early exchange transactions, one should not simply look for isolated references to bills of exchange, but seek cases that actually involved efforts to enforce the rights of the parties in an exchange transaction. The most detailed printed record of an early English case arising out of an exchange transaction is the London Mayor's Court case of *Burton*

[3] Y.B. Hil. 5 Hen. V, f. 4, pl. 10 (1413).

v. *Davy* (1437).[4] The case arose out of a typical import financing transaction: a London mercer's agent in the Low Countries borrowed money on his principal's account in order to finance the purchase of goods shipped to London.

The facts in *Burton* were that John Audeley, described as the 'factor and attorney' of the London mercer Elias Davy, took up money in Bruges from Thomas Hanworth, who was acting as factor of the Norwich merchant John Burton. The funds were used to pay for merchandise which Audeley purchased and shipped to Davy. Audeley drew a bill of exchange on Davy payable to Burton or bearer.[5] Davy failed to pay the bill of exchange. Suit was brought 'in the name of . . . John Burton' by one John Walden, and the London Mayor's Court gave judgment against Davy for the amount specified in the bill.

The aspect of *Burton* v. *Davy* that has attracted the attention of legal historians is that the court made several references to the law merchant in permitting Walden to prosecute the action as bearer of the bill.[6] This has led some commentators to interpret *Burton* as evidence that the mercantile courts recognized modern principles of negotiability.[7] That is a very dubious reading. In the first place, the court's judgment was that the drawee was to pay the amount of the bill 'to the before mentioned supplicant [Burton] *or* to John Walden, the bearer of the same letter (who is held in his place in this case, etc. according to the law merchant and custom before-

[4] *Select Cases Law Merchant*, 49 SS 117.
[5] The bill of exchange read as follows:

> To my very honoured master Elias Davy, mercer, at London, let this be given: Very honoured sir, please it you to know that I have received here of John Burton, by exchange, £30 payable at London to the aforesaid John or to the bearer of this letter of payment on the 14th day of March next coming, by this my first and second letter of payment. And I pray you that it may be well paid at the day. Written at Bruges, the 10th day of December, by your attorney.

> John Audeley, etc.

[6] 49 SS at 118, 119.
[7] Beutel remarked that the *Burton* case showed 'the complete development of the negotiable bill of exchange'. Beutel, 'Development of Negotiable Instruments', 831. Holden was somewhat more cautious, suggesting that while *Burton* showed that the mercantile courts recognized free assignability, it did not indicate whether a bona fide purchaser took free from claims and defences. Holden, *History of Negotiable Instruments*, 23–25.

said'.[8] The fact that the original payee, Burton, retained a right to payment is hardly consistent with surmise that the instrument had been transferred outright to Walden, or that the court treated the bearer as entitled to sue in his own right. It is far more likely that Walden was acting only as a collection agent for Burton.

There is, however, a far more basic flaw in the conventional interpretation of *Burton* v. *Davy*. The most fundamental concept of modern negotiable instruments law is the notion of liabilities 'on the instrument', that is, the parties to negotiable instruments incur legal obligations simply by signing the instruments, independent of whatever obligations might arise in the underlying transaction. Whether consciously or not, lawyers and legal historians who speak of a certain case as being an action *on* a bill of exchange, and hence as being a significant event in the development of the law of *bills* of exchange, are assuming that the case in question is one in which the obligations enforced were of this nature. There is, however, nothing in *Burton* v. *Davy* to suggest that the court or parties entertained any concept of independent liabilities on the instrument.

In the language of modern negotiable instruments law, *Burton* v. *Davy* would be described as an action by the holder against the drawee. In modern negotiable instruments law the drawee incurs no liability to anyone on the instrument unless he accepts it. Yet in *Burton* there is no mention of acceptance of the bill by Davy, nor of any sort of promise or undertaking by him to pay the bill. Instead, there is a full recitation of the facts of the underlying transaction. The complainant alleged that John Audeley was acting as the factor and attorney of Elias Davy, that Audeley took up the money in order to pay for merchandise bought by Audeley for Davy and shipped to him, and that the money had been advanced in Bruges by Thomas Hanworth acting as factor for the named payee, John Burton. Similarly, the description of the trial portrays a proceeding directed not at the *bill* but at the facts of the underlying transaction:

Elias ... tried and examined concerning the premises, does not deny that the said John Audeley at the time of the taking up of the £30 aforesaid and

---

[8] *Select Cases Law Merchant*, 49 SS 118 (emphasis added). Beutel falsely states that 'the judgment was given directly to the holder, and, as the court goes to some length to explain, in his own name'. Beutel, 'Development of Negotiable Instruments', 831.

of the making of the letter of payment for the same, and long after, had been his factor and attorney; nor that he had laid out the same £30 upon merchandises bought to the use of him, Elias, and [which had] come into his possession, as is premised.

And hereupon, because as well by the oath of the said Thomas Hanworth who delivered, as of the aforesaid John Audeley who received the moneys aforesaid by exchange in the form aforesaid, and other numerous kinds of proofs manifestly declaring the truth of the matter aforesaid, it appears to this court here sufficiently clear that all the premises were and are true.[9]

Thus, although *Burton* may indicate that the London Mayor's Court was willing to accept possession of a bill of exchange payable to bearer as sufficient evidence of the plaintiff's authority to prosecute the action, the cause of action seems to have been regarded as grounded not on the bill of exchange but on the obligations arising out of the underlying exchange lending transaction.

There are numerous other cases in the London Mayor's Court records that reflect the same approach to exchange contracts as *Burton*. *Burton* was an action against the person on whom the bill was drawn. An even simpler form of legal dispute arising out of an exchange transaction would be an action by the deliverer against the taker. Suppose, for example, that someone in London borrowed money, giving the lender a bill of exchange directing the borrower's agent abroad to repay the loan to the lender's foreign representative. If the money was not repaid, the deliverer in London might bring an action against the party who had received the funds. No sophisticated legal theory would be required to resolve the dispute. It would simply be an action by a creditor against a debtor. There are many instances of such cases in the records of the London Mayor's Court. For example, in 1462 a Genoese merchant brought 'an original bill of debt for £66 5s 8d against Laurence Grill, merchant of Genoa . . . in respect of sums paid to him by the plaintiff by way of exchange'.[10] Presumably the borrower, Laurence Grill, had given the lender a bill of exchange drawn by Grill on his representative abroad, and the bill had been dishonoured. Similarly, in 1364 the Lombard merchant Vane Camby brought an action alleging that 'he had bought a letter of exchange in London for £30 from Nicholas Sardouch of Lucca,

---

[9] *Select Cases Law Merchant*, 49 SS 118–19.
[10] *Salvaigus* v. *Grill* (1462), *Calendar of London Plea and Memoranda Rolls*, 6: 21.

Lombard, which letter was to be payable to himself or his attorney at Bruges in the form of 200 scudos, each scudo being worth 3s; that he had given the letter to his attorney John Paule, and that the latter had been refused payment in Bruges'. Sardouch contended that he had been instructed to pay the money 'to Sir Paul Johan of Pistoja or to a certain John Paule' and had done so; the case was adjourned to permit Sardouch to produce evidence of the payment from the municipal authorities of Bruges.[11] Although the nature of the transaction is not made absolutely clear from the entry, the most probable interpretation is that Sardouch had taken up £28 15s from Camby in London giving a bill of exchange calling for repayment in Bruges in the amount of 200 scudos.

In these simple cases brought by the deliverer against the taker, the bill of exchange itself would have played little role in the lawsuit. Thus, although cases such as *Camby* v. *Sardouch* have been referred to as actions 'on bills of exchange',[12] that is a singularly inapt description. The plaintiff in such an action would not be the one to whom the bill was made payable. He would not even be a party to the bill, in the sense of modern negotiable instruments law. Rather, he would be mentioned in the bill only as the party from whom the drawer received the value. Nor would the plaintiff be appropriately described as a 'holder' of the bill. If the deliverer had physical possession of the bill at all, it would be because it had been returned to him along with the protest of the bill for nonpayment. Indeed, in the proceedings brought by Camby against Sardouch there is not even any mention of what happened to the bill. Rather, the entry suggests that what the London Mayor's Court thought was important was not where the piece of paper was, but whether or not the payment that the bill called for had actually been made.

Cases such as *Burton*, where merchants were sued for money borrowed by their foreign representatives in exchange transactions, presented only slightly more complex legal issues. If the agent's authority to borrow was established, as in *Burton* and a number of similar cases in the London Mayor's Court,[13] the legal

---

[11] *Camby* v. *Sardouch* (1364), *Calendar of London Plea and Memoranda Rolls*, 2: 10.

[12] Beutel, 'Development of Negotiable Instruments', 830 n. 85.

[13] *Calendar of London Plea and Memoranda Rolls*, 2: 242 (1377) (entry of recording of a letter of attorney appointing representative to collect from English merchant

issue would be no more complex than any other action in which a principal was sued for a debt contracted by his agent. Disputes about the agency relationship might, however, make these cases somewhat more complex. For example, in a fourteenth-century case, two German merchants brought an action against an English pepper merchant for money borrowed in Bruges by one who represented himself as the English merchant's factor. The merchant disputed liability, contending that the person in Bruges was not 'his attorney, or his factor or apprentice, but had merely been sent to him by . . . the King's Treasurer, on trial, to discover whether he was able to learn the defendant's trade, and thus he was not entitled to borrow on his behalf'.[14] There are also a number of cases where someone sued on an exchange debt contracted by his foreign representative asserted that his representative abroad had already repaid the loan.[15]

Unlike the deliverer-versus-taker cases, *Burton* and other cases against principals for whose account the money was taken up were actions against someone who was a party to the bill of exchange. In the language of modern negotiable instruments law, these would be actions against the drawee, who would incur liability on the instrument by accepting it. There is nothing in these cases, however, to suggest that liability was based on the bill rather than

'the sum of 400 scudos, valued at 26d English each scudo, that amount being due on an exchange made at Bruges' to the English merchant's servant); ibid., 4: 195 (1426) (entry relating to settlement of a claim of Venetian merchants Alexander de Boromeis and Lazarus Johannis against Ector Belhono for '1000 ducats, which amount to £178 2s 6d sterling' that one George de Orsellis 'as factor of the said Ector had taken up by exchange at Venice from the said Alexander and Lazar').

[14] *Glemerod* v. *Brounesford* (1345), *Calendar of London Plea and Memoranda Rolls*, 1: 217. See also *Holmton* v. *Walworth* (1390), ibid., 3: 176 (alleging that Holmton's agent abroad had lent money to Walworth's agent abroad 'under the condition that the money be repaid in England'; Walworth's agent confessed that he had borrowed the money for his own use; not for his master's account).

[15] *Calendar of London Plea and Memoranda Rolls*, 4: 195 (1426) (Italian merchant sued for money taken up by his agent in Venice gave bond that he would pay if he was unable to produce evidence from municipal authorities of Venice certifying that his agent in Venice had already settled with deliverers). Agency issues might also arise on the lender side of the transaction, as in a 1386 case, ibid., 3: 125, where an English merchant's agent in Middleburgh had borrowed money on his behalf, sending a letter of payment calling for repayment of the loan to the London principal of the Middleburgh lender. The Middleburgh lender had died, and the dispute was whether the loan should be paid to the person named in the bill of exchange or to one who claimed an interest in the funds in association with the Middleburgh lender.

on the underlying loan. None of the London Mayor's Court cases describe the defendant as the acceptor of the bill or even make any mention of acceptance. Indeed, the usual allegation is that the defendant refused to pay when the bill was shown to him. Thus, the 'drawee's' liability seems to have been based entirely on the fact that his authorized agent had obtained the loan on his behalf.

The distinction illustrated by *Burton* and the other London Mayor's Court cases between enforcing the obligations arising out of an exchange contract and enforcing obligations on a bill of exchange is the key to understanding the early history of English law on exchange transactions. Until the seventeenth century there is virtually no evidence that any of the courts in England treated bills of exchange as themselves creating legal obligations distinct from the obligations arising out of the underlying exchange transaction. In this era, it is an anachronism to speak of a law of bills of exchange; at most there was a law of exchange contracts.

EXCHANGE CONTRACTS IN THE ADMIRALTY COURT

It is sometimes said that the Admiralty Court played a key role in the development of the law of bills of exchange in England, particularly in the sixteenth century.[16] There is, however, little evidence to suggest that the Admiralty Court developed or applied any special body of law governing bills of exchange.

The only data on early Admiralty Court proceedings available in published form are in the two-volume collection of excerpts from the records of the Admiralty Court edited by R. G. Marsden for the Selden Society. This collection includes only one case directly dealing with enforcement of an exchange contract, *Fuller* v. *Thorne* (1533).[17] The underlying transaction was a typical exchange contract. Thomas Fuller, an English wool merchant, delivered money at Calais to Thomas Thorne, a London haberdasher, who agreed

16 Marsden, Introduction to *Select Pleas Admiralty*, 6 SS lxvii. See also Beutel, 'Development of Negotiable Instruments', 834–37; Holden, *History of Negotiable Instruments*, 25–27; Holdsworth, *History of English Law*, 1: 552–59.
17 *Select Pleas Admiralty*, 6 SS 38–41, 179–81. There are two other cases incidentally involving bills of exchange, *Denaker* v. *Mason* (1564), *Select Pleas Admiralty*, 11 SS 73, 126, and *Le Fort* v. *Le Fort* (1599), *Select Pleas Admiralty*, 11 SS 192, but neither gives any indication of how the Admiralty Court analysed exchange contracts or bills of exchange.

to repay the advance in London. The case was the simplest form of action to enforce an exchange contract – a suit by the deliverer against the taker who had failed to repay the full amount. This was clearly not, in any sense, an action on a bill of exchange, for there is no indication that any writing in that form was used in the transaction. Rather, the bill obligatory executed by the taker was in the form of a sealed bond. As in the London Mayor's Court cases discussed above, the defendant's liability seems to have been based on the debt arising out of the underlying exchange contract.

There are also various records in the published Admiralty Court records concerning a form of contract related to exchange contracts, the sea loan or *foenus nauticum*.[18] In a sea loan contract, funds were borrowed for the expenses of a voyage, but the obligation to repay was contingent upon safe arrival of the ship at its destination. Usually the ship and/or goods were pledged to secure the loan.[19] Sea loans and exchange contracts were closely related. Both were means of financing trade ventures, the difference being that in the typical sea loan the ship or cargo was pledged as security and the investor bore the risk of successful completion of the voyage. It is, then, not surprising that hybrids of the two transactions developed in which money was taken up by way of exchange in one currency to be repaid in another, with the lender bearing the risk of the voyage.[20] Eventually, the paths of development diverged. The sea loan always remained close to its roots. The modern descendant of the ancient *foenus nauticum* is the bottomry contract, which by the late sixteenth century had developed into a standard form of a sealed bond for money borrowed on the security of the 'bottom' or keel of the ship, with payment contingent upon arrival. By contrast, the exchange contract eventually gave birth to the bill of exchange, which came to be used in a wide variety of credit and payment transactions. In the sixteenth century, however, it appears that sea loans and exchange contracts were still close cousins. In that kinship lies some evi-

---

18 *Thorne* v. *Vincent* (1541), *Select Pleas Admiralty*, 6 SS 92; *Austen* v. *Castelyn* (1541), *Select Pleas Admiralty*, 6 SS 106.
19 Malynes, *Lex Mercatoria*, 122–23; Molloy, *De Jure Maritimo*, 288–98; Beawes, *Lex Mercatoria Rediviva*, 127–29. On the development of the sea loan contract in Italy, see Lopez and Raymond, *Medieval Trade in the Mediterranean World*, 168–72.
20 Early works on exchange contracts refer to these as 'conditional exchange'. Forbes, *Bills of Exchange*, 5–7; Scarlett, *Stile of Exchanges*, 250–59.

dence of the Admiralty Court's treatment of exchange and bills of exchange.

The various sea loan contracts printed in Marsden's collection show extreme variation in their form. One example is in the ancient form of lengthy formal notarial instrument.[21] Others are simple sealed bonds acknowledging receipt of the money and the obligation to repay, contingent on completion of the voyage, with clauses binding the ship or cargo.[22] By the latter part of the century, some of these sealed bonds had taken on the standardized language of bottomry.[23] For present purposes, however, the most interesting forms of documentation are those which combine the characteristic sea loan provisions with some of the language of exchange contracts or bills of exchange. For example, there is a ship loan contract dating from 1533 in which the master of the ship acknowledges that for the necessary use of the ship he has 'received and had by exchange and in the name of exchange' 192 ducats in Sicily, 'which said ducats ... shall go in all this voyage at the adventure and peril as well of god as of the sea'.[24] Another, dated 1536, takes the form of a simple unsealed bill obligatory, with the typical 'be it known unto all men by this ... that I owe' language, but it shows that it was executed as one of a set of three, and adds a clause that on default, the borrower binds himself 'to pay change and rechange'.[25] There are even a number of sea loan instruments which explicitly denominate themselves as bills of exchange, even though they are not orders for payment, but acknowledgments of debts with engagements to repay in the usual language of bonds.[26] The use of widely varying forms of instruments in the same underlying transaction pattern suggests, albeit somewhat obliquely, that the focus of legal analysis was the underlying transaction rather than the specific writing used to implement the transaction. The Admiralty records show that the term 'bill of exchange' was promiscuously used for a wide variety of instruments, and that a particular type of transaction, the sea loan, might

[21] *Select Pleas Admiralty*, 11 SS 65–68.   [22] Ibid., 6 SS 29, 61, 195.

[23] Ibid., 11 SS 75–76, 77.

[24] Ibid., 6 SS 93–94.

[25] Ibid., 6 SS 55–56. Similarly, the 1533 contract for the ship loan advance received 'by exchange' adds a clause in which the borrower agrees that on default of payment, the lender can 'take the said money at exchange and rechange for four parts of the world' at the expense of the borrower. Ibid., 6 SS 94.

[26] Ibid., 11 SS 68–69, 70–71, 72.

be implemented by means of a wide variety of different forms of instruments, some styling themselves 'bills of exchange' and others not.[27]

Thus, while it is undoubtedly the case that the Admiralty Court enforced obligations arising out of exchange contracts, there is no evidence to suggest that the Admiralty Court had developed any special body of law concerning bills of exchange.

EXCHANGE CONTRACTS IN THE COMMON LAW COURTS

The conventional wisdom is that the common law courts, as opposed to mercantile courts such as the London Mayor's Court or Admiralty Court, did not handle cases concerning bills of exchange until the seventeenth century. In fact, the common law courts enforced obligations arising out of exchange transactions long before the era of the so-called 'incorporation' of the law merchant in the seventeenth century.

It is true that it is not until the seventeenth century that one finds explicit mention of the legal effect of bills of exchange in the records of the common law courts. That, however, does not distinguish the common law courts from the mercantile courts. The cases from the London Mayor's Court and Admiralty Court were not actions 'on bills of exchange', but actions to enforce the obligations arising out of the underlying exchange lending transaction. To find analogues in the common law courts of cases such as *Burton* v. *Davy,* one should look not for mention of bills of exchange, but for actions arising out of the basic factual pattern of exchange lending: someone borrowed money in one location agreeing that the advance would be repaid in a different country and currency.

For the simplest sort of exchange case, an action by the deliverer

---

27 Although this seems incredible given the remarkable variation in the form of the bills of exchange included in the Selden Society's collection, the principal conclusion that some have drawn from these records is that by the sixteenth century the form of bills of exchange had become quite settled. Holdsworth refers to the Admiralty records as showing that the sixteenth-century English bills of exchange 'were drawn in the same stereotyped form as in other parts of Europe'. Holdsworth, *History of English Law,* 8: 152. Holden concludes from the Admiralty records that the 'bills are similar in form to those used on the Continent'. Holden, *History of Negotiable Instruments,* 26.

against the taker to recover the amount advanced, there would be little difficulty fitting the case within the procedural categories of the common law. As a simple action for recovery of a liquidated sum of money, an action of debt would lie. An action against a principal for money taken up by exchange by his authorized agent might also be accommodated within the common law system. A case like *Burton* v. *Davy,* where an agent acting on behalf of his principal obtained value which came to the principal's benefit, called for only the simplest form of agency law. As early as the fourteenth century, the common law courts allowed actions in debt against principals for goods purchased by their agents which came to the principal's use.[28]

The principal difficulty in finding evidence of such cases in the records of the common law courts is the nature of the records. As Baker has pointed out,[29] documentary evidence of obligations, other than formal sealed bonds, would generally not be mentioned in the pleadings in the actions of debt, and hence would not be recorded in the plea rolls. Thus, even if exchange obligations had been enforced in the common law courts in debt actions in the fifteenth, sixteenth, and seventeenth centuries, the written records of the cases might consist of nothing more than skeletal entries of writs of debt for certain sums. Baker notes that if a sealed writing had been used to evidence an exchange obligation, then it might be recited in the pleadings and hence recorded. Although the bill of exchange in its classical form was a simple unsealed instrument, the Admiralty records show that forms were by no means standardized in the sixteenth century, and sealed instruments explicitly called bills of exchange were in use. Baker has found at least one instance of a King's Bench action in the mid-sixteenth century on a sealed ship loan bill of exactly the same sort as are recorded in the Admiralty records of the same era.[30]

The most likely obstacle to bringing such actions in the common law courts was not a deficiency of substantive law, but the limits of territorial jurisdiction. An action on a contract made abroad, such

---

[28] *Stowey* v. *Prior of Bruton* (1378), Y.B. 2 Rich. II (Ames Ser.) 11 (per Belknap, C. J., 'If you have a bailiff or a servant who is known to be your servant and you send him to a fair or market to buy sheep or other goods, it is reason that you be charged for the payment if the goods come into your use').

[29] Baker, 'Law Merchant and Common Law', 350.

[30] *Walker* v. *Myddylton* (1542), K.B. 27/1122, m. 105d, printed in Baker, 'Law Merchant and Common Law', 351.

as was involved in *Burton* v. *Davy*, could not be brought in the common law courts because of the rule that cases had to be tried by juries from the place where the action arose.[31] Once it became standard practice to evade the venue requirement by a fictitious allegation that the foreign place was located in England,[32] the common law courts might well have enforced exchange lending obligations. There are several tantalizing, though inconclusive, hints in the reported decisions in the sixteenth and seventeenth centuries that exchange lending obligations may have been enforced in the action of debt. In *Bagshaw* v. *Playn* (1596),[33] the plaintiff brought an action of debt upon an obligation denominated in Flemish currency, alleged to amount to a stated sum in English money. It is, however, not clear from the report in *Bagshaw*, or a number of similar cases,[34] whether the underlying transaction was an exchange lending contract or whether it was simply a foreign obligation intended to have been repaid in the foreign currency.

As the action of *assumpsit* came to replace debt as a vehicle for enforcing contractual obligations in the sixteenth and seventeenth centuries, the records of the common law courts begin to reveal greater detail about the transactions that gave rise to the cases.[35] Reported decisions of the central courts provide some evidence of the approach taken by the central courts in cases involving exchange and bills of exchange, though the reports tend to be very sketchy. Published collections of precedents of declarations provide considerably more detail, though there are some questions about the reliability of formbooks as evidence of contemporary legal doctrine. One cannot be entirely sure that the published forms were accurate transcriptions of pleadings that had been used

---

[31] An action on a foreign debt could, however, be brought in Chancery. Barbour, *History of Contract in Early English Equity*. Barbour cites many examples from the Chancery rolls of proceedings to collect loans made abroad. Many of these could well have been exchange loans, though the information given by Barbour does not permit confident conclusions. Ibid., 76–77. At least one of the fifteenth-century Chancery cases clearly was an action on an exchange loan: an English Merchant of the Staple sought to collect from a London grocer for a loan made to the grocer's factor in Bruges, for which the factor had drawn a bill on the grocer. *Grene* v. *Warde* (*c.* 1460), ibid.

[32] Baker, *Introduction to English Legal History*, 141.

[33] Cro. Eliz. 536, Moore 704.

[34] *Ward* v. *Kedsgrove* (1625), Latch. 4, W. Jones 69; *Rands* v. *Peck* (1621), Cro. Jac. 618; *Peirson* v. *Ponuteis* (1608), 1 Brownl. & Golds. 102.

[35] Baker, 'Law Merchant and Common Law', 354–56.

successfully in actual cases. Nonetheless, since the formbooks were typically published by established lawyers, judges, and clerks, and were designed specifically to provide models for practising lawyers, it does seem safe to assume that the forms published in respected works of the genre are at least representative of pleadings that had been held sufficient in litigation.[36] From the similarities and differences among the various precedents for such actions in the formbooks, one can form fairly confident conclusions about how the common law courts treated exchange contracts in the latter part of the sixteenth century.

Let us examine and compare six such pleadings. The first three are examples of the simplest sort of action arising out of an unpaid exchange transaction, suits by the deliverer against the taker seeking repayment of the money advanced. The second three are examples of a slightly more complicated sort of exchange dispute, actions against English merchants for money taken up abroad by their factors or agents.

1. *Anon* (*c.* 1560s).[37] Action against taker. The first edition of Rastell's *Entrees*, published in 1566, contains an undated precedent in which the plaintiff alleges that his agent had delivered £110 8s 4d of English money to the defendant, in consideration of which the defendant promised that a certain John of G. would pay 113½ ducats to another of the plaintiff's agents, one Reginald S. The declaration alleges that if the 443½ ducats had been paid to Reginald S., they would have come to the use of the plaintiff, but that John of G. failed to pay, whereupon the plaintiff lost the benefit of his £110 8s 4d as well as profits that he might have made with it.

2. *J. L.* v. *E.* (1594).[38] Action against taker. A slightly different form of declaration arising out of the same sort of transaction is

---

[36] Dating the pleadings is somewhat more difficult. In some cases the pleading books include specific references to the rolls, so that one can date them with fair confidence. In other instances, one must rely on the dates given in the text of the pleadings, yet one cannot be entirely sure that these have not been changed by the author. To give an extreme example, several of the pleadings contained in Brown, *Vade Mecum* (1678), dating from the late sixteenth and early seventeenth centuries, also appear in Bohun, *Declarations* (1733), with the dates changed to the 1730s.

[37] Rastell, *Entrees*, 10r. A translation of the entry is printed in Cranch, 'Promissory Notes', 375–76 and Holden, *History of Negotiable Instruments*, 324–25.

[38] Rastell, *Entrees*, 3rd edn, 338r. Rastell gives a citation to the rolls of Trinity, 37 Eliz. Rot. 597.

given in the third edition of Rastell's *Entrees*, published in 1596.
This precedent, apparently dating from 1594, alleges that the
plaintiff J. L. had delivered £150 of English money to the
defendant E., and that in consideration thereof the defendant
assumed and faithfully promised that his factor at Hamborough
would pay to one H. L., to the proper use of J. L., the sum of
£182 10s of the money of Hamborough by way of exchange according to the use of merchants ('*per viam excambii secundum usum
mercatorum*').

   3.   *Toft* v. *Garraway* (1613).[39] Action against taker. Yet a third
form of declaration against the taker in an exchange transaction is
found in Brown's *Vade Mecum*. The declaration, which appears to
date from 1613, alleges that Robert Toft paid £45 to William
Garraway in England, that for the £45 Garraway made and gave to
Toft a set of bills of exchange on one Thomas Cole in Venice,
directing Cole to pay 200 Venetian ducats to Toft two days after
sight of the bill, and that in consideration thereof, Garraway
assumed and faithfully promised to Toft that Cole would pay the
200 ducats. The allegations of nonperformance and damage are
that Cole did not pay the 200 ducats when the bill of exchange was
shown to him, that Garraway had not paid the 200 ducats by the
hands of Cole or otherwise, and that the 200 ducats amounted to
the value of £45 16s 8d English.

   4.   *C. W.* v. *J. B.* (1595).[40] Action against taker's principal. The
third edition of Rastell's *Entrees* also includes a declaration against
an English merchant for money taken up abroad by his factor. The
declaration alleges that on 10 June 1595, at Rochelle in France, the
plaintiff's factor delivered 1,400 French crowns to the defendant's

---

[39] Brown, *Vade Mecum*, 27. The pleading states only that the transaction occurred
in the tenth year of the present king, which might either be 1613 or 1635,
depending on whether the reference is to James I or Charles I. Plausible
surmises about the identity of the parties suggest that it was 1613. The declaration alleges that one Robert Toft delivered money to William Garraway, who
gave a bill drawn on Thomas Cole in Venice. The *Dictionary of National
Biography* (*DNB*) has a listing for a Robert Tofte (*d.* 1620), a poet who
published many translations of Italian poetry. The *DNB* article on Sir Ralph
Cole (1625–1704) refers to his uncle Thomas Cole (*d.* 1620) as having 'amassed a
large fortune in bills, bonds, &c.'. The *DNB* article on Sir Henry Garraway,
1575–1646, Lord Mayor of London, lists his father as Sir William Garraway,
chief farmer of the customs.

[40] Rastell, *Entrees*, 3rd edn, 338r. A translation of the entry is printed in Cranch,
'Promissory Notes', 377 and Holden, *History of Negotiable Instruments*, 326.

factor, 'to the proper use of' the defendant, at the rate of 5s 11d English per French crown. Thereupon, the defendant's factor delivered to the plaintiff's factor a set of bills of exchange directing the defendant J. B. to pay the plaintiff C. W. £414 3s 4d thirty days after sight of the bills. The declaration then states that the defendant, 'on the day and year first aforesaid, at the city of E. ... in consideration thereof assumed and to the plaintiff then and there faithfully promised that he, the defendant, well and faithfully would pay to the plaintiff, to the plaintiff's use at the city of E. aforesaid by way of exchange according to the usage of merchants, the aforesaid £413 3s 4d lawful money of England, at the end of thirty days next after sight of any of the bills of exchange aforesaid'. The declaration then states that afterwards, on 1 September of the same year, the first of the set of three bills was shown to the defendant, but 'his promise and undertaking not regarding', he did not pay the money.

5. *Hampton v. Calthrope* (1584).[41] Action against taker's principal. Brown's *Vade Mecum* has a similar declaration on an exchange contract from Antwerp to London dating from 1584. The plaintiff Robert Hampton, an alderman of London and Merchant Adventurer, alleged that his factor in Antwerp had delivered £170 6s 8d Flemish to the defendant's factor 'to pay to the plaintiff in consideration thereof seventy pounds Sterling at double usance according to the use of merchants, that is to say, at the end of two months then next following, by way of exchange, that is at the rate of 30s 8d Flemish per pound Sterling'. On receipt of the £170 6s 8d Flemish, the defendant's factor drew a set of bills of exchange on his master, Martin Calthrope, directing him to pay £70 sterling to the plaintiff. The declaration goes on to state that one of the bills was shown to the defendant, and that in consideration of the premises the defendant assumed and faithfully promised that he would pay the £70, but that he had paid only £40.

6. *Williamson v. Holiday* (1611).[42] Action against taker's principal. The last example to be considered here also comes from Brown's *Vade Mecum*. The declaration alleges that on 31 March 1610 the plaintiff's factor at Middleburgh paid to the defendant's

---

[41] Brown, *Vade Mecum*, 23. A rough translation, with dates altered to the 1730s, is printed in Bohun, *Declarations*, 56.

[42] Brown, *Vade Mecum*, 26. Brown gives a citation to the rolls of Trinity, 9 Jac. Rot. 712.

factor a sum of Flemish money that amounted to £200 English money to pay to the plaintiff in London at double usance by way of exchange according to the use of merchants. Thereupon the defendant's factor delivered to the plaintiff's factor a set of bills of exchange directing the defendant to pay the plaintiff the £200 sterling at double usance. The declaration then states that thereafter, on 20 May 1610, the plaintiff Abraham Williamson showed the first bill of exchange to the defendant Leonard Holiday at London, and that the defendant accepted the first bill of exchange and in consideration of the premises assumed and faithfully promised to pay the plaintiff the £200 sterling at double usance according to the tenor of the first bill of exchange. The defendant, however, did not pay.

From these declarations it is evident that at least by the end of the sixteenth century the central courts of the common law enforced exchange contracts in *assumpsit* actions without any conceptual or doctrinal difficulties. Unpublished records suggest an even earlier date. Baker has found entries in the King's Bench plea rolls of actions in *assumpsit* dating from the beginning of the sixteenth century that are almost certainly suits by deliverers against takers for unpaid exchange contracts.[43]

The slight variations among the examples of declarations on exchange contracts described above provide persuasive evidence of the thesis advanced herein that courts at this time, both common law and mercantile, regarded the obligation in exchange transactions as based on the value given in the transaction, not on the bill of exchange. Consider first the three examples of declarations in actions by deliverers against takers. The transaction in each seems to be the same. A merchant delivered currency of one country to another merchant, who engaged that his factor or representative abroad would repay the value in another currency. The repayment was not made, and the merchant who had delivered the money sued the merchant who received it. The essential allegations of each declaration are the same: (i) the

---

43 *Blanke* v. *Spinula* (1520), K.B. 27/1036, m. 75, described in Baker, 'New Light on Slade's Case', 400 n. 42; *Maynard* v. *Dyce* (1542), K.B. 27/1125, m. 110, described in Baker, 'Law Merchant and Common Law', 357–58. Baker has also pointed out that in the arguments in *Slade's Case*, it was suggested that an action on an unpaid exchange contract may have been the first instance of the use of *assumpsit* to enforce a simple promise for the payment of money. Baker, 'Law Merchant and Common Law', 354, 354 n. 50.

plaintiff delivered money to the defendant; (ii) in consideration thereof the defendant undertook that money would be paid abroad to the plaintiff or his representative; but (iii) the money was not paid abroad. There is, however, some variation in the extent and manner of the description of the events as an exchange or bill of exchange transaction. The earliest example, the anonymous declaration in the 1566 first edition of Rastell's *Entrees*, makes no mention at all of exchange or bills of exchange. The declaration in *J. L.* v. *E.* (1594), in the third edition of Rastell's *Entrees*, does use the word exchange in describing the transaction, but does not refer to any bill of exchange. Rather, the phrasing is that the plaintiff delivered English money to the defendant 'to pay [to the plaintiff's factor abroad] by way of exchange according to the use of merchants', and that the defendant assumed and promised that his factor abroad would pay 'by way of exchange according to the use of merchants'. This phrase – 'by way of exchange (*per viam excambii*)' – appears very frequently in the declarations of the late sixteenth and early seventeenth centuries. It is important to note that the phrase does not refer to any *bill* of exchange. '*Per viam excambii*' referred to the underlying exchange transaction rather than the piece of paper used to implement the transaction. To say that someone had undertaken to pay 'by way of exchange' meant that he had received money in one place and currency to be repaid in another location and currency. The transaction would, of course, usually have been effectuated by having the taker draw a bill of exchange directing his foreign representative to make the payment, but when pleaders of this era wished to refer to bills of exchange they did so explicitly, using the term '*per billam excambii*' not '*per viam excambii*'. The distinction is particularly clear in *J. L.* v. *E.*, for although the declaration avers that the plaintiff delivered money to the defendant to pay *per viam excambii* and that the defendant assumed that his factor would pay *per viam excambii*, the declaration never mentions any bill of exchange. Thus, while it is clear that the action was thought of as an action arising out of an exchange transaction,[44] it is equally clear that the legal obligation was not based on the execution of a bill of exchange. Rather, the plaintiff's right of recovery seems to have been based on the

---

[44] Indeed, in Rastell's alphabetical organization, this declaration appears under the letter E, subheading 'Exchange'.

ground that the plaintiff delivered money to the defendant, that the money was supposed to be repaid abroad, and that this did not happen.

The same conception of the basis of the obligation is evident even in declarations by a deliverer against a taker which do mention the bill of exchange, as in *Toft* v. *Garraway* (1613). The essential allegation still seems to be that the plaintiff delivered money to the defendant that was to be repaid abroad. The declaration does allege that on delivery of the money, the defendant gave the plaintiff a set of bills of exchange drawn on someone in Venice, and that one of the bills was shown to the drawee but was not paid. Yet it still seems inapt to speak of this as an action 'on the bill of exchange'. The bill is mentioned only as the mechanism by which the £45 delivered in England was to have been repaid in Venice. The plaintiff's right against the defendant seems to be based, as in the earlier declarations, on the ground that the plaintiff delivered the money to the defendant.

The precedents for actions in *assumpsit* against English merchants for money taken up abroad by their factors or agents provide even stronger evidence that the bill of exchange was not at this time regarded as having independent legal significance. The declarations described above as examples 4 to 6 all arose out of the same form of transaction. An English merchant's foreign factor had taken up money by exchange for his principal's use, but the English merchant failed to repay the value. In each case, the declaration uses the standard phrase 'to pay *per viam excambii*' to describe the underlying transaction, although it then goes on to mention the bill or bills of exchange given in the transaction. Thus, the essential allegations of each declaration are the same: (i) the plaintiff's factor abroad delivered a sum of foreign money to the defendant's factor; (ii) in consideration thereof the defendant undertook that he would pay money to the plaintiff in England; but (iii) the money was not paid.

The interesting aspect of these three declarations is how one should interpret the allegation that the plaintiff undertook to pay the money. Was the allegation of an undertaking to pay based on acceptance of the bill of exchange, as in modern negotiable instruments law, or on the receipt of value by the defendant's agent in the underlying exchange transaction? Only one of these three pleadings,

Williamson v. *Holiday* (1611), specifically alleges that the defendant 'accepted' the bill. The declaration states that 'said defendant, then and there ... accepted the first bill of exchange and then and there, in consideration of the premises, took upon himself and then and there faithfully promised that he would pay said plaintiff the two hundred pounds sterling at double usance according to the tenor of the first bill of exchange'. In the two earlier declarations, by contrast, the phrase 'accept' is not used in the allegation of the defendant's undertaking or *assumpsit*. Thus, the declaration in *Hampton* v. *Calthrope* (1584) alleges that the defendant's factor received money from the plaintiff's factor and drew a set of bills of exchange on the defendant, that the first bill was shown to the defendant, and that 'in consideration of the premises, [the defendant] took upon himself and to plaintiff then and there faithfully promised that he would well and faithfully pay and content unto plaintiff the said £70 at the end of said two months according to the tenor of the bill'. In *C. W.* v. *J. B.* (1595), the wording of the assumpsit allegation is somewhat different. After setting out the facts of the underlying exchange transaction and the drawing of the bills for £414 3s 4d, the declaration alleges that the defendant 'in consideration thereof took upon himself and to the plaintiff then and there faithfully promised that he the defendant well and faithfully would pay to the plaintiff to the plaintiff's use ... by way of exchange according to the usage of merchants, the aforesaid £414 3s 4d'.

Perhaps the most interesting aspect of these three declarations is the internal chronology of the pleading in *C. W.* v. *J. B.* (1595). The declaration states that on 10 June the plaintiff's factor delivered money to the defendant's factor at Rochelle, France, and the defendant's factor drew a set of bills on the defendant. The allegation that the defendant, in England, assumed upon himself and faithfully promised to pay, is also laid as occurring *that same day*. The declaration then goes on to say that afterwards, on 1 September, the bills were shown to the defendant, but the defendant 'not regarding his promise and assumption' refused to pay them. To be sure, the dates in declarations in *assumpsit* do not necessarily correspond with the actual chronology of the events, so that this allegation of a physical impossibility – that the defendant in England accepted a bill on the same day it was drawn in France –

might be explained as an example of the practices of early *assumpsit* pleading where all of the essential events were laid as having occurred on the same day.

There is, however, a far more plausible explanation of the chronological oddity. The allegation that the defendant 'assumed upon himself and faithfully promised to pay' the £414 3s 4d can be interpreted not as an allegation of fact, but an assertion of law, in the conventional language of *assumpsit* pleadings. The facts alleged in the 'whereas' clauses – that the plaintiff's factor delivered money to the defendant's factor, and that the defendant's factor drew bills of exchange on the defendant payable to the plaintiff – explain why the defendant should be bound to pay the money. The allegation of an *assumpsit* by the defendant is simply the legal mechanism by which the obligation is enforced. This interpretation seems particularly plausible given that these early *assumpsit* pleadings on exchange dealings date from exactly the same era as the developments, culminating in *Slade's Case* (1602),[45] which permitted a wide variety of obligations to be enforced in *assumpsit* by the device of pleading an implied *assumpsit*.

Indeed, viewed in light of the problem eventually resolved in *Slade's Case* – whether *assumpsit* could be used in cases where debt would lie – it seems particularly likely that the *assumpsit* allegation in *C. W. v. J. B.* is an assertion of law, not a chronologically muddled assertion of fact. If there was any possibility that the exchange contract could have been enforced by an action in debt, a pleader would have wanted to distinguish the promise from the underlying transaction, as in the somewhat later form of *indebitatus assumpsit* pleadings which alleged that the defendant, being indebted, afterwards assumed to pay. Thus, if the defendant in *C. W. v. J. B.* really did accept a bill which had previously been drawn by his factor for money taken up for the defendant's use, a late-sixteenth-century pleader would have had every reason to emphasize, not obscure, the chronological separation between the underlying transaction and the promise.

Even if the defendant in these actions had made an actual promise to pay, as seems to have been the case in *Williamson* v. *Holiday,* and may have been the case in *C. W. v. J. B.*, it does not

[45] 4 Co. Rep. 92. *Slade's Case*, or the interpretation thereof, plays a major role in the history of English contract law. For an overview, see Baker, *Introduction to English Legal History*, 374–408.

follow that the defendant was legally bound because he made that promise. Neither in the sixteenth century nor at any time since then has it been the case that a promise to pay money or perform any other act is enforceable in *assumpsit* simply because the promise was made. Rather, the whole point of the substantive law of contract, or of the pleading rules in *assumpsit*, is to distinguish enforceable from unenforceable promises. From that perspective, the important thing about the three examples of pleadings against drawees described above is not what they say about the defendant's undertaking but what they say about the circumstances that gave rise to the undertaking. In that respect the three pleadings are identical. They set out in detail the facts of the underlying exchange transaction in which the defendant's factor received money from the plaintiff's factor, taking particular pains to make it clear that the transaction abroad was conducted on behalf of the plaintiff and for the benefit of the defendant. The typical phrasing is not that the bill was drawn on the defendant by a person who happened to be the defendant's factor, or that a person who happened to be the plaintiff's factor delivered money to a person who happened to be the defendant's factor. Rather, the phrasing is singularly designed to characterize the events as a transaction between plaintiff and defendant, albeit conducted through intermediaries. For example, the opening words of the description of the transaction in *Hampton* v. *Calthrope* are that 'on September 10, 1584, at Antwerp in parts beyond the seas, Robert [Hampton, the plaintiff] *by the hands of* one Richard Ifield, then the factor of the said Robert, at the special instance and request of one Edward Chamberlain, servant of the said Martin [Calthrope, the defendant] ... delivered to said Edward Chamberlain ... *to the proper use of* said Martin, the sum of £107 6s 8d Flemish money to pay to said Robert in England in consideration thereof £70 sterling'. If these had been thought of as actions 'on bills of exchange' against the 'acceptors' of the bills, none of these allegations would have been necessary.

The conclusion that these sixteenth-century cases were actions to enforce the obligations arising out of the underlying exchange contracts, rather than actions on bills of exchange, undercuts a great deal of the traditional account of the early history of bills of exchange in the common law courts. The pleadings described above, particularly the declaration in *C. W.* v. *J. B.* from Rastell's

Entrees, have been analysed and discussed in considerable detail in previous works on the history of the English law of bills and notes. The conventional interpretation, however, is that these pleadings represent the first clumsy efforts to fit the law of bills and notes, which had previously been enforced in the mercantile courts, into the ill-fitting categories of the common law. The theory seems to have originated with Judge Cranch, writing in 1804,[46] and has been followed by Street,[47] Holdsworth,[48] and Holden.[49] Holden explains it as follows:

One instance will suffice, for the moment, to show how the technicalities of the common law were ill-suited to the handling of problems on bills of exchange. Suppose that a bill, which had been accepted, was dishonoured by non-payment. The payee wished to sue the acceptor. He was faced with this difficulty: at common law the general rule is that the only person who can sue on a promise is the person from whom the consideration moves. This, and other problems, were solved by the ingenuity of the common lawyers ...
The inventiveness of the common lawyers is seen at its best when they attempted to frame an action by the payee ... against the acceptor ... The pleading given in *Rastell's Entries* ... proceeds, in abbreviated form, as follows. The purchaser paid money to the drawer. The drawer drew a bill on the drawee. The drawee undertook to make payment to the payee. He has failed to do so. If the pleading had stopped at this, there is no doubt that, at common law, the payee would have had no action against the acceptor; the consideration for the promise of the acceptor did not move from the payee. Therefore, the pleader added a fictitious allegation that the purchaser was the agent of the payee; and a further allegation that the drawer was the agent of the acceptor. The position then reached was as follows: the payee was being 'identified' with the purchaser (who gave value) and the drawer was alleged to be the agent of the acceptor. All this was done to create 'that degree of privity between the payee and the acceptor which at that time was supposed necessary to support the action of assumpsit'.[50]

Baker has pointed out one major problem with this account; the requirements about consideration and privity that these pleadings were supposedly designed to fit did not evolve until nearly a century later.[51] The basic fallacy, however, is the far more funda-

---

[46] Cranch, 'Promissory Notes', 376–80.
[47] Street, *Foundations of Legal Liability*, 2: 343–45.
[48] Holdsworth, *History of English Law*, 8: 159–60.
[49] Holden, *History of Negotiable Instruments*, 27–29.
[50] Ibid., 27, 28–29. The quotation in the last sentence is from Cranch, 'Promissory Notes', 378.
[51] Baker, 'Law Merchant and Common Law', 357.

mental anachronism of assuming that bills of exchange and exchange transactions in the sixteenth century were used in the same fashion as in the eighteenth or nineteenth century. If one assumes that the transaction in *C. W.* v. *J. B.* was one in which someone in France who needed to make a payment to someone in England went to a banker or other financial professional to buy something like a bank draft to send to his creditor in England, then the allegations that the drawer of the bill in France was the agent of the payee do seem very odd. On the other hand, the allegations in *C. W.* v. *J. B.* make perfect sense on the assumption that the case arose out of a typical early exchange transaction in which a merchant's factor abroad borrowed money to finance a shipment of goods to his principal. Ironically, the conventional account puts matters precisely backwards. The allegations of agency have been regarded as fictitious allegations of fact, designed to make the acceptor's promise to pay the bill enforceable in the common law action of *assumpsit*. In reality, the allegations of a delivery of money by the plaintiff's agent to the defendant's agent were literally true and formed the basis of the defendant's obligation to pay the amount specified in the bill. The only fictitious allegation was that the drawee had promised to pay.

The conventional account of the early common law actions involving bills of exchange is an effort to solve a non-existent problem. The assumption has been that from medieval times merchants had been dealing with bills of exchange in essentially the same fashion as merchants of the late eighteenth century, and that the mercantile courts resolved disputes arising out of these transactions by applying a fully developed law of bills of exchange. The problem that the merchants faced was that the common law courts did not understand and would not enforce the legal obligations that arose by virtue of the execution of bills of exchange. Yet so far as one can tell from the published records of court proceedings, the supposed disparity between the law merchant and the common law does not exist. The most plausible conclusion about English cases involving exchange or bills of exchange before the seventeenth century is that they were handled in very much the same way regardless of which court they were in. To take a particularly striking example, the London Mayor's Court case of *Burton* v. *Davy* in 1437 is all but indistinguishable from the common law case of *Hampton* v. *Calthrope* in 1584, described above as example 5. In each case an English merchant's factor in the Low Countries took up money by exchange, giving a bill of exchange on his principal. Neither case can be described as an action 'on a bill of exchange'. Rather, both were cases to enforce the obligations arising out of the underlying exchange contract. In both cases, the defendant's obligation to pay was based not on acceptance of the bill, but on the fact that the defendant, through his agent, had received value from the plaintiff.

4

EARLY EXCHANGE TRANSACTIONS:
PUBLIC LAW AND POLICY

The cases examined in the previous chapter suggest that from the fifteenth to the early seventeenth centuries various English courts enforced the monetary obligations that arose out of exchange contracts, but no special body of law had developed concerning bills of exchange. Indeed, it may even be stretching the imagination to speak of a law of exchange contracts prior to the seventeenth century, if that phrase is taken to suggest that disputes arising out of exchange contracts were governed by a special body of law distinguishing exchange contracts from other monetary engagements. Rather, the cases are most aptly described as applications to exchange transactions of general concepts and procedures for enforcement of simple monetary obligations.

Although exchange contracts and bills of exchange do not seem to have raised any special problems in this period from the standpoint of private law analysis, that is not to say that exchange dealings were regarded as wholly unproblematic. Quite the contrary, if we shift focus from private law to public law, we find that exchange transactions in particular, and commercial affairs in general, were the subject of intense public controversy in the sixteenth and early seventeenth centuries. A satisfactory account of the history of commercial law in general, and bills and notes in particular, requires careful consideration of the relationships between legal issues and controversies concerning economic policy and morality. This chapter attempts to portray some of the richness and complexity of the relationship between law and commerce in the era in which the law of exchange contracts and bills of exchange developed by examining two major issues of public policy raised by early exchange transactions: usury and monetary policy.

THE DEBATE OVER USURY IN EXCHANGE

In describing exchange transactions as a means of finance, it was suggested that taking up money by exchange could be understood as a means of borrowing money at interest, where the interest charged for the use of the funds was expressed in the exchange rates between the two currencies. In the sixteenth century these would have been fighting words. At least until the Reformation era, the Church condemned as usury any fixed charge for the use of money.[1] Whether the profit on exchange transactions was a charge for the use of money was a matter of intense controversy from the Middle Ages until the end of the seventeenth century.[2]

The essential equivalence of funds transfer and finance in early exchange transactions posed particularly thorny problems for the usury analysis. No one disputed that simple money changing, that is, the immediate exchange of coins of one state for those of another, was both essential and legitimate and that the usury proscription did not preclude just charges and profits for such services. By the sixteenth century, the institutions of international trade had developed to the point that exchange by bills was no less essential. Even the most rigid moralists, such as the sixteenth-century English civil lawyer Thomas Wilson, conceded that exchange in the sense of simple funds transfer was lawful, so long as the currencies were rated at their just values without profit for the mere use of money: 'all such exchange is necessary, and worthy to be maintained and cherished, if we will have traffic and society to be continued betwixt all sorts of men and countries'.[3]

The problem was that it was extremely difficult to distinguish the profits in exchange dealings attributable to the mere use of funds for time from the profits that might legitimately be derived from fluctuations in the value of the respective currencies. According to standard usury doctrine, contracts where the lender established a charge for the use of money which was certain from the

---

[1] Ashley, *English Economic History*, 2: 377–488; Jones, *God and the Moneylenders*; Noonan, *Scholastic Analysis of Usury*; Tawney, Historical Introduction to Wilson's *Discourse upon Usury*, 105–34.

[2] de Roover, *Gresham on Foreign Exchange*, 99–102, 161–65; de Roover, 'Cambium ad Venetias'; Grice-Hutchinson, *School of Salamanca*; Grice-Hutchinson, *Early Economic Thought in Spain*, 81–121; Noonan, *Scholastic Analysis of Usury*, 175–92, 311–39; Savelli, 'Between Law and Morals: the Dispute on Exchanges'.

[3] Wilson, *Discourse upon Usury*, 300.

outset were usurious, while contracts in which the investor's profits were subject to risk and fluctuation, such as investments in partnership with trading merchants, could be legitimate. Exchange dealings, even seen as a form of finance, fell somewhere between the poles of certain gain on a loan and uncertain return on an investment.

One respect in which the system of exchange finance of the fifteenth or sixteenth century differs dramatically from modern credit transactions involving bills of exchange is that exchange transactions were inherently speculative. A merchant or banker who advanced money by exchange could never be entirely certain at the outset what his gain on the transaction would be. For example, in the hypothetical transaction described in chapter 2 in which a London banker lent £100 English at 22s 6d Flemish to the pound, the banker might have known at the time of the loan that the most recent rate in Antwerp that had been reported to him was 22s 2d, but his gain on the transaction would be determined by the spread between the 22s 6d rate at which he lent and the rate prevailing in Antwerp one month later when his correspondent lent out the money in the rechange transaction. By the time the banker's correspondent in Antwerp made the rechange loan, the exchange rate might have changed, in response either to conditions affecting the relative valuation of the Flemish and English currencies or factors affecting prevailing interest rates. Indeed, it was even possible, though generally unlikely, that the lender would make nothing or lose money on the transaction. Suppose, for example, that the Flemish pound was rising in relative valuation against the English pound. If the exchange rate in Antwerp at the time of the rechange loan had risen to 22s 6d – the same as the London rate a month before – then at the end of the two-month period of the exchange and rechange the London banker would be paid back exactly the £100 he started with.[4] If the Antwerp rate had risen still further, he might even receive less than his original £100. As Malynes put it, 'Know ye therefore, that the benefit or profit of Exchange is never known directly, but by the rechange thereof'.[5]

---

[4] de Roover gives an example of such a transaction in which the Medici Bank ended up receiving no interest for a loan, due to adverse fluctuations in the exchange rate in 1441. de Roover, 'What is Dry Exchange?', 195–96.

[5] Malynes, *Lex Mercatoria*, 256. See also Scarlett, *Stile of Exchanges*, preface p. 8 ('nor do they always gain by Exchanges, nor can they that observe the lawful

By the sixteenth and seventeenth centuries, many, if not most, theologians, canonists, and jurists, were able to conclude that exchange dealings, conducted honestly and within proper bounds, were not usurious, because the exchange contract was not a simple loan but an exchange of one coin for another in which the profit was uncertain.[6] That opinion, however, was by no means universal. Even those who found exchange dealings legitimate warned that practitioners faced a serious risk of crossing the line into sinful usury, and throughout the period there remained a minority of moralists who adhered to the rigorous view that any profit on exchange as a form of finance was usurious. Thus, for Dominic Soto, a Dominican professor at Spain's leading university in the mid-sixteenth century, and for Thomas Wilson, the English civil lawyer of about the same era, the contention that exchange profits were not usury simply could not be squared with basic facts about the transactions, particularly that a higher charge was invariably made for bills at double or triple usance than for those payable at a shorter time, and that bankers' profits from exchange dealings, though theoretically uncertain, were in practice predictably large.[7]

Some forms of exchange, however, were universally condemned. Suppose that someone in London wished to borrow money for some purely local need. There were merchants and bankers in London willing to deliver money by exchange on Antwerp, but the borrower would have to have some means of repaying the advance in Antwerp. Suppose however that someone in Antwerp was willing to act as a strawman for the borrower, agreeing to pay the bill drawn on him by the London borrower. The strawman, of course, would need some source of funds to pay the bill. Suppose that it was agreed that when the bill came due, the strawman would obtain the necessary funds by going to the Antwerp bourse and taking up money by exchange for London,

Course of Exchanges know certainly that they shall gain ... yet such is the variableness of the Course, that till they have the Moneys in Cash again, which they gave out on Exchange, they cannot know whether it be to their loss or profit'). In the appendix to *Gresham on Foreign Exchange*, de Roover sets out a compilation of quotations from jurists and moralists noting the point that exchange profits were inherently uncertain.

[6] Noonan, *Scholastic Analysis of Usury*, 311–39; de Roover, *Gresham on Foreign Exchange*, 173–77.

[7] Noonan, *Scholastic Analysis of Usury*, 313–14 (describing Soto's views); Wilson, *Discourse upon Usury*, 298–314.

drawing a bill on the original borrower in London payable to the original lender. The exchange and rechange transactions would be merely formal steps in what amounted to a purely local loan from the London borrower to the London lender. Indeed, the strawman in Antwerp was not really necessary. The original bill could have been drawn not on some formal representative of the *borrower* in Antwerp, but on the *lender's* representative in Antwerp. The lender's representative in Antwerp would not even have to bother with any actual payment and reborrowing in Antwerp. He could act both as the drawee who was to pay in the original transaction, and as the deliverer who advanced the funds in the rechange. No money need actually change hands in Antwerp at all; the Antwerp transaction could simply be a book entry. Indeed, one could even dispense with sending the bills back and forth from London to Antwerp. The borrower in London could simply agree to repay the amount that would have become due if he had drawn a bill on someone in Antwerp which had been paid by a rechange bill drawn on him.

Although the terminology was by no means uniform, the term 'dry exchange' was generally used to describe transactions in which the bill given for a loan was drawn on the lender's own representative abroad, with the understanding that instead of actually paying the bill, the lender's representative would simply redraw on the original borrower.[8] Transactions in which the lender and borrower did not even bother to send bills back and forth, but used the exchange merely as a means of computing the charge for the loan, were commonly called 'fictitious exchange'.[9] Virtually every six-

[8] 'This *Cambio sicco*, alias called dry Exchange, is in this manner: A Merchant hath occasion to use ... one hundred pounds, which they will deliver him in London, to be paid unto their Factor at Stoad: But having there no Factor of his own, the said Merchant is content to make his Bill of Exchange upon the Bankers Factor, payable to him the said Factor, with order and advice, that when the said Bill shall be due, he shall charge him by Exchange again, and take up the Money there, and he will pay the same with the rechange and charges of Factorage and Brokerage: Wherein they will be sure to make him pay very great Use or Interest, of fifteen or twenty in the 100 for the taking up of this Money'. Malynes, *Lex Mercatoria*, 261. Other sixteenth- and seventeenth-century English sources give similar definitions. Marius, *Bills of Exchange*, 3; Molloy, *De Jure Maritimo*, 274–75; Wilson, *Discourse upon Usury*, 305.
[9] Molloy, *De Jure Maritimo*, 275: Malynes, *Lex Mercatoria*, 261; Marius, *Bills of Exchange*, 4; Molloy, *De Jure Maritimo*, 275. Wilson does not seem to distinguish between dry and fictitious exchange. Wilson, *Discourse upon Usury*, 305.

teenth- and seventeenth-century theologian, canonist, and jurist agreed that dry and fictitious exchange were nothing more than simple usury cloaked in the guise of exchange.[10] Yet as in so many ethical disputes, there was far greater agreement on the names of the sins than on their definition. 'Dry exchange' and 'fictitious exchange' were usury; 'real exchange' or 'merchants' exchange' was not. The distinction between the categories was a matter of endless dispute.

The most difficult aspect of understanding the debate over usury in exchange is trying to assess the relationship between the ethical debate and the actual practice of merchants and bankers. This is not the place to enter into the perennial scholarly debate about the role of the usury proscription on the development of financial techniques. At the least, though, one should be wary of assuming that merchants and bankers of the era cared nothing about the ethical problem and simply looked for means to evade the usury prohibition. There is evidence that bankers and merchants themselves cared about the usury problem. In 1532 the Spanish colony of merchants in Antwerp specifically requested the opinion of the theology faculty of the University of Paris on the legitimacy of exchange dealings.[11] Whether they changed their conduct in response to the negative answer they received may be doubted, but that they asked is itself revealing. Similarly, merchants themselves participated in some of the principal debates in Genoa and other Italian cities on the legitimacy of exchange.[12] Moreover, even if one concludes that the merchants and bankers themselves were prepared to proceed despite the conclusions of the theologians, their behaviour does not necessarily reflect broader cultural attitudes. Rather, the controversy over the usury analysis of exchange seems to reflect deeply felt concerns about the ethical implications of the major developments in commercial and financial affairs that were occurring.

[10] In 1571 Pope Pius V issued the bull *In eam* which condemned as usury all dry exchange, without providing detailed specification of what the term meant. Noonan, *Scholastic Analysis of Usury*, 332–33.
[11] Excerpts from the merchants' questions and the theologians' response are printed in Grice-Hutchinson, *School of Salamanca*, 120–26.
[12] Savelli, 'Between Law and Morals: the Dispute on Exchanges'.

THE EXCHANGE CONTROVERSY IN ENGLAND

The literature in the continental tradition provides ample evidence of the conflicts and tensions produced by the evolution of exchange transactions in the early modern era. In England the situation is somewhat less clear. In the English tradition there is nothing comparable to the detailed, systematic treatment of the ethical and legal analysis of exchange contracts that one finds on the continent. The general problem of usury was certainly an issue of major concern in English moral debate in the sixteenth century. Numerous treatises and tracts on usury were published by English theologians and moralists, and the prohibition or control of usury was the subject of frequent legislation.[13] Yet Thomas Wilson's *Discourse on Usury*, published in 1572, is perhaps the only work by an English moralist that treats the problem of usury in exchange in any detail. The English legal literature shows even less evidence of the impact of ethical and social issues posed by exchange. Exchange transactions did not even become a topic of discussion in legal works until the late seventeenth century, by which time the usury dispute had in large measure died out.

It is, however, a mistake to assume that ethical and social issues can be ignored in examining the early history of English law of exchange contracts. Although the dispute about whether exchange was usurious may not have given rise to a rich theoretical literature in England, that is not to say that exchange transactions were not controversial. Quite the contrary, as a matter of economic policy, if not theology, exchange transactions were a matter of major social concern in England.

Until the sixteenth century, discussion of exchange transactions in English sources was intertwined with concerns about regulation of coinage.[14] The earliest reference to exchange of any form found in the printed collections of statutes is the Statute concerning False Money,[15] enacted as part of the recoinage measures in 1299.[16] As is typical of early English legislation concerning exchange, the 1299 statute contemplated only petty exchange, that

[13] Tawney, Historical Introduction to Wilson's *Discourse upon Usury*, 105–72.
[14] On early English regulation of coinage, see Munro, 'Bullionism and the Bill of Exchange in England'; de Roover, *Gresham on Foreign Exchange*, 31–93.
[15] 27 Edw. I (1299), *Statutes of the Realm*, 1: 131.
[16] Feavearyear, *Pound Sterling*, 12–13.

is, the immediate swap of coins of one realm for those of another. Nothing in the statute referred or alluded to any form of exchange by bills. Statutory regulation of petty exchange seems to have been based on a fear that much of the base coin in circulation had been imported by foreign merchants. Accordingly, the statute prohibited the import of false coins and also prohibited the export of good coin or silver bullion or plate without licence from the king. The statute further directed that tables be set up at Dover and elsewhere, where the king's appointed exchangers would exchange foreign and domestic coin for merchants and travellers. Similarly, various other early-fourteenth-century statutes regulating or prohibiting the import and export of coin and bullion seem to have been primarily directed at the concern that foreign merchants would take good coin and bullion out of the realm and import or smuggle false, clipped, and counterfeit coin. Thus the usual regulations were prohibitions of the export of good coin and bullion and of the import or circulation of foreign or base coins, coupled with requirements that foreign coins be changed only at the tables of the king's exchangers.[17]

By the late fourteenth century, there is some evidence of concern with public policy toward true exchange transactions, in the sense of the delivery of money in one place for payment abroad, as distinguished from simple coin changing. In 1381, the officers of the mint were asked to report on the causes of the flow of bullion from England to other realms.[18] The mint officers' analysis was surprisingly modern in some respects, for their conclusion was that the principal cause of bullion export was that English imports exceeded exports. The remedies suggested were that the export of bullion be prohibited and that trade be strictly regulated to ensure that merchants importing goods to England made their returns abroad in goods rather than money. The mint officers' discussion of exchange, by contrast, was quite primitive. Exchange transactions are mentioned not as an institution of trade, but in connection with payments of revenues due to the Pope. One of the causes of bullion export, they reported, was 'exchanges made to the Court

---

[17] Statute concerning Money (uncertain date), *Statutes of the Realm*, 1: 219; 9 Edw. III, stat. 2 (1335), *Statutes of the Realm*, 1: 273; 17 Edw. III (1343), *Statutes of the Realm*, 1: 299.

[18] The mint officers' report is printed in Bland, Brown, and Tawney, eds., *English Economic History: Select Documents*, 220–23.

of Rome in divers ways',[19] and the remedy suggested was that 'the Pope's money [should] be sent to him in merchandise and not in money'.[20]

The immediate response to the mint officers' report was a 1381 statute prohibiting, with certain exceptions, the export of gold and silver.[21] This act also dealt incidentally with exchange transactions, though it reflected a peculiar understanding, or misunderstanding, of exchange. The exchange regulation seems to have been prompted by a concern that exchange transactions were being used not as an alternative to the shipment of bullion, but as a cloak for the actual physical export of bullion. The statute first establishes a flat prohibition on the export of bullion except for the payment of the expenses of the king's fortresses abroad, stating that no one shall 'privily or openly send nor carry, nor cause to be sent or carried out of the said realm, any gold or silver in money, bullion, plate, or vessel, neither by exchanges to be made, nor in other manner'. The statute then provides that when prelates or others do have legitimate need to make payments abroad, 'that of the same payments only they [may] make exchanges in England, by good and sufficient merchants to pay beyond the sea, and first special leave and licence had of the King, as well for the exchangers as for the person which ought to make the payments, containing expressly the sum which shall be so exchanged'. The merchants making such licensed exchanges, however, were subject to examination and required to swear 'that they shall not send beyond the sea any manner of gold nor silver under the colour of the same exchange'.[22]

The proscription of bullion export was shortly supplemented with affirmative prescriptions about how merchants bringing goods to England should make returns of the proceeds of their sales. The 1381 mint officers' report had suggested that since the cause of the export of bullion was that imports exceeded exports, 'the remedy seems . . . to be that each merchant bringing merchandise into England take out commodities of the land as much as his

---

[19] Ibid., 220.   [20] Ibid., 222.
[21] 5 Rich. II, stat. 1, c. 2 (1381), *Statutes of the Realm*, 2: 17.
[22] The prohibition of bullion export was confirmed and supplemented in a series of fifteenth-century statutes, though these make no mention of exchange transactions. 2 Hen. IV, c. 5 (1400), *Statutes of the Realm*, 2: 122; 4 Hen. IV, c. 15 (1402), *Statutes of the Realm*, 2: 138; 2 Hen. VI, c. 6 (1423), *Statutes of the Realm*, 2: 219; 17 Edw. IV, c. 1 (1477), *Statutes of the Realm*, 2: 452.

78 _Early history of the law of bills and notes_

merchandise ... should amount to'. The first of the acts imposing
such a requirement, known as 'statutes of employment', was
adopted in 1390. It provided that every foreign merchant 'that
bringeth any merchandise into England, shall find sufficient sureties before the customers, in the port where the merchandise shall
be brought, to buy other merchandise, to the value of half the said
merchandise so brought, at the least, as wools, woolfells, lead, tin,
butter, cheese, cloths, or other commodities of the land'.[23] In
1402, the requirement was extended to English as well as foreign
merchants, and all were required to invest the full value of their
sales in English goods for export.[24] As was the case with the bullion
export prohibitions, some of the statutes of employment also dealt
with exchange transactions, reflecting the same concern that
exchange was being used as a means of secretly exporting bullion.
The 1390 Act, for example, required 'for every exchange that shall
be made by merchants to the Court of Rome, or elsewhere, that the
said merchants be firmly and surely bound in the chancery, to buy
within three months after the said exchange made, merchandises
of the staple ... or other commodities of the land, to the value of
the sum so exchanged, upon pain of forfeiture of the same'.[25]
Presumably the idea of the exchange provision was that one who
took up money by exchange should use the money to buy English
commodities for export, rather than exporting the bullion itself.

These legislative measures of the late fourteenth century set the
pattern for English exchange control policy for the next century.
During the fifteenth century, the bullion export prohibitions and
statutes of employment were frequently confirmed and strength-
ened, but there is no indication of any change in the understanding
of or policy toward exchange transactions. The legislative enact-
ments of this period seem to proceed on the assumption that trade
was or could be organized in the simple fashion of the age-old
travelling merchant system. English commodities, principally
wool, should be carried abroad by English merchants and sold at
the foreign marts for bullion to be minted into good English coin
for domestic circulation. Foreign merchants wishing to import
goods to England should be watched cautiously to see that the
proceeds of the sale of any goods that they brought to England

[23] 14 Rich. II, c. 1 (1390), _Statutes of the Realm_, 2: 76.
[24] 4 Hen. IV, c. 15 (1402), _Statutes of the Realm_, 2: 138.
[25] 14 Rich. II, c. 2 (1390), _Statutes of the Realm_, 2: 76.

were invested in English commodities for export. Such regulations of exchange as one finds are incidental to the concern that the desired pattern of trade not be disrupted, reflecting the old fear that exchange transactions were being used as cover for bullion shipments.

The medieval system of exchange and trade regulation was summed up in a group of economic and trade measures adopted at the parliament held in the third year of Henry VII's reign in 1487.[26] Various earlier bullion export prohibitions and statutes of employment were recited, noncompliance was lamented, and the statutes were once again directed to be put into execution. The statutes give no indication of why it might be thought that this effort would be any more effective than previous ones, let alone any indication that new measures might be necessary. The 1487 measures do, though, contain at least a hint of recognition that developing trade and financial practices were raising new issues of economic morality and policy. One of the statutes enacted that year was an 'Act against Usury and Unlawful Bargains', which broadly prohibits any form of usury, mentioning dry exchange in a parenthetical remark as one of the prohibited forms of disguised usury.[27]

By the beginning of the sixteenth century disputes about exchange transactions became more prominent in England. A representative example of early-sixteenth-century public attitudes on the issue can be found in 'A Treatise concerninge the Staple and the Commodities of this Realme', attributed to Clement Armstrong.[28] Exchange transactions were depicted by Armstrong as one aspect of the subversion of the natural order of English economic life by private greed. His argument began from the premise that in the fourteenth and fifteenth centuries sheep were raised and wool produced only on the best pasturage, leaving the

---

[26] 3 Hen VII, cc. 5, 6 & 8 (1487), *Statutes of the Realm*, 2: 514–18.
[27] 'If hereafter any bargain, covenant by buying of any obligation or bill or by any pledge put for surety or by bill or otherwise, by the name of dry exchange or otherwise, whereby any certain sum shall be lost by any covenant or promise betwixt any person or persons . . . or of any bargain or loan whereby any of the parties shall lose or pay for any sum certain . . . that all such bargains, covenants, promises and sureties therefor made, and all thing thereof depending, be utterly void and of none effect'. 3 Hen VII, c. 5 (1487), *Statutes of the Realm*, 2: 514.
[28] Printed in *Tudor Economic Documents*, 3: 90–114. For discussion of its authorship and dating see Bindoff, 'Clement Armstrong and his Treatise'.

rest of the realm to tillage for the support of the populace. There were only as many merchants as were needed to deal in the natural produce of the realm, and only as much wool was produced as could be sold in the market at Calais for ready money and bullion. In time, though, greed led to a great increase in the volume of the trade – a growth which Armstrong viewed as in all respects pernicious. Too many wool merchants bid up the price of wool; the higher price of wool led landowners to enclose their pastures for sheep raising, destroying the livelihood of those who had tilled the soil; more wool was taken to Flanders than could be sold for ready money, so the merchants had to sell cheaply and on long credit terms. On and on goes Armstrong's lament of the dire consequences produced by the efforts of those who would foolishly seek to 'have more plenty of wool by men's wisdom than God by his wisdom first ordained'.[29]

Exchange transactions figure quite prominently in Armstrong's analysis of England's economic woes. According to Armstrong, since the time that exchange transactions developed, the 'staplers ... never used for their wool to bring no money into England, as they did before, but always practised and covenanted with the adventurers in London to deliver their money, that rose of their wool sales, to them by exchange. So began the staplers and adventurers for their own singular profit to make their exchange together in keeping out of the realm all such money as yearly should be brought into the realm for our rich commodities'.[30] Armstrong's analysis is at least a slight advance over the view manifest in earlier legislation that those taking up money by exchange in England were somehow secretly exporting it abroad. Unlike those who framed the legislation of the fourteenth and fifteenth centuries, Armstrong clearly understood that exchange transactions did not involve shipment of specie, but simply allowed receipts from English exports to be used to pay for English imports. Yet he remained firmly convinced that exchange transactions were an impediment to policies designed to bring bullion to the realm.

The key to Armstrong's analysis of exchange was the view that export revenues were the natural fruit of England's resources while payments for imports were a waste of treasure on foreign trifles. The sale of England's wool and cloth should yield specie, enriching

[29] *Tudor Economic Documents*, 3: 90.   [30] Ibid., 93–94.

the treasure of the realm. Instead, by exchange transactions the proceeds of the sale of England's goods were delivered to merchants who 'receiveth the staplers money beyond sea and there bestow it upon strange merchandise and bringeth it into the realm, which else by the stapler ought to be brought into the realm in ready money'.[31] Although Armstrong's implication that exchange transactions were responsible for the import of trifles may be an extreme example, even for sixteenth-century economic writing, of confusion between cause and effect, the notion that imports were generally undesirable was commonly held in Armstrong's time and long thereafter.[32]

Armstrong's view that the development of exchange transactions was a lamentable modern departure from traditional methods of trade must have been commonly held in sixteenth-century England. On several occasions, efforts were made to cure perceived economic ills by recreating the trading conditions of the late fourteenth century. In 1530 Henry VIII directed his advisers, including the Lord Chancellor and Chief Justices of the king's courts, to consider legislative measures to prevent loss of bullion. The advisers concluded that 'all the statutes should be insearched to see, whether there were any statute or law able to serve for the purpose'.[33] The result was a royal proclamation reviving the statute of 1381 prohibiting bullion export and confining exchange transactions to the king's licensed exchangers. What effect the proclamation had can probably never be known, but those knowledgeable in matters of trade and exchange evidently thought it foolish. Sir Richard Gresham, father of Thomas Gresham, noted that 'merchants can no more be without exchanges and rechanges, than the ships in the sea without water', and pointed out that far

---

[31] Ibid., 95.

[32] Another writer of the same era excoriates as 'Ill-occupied ... all such merchants which ... bring ... in vain trifles and conceits, only for the foolish pastime and pleasure of man'. Starkey, *England in the reign of King Henry the Eighth*, quoted in Viner, *Theory of International Trade*, 30. Nearly a century later, Malynes noted caustically that 'some men do wonder at the simplicity of Brasilians, West-India, and other Nation ... in giving good Commodities of their Countries, yea Gold, Silver, and precious things, for Beads, Bells, Knives, Looking-Glasses, and such toys and trifles [yet] we ourselves commit the same, in giving our staple wares for Tobacco, Oranges, and other corruptible smoking things, or superfluous Commodities at dear rates, to the loss of the Common-wealth'. Malynes, *Lex Mercatoria*, 62.

[33] Schanz, *Englische Handelspolitik*, 2: 631.

from being a cause of the loss of bullion, 'these exchanges and
rechanges do much to the stay of gold in England, which would
else be conveyed over'.[34] In 1538, the exchange prohibition was
withdrawn, in a proclamation acknowledging that unless merchants have 'free liberty to exchange and rechange ... great
damage might grow to the common wealth of this realm'.[35]

The 1530s measures, however, were only the first skirmish in the
lengthy controversy over the legitimacy of exchange transactions
that raged in England for another century. Throughout the period
exchange transactions were deeply mistrusted. Even if exchange
was not regarded as inherently pernicious, it was widely felt that in
practice exchange transactions were conducted in a fashion detri-
mental to English national interests. In the late sixteenth and early
seventeenth centuries it was widely believed that English money
was underrated in exchange transactions, especially against the
coin of the Low Countries. The 'undervaluing' of English money
was commonly cited as one of the principal causes of the loss of
treasure from England and decay of its trade. The argument
seemed quite simple. If English coin was valued in exchange
transactions below the mint par, then those who needed to send
money from London to Antwerp would prefer to export bullion
rather than deliver the money in exchange transactions at an
unfavourable rate. Similarly, those who had money in Antwerp to
be returned to London would be discouraged from doing so in
bullion since they could make the transfer more advantageously by
exchange. Numerous writers of the period offered their analyses of
the causes of the problem and proposals for cures. The issue was
evidently a matter of major public concern, for on at least five
occasions, in 1564, 1576, 1586, 1600, and 1621, Royal Commissions
were established to investigate the problem of the exchanges and
make recommendations for reforms.[36]

---

[34] Letter of 25 July 1538, printed in ibid., 632–33.
[35] Proclamation of 30 July 1538, printed in ibid., 634. In 1551, the exchange
prohibition statutes were again revived by royal proclamation, this time for a
period of only a few months. Tawney, Historical Introduction to Wilson's
Discourse upon Usury, 145–46.
[36] For more detailed accounts of the English exchange controversy, see Buckley,
'Sir Thomas Gresham and the Foreign Exchanges'; de Roover, *Gresham on
Foreign Exchange*, 173–274; Lipson, *Economic History of England*, 3: 62–116;
Supple, *Commercial Crisis and Change in England*, 89–96, 163–224; Tawney,
Historical Introduction to Wilson's *Discourse upon Usury*, 134–54.

A common theme of the controversy over the exchanges in the late sixteenth and early seventeenth centuries was the suspicion that unfavourable exchange rates were caused by the manipulations of bankers and foreign merchants. As early as the 1530s, Armstrong had suggested that the Dutch manipulated exchange rates so that 'rather than the staplers should carry their money for their wool into England, they should gain more profit to deliver it by exchange to adventurers of London for 8d or 12d less in the pound to win so much by that exchange in every pound, to receive their money after they come home'.[37] The charge of manipulation was elaborated in an anonymous memorandum known as 'For the Understanding of the Exchange', which is thought to have been written some time between the mid-1550s and mid-1570s.[38] The memorandum contains a section on the 'feats Merchants devise by exchange', which comprises a rather full catalogue of popular suspicions about exchange. The charges against those engaged in exchange transactions ranged from the old fear that they use exchange 'to hide their carrying away of any Princes money', to the perennial mistrust of those who leave off trade and specialize in financial affairs, to the special late-sixteenth-century concern that they 'conspire together so to rule the exchange'. The memorandum evidently enjoyed wide notoriety in the late sixteenth and early seventeenth centuries, and the views it expressed seem to have been commonly held.

The 1564 Royal Commission on Exchanges recognized that exchange rates were in some measure the product of market forces, but still adhered to the view that exchange rates were fixed by 'conspiracy of the great bankers'.[39] A memorandum prepared for the Commission noted that 'because the keeping of the exchange low is the common benefit of the Low countries gained upon the common detriment of the realm of England, therefor it seemeth

---

[37] 'Treatise concerninge the Staple', in *Tudor Economic Documents*, 3: 94.

[38] The text of the memorandum is printed in de Roover, *Gresham on Foreign Exchange*, 290–309. de Roover concluded that the memorandum was written by Sir Thomas Gresham, some time around 1559 or 1560. Ibid., 3–18. Others have disputed that attribution, suggesting it was written by either Sir Thomas Smith or Richard Martin some time between the 1550s and 1570s. Dewar, 'The Memorandum "For the Understanding of the Exchange": Its Authorship and Dating'; Fusfeld, 'On the Authorship and Dating of "For the Understanding of the Exchange"'.

[39] 'Memorandum Prepared for the Royal Commission on the Exchanges, 1564', in *Tudor Economic Documents*, 3: 352.

that the Council of the Finances in the Low countries have con-
tinually spurred the bankers of Antwerp to keep the exchange
lower than the just proportion of the values of the moneys of either
realm hath duly required'.[40] The conspiracy theory apparently
figured even more prominently in the deliberations of the 1576
Royal Commission on Exchanges, with disastrous consequences.
In response to the Commission's report, the old exchange regulations of the late fourteenth century were again reimposed; private
exchange business was prohibited, and all exchange transactions
were to be effected through three licensed exchangers, at substantial fees.[41] A group of Italian merchants prepared a memorandum opposing the exchange control measures, explaining in some
detail that their exchange operations were not devices for drawing
treasure out of England but were essential to English trade.[42] A
group of English merchants also prepared a protest, pointing out
that the medieval statutes dealt with simple coin changing, and
were wholly unsuited to late-sixteenth-century conditions.[43]
Within a year, the scheme seems to have collapsed.[44]

Despite the failure of the periodic efforts in the sixteenth
century to control exchange rates by prohibiting unregulated
exchange transactions, the theory that England's economic woes
were caused by manipulation of the exchanges continued to be
vigorously advanced through the early part of the seventeenth
century. The theory was articulated forcefully by one of the most
intriguing figures in early English commercial policy and law,
Gerard Malynes. Malynes is known to legal historians primarily as
the author of a book published in 1622 entitled *Consuetudo, vel,
Lex Mercatoria*, which is usually described as the first English
book on commercial law. Malynes was not, however, a lawyer by
profession. Indeed, one of the keys to understanding his role in the
development of English law is the realization that law, at least in
the narrow sense of private law, was but a small part of his concern.
Malynes was a merchant – though apparently not always a successful one – but also had wide knowledge of contemporary and
scholastic literature. Throughout his life he acted as an advisor to

---

[40] Ibid.
[41] 'Proclamation Prohibiting Private Exchange Business and Establishing a Public
     Exchange Office, September 27, 1576', in *Tudor Economic Documents*, 2: 167–69.
[42] Ibid., 169–73.   [43] Schanz, *Englische Handelspolitik*, 2: 646.
[44] de Roover, *Gresham on Foreign Exchange*, 210–18.

the government, by request and on his own volition, on matters of trade, economics, and other matters of public policy.[45] In short, he was a typical example of what the economic historian George Unwin cleverly termed 'that class of volunteer statesmen who were encouraged ... by the growing administrative activity of the Crown to offer their schemes for the benefit of the commonwealth ... with an accompanying prayer that they might be chosen as humble instruments to carry out the good work which they had recommended'.[46]

The dominant concern in all of Malynes' writings and public activities was monetary policy, particularly control of exchange transactions. His first published work, *A treatise of the Canker of England's Common wealth*, printed in 1601, was devoted to showing that the abuse of exchange transactions and manipulation of exchange rates was the cause of the decay of England's trade, and therefore that reformation of exchange was the key to ensuring her prosperity. He advocated these views as a member of the Royal Commissions on Exchange in 1600 and 1621, and in his well-known literary battle with the mercantilist writers Edward Misselden and Thomas Mun in the early 1620s.[47]

Malynes accepted enthusiastically the common view that bankers and foreign merchants manipulated exchange rates to the detriment of England. In several of his published works on exchange, Malynes included the passage on the feats of bankers contained in the anonymous memorandum 'For the Understanding of the Exchange', and he was unapologetic about heaping abuse

---

[45] On Malynes' life, activities, and thought, see de Roover, 'Gerard de Malynes as an Economic Writer'; Johnson, *Predecessors of Adam Smith*, 41–54; Muchmore, 'Gerrard de Malynes and Mercantile Economics'; Supple, *Commercial Crisis and Change in England*, 201–11.

[46] Unwin, *Industrial Organization in the Sixteenth and Seventeenth Centuries*, 137–38. On at least one occasion Malynes suffered the fate of the ancient curse, 'May all your wishes come true'. In 1619 he succeeded to a patent issued by James I for private coinage of copper farthings. The project was a financial disaster, bringing Malynes only massive debts arising from his obligation to convert the copper farthings into silver on demand. Malynes ended up imprisoned for debt in the Fleet, a fate which apparently had befallen him before from mercantile activities. Johnson, *Predecessors of Adam Smith*, 42–43; de Roover, 'Gerard de Malynes as an Economic Writer', 349. It may then be no coincidence that his 1622 work *Lex Mercatoria* contains an eloquent plea for abolition of the English practice of imprisonment for debt.

[47] Johnson, *Predecessors of Adam Smith*, 66–69; Supple, *Commercial Crisis and Change in England*, 198–221.

on the exchange bankers. 'Some men of judgment have found my Writing to be invective and pathetical against Bankers, wherein they are not mistaken; for the use of Banks ... are not to be suffered in any well ordered Common-wealth'.[48] For Malynes, however, the conspiracy theory of exchange was not simply an expression of the characteristic human trait of attributing to villainy that which one does not understand. Malynes had a detailed and comprehensive understanding of the operation of exchange transactions and monetary matters, and integrated the charge of exchange manipulation into a theory of exchange, trade, and monetary policy that was, for its time, quite systematic and comprehensive, even if it was soon to fall into disrepute.

In common with virtually all other economic writers of the era, Malynes' prime concern was the organization of foreign trade. He believed that foreign trade should be conducted in such fashion that bullion came to and remained in the realm. Exports should exceed imports, and exchange transactions should not impede these objectives. Where Malynes parted company with his opponents was in his assessment of the causal links. Malynes maintained that the underrating of English money in exchange was not a symptom of other economic conditions, but was itself the cause of the loss of bullion. As he put it in his first published work, 'this course of exchange being abused ... is become predominant or doth over-rule the course of commodities and money, and is the very efficient cause of this overbalancing of commodities ... and consequently of the decrease of our wealth and exportation of our monies'.[49] To Malynes, the point seemed self-evident. Whatever happened to the state of imports or exports, the payments must

---

[48] Malynes, *Lex Mercatoria*, 280.
[49] Malynes, *Canker of England's Common wealth*, in *Tudor Economic Documents*, 3: 389. He made the point repeatedly in his later writings. For example, in an unpublished work on exchange written in 1610, he noted 'that the exchange for money between us and other nations is a thing *active* and that commodities and money are things *passive* upon which ... the operation of exchange doth work incredible loss of the Realm'. *Treatise of Tripartite Exchange According to the Three Essential Parts of Traffique* (1610), quoted in de Roover, 'Gerard de Malynes as an Economic Writer', 363 n. 79, Similarly, in *Lex Mercatoria* he spoke of the 'over-balancing of Commodities in price, and quality, and not in quantity; whereby in effect, Monies are given to boot, and as it were over and above the reasonable estimation of things; and herein is the course of Exchanges by Bills predominant, and over-ruling both the course of Commodities, and Money'. Malynes, *Lex Mercatoria*, 44.

ultimately be made either by exchange or in bullion. If exchange rates are unfavourable, then payments necessarily will be made by shipment of bullion. 'If the exchange with us here be low, so that more will be given for our money being carried in specie, than by bill of exchange can be had, then our money is transported; whereas otherwise no man would adventure the money, and stand in danger of the law to lose treble the value, if by a simple bill of exchange he might have as much paid him beyond the seas, for in truth gain is the cause of exportation of our monies.'[50] The later mercantilists, such as Misselden and Mun, contended that the only sensible focus of policy was the balance of trade, since if exports exceeded imports, the net difference would necessarily come to England in bullion. They believed that it was foolish to worry about the exchange rate in itself, for they contended that exchange rates were determined simply by the supply of and demand for transfers to pay for imports and exports. As Mun put it, 'In vain therefore hath Gerard Malines laboured so long, and in so many printed books to make the world beleeve that the undervaluing of our money in exchange doth exhaust our treasure, which is a mere fallacy of the cause, attributing that to a Secondary means, whose effects are wrought by another Principal Efficient.'[51]

Malynes was clearly the loser in the debate over the role of the exchanges in the formulation of economic policy. By the mid-seventeenth century the debate over exchange control had largely died out. There was a brief final effort to disinter the ancient device of confining exchange to the royal exchange early in the reign of Charles I, but the controversy had by then passed into history, and the occasional revivals of the contention that exchange control was the key to prosperity 'were now dismissed as "old inconsiderate fancies, sufficiently refuted before"'.[52] So too, in the literature on early English economic thought, Malynes is known principally as the man who lost the debate with Misselden and Mun, providing the foil against which they formulated the general theory of the balance of trade. What is important for present purposes, however, is not to assess the merits of the positions taken

---

[50] Malynes, *Canker of England's Common wealth*, in *Tudor Economic Documents*, 3: 392.

[51] Mun, *England's Treasure by Forraign Trade*, 42.

[52] Lipson, *Economic History of England*, 3: 84, quoting *Britannia Languens* (1680), 236.

by Malynes but to see that they reflected attitudes toward exchange transactions that were very deeply held in the sixteenth and early seventeenth centuries.

THE SIGNIFICANCE OF THE PUBLIC CONTROVERSY OVER EXCHANGE

The realization that exchange transactions in particular, and commercial affairs in general, were the subject of intense public controversy in the sixteenth and early seventeenth centuries is essential in understanding the development of the law of bills of exchange. Consider, for example, the way that the conventional accounts of the early history of the law of bills and notes have treated Gerard Malynes' 1622 work, *Consuetudo, vel, Lex Mercatoria: or, The Ancient Law-Merchant.* This book has been referred to as 'the oldest book . . . extant in the English language on the subject of the law-merchant'; 'the first general English treatise on commercial law'; 'the first work on the Merchant Law in England'; and 'the earliest English work on bills'.[53] Legal historians have regarded the very fact of its publication as one of the most significant events in the early development of English law of bills and notes, for it seems to provide a good indication of the date at which the rules of mercantile law were first laid out in a systematic fashion in England.[54]

The conventional depiction of Malynes' *Lex Mercatoria* as the seminal book on English commercial law is, however, profoundly misleading. In modern usage the phrase 'commercial law' refers to the body of private law specifying the rights and duties of participants in commercial transactions. To state the obvious, modern commercial law is both commercial and it is law. To speak of commercial law is to distinguish commercial activity from other aspects of social life, and law from other aspects of public concern such as economic or ethical policy. In Malynes' era, the focus of

---

[53] The quotations, respectively, are taken from: Cranch, 'Promissory Notes', 376; Plucknett, *History of the Common Law*, 660; Scrutton, *Elements of Mercantile Law*, 5; and Kent, *Commentaries on American Law*, 3: 89.

[54] Holden, *History of Negotiable Instruments*, 36–42, 66–70; Holdsworth, *History of English Law*, 5: 129–35, 8: 146–59; Street, *Foundations of Legal Liability*, 2: 354–59.

discussions of exchange was not the private law rules about the obligations of parties to bills, but the issues of ethical and economic policy raised by exchange transactions.

To be sure, Malynes' book does discuss the rights and obligations of participants in exchange transactions as well as other commercial relations, such as the suretyship, factors, charter parties, bills of lading, insurance, and sea law. Yet these passages that can aptly be characterized as commercial law in the modern sense account for no more than a quarter or a third of the book. The book deals with a wide variety of topics of private and public concern in connection with commerce. One cannot maintain the image of this as a book on commercial law, in anything like the modern sense, in the face of the extensive passages of practical advice for the conduct of business, description of world trade, explanation of the coinage of various countries and operations of the mints, discussion of Church teaching on usury and various practical proposals for the provision of loans to the needy poor, description of the best current methods of maintaining accounting records, trenchant criticism of the English practice of imprisonment for debt, and, above all, exposition of Malynes' own theories of economic policy.[55] To regard the discussion of these other topics in Malynes as merely appendages to a work fundamentally dedicated to private commercial law is to miss what is perhaps most interesting about Malynes and his era. Rather than being the first English book on commercial law, Malynes' *Lex Mercatoria* is the archetype of a work on mercantile affairs in the era predating the separation of private law from the public issues raised by the transition to an era dominated by commerce.

Although exchange transactions were controversial throughout Europe, the nature of the controversy seems to have differed on the continent and in England. There are some indications that English writers and authorities were concerned with the problem of the usury analysis of exchange,[56] but for the most part the concern

---

[55] As if Malynes' work were not itself a sufficiently heterogeneous mix, it was in the later editions bound together with a collection of works by other authors, including several lengthy treatises on accounting, a brief guide to practice in exchange transactions written by an English notary, John Marius, various collections of sea laws, and several polemical tracts on the jurisdiction of the Admiralty Court and the sovereignty of England over the surrounding seas.

[56] 3 Hen. VII, c. 5 (1487), *Statutes of the Realm*, 2: 514 (prohibiting dry exchange along with other forms of disguised usury); Memorandum Prepared for the

with the morality of exchange seems to have been subordinate to the concern over the economic effects of exchange. Those who earned their living from exchange were often condemned, though more because they no longer engaged in productive activity than because their new calling was sinful. For example Clement Armstrong complained that specializing in exchange finance 'is not only plain usury, but it hath and yet doth help to destroy the wealth of the king, of his lords and commons', since the rich 'old merchants who forsake occupying of cloths to occupy their money by exchange ... never bestow their money upon no English cloth nor other things, whereby to win money as upon merchandise outward, to pay any custom to the king's profit or for any profit of the realm, but only to win lucre as upon the loan and forbearing of his money'.[57] Another characteristic concern in the English writing on exchange finance was that whether or not charging for loans was sinful, agreeing to pay the charges was imprudent. Sir Thomas Gresham complained that young merchants who had insufficient capital financed their trade by taking up money by exchange, and that the necessity of paying the charges for their exchange loans forced them into rash sales, harming the trade in general as well as leading them to ruin.[58]

If one looks beneath the surface of the particular arguments and issues, one can see a connection between the English exchange controversy and the continental usury debate. Both disputes can be interpreted as manifestation of the same basic social concern over the explosion of financial activity and transformation of economic life in early modern times. From this perspective, it is particularly interesting to compare the writings of the conservative economist Malynes and the conservative lawyer Wilson.

In all of his writings, Malynes maintained that since the cause of England's troubles was the underrating of its money in exchange, the cure was to ensure that exchange transactions were conducted at values determined strictly in accordance with the gold and silver content of the respective coins. 'The true royal exchange for money

Royal Commission on the Exchanges, 1564', in *Tudor Economic Documents*, 3: 349 ('here you may perceive that this necessary and fair name exchange might be truly termed by the odious name of buying and selling of money for time, otherwise called usury'); Fenton, *Treatise of Usurie*, 24.

[57] *Tudor Economic Documents*, 3: 107.
[58] Burgon, *Sir Thomas Gresham*, 1: 464.

(by bills of exchange) is grounded upon the weight, fineness, and valuation of the money of each country, according to the Par, which is, value for value'.[59] If all exchanges were conducted according to this fundamental principle of *par pro pari* then all of the adverse consequences he attributed to exchange manipulation would necessarily disappear. 'Having found out the efficient cause, the remedy is easy, . . . every man of judgment may easily gather that the exchange for all places ought to be kept at a certainty in price, according to value for value.'[60] Malynes' position on how this goal would best be attained varied in his writings over the years, but he never wavered in his insistence that exchange trans-actions should be conducted solely on the basis of the inherent specie values of the currencies. Thus, in Malynes' view, the funda-mental cause of England's woes was that greedy merchants and bankers had perverted exchange from its foundation as an exchange of monies in accordance with their natural valuation.[61]

Thomas Wilson's *Discourse upon Usury*, published in 1572, contains a discussion of the morality of exchange that is remark-ably similar in tone and content to Malynes' work. Wilson found nothing usurious or otherwise ethically problematic about exchange transactions entered into simply for the purpose of avoiding the danger and expense of the transfer of money.[62] By contrast, Wilson condemned any form of 'merchandizing exchange', where 'merchants do only themselves set and appoint the prices and values of money so exchanged'.[63] Wilson understood quite clearly that as exchange was then conducted, those who delivered money by exchange were typically lending the money and charging for the use of the funds, 'which over gaining and excessive taking in this sort is, in my opinion, most biting usury'.[64] In a passage which could just as easily have been written by Malynes, Wilson laments that in their pursuit of gain the mer-chants of his time had abandoned the true valuation on which exchange should be based. 'I grant still that real exchange is honest and lawful where money is delivered to be paid again at sight, or at two or three months, according to the just and public valuation of

[59] Malynes, *Lex Mercatoria*, 262.
[60] Malynes, *Canker of England's Common wealth*, in *Tudor Economic Documents*, 3: 397.
[61] Ibid., 389.   [62] Wilson, *Discourse upon Usury*, 298–300.   [63] Ibid., 303.
[64] Ibid., 305.

money, to what country soever the exchange is made. But this kind of exchange pleaseth not merchants, the same having no such savor of lucre and gain as the rechange and the dry exchange have, which two kinds of dealings are very hurtful to all occupiers, and destroy all trade, when such often returns are made of money, either the one way or the other'.

The similarity between Malynes and Wilson is not simply that both lamented modern conditions as degenerate. Depicting current practices as a corruption of the purity of the past is a common metaphor of social commentary in all ages. The significant aspect of the similarity is that both Malynes and Wilson singled out one very specific change as the source of the evils of their times: the notion that money can be regarded as merely another commodity, with a price that fluctuates in accordance with ordinary market forces.

The dispute over exchange dealings, even more than other aspects of the general problem of usury, placed into sharp focus the transformation that was occurring in the basic concepts of money and the monetary economy.[65] The argument that exchange finance was not usurious turned on seeing exchange dealings as sales or exchanges of one form of property for another, rather than as loans. Yet the property in question was money. Thus, to describe exchange as anything other than a loan required a conception of money as simply another commodity, with a price set by market forces as with any other commodity. That struck at the very root of the principal natural law arguments against usury which were based on the view that money was a measure, not a commodity. This aspect of the problem is very prominent in Wilson's discussion.[66] So too, the dominant theme of all of Malynes' writing on exchange was that the source of England's economic woes was that the exchangers had abandoned the natural use of money, and no longer valued it in exchange according to the principle of *par pro pari.*

---

[65] Noonan, *Scholastic Analysis of Usury*, 317–27; Grice-Hutchinson, *School of Salamanca*, 52–58; Grice-Hutchinson, *Early Economic Thought in Spain*, 102–06.

[66] 'The exchange in these days is no other thing than a ... device of buying and selling coin and money ... an art as is against nature. For the occupiers thereof do give and sell money for money, which was not invented and ordained to the end that either it should price itself by itself, or be ... esteemed by way of

Perhaps, then, the explanation for the apparent difference between the continental and English developments concerning exchange is simply that the underlying concern was manifested in different languages. Indeed, one might speculate that differing economic circumstances influenced the difference in the discourse. In Antwerp or Genoa, where fabulous wealth was attained through exchange banking in the sixteenth century, social commentary on exchange focused on the development of a moral theory that would justify the wealth that had been attained by the revolution in financial techniques. In England, which throughout much of the sixteenth and early seventeenth centuries lived in fear of trade decline and economic domination by the Low Countries, the development of exchange finance was perceived as a problem in national economic policy. In any event, it is probably impossible to underestimate the significance of the transformation in basic concepts and attitudes toward money and finance that were associated with the development of exchange finance. Indeed, even half a millennium later, it is not entirely clear that society has fully accustomed itself to the concept of money as a mere commodity. We do, to be sure, speak easily of the 'money market'; yet one still cringes a bit to hear descriptions of contemporary banking in which loan officers unflinchingly describe themselves as salesmen whose product happens to be money.

merchandise, but that all other things should receive their prices and value of it'. Wilson, *Discourse upon Usury*, 307.

5

FROM EXCHANGE TRANSACTIONS TO BILLS OF EXCHANGE: THE TRANSFORMATION OF COMMERCIAL PRACTICE

Though there is always a risk of oversimplification in dividing history into chronological periods, the middle of the seventeenth century serves as a convenient dividing line in the history of commercial practice concerning bills of exchange. The periods before and after the mid-seventeenth century might be called the era of exchange transactions and the era of bills of exchange, respectively. In the earlier era, exchange was a contract between the deliverer and the taker, which happened to have been carried out by means of a bill of exchange. In the later era a bill of exchange was an instrument that created and embodied an obligation binding the drawer (and, after acceptance, the drawee) to pay money to the payee or other holder; whether it happened to have been issued in a transaction akin to the exchange transactions of earlier times was of little significance.

THE ERA OF EXCHANGE TRANSACTIONS AND THE ERA OF BILLS OF EXCHANGE

The differences in commercial practice in the periods before and after the mid-seventeenth century can be seen quite clearly by contrasting portrayals of typical transactions in the two periods. In a seventeenth-century book on commerce, Lewes Roberts described a typical exchange transaction as follows:

Exchange ... is ... the giving of so much *Moneys* in one place to one, who should cause it to be again repaid in another place by another for him; as for example, *Edward* hath here in London one thousand pounds, and desireth to remit the same, or have it in the hands of *Joseph*, who resideth in Venice; and *Lodowick* hath one thousand pounds in Venice, in the custody and hands of *Thomas*, which he would get, receive, and recover out and have them here: it happeneth that *Edward* meeteth with

Lodowick, to whom he delivereth and payeth the said one thousand pounds; and thereupon *Lodowick* writeth to *Thomas*, that he pay the said thousand pounds to *Joseph*, and thus each party comes to be both satisfied and accommodated; by which it may be discerned, that in all *Exchanges*, there is concluded two payments, two places, and four distinct persons; as he who payeth in the one place, and he who receiveth in the other; and he who receiveth in the one place, and he who payeth in the other; and from hence it consequently followeth, that no man can *remit*, except there be another to *draw*; nor no man can in the second place *receive*, except there be another authorized to *pay*.[1]

In a work on banking theory published in 1802, Henry Thornton described the function of bills of exchange as follows:

Bills, though professedly drawn for the purpose of exchanging a debt due to one person for a debt due to another, are, in fact, created rather for the sake of serving as a discountable article, and of forming a provision against contingencies . . . by being at any time convertible into cash (that is, into either money or bank notes) they render that supply of cash which is necessary to be kept in store much less considerable.

But they not only spare the use of ready money; they also occupy its place in many cases. Let us imagine a farmer in the country to discharge a debt of £10 to his neighbouring grocer, by giving him a bill for that sum, drawn on his cornfactor in London for grain sold in the metropolis; and the grocer to transmit the bill, having previously indorsed it, to a neighbouring sugar-baker, in discharge of a like debt; and the sugar-baker to send it, when again indorsed, to a West India merchant in an outport, and the West India merchant to deliver it to his country banker, who also indorses it, and sends it into further circulation. . . . A multitude of bills pass between trader and trader in the country in the manner which has been described; and they evidently form, in the strictest sense, a part of the circulating medium of the kingdom.[2]

One obvious difference between Roberts' description and Thornton's is that Roberts did not mention the transfer of bills while the main point of Thornton's remarks was to show the role transferable bills in the monetary system of his time. The practice of transferring and discounting bills is, to be sure, an important aspect of the transformation that occurred between the times that Roberts and Thornton wrote, but it is by no means the only, or even most important point about the changes in commercial practice that must be considered in understanding the development of the law of bills.

---

[1] Roberts, *Merchants Map of Commerce*, 7.
[2] Thornton, *Paper Credit of Great Britain*, 91–92.

The first point to note about the difference in the treatment of bills of exchange in the periods before and after the mid-seventeenth century is the general tone of the discussion. In the earlier period, exchange was described as an arcane and highly specialized matter. Malynes delighted in pointing to the 'Feats of Bankers performed by Exchanges', and even less polemical writers observed that exchange was an esoteric topic. Roberts noted that exchange is 'the most mysterious part of the Art of Merchandizing and Traffique',[3] and similar comments are found in many of the other works of this era.[4] These comments were not at all inaccurate. The exchange business of the sixteenth and early seventeenth centuries was indeed extremely complex. Success in exchange dealings required an intimate knowledge of the value of the coins of various states, command of rather difficult computational techniques, familiarity with the patterns of fluctuation in exchange rates caused either by regular seasonal variations in trade or by unpredictable circumstances, and access to a network of information on which to base the guesses about future exchange rates that were the key to profitable exchange dealings.[5] One of the main points of the early works on exchange was to provide some of this information. The books commonly included lengthy passages explaining the denomination and fineness of the coin of all nations and the methods for computation of exchange rates and the profits on exchange dealings.

By the eighteenth century this sense of mystery had disappeared. Prefaces to books on the law of bills of exchange commonly noted that all persons dealt with bills in their ordinary financial affairs.[6] Indeed, as early as 1687, Chief Justice Holt had

---

[3] Roberts, *Merchants Map of Commerce*, 39.
[4] 'Exchange is by some held to be the most mysterious part of the Art of Merchandizing and Traffick'. Marius, *Bills of Exchange*, 1. 'To many, if not to most Merchants, [exchange] remains a Mystery, and is indeed the greatest and weightiest Mystery that is to be found in the whole Map of Trade.' Scarlett, *Stile of Exchanges*, preface, p. 1. '''Tis universally own'd that in this vast body of Laws or Customs, there be none more intricate, and involv'd than those concerning Exchange.' Forbes, *Bills of Exchange*, 1–2.
[5] de Roover, *Gresham on Foreign Exchange*, 165–72.
[6] 'At this period few men are exempt from the necessity of passing and receiving *Bills of Exchange*, or Promissory Notes, in the course of their ordinary dealings; and in every place of trading, from the highest branches of import and export, to the smallest concerns of buying and selling, payments are made and settlements effected by means of those highly-regarded instruments. A plain digest, therefore, of the Laws and Usages respecting Bills and Notes, cannot be unacceptable

remarked that 'we all have bills directed to us, or payable to us'.[7]
Many of the eighteenth-century legal treatises on the law of bills
state that they were designed to be usable by lay people and
common traders rather than only by lawyers or sophisticated merchants.[8] By the end of the eighteenth century, there was even a
market for cheap, pocket-sized handbooks on the law of bills and
notes to serve as a ready reference for 'the Merchant and Man of
Business, whether in his compting house or travelling to any
distant part of the country'.[9]

The most fundamental difference, however, is that in the earlier
period the focus of the discussion was the exchange contract, while
in the later period the focus was the bill of exchange itself.
Roberts' description of exchange centred on the transaction in
which the bill was issued, not the bill itself. Roberts did not even
use the term 'bill of exchange' in the passage quoted above. He
spoke only of Lodowick in London writing to his correspondent
Thomas in Venice directing him to repay the money that had been
delivered to Lodowick. For Roberts, the bill of exchange was only
the mechanism by which the contract between the deliverer and
taker was carried out, and therefore it deserved no special emphasis. This focus on exchange transactions, rather than bills of
exchange, is characteristic of the English literature on exchange
and mercantile practice in the seventeenth century. The discussion usually began with an explanation of the nature of exchange
transactions, and then proceeded to a categorization of the different varieties of exchange, such as petty exchange, real exchange,
dry exchange and fictitious exchange.[10] Exchange was character-
istically described as a transaction involving four persons: the
deliverer (or remitter) and the taker in one location, and the
parties who are to make and receive the repayment in the other

---

to the public.' Tisdall, *Laws Respecting Bills of Exchange*, iii–iv. See also Love-
    lass, *Law Concerning Bills of Exchange*, iii; Glen, *Law of Bills of Exchange*,
    preface.
[7] *Sarsfield* v. *Witherly* (1689), 1 Show. 125, 2 Vent. 292, Holt 112, Carth. 82,
    Comb. 45, 152.
[8] E.g., Lovelass, *Law Concerning Bills of Exchange*, iii; Kyd, *Law of Bills of
    Exchange*.
[9] Maxwell, *Pocket Dictionary of the Law of Bills of Exchange*. See also Rolle, *Pocket
    Companion to the Law of Bills of Exchange*.
[10] Malynes, *Lex Mercatoria*, 260–61; Marius, *Bills of Exchange*, 1, 3–5; Molloy, *De
    Jure Maritimo*, 274–75; Scarlett, *Stile of Exchanges*, 1–7; Forbes, *Bills of
    Exchange*, 3–5.

location.[11] Of the four parties, however, two were the focus of the transaction: the deliverer (or remitter) and the taker (or drawer). Indeed, exchange was commonly defined as a contract between the deliverer and the taker. John Scarlett's *The Stile of Exchanges* (1682) defined the subject as follows:

Exchange that is done by Bills of Exchange, consists in a Contract and Agreement betwixt two Parties, whereby the one Party gives his Bill for the Payment of a certain precise Sum of Moneys, at a certain and limited time, in a certain and limited place, for the value of the same Sum already received, or presently to be paid by the other Party.[12]

All of the legal obligations in exchange transactions were described as flowing from the delivery of money. John Marius' *Advice Concerning Bills of Exchange* (1651) stated that a lawsuit against the drawer of a bill must be brought in the name of the deliverer of the money rather than in the name of the payee of the bill.[13] Marius did say that the acceptor of a bill incurs an obligation to the holder, but in his view the acceptor's obligation was of a different nature to the drawer's obligation.[14] So long as one thinks of exchange as fundamentally a contract between the deliverer and the taker, Marius' conceptualization of the obligations of the parties makes sense. The drawer was liable because he had received the money from the deliverer, and so his obligation ran to the deliverer. The acceptor, by contrast, was liable only by virtue of his acceptance of the bill, and thus his obligation ran to the person to whom the bill was payable. Aside from situations where the parties stood in some special agency relationship, these two species of obligation were conceptually and practically distinct.[15]

11 Marius, *Bills of Exchange*, 2; Scarlett, *Stile of Exchanges*, 5; Forbes, *Bills of Exchange*, 27.
12 Scarlett, *Stile of Exchanges*, 3. See also Forbes, *Bills of Exchange*, 27–28.
13 Marius, *Bills of Exchange*, 26–27.
14 Ibid.
15 Marius' analysis was essentially the same as the medieval continental analysis of the legal relationships of the parties to exchange contracts. See Usher, *Early History of Deposit Banking*, 86–89; de Roover, *Medici Bank*, 140. His treatment may well have been outdated even by the time he wrote and certainly was archaic by the time that the later editions of his treatise were published. Despite Marius' contention that 'if . . . there be occasion to commence a Sute in Law against the Drawer, it must be entered in the name of the Deliverer', there is a reported decision in the King's Bench in 1663 of a successful action by the payee against the drawer of a dishonoured bill, with no mention of any deliverer. *Edgar* v. *Chut* (1663), 1 Keb. 592, 636.

By the eighteenth century, the focus of attention had shifted to the bill of exchange itself. Thornton, for example, did not speak of an exchange transaction in which the farmer in the country received money from someone and directed his cornfactor in London to repay the funds to another. Rather, Thornton spoke of the farmer drawing a bill of exchange on his cornfactor, which bill could then be used in a multitude of other transactions. The difference is that in Thornton's example there was no 'delivery' of money; that is, there was no exchange transaction. The farmer did not give the bill to someone who had handed him funds for transmission to London; he drew the bill as a way of using his London funds to pay his debt to the grocer. The original, and only, obligation represented by the bill was the obligation to the holder.

Discussions of bills in this later era are frequently characterized by an explicit emphasis on the idea that pieces of paper had come to have major economic and legal significance. The preface of an 1801 book on the law of bills notes that 'paper is now become the grand currency in commercial dealings, and an ample substitute for cash; insomuch that it has almost superseded the circulation of specie. We are convinced of the propriety of what has been asserted by a certain exalted character, "That we eat and drink paper, and live upon paper".'[16] By the late seventeenth century, judges and lawyers spoke explicitly of actions '*on* bills of exchange', and it was well established that people who drew, accepted, or indorsed bills of exchange incurred enforceable legal obligations independent of obligations that might have arisen in the underlying transaction in which the bills were used. No eighteenth-century English lawyer would have described obligations on bills in the way that Marius did, carefully distinguishing the obligation of the taker to the deliverer from the obligation of the acceptor to the payee. Indeed, no one would have spoken about the rights of 'deliverers' at all. Rather, they would have spoken of the rights and obligations of parties to the bill. As Chitty put it in his 1799 treatise, 'the holder of a bill, check, or note, may in general maintain an action thereon against all the parties to it, who became so previously to himself'.[17]

---

[16] Manning, *Law of Bills of Exchange*, preface.
[17] Chitty, *Law of Bills of Exchange*, 179–80.

THE MIDDLEMAN ECONOMY AND THE DEVELOPMENT OF INLAND BILLS

The striking differences in the treatment of exchange and bills of exchange in the periods before and after the mid-seventeenth century are probably attributable, at least in part, to the passing of the clouds of ethical and economic suspicion that had hung over exchange transactions in the earlier period. By the seventeenth century, the theory that any fixed charge for the use of money was usurious had largely been displaced by the view that there was nothing sinful about charging interest, so long as the rate was moderate. Thus, one of the principal functions of early foreign exchange transactions – providing a means of finance in which the charge for the loan could be concealed, or justified, by reference to exchange rate fluctuations – had become essentially irrelevant. So too, by the mid-seventeenth century, the controversy in England over the role of exchange transactions and exchange rates as a causative factor in the balance of trade had largely died out. Freed from the suspicion that exchange transactions and bills of exchange were either cloaks for usury or a means by which foreign bankers and merchants manipulated exchange rates to the detriment of English trade, bills of exchange could come to be seen as a useful, indeed indispensable, mechanism for the transmission of funds and settlement of foreign obligations.

The seventeenth century also seems to have been the period when a comprehensive international settlement mechanism via bills of exchange developed. Bills had long been used in dealings between the major commercial and financial centres of Europe, but before the mid-seventeenth century there were important areas of English foreign trade, such as the trade to the Baltic regions, where no regular course of bill transactions had developed. By the late seventeenth century, the Baltic regions as well as other areas were linked in a system of international finance and payment so that trade transactions with virtually all areas of Europe could be settled by bills on Amsterdam or London.[18]

---

[18] The development of bills as a means of settlement in the Baltic trade is traced in a series of articles in the *Economic History Review*, beginning with a controversy between Charles Wilson and Eli Heckscher over the extent to which the Baltic trade was settled by bilateral or multilateral mechanisms. Wilson, 'Treasure and Trade Balances'; Heckscher, 'Multilateralism, Baltic Trade, and the Mercanti-

Though the increasing use of bills in international trade certainly accounts for some of the change in the conception of exchange and bills that we see in the seventeenth century, a major factor in the transformation of bills from the exotic to the everyday must have been that bills came to be used in English domestic trade and finance as well as in international commerce. Thus, in seeking an understanding of the changes in economic conditions and institutions that were associated with the transition from the era of exchange transactions to the era of bills of exchange, it is worthwhile to examine the development and use of 'inland bills', that is, bills of exchange drawn and payable entirely within England.

It is difficult to determine precisely when inland bills came into use in England. Lawsuits involving inland bills do not seem to have become common until the mid-seventeenth century,[19] but other evidence suggests that they were used as early as the beginning of the century.[20] Asking when domestic traders began to adopt their international brethren's practice of using bills of exchange is, however, a rather misleading way of considering the phenomenon of the appearance of bills in English domestic trade. As the economic historian M. M. Postan pointed out, explaining the appearance of an economic institution in one setting as the result of a borrowing from another setting only evades the real issue – identifying the changes in economic conditions that presented the need or opportunity for the use of the institution.[21] Thus, dating the appearance of inland bills is of interest only as it may help in identifying the economic changes that made it possible for bills of exchange to develop and flourish in the internal financial structure of seventeenth-century England.

lists'; Wilson, 'Treasure and Trade Balances: Further Evidence'; Price, 'Multilateralism and/or Bilateralism'; Sperling, 'The International Payments Mechanism in the Seventeenth and Eighteenth Centuries'.

[19] In *Buller* v. *Crips* (1703), 6 Mod. 29, Chief Justice Holt remarked that he remembered that actions on inland bills were first heard at the time that Matthew Hale was one of the judges (1654–76).

[20] In the correspondence of a London cloth merchant in the period 1606 to 1618 there are references to bills of exchange that he was sending along to his wife in London for collection while he was travelling about the countryside. Willan, *Inland Trade*, 123–26. Numerous examples of inland bills of exchange from the early seventeenth century are described in Kerridge, *Trade and Banking in Early Modern England*, 45–75.

[21] Postan, 'Private Financial Instruments in Medieval England', 58–59.

In seeking the economic causes of the development of inland bills, it may be worthwhile to reiterate that the need that bills of exchange answered was not, or at least was not initially, merely a desire for written evidences or embodiments of debt obligations. Credit, both for money borrowed and for the price of goods sold, was an essential part of English domestic commerce from earliest times.[22] To a large extent these credit transactions, particularly credit sales of goods, were conducted without any written debt instruments other than the account books of the seller. Yet where some specific written evidence was needed, there was no shortage of suitable forms of legally recognized debt instruments, such as sealed bonds, statutory recognizances, and the like.[23] Such instruments, as well as other less formal writings, had been a common feature of English commercial practice and English law for centuries before the appearance of the inland bill of exchange. The point that must be borne in mind is that the bill of exchange was not, or not merely, a written evidence of the obligation of a debtor to a creditor. Rather, even in the domestic version, it was a bill *of exchange* – not, of course, in the sense of an exchange of currencies, but of an exchange of value in one location for an obligation payable in another location. To understand why bills appeared in English domestic trade in the seventeenth century, one must ask how it came to be that traders in England at that time would find themselves in the position of having funds due to them in the hands of persons in other locations within England, and why instructions for the payment of these funds to others would have been necessary or useful.

Posing the question in this fashion suggests that the economic causes of the appearance of bills in seventeenth-century English domestic trade might well have been analogous to the economic causes of the development of exchange transactions in foreign trade in the thirteenth and fourteenth centuries – the rise of a system of trade in which merchants or other participants in economic affairs traded through permanent representatives in other locations. That change in patterns of distribution was one

---

[22] Postan, 'Credit in Medieval Trade'; Salzman, *English Trade in the Middle Ages*, 25–42.
[23] Simpson, *History of the Common Law of Contract*, 88–135.

aspect of what economic historians have often referred to as the transition from the town economy to the national economy.[24]

As late as the sixteenth century, the domestic trade of England was conducted in such fashion that there would rarely be either need or opportunity for the use of bills, for the great bulk of economic activity was purely local. The largest portion of any household's economic needs was met by its own production. Those items that were purchased were also produced locally and distributed in a system characterized by direct contact between producer and consumer. Most of the relatively limited stock of manufactured goods that were used were produced by craftsmen in the towns who sold their wares directly from their shops. The most significant items of domestic commerce, foodstuffs, were sold at local markets and the larger periodic fairs, where farmers brought their surplus production and offered it for sale directly to consumers.

Bills of exchange presuppose an economy in which it is common for producers or merchants to have shipped their goods to representatives in other locations and thereby acquired credits in distant hands on which they can draw bills of exchange. In the medieval town economy, such transactions were not only uncommon, they were positively discouraged. In most settings in the medieval economy, those who engaged in the activities that are now the life-blood of domestic commerce – wholesale trade in which merchants buy goods for resale – would have been guilty of the penal offences known as 'forestalling', 'engrossing', or 'regrating'.[25] The ideal of medieval market regulation was that goods should be sold directly from producer to consumer, in openly conducted sales at well-regulated public markets or in the shops of the craftsmen who produced them. Any other form of distribution was regarded with hostility. The laws against forestalling, engrossing, or regrating were of particular significance in connection with food distribution, but the hostility they represented toward the activities of middlemen was quite general.

In time, the town economy gave way to the national economy. No longer was each town or local community a self-sufficient

[24] See generally Ashley, *English Economic History*, 2: 42–54; Unwin, *Industrial Organization in the Sixteenth and Seventeenth Centuries*, 70–102.
[25] Blackstone, *Commentaries*, 4: 158–59; Illingworth, *Laws respecting Forestalling, Regrating, and Ingrossing*.

whole, in fact or aspiration. Various regions began to specialize in the production of particular types of goods, which were distributed for sale throughout the country. Needless to say, this was a gradual development, extending over a long and not easily specified period of time. For purposes of the present inquiry, it suffices to note that the development of the national economy is usually regarded as a phenomenon of the sixteenth and seventeenth centuries. One aspect of the development of a national economy was an increase in the complexity of the channels of production, distribution, and sale, and that inevitably brought with it the development of economic actors who neither produced, improved, nor transported the goods in which they dealt, but simply passed goods from one stage to the next; in short, the rise of the middleman.[26] A particularly well-known and well-documented instance of such a development was the rise of the so-called 'Blackwell Hall factors' in the cloth trade in the seventeenth century.

As early as the late fourteenth century, a market for woollen cloths was established at Blackwell Hall in London, and in time it became the principal market for the sale of woollen cloth in England.[27] In the usual pattern of early trade regulation, municipal ordinances established detailed regulations governing the time and manner of sale at the regular weekly market and prohibited the sale of cloth out of the market. The cloth manufacturers, or 'clothiers' as they were called, brought their cloths to the market from areas around London and throughout the country and offered it for sale to the cloth merchants, or 'drapers'. During the seventeenth century, however, the pattern of direct sales from clothiers to drapers changed. Rather than themselves travelling to London, clothiers began to ship their product to factors at Blackwell Hall who sold it for them on a commission basis. As the practice became more and more common, the factors achieved an important, if not dominant, position in the cloth market. During the latter part of the seventeenth century, the clothiers waged a vitriolic campaign against the factors, which at times resulted in ordinances, largely ineffectual, designed to regulate or limit their activities. In large measure, the clothiers' protests grew out of the credit practices that developed with the factor system. The factors allowed drapers

---

[26] Westerfield, *Middlemen in English Business.*
[27] Lipson, *Economic History of England*, 1: 464–65; Ashley, *English Economic History*, 2:19–20, 214–15.

to purchase on very long credit terms, ranging from six months to more than a year. Since the clothiers did not receive the money from the sale of their cloth for a long period, they in turn had need of credit for the purchase of wool, and the factors came to provide that service as well. By providing the clothiers with their raw materials on credit and acting as the distributor of their output, the factors achieved a position of economic dominance over their principals.[28]

The development of the Blackwell Hall factors, and similar changes in trade organization in other branches of commerce, created the conditions essential to the use of bills of exchange in domestic trade. A clothier in the countryside who sold his goods through a London factor would build up balances in the factor's hands in London. He could make return of those funds to the country by engaging in exchange transactions. For example, in the 1640s the Lancashire clothiers Abraham and John Rodes regularly received money from Samuel Wyld, a local mercer, giving him bills of exchange drawn on their Blackwell Hall factor William Ryder, which Wyld used to make payments to his suppliers in London.[29] During a three-year period in the 1680s Jonas Buckley, the London factor of another Lancashire cloth dealer, Thomas Marsden, paid out more than £50,000 on bills drawn by Marsden.[30] The importance of such transactions in the English economy is illustrated by the role of domestic exchange in the tax collection system. Tax collectors in the country received collections in specie and needed to transmit the funds to the central government in London. The remittance needs of the tax collectors could easily be met by cloth dealers and other merchants and manufacturers in the countryside who had funds in the hands of their London representatives. For example, in 1657 Thomas Salmon, a tax collector in

[28] Lipson, *Economic History of England*, 2: 27–29. This was a rather common pattern of development; indeed, the clothiers of the sixteenth and seventeenth centuries owed their own position of economic power to a similar phenomenon. As exemplars of the pattern of industrial organization commonly known as the 'domestic system' the clothiers were not artisans-producers but capitalist organizers of production. The weavers and other craftsmen who produced and finished the cloth got their raw materials from the clothiers and turned over the finished product to them for distribution. Ibid., 2: 2–18; Ashley, *English Economic History*, 2: 218–37; Westerfield, *Middlemen in English Business*, 273–95.

[29] Willan, *Inland Trade*, 113.

[30] Wadsworth and Mann, *Cotton Trade and Industrial Lancashire*, 94–95.

Somerset, transmitted thousands of pounds to London via Richard Burt, the London factor of various local clothiers.[31] In the early eighteenth century, Daniel Defoe observed that 'a very great part of the bills drawn out of the several counties in England upon the tradesmen in London, such as factors and ware-housekeepers, are made payable to the General Receivers of the several taxes and duties, Customs and excises which are levied in the country in specie, and the money is remitted by those collectors and receivers on account of those duties'.[32]

Domestic exchange transactions of the sort considered thus far were still a means by which a merchant or manufacturer could make return of the proceeds of the sale of his goods in a distant location, and they still followed essentially the same pattern as the four-party exchange transactions of earlier times. In seventeenth-century domestic trade, however, one also finds evidence of forms of bill dealings that differ somewhat from the old model of exchange. To begin with, there are many instances of country merchants and manufacturers paying out money in the country and taking in return bills drawn on London payable to their factors or other representatives. In a typical example of such remittance transactions, the Lancashire cloth dealer John Rodes paid £200 to a Mr Wrigley in Lancashire, receiving in exchange a bill for that amount drawn on one Joseph Hunton in London, payable to William Ryder, the Rodes' factor in London.[33] If exchange transactions are thought of as a means of making returns, this transaction seems peculiar. One would expect that a merchant or manufacturer who sent goods to a distant location for sale would be seeking ways of returning funds from the distant location, rather than sending additional amounts there. Yet it is clear that remittances to London were an important part of the financial dealings of the country merchants and manufacturers. In the late 1640s the Rodes brothers were sending from £500 to £1,000 a year to London, both in bills and in cash. That was a rather large sum for them, considering that their annual volume of cloth sales in the same period was in the range of £3,000 to £5,000.[34] The same pattern of transactions is found in accounts of the business of other

---

[31] Mann, *Cloth Industry in the West of England*, 66. See also Wadsworth and Mann, *Cotton Trade and Industrial Lancashire*, 93.
[32] Defoe, *Complete English Tradesman*, 1: 362.   [33] Willan, *Inland Trade*, 112.
[34] Ibid., 110–14.

seventeenth-century country merchants and manufacturers.[35] Evidently, then, making return of funds held in one's representative's hands in a different location was no longer the sole or even principal reason for exchange dealings. To understand this aspect of seventeenth-century exchange dealings, one must consider why manufacturers and merchants in the country would have found it desirable to build up balances in the hands of their London agents beyond the extent of the proceeds of their mercantile activities.

The answer may well lie in the enormous growth of London and the dominant position in the commercial and financial life of England that it had attained by the end of the seventeenth century. At the beginning of the sixteenth century, the population of London was only about 30,000. By the late seventeenth century, London was the largest city in western Europe with a population of half a million or more.[36] By the end of the seventeenth century, perhaps one-tenth of the population of England lived in London,[37] and that figure probably understates the role of the city in the economic life of the country. Most of the external trade of England passed through London, and the enormous demand of the London population provided a market for a large part of the internal production of the country.[38] Moreover, London was the hub of all domestic trade. Manufactured goods and surplus production of the various regions of the nation generally passed through the hands of factors, warehousemen, and merchants in London on their way toward the ultimate consumers elsewhere in England.[39] Indeed, London's position in the national economy was so dominant as to provoke concern, or more likely jealousy, from those outside the capital. 'Some landed men say, that the immoderate growth of London undoes and ruins all the country ... that the Kingdom is like a rickety body, with a head too big for the other members'.[40]

With so much commercial and financial activity centred in London, it is easy to see why merchants and manufacturers in the country would often have been content to leave the funds generated from the proceeds of their sales in London rather than

---

[35] Wadsworth and Mann, *Cotton Trade and Industrial Lancashire*, 94–95.
[36] Coleman, *Economy of England*, 20.
[37] Wilson, *England's Apprenticeship*, 47.   [38] Hill, *Century of Revolution*, 22.
[39] Braudel, *Civilization and Capitalism*, 3: 365–68.
[40] Rolt, *New Dictionary of Trade and Commerce*, s.v. 'London'.

returning them to the country. If the merchant or manufacturer bought his raw materials or inventory in London, he could himself use his London funds to make payment to his suppliers. Even if he purchased his supplies in the country, his suppliers might prefer to receive payment in London funds. For example, in the 1640s the Rodes brothers regularly paid their local suppliers of cloth in Lancashire by means of bills of exchange drawn on their London factor, William Ryder.[41] Moreover, if virtually everyone in the country had use for bills drawn on London as a means of making payment for their transactions, the demand for London funds could well present such a profitable opportunity for those who could supply bills on London that country traders might find that they could sell far more bills on London than they could supply from the proceeds of their own sales.

Although the concentration of trade and financial activity in London may well have been an important factor in the development of inland bills and the transformation of the focus of bill dealings from the exchange contract to the bill of exchange, that is not to say that these changes were limited to inland bills or to bills drawn on London. The general point about the seventeenth-century development is that as the economy moved from the stage of independent local activity to a national or international economy, the manufacturers and merchants of any one area had continuing relationships with factors, merchants, and other middlemen in other parts of the country or the globe, and the balances that they held in the hands of their correspondents came to play an important role in the payment system.

THE ECONOMIC FUNCTIONS OF BILLS IN THE SEVENTEENTH AND EIGHTEENTH CENTURIES

Having examined some of the changes in commercial and financial practice associated with the shift in the conception of exchange and bills of exchange that occurred during the seventeenth century, it may be worthwhile to survey the various roles that bills came to play in English trade and finance by the end of the seventeenth and eighteenth centuries.

---

[41] Willan, *Inland Trade*, 113–14.

Bills as payment media

In the seventeenth and eighteenth centuries, bills played an important role in the payment system. One must, however, be careful to avoid anachronistic assumptions in considering the role of bills as payment media. Modern books on negotiable instruments law often begin with a brief outline of the stages of development of media of exchange. In the beginning people exchanged by barter and the only tokens of value were commodities such as cattle, animal skins, or salt. Next came the stage where people realized the convenience of using precious metals as tokens of value, and made payments in coin. Finally, came 'the commercial paper or negotiable instruments stage . . . when credit as evidenced by negotiable instruments is able to pass from hand to hand as the representative of value or money'.[42] The anachronism of such accounts is that they take as universal the modern phenomenon of a payment system that is so pervasive and sophisticated that each commercial transaction can easily be settled by a corresponding payment transaction. In examining the mechanisms of payment used before the development of modern payment media, it is misleading to frame the question as 'What did they use in making payments instead of paper currency or bank credit?' Rather one must ask how people engaged in economic exchange even though they frequently did not have anything to pass around as a payment medium.

Consider, for example, a frontier community which has not yet developed any sophisticated commercial or financial institutions. The community would be dependent upon more developed economic centres both for the materials and supplies needed for its agricultural or other production and for marketing its produce. Yet such a community is unlikely to have a sufficient volume of specie or specie substitutes to settle all of its transactions, both within the community and with the outside world. The general storekeepers would need money to pay for the ploughs, cloth, sugar, and coffee they buy from merchants in commercial centres; the local farmers would need money to pay for their purchases from the storekeepers; and the merchants who buy the produce

---

[42] Ogden, *Law of Negotiable Instruments*, 14–15.

from the farmers for shipment to markets elsewhere would need money to pay the farmers.

There is, however, a very simple solution to the payment problems of such a community. The general storekeeper and the exporting merchant are the same person. The storekeeper buys his supplies, usually on very long credit terms, from suppliers in the commercial centres and sells them in his community on open account credit. At the end of the growing season, the farmers, who are heavily in debt to the storekeeper, sell him their produce, receiving payment in the form of cancellation of the debts. The storekeeper then sells the produce to merchants in the commercial centres, perhaps the same ones from whom he purchased his inventory, thereby settling, or acquiring the funds to settle, the debts he incurred to lay in his supplies. The vast bulk of the payments of the internal economy of the frontier town could consist of nothing more than entries on the account books of the frontier merchant, without the circulation of either specie or any form of specie substitute.

This model of local exchange without payment media seems to have been quite common. Lewis Atherton has described in detail the operations of such storekeeper-merchants in early-nineteenth-century America, both in the cotton economy of the South and in the foodstuffs economy of the Midwest.[43] Thomas Jefferson remarked in 1813 that 'a farmer with a revenue of ten thousand dollars a year may obtain all his supplies from his merchant and liquidate them at the end of the year by the sale of his produce to him without the intervention of a single dollar of cash'.[44] The same pattern can even be found in medieval trade. The ledgers of a fourteenth-century merchant in a small town in southern France show that a typical customer's account consisted of a long series of debits throughout the year in varying small amounts for cloth and other items, followed by one credit entry in a large sum for barley sold to the merchant by the customer.[45] The use of running counter accounts was by no means limited to frontier storekeepers. In the modern world in which businesses commonly specialize in a limited range of goods, it is hard to imagine that opportunities for

[43] Atherton, *Southern Country Store*, 14; Atherton, *Frontier Merchant in Mid-America*, 18–19, 125.
[44] Quoted in Hammond, *Banks and Politics in America*, 71.
[45] Lopez and Raymond, *Medieval Trade in the Mediterranean World*, 98–100.

settlement by netting out counter accounts would often arise. In the past, however, merchants were far less specialized than they are today. In transactions among general merchants, each of whom dealt in a wide variety of goods, opportunities for barter would be far more common.[46]

The evolution of the system of trade through factors and other middlemen greatly increased the opportunities for making settlements through running counter accounts. As has been noted, the clothiers who sold their cloth through the Blackwell Hall factors often purchased the wool that they used as raw material through the same factors. Thus, clothiers' debts for wool purchases could be settled by netting them against the amounts that the factors collected from the sale of the finished cloth. In many lines of trade, factors came to serve as the conduit for a large portion of the financial dealings of their customers. For example, in the early nineteenth century, American plantation owners commonly sold all of their cotton through factors in the principal cities of the southern states. The cotton factors also acted as agents for the plantation owners in the purchase of supplies and in virtually all other financial dealings, so that little or no currency or other media of exchange were needed to settle all of the transactions between the plantation owners and the rest of the world.[47]

In the simplest form, settlement by counter accounts is feasible only to the extent that the two parties regularly conduct transactions running in opposite directions. Once the bill of exchange had developed into a payment device independent of exchange contracts, a multilateral version of the system of settlement via counter accounts became possible. If a Lancashire clothier purchased his wool from someone other than the factor through whom he sold his cloth, the clothier could not pay for his supplies by a direct entry on the books of the factor. He could, however, indirectly use the proceeds of the sale of his cloth to pay for his wool by drawing a bill on his factor payable to his wool supplier. Once bills became generally acceptable as media of payment,

[46] An example cited in a history of mid-eighteenth-century New York merchants illustrates the point. 'A shipment of sugar to Virginia was paid for by a cargo of wheat or corn, the cargo being sold by the original shipper on commission; the cost of shipment, together with the commissions was deducted from the proceeds, and the remainder, if any, placed to the credit of the payee.' Harrington, *New York Merchant on the Eve of the Revolution*, 88.
[47] Woodman, *King Cotton and his Retainers*.

balances that one trader held in the hands of any factor or middle-man became usable to settle transactions with any other trader.

Although bills could serve as a medium of payment even when they were paid directly to the original payee, the fact that bills were transferable significantly facilitated their use as payment media. A country merchant or manufacturer would probably find that his local suppliers or creditors were willing to take bills on London in payment whether or not they themselves had any immediate need for London funds, since they could indorse the bill to someone else who might have need of London funds. At each stage on its path toward London, it could be used to settle a local transaction. Circulation of bills in this fashion played a key role in the English payment system. All through the eighteenth century, including the period of enormous economic expansion in the Industrial Revolution of the later part of the century, private bills of exchange were the principal circulating medium of exchange in Lanca-shire.[48] In 1826 a Manchester banker gave evidence to a Parlia-mentary Committee that he had seen bills that had been indorsed by fifty or more people as they circulated, 'I have seen slips of paper attached to a bill as long as a sheet of paper could go, and when that was filled another attached to that.'[49]

Bills as credit media

In the era of the exchange contract, delivering money by way of exchange was a way of providing credit as well as a way of trans-mitting funds. So too, credit was an important aspect of bill dealings in the era of bills of exchange. Just as in the earlier era, whether a particular bill transaction of the seventeenth or eighteenth century is described as a payment or credit transaction is often only a matter of perspective.

Earlier in this chapter it was noted that a country manufacturer or trader could make use of the funds that his London factor received on sale of his goods by drawing a bill on his factor and

---

[48] Ashton, 'Bill of Exchange and Private Banks in Lancashire'; Pressnell, *Country Banking in the Industrial Revolution*, 170–80; Edwards, *British Cotton Trade*, 218–19.

[49] Report of Sel. Comm. of the House of Lords ... into the Circulation of Promissory Notes, 1826–27, quoted in Pressnell, *Country Banking in the Indus-trial Revolution*, 173.

either selling the bill to someone in the country who wished to transmit funds to London or using the bill to pay his own suppliers or creditors. If the bill was drawn, accepted, and paid after the factor had sold the goods and collected the proceeds of the sale, the transaction could be described purely as funds transfer or payment. If, however, the factor permitted the country trader or manufacturer to draw bills in advance of the sale of the goods, the transaction takes on a different appearance. If the factor paid the bill in advance of the sale, the credit aspect is clear. The factor would effectively be lending money to the country trader, and the loan would be repaid from the sale of the goods. Even if the factor did not actually pay the bill until he had received the proceeds of the sale, he might be providing a form of credit. Suppose for example, that the country trader drew a bill on his London factor payable sixty days after sight, and the London factor accepted it. The holder of the accepted bill might then have used it to make payments in London or discounted it for cash. Even if the factor was able to sell goods to the extent of the bill by the time it came due, he would have provided a financial accommodation to the country trader by lending his credit to the bill and thereby enhancing its value. He would, of course, also have run the risk that the transaction would become an outright loan if he could not sell the goods before he had to pay the bill.

Instances of this form of finance can be found in accounts of domestic trade in the later part of the seventeenth century,[50] and by the eighteenth century acceptance finance was one of the most important functions of bills in domestic and foreign trade. In the early eighteenth century, Daniel Defoe noted the practice with concern. 'It is the great error of our country manufacturers, in many, if not most parts of England at this time; that as soon as they can finish their goods they hurry them up to London to their Factor, and as soon as the goods are gone, immediately follow them with their bills for the money.'[51] Acceptance finance was one of the mainstays of the international trade centred in Amsterdam in the eighteenth century.[52] The merchants of Amsterdam rose to dominance in European trade in the seventeenth century on the basis of their role as commission sales agents. Goods from all over

50 Mann, *Cloth Industry in the West of England*, 80.
51 Defoe, *Complete English Tradesman*, 1: 353.
52 Wilson, *Anglo-Dutch Commerce and Finance*, 24–27.

Europe, and indeed, the world, were shipped to Amsterdam and resold there. Gradually, however, the role of the Amsterdam merchants shifted to pure finance.[53] The merchants of Amsterdam who acted as commission agents for other merchants throughout the world were often far wealthier, more creditworthy, and more powerful than their principals. Accordingly, a merchant whose own credit would have counted for little might well have found a ready market for his bills of exchange if he drew on an Amsterdam house that regularly accepted his bills. As London came to rival Amsterdam as a centre of world trade and finance in the eighteenth century, the acceptance business became a major part of the business of the great merchant banking houses of London that financed Anglo-American and world trade in the eighteenth and nineteenth centuries.[54]

Acceptance finance, though extremely important, was but one aspect of the credit operations carried out through bills of exchange. Just as factors and commission merchants evolved into finance houses, the same development occurred in the business of the country manufacturers and merchants. Wadsworth and Mann's account of the financial activities of Thomas Marsden, a Lancashire cloth manufacturer and merchant in the 1680s and 1690s, is illustrative.[55] The simplest form of financial business for a country manufacturer or merchant such as Marsden would have been to make use of his London balances by selling bills to tax collectors and others who needed to transfer funds to London or make payments in London. This form of remittance business could easily develop into finance. Marsden did not always demand cash for the bills; he regularly sold bills on credit to persons in the country, charging interest on the amount of the bill until the

---

[53] Conservative merchants and public officials in Amsterdam generally frowned on the transformation of the Amsterdam merchants from goods merchants into pure finance houses, believing it important to the prosperity of Amsterdam that the goods actually pass through the Amsterdam warehouses. Ibid., 10–11. Even aside from concerns of public economic policy, a merchant banking house might well want to ensure that it received the commission sales business as well as the acceptance business, for the commission earned on the sale of the goods generally exceeded the commission earned for accepting bills. Hidy, *House of Baring*, 105.

[54] Buck, *Organization of Anglo-American Trade*, 12–14; Hidy, *House of Baring*, 134.

[55] Wadsworth and Mann, *Cotton Trade and Industrial Lancashire*, 91–96.

purchaser was able to pay for the bill.[56] Inasmuch as a bill on London was as good or better than cash as a medium of exchange in Lancashire, such transactions are all but indistinguishable from simple loans of money from Marsden to the borrowers.

Marsden also provided credit to borrowers in the country by advancing cash to them in return for bills that the borrowers drew on their London correspondents.[57] Transactions of this form show how elusive the characterization of bill dealings might be. One might describe such a transaction as a way for Marsden to send money to his London correspondent, perhaps because the business of selling bills on London was so profitable that Marsden wanted to build up balances in London beyond the extent generated from his cloth trade. Undoubtedly that was one motive for the transactions, for Marsden and other Lancashire traders regularly sent cash to London hidden in packets along with their cloth.[58] The same form of transaction, however, might as aptly be described as one in which Marsden was lending money to people in the country, with the advances repaid by the borrowers' correspondents in London. Or, to say the same thing in slightly different language, one could describe this form of Marsden's business as discounting the bills of other local traders.

It is not difficult to see how the financial activities of someone in Marsden's position could grow to overshadow his mercantile business. A country merchant or manufacturer might start by selling bills to tax collectors or others as a means of making return of the balances in the hands of his cloth factor and then realize that the demand for such bills exceeded the amount that he could provide for from the sale of his cloth. He might send cash down to London to permit the expansion of his remittance business, but that must have been somewhat risky and also had the disadvantage that it generated no return on the Lancashire to London side of the circuit. A far more profitable way of building up London balances would be to make loans in the country, taking in return bills drawn by the borrowers on their London correspondents. Surely it would not take long for the trader to realize that these two lines of business were perfectly complementary. He could take money from tax collectors or others who needed to remit to London, giving them bills that he drew on his London correspondent.

[56] Ibid., 93.   [57] Ibid.   [58] Ibid., 94; Willan, *Inland Trade*, 112–13.

Then, he could take the money that he received from the tax collectors and lend it to others in the country, to be repaid in London. For example, he might discount bills that other local manufacturers had drawn on their London factors. The money that his London correspondent received in repayment of the discounts could provide the balances that he needed to pay the bills that he had sold to the tax collectors.[59]

Bills and banking

A final aspect of the transformation in the conception of bills that warrants some consideration is the relationship between the development of banking institutions in England and the development of the law of bills. The early history of banking in England is a complex matter.[60] What is important to realize for present purposes is that there was no single source of the development of banking institutions. Although it is commonly said that banking in England began with the goldsmiths in the mid-seventeenth century, Tawney pointed out that the goldsmiths 'merely supplied one tributary to a stream which was fed from a multitude of sources'.[61] Moreover, not only were there a multitude of antecedents, but the appearance of banks was less a matter of creation of new financial techniques than an institutional rearrangement in which certain firms came to specialize in financial dealings which had long been performed as adjuncts to mercantile or other activities.[62]

To some extent, the difficulty in identifying the beginnings of banking institutions is a matter of definition. If money lending is

---

[59] Marsden in fact engaged in all of these activities in the 1680s and 1690s. Wadsworth and Mann, *Cotton Trade and Industrial Lancashire*, 92–95. See also Pressnell, *Country Banking in the Industrial Revolution*, 77–78; Feavearyear, *Pound Sterling*, 161–62.

[60] Ashton, 'Bill of Exchange and Private Banks in Lancashire', 167–200; Clapham, *Bank of England*; Clark, 'Restoration Goldsmith-Banking House: The Vine on Lombard Street'; Feavearyear, *Pound Sterling*, 99–118; Joslin, 'London Private Bankers'; Lipson, *Economic History of England*, 2: 227–46; Pressnell, *Country Banking in the Industrial Revolution*; Richards, *Early History of Banking in England*; Tawney, Historical Introduction to Wilson's *Discourse upon Usury*.

[61] Tawney, Historical Introduction to Wilson's *Discourse upon Usury*, 101.

[62] Ashton, *Economic History of England: the Eighteenth Century*, 179–80; Joslin, 'London Private Bankers', 183; Pressnell, *Country Banking in the Industrial Revolution*, 12; Tawney, Historical Introduction to Wilson's *Discourse upon Usury*, 86–87.

regarded as the principal banking function, one can find banking institutions, or at least banking functions, as far back as one likes. Credit, both in the form of giving time for payment for goods and actual advances of money, was an important aspect of English trade, agriculture, industry, and financial life even in the Middle Ages.[63] Even if one defines a bank or banker in a more limited sense, as one who specializes in money lending, or specializes in lending not only his own capital but also funds that he has taken up from others, one can find firms meeting that description well before the seventeenth century. By the sixteenth century if not before, foreign as well as English merchants were actively engaged in the business of delivering money in exchange transactions as a form of finance. To the extent that exchange lenders financed their operations by themselves taking up money by exchange, the exchange finance business could fit a fairly narrow definition of banking. So too, even in the less exotic field of domestic lending, one can find classes of people whose business was to receive money from some and lend it to others. A prominent example were the 'money scriveners', who originated as the English equivalent of notaries, preparing legal documents such as bonds and mortgages, but often developed into financial intermediaries soliciting surplus funds from investors and lending it to others on mortgages.[64]

The common notion that the goldsmiths began the business of banking is probably attributable to the fact that the particular path of development that their financial activities took happened to have involved the issuance of notes – the attribute that was regarded in the nineteenth century as the pre-eminent characteristic of banking. During the course of the seventeenth century, many of the goldsmiths of London evolved from artisans whose medium was precious metal into finance houses that accepted deposits, used the funds in making loans, and provided transfer banking services by means of circulating notes and written transfer orders.

Exactly why, how, or when the goldsmiths developed into

---

[63] Postan, 'Credit in Medieval Trade'; Salzman, *English Trade in the Middle Ages*, 25–42.

[64] Tawney, Historical Introduction to Wilson's *Discourse upon Usury*, 96–101; Richards, *Early History of Banking in England*, 14–22; Pressnell, *Country Banking in the Industrial Revolution*, 36–44; Melton, *Sir Robert Clayton and the Origins of English Deposit Banking*.

bankers is not clear. There is a persistent myth that the precipitat-
ing cause of the evolution was that in 1640 Charles I forcibly
'borrowed' some £200,000 from the vaults in the Tower of London,
where merchants had been accustomed to keeping their money,
prompting them to look elsewhere for safe deposit services.[65] This
story is largely the result of a misunderstanding of early monetary
systems. The Tower was not a place of safekeeping for cash; it was
the location of the mint. Anyone having bullion could, if they
wished, have it minted into coin at the Tower, at the cost of the
customary seignorage. Given the primitive technology of coin-
making, the process took some time. One delivered the bullion to
the mint, but received the coins some days or weeks later. When
the crown's finances were tight, the mintmasters sometimes happened to become even slower than usual, for the crown could make
temporary use of the bullion left for minting. That was essentially
what happened in 1640. Being short of money, Charles I
announced that the coins that were to have been minted from a
shipment of silver from the mines of the New World would not be
released to the London agents of the Spanish merchants and their
Italian bankers; instead, they would receive interest bearing
exchequer receipts. When the merchants protested, the king
quickly relented, releasing two-thirds of the coin at once and the
balance, with interest, in six months. To be sure, the event made
London merchants wary of financial dealings with the crown, but it
had nothing to do with money supposedly deposited at the Tower
for safekeeping or with the development of the goldsmiths'
business.[66]

A more likely explanation of the goldsmiths' interest in becom-

---

[65] The legend may have originated with Anderson's *Historical and Chronological
Deduction of the Origin of Commerce* (1762), 2: 512. It has been repeated in many
sources, including the standard works on the history of the law of bills. Cranch,
'Promissory Notes', 384–85; Holden, *History of Negotiable Instruments*, 70–71;
Street, *Foundations of Legal Liability*, 2: 367. Anderson's account of the goldsmiths was largely based on the anonymous pamphlet *The Mystery of the New
Fashioned Goldsmiths or Bankers* (1676), an unremarkable tract of the sort that
seems to have been common in every age of financial history, the basic thesis of
which was that a group of evil men were making personal fortunes at the expense
of the commonweal from some new form of financial dealing which violated basic
principles of law and morality. The story of Charles I's seizure of the merchants'
money from the Tower, however, seems to have been Anderson's embellishment, for it is not found in the *Mystery*.

[66] Feaveryear, *Pound Sterling*, 92–93; Supple, *Commercial Crisis and Change in
England*, 125–26.

ing cash keepers was that they were accustomed to dealing in precious metal, and given the bad state of the coinage in the seventeenth century there was a profit to be made by culling out the heavier weighted coins from the circulation and melting them down into bullion. The more coins passed through one's hands, the more opportunity one had to cull.[67] On the side of the depositors, the incentive was probably convenience and interest. Moreover, the practice of leaving cash and plate for safekeeping in London may have seemed particularly attractive in the turbulent era of the Civil War, particularly for people in the country whose sympathies lay with Parliament.[68] As to the chronology of the development of goldsmith bankers, there is evidence that goldsmiths may have been accepting deposits even in the early seventeenth century. The records of Hoare's Bank include a receipt for a deposit of £3 5s of current coin dated 1 December 1633. By the 1670s and 1680s, the practice of leaving one's cash with goldsmiths seems to have become quite general. Macaulay noted that Sir Dudley North reacted with surprise to the changed financial arrangements of London when he returned to England in 1680 after an absence of some two decades. 'He found that he could not go on Change without being followed around the piazza by goldsmiths, who, with low bows, begged to have the honour of serving him. He lost his temper when his friends asked where he kept his cash. "Where should I keep it," he asked, "but in my own house?"'[69]

Funds on deposit with the goldsmiths could be transferred in two ways. Those who maintained 'running cash' accounts would simply write a brief letter to the goldsmith, directing him to pay money to another, just as in an earlier era one might have written such a letter to one's steward directing him to pay money out of one's strongbox. By the end of the seventeenth century, these 'drawn notes', though still handwritten, developed into a fairly standardized form, akin to modern cheques, directing the banker to pay a given sum to the designated person or his order or bearer.[70] In the other form of account, the depositor received one or more receipts totalling the amount of the deposit. One made

---

[67] Feavearyear, *Pound Sterling*, 102–04.   [68] Ibid., 105.
[69] Macaulay, *History of England*, 4: 541–42.
[70] Feavearyear, *Pound Sterling*, 109–10; Richards, *Early History of Banking in England*, 50–52; Holden, *History of Negotiable Instruments*, 209–10.

withdrawals by returning the receipt, and the amount of the withdrawal, if less than the account balance, would be noted on the receipt. The practice of giving such receipts seems to have evolved into the issuance of transferable notes representing deposits. There are examples of handwritten notes of this sort, in which the banker promises to pay a specific sum to the named payee or bearer, as early as the 1680s, and engraved forms were in use by the early eighteenth century.[71]

The advantages to trade and finance of the development of banking institutions must have been apparent, for during the mid- and late seventeenth century there was a veritable explosion of publication of schemes and proposals for the establishment of various forms of banks.[72] Some of these were little more than the latter day equivalent of the dreams of alchemists – banks create money, people with lots of money are rich, we would like to be rich, therefore let us have lots of banks![73] Many, though, were serious efforts to devise ways of improving the credit, payment, and remittance system, so that the benefits of the kind of banking facilities that the goldsmith had provided in London could be enjoyed throughout the country. Oddly enough, the proposal that bore fruit in the creation of the Bank of England in 1694 must at its inception have seemed among the most inauspicious, if not out-right suspicious. As Bagehot put it, the proposal was little more than a 'Whig finance company ... founded by a Whig Government because it was in desperate want of money, and supported by the "City" because the "City" was Whig'.[74] For the government, the point of the scheme was a loan of £1,200,000. The 8 per cent annual interest expense was to be paid from a new customs duty, and as an added incentive the subscribers to the loan were to be granted a charter of incorporation, under the style of 'The Governors and Company of the Bank of England'. 'It was', notes Macaulay 'not

<hr/>

[71] Feavearyear, *Pound Sterling*, 107–8; Richards, *Early History of Banking in England*, 40–41; Holden, *History of Negotiable Instruments*, 72–73.
[72] Richards, *Early History of Banking in England*, 92–131; Horsefield, *British Monetary Experiments*, 93–217.
[73] John Driscoe, a proponent of a land bank scheme in the late seventeenth century, rejected out of hand the objection that the bank might issue too many notes. 'These bills being a new species of money, and to all intents and purposes answering the end of money; we may as well fear that we shall have too much money in the nation, which no wise man will complain of.' Driscoe, *A Discourse on the Late Funds*, 63–64, quoted in Mints, *History of Banking Theory*, 15.
[74] Bagehot, *Lombard Street*, 92.

easy to guess that a bill, which purported only to impose a new duty on tonnage for the benefit of such persons as should advance money towards carrying on the war, was really a bill creating the greatest commercial institution that the world had ever seen.'[75] Once the Bank was established, the private side of its business was conducted in the same fashion that the goldsmiths had earlier developed. The Bank issued circulating notes as well as accepting deposits which could be transferred by cheque, and it made loans on various forms of security.[76]

The development of the goldsmith bankers and the Bank of England must have greatly eased the process of making payments in London. That in turn would have facilitated financial dealings throughout the country, since London was the centre of the web of the English domestic financial system. We have seen the various ways in which country manufacturers and merchants could make use of balances in the hands of their London factors by drawing bills of exchange on them. With the development of deposit and transfer banking in London, the factors would no longer need to keep cash on hand to pay such bills. Marius, writing in 1651, observed that when the person to whom a bill of exchange is payable presents it for payment, the acceptor will commonly 'write him a Note to go to a Gold-smith, or to such a place to such a man, and there orders the Money to be paid'.[77] The economic historian James E. Thorold Rogers noted that by the late seventeenth century 'all foreign and inland bills of exchange and all great payments were made in [bank] notes and very seldom any considerable sum was paid or received in money'.[78]

The London banking facilities of the late seventeenth and early eighteenth centuries must also have provided much needed credit facilities for the expanding domestic trade and manufacture. One of the principal means by which the goldsmiths and the Bank of England made loans was by discounting bills of exchange. The system of domestic payment and credit based on bills that was described earlier in this chapter must have benefited greatly from

---

[75] Macaulay, *History of England*, 4: 547.
[76] On the formation and early operations of the Bank of England, see Clapham, *Bank of England*; Rogers, *First Nine Years of the Bank of England*; Horsefield, *British Monetary Experiments*, 125–43; Lipson, *Economic History of England*, 2: 240–43; Richards, *Early History of Banking in England*, 132–88.
[77] Marius, *Bills of Exchange*, 6.
[78] Rogers, *First Nine Years of the Bank of England*, 75.

this development. Bills on London would have seemed even more attractive once the discounting facilities of the London bankers made them readily convertible into cash. Indeed, Henry Thornton's remarks, quoted at the beginning of this chapter, suggest that by the late eighteenth century, one of the principal functions of bills of exchange was to serve as a means of obtaining loans from banks.[79]

One should, however, be wary of overstating the impact of the development of banks on the domestic financial system and the development of practice and law concerning bills of exchange. While specialized banks played a key role in credit and payments in London by the end of the seventeenth century, it was not until a century or so later that the development spread to the rest of the country. Edmund Burke remarked that when he arrived in England in 1750, there were not more than a dozen bankers' shops outside of London, and his estimate has generally been credited by modern historians of banking.[80] In the second half of the eighteenth century there was enormous growth in country banking; estimates of the number of country bankers established by the end of the century range from 300 to 400.[81] Nonetheless, some areas of the country remained largely untouched. Surprisingly, the most economically advanced part of the country – the Lancashire region in which the great cotton industries of the Industrial Revolution developed – was among the last to see the establishment of specialized banking institutions. Even in the late eighteenth century, there were few banking houses in Lancashire

---

[79] 'Bills, though professedly drawn for the purpose of exchanging a debt due to one person for a debt due to another, are, in fact, created rather for the sake of serving as a discountable article.' Thornton, *Paper Credit of Great Britain*, 91. In another passage, he makes the point even more explicitly. 'When a merchant in this country sells his goods on credit, it is, perhaps, not very important to him that he should receive from the buyer a promissory note (or an accepted bill, which is the same thing), if the only object of taking the note is the ascertainment of the exact amount of the debt, and of the period of payment', since an open book debt would suffice nearly as well for those purposes. The reason that a merchant might prefer a bill is that it 'is a discountable item. It may be turned, if circumstances require, into money; or into bank notes, which answer the same purpose.' Bills and notes, according to Thornton, 'are created for the purpose of being discounted'. Ibid., 83–85.

[80] Pressnell, *Country Banking in the Industrial Revolution*, 4; Clapham, *Bank of England*, 1: 157.

[81] Pressnell, *Country Banking in the Industrial Revolution*, 4–11; Clapham, *Bank of England*, 1: 157–72.

and little circulation of Bank of England notes; the circulating medium of the region consisted primarily of mercantile bills of exchange.[82]

The late appearance of banks in Lancashire is a good illustration of the point that one must not confuse banking institutions with banking functions. The merchants and manufacturers of seventeenth- and eighteenth-century Lancashire probably had no less ready access to local banking services than their London counterparts; the difference was only that banking functions in Lancashire were still performed as an adjunct to other commercial activities. The activities of Thomas Marsden in the 1680s and 1690s, noted earlier in this chapter, are illustrative. Though he was described at the time as 'a great dealer in fustians, linen and woollen cloth, and in yarne and other things of the like nature',[83] his financial dealings may well have been a more important source of earnings than his cloth manufacture and dealing. As we have seen, he provided remittance services to London, he made loans to local traders both in bills on London and in cash, and he discounted their bills. Moreover, he carried on these financial activities not only with his own capital, but with the funds he received from tax collectors and others. In short, he was a banker in all but name, and in that respect was typical of many successful merchants, manufacturers, and others. As Pressnell has shown, the firms that became known as banking houses in the late eighteenth century were outgrowths of the business of manufacturers, merchants, tax collectors, scriveners, and others. 'Country banking was less an innovation than a specialization in existing financial techniques.'[84]

Thus, although it is clear that banks developed and became important institutions of English trade and finance in the seventeenth and eighteenth centuries, and that bills of exchange played a key role in the lending practices of English banks, it is not so clear that the development of banks and bank notes in the late seventeenth century was itself a major factor in the development of the law of bills and notes. The development of bank notes may,

[82] Wadsworth and Mann, *Cotton Trade and Industrial Lancashire*, 92; Edwards, *British Cotton Trade*, 216–25; Pressnell, *Country Banking in the Industrial Revolution*, 170–80; Ashton, 'Bill of Exchange and Private Banks in Lancashire', 37–43.

[83] Wadsworth and Mann, *Cotton Trade and Industrial Lancashire*, 83.

[84] Pressnell, *Country Banking in the Industrial Revolution*, 12.

however, have had a subtle influence on attitudes toward bills in that as people became increasingly familiar and comfortable with paper money it must have seemed more and more natural to regard bills of exchange as items of sufficient economic importance to warrant special attention in law. Thus, the development of bank paper may have reinforced the tendency, already well under way as a result of other forces, to separate bills of exchange from exchange contracts.

The important point about the economic changes associated with the development of the English law of bills is that bills of exchange provided a flexible and convenient means by which credits arising out of trade – whether in the form of collected balances held in the hands of one's factor, debts due from customers, or merely the willingness of trading correspondents to provide accommodation – could be used to make payments and obtain credit. The development of specialized banking institutions unquestionably made it much simpler and more convenient to use trading credits in these ways. A mid-seventeenth-century country merchant or manufacturer who had balances in the hands of his London factor could use those credits to make payments, but to do so he either had to convert them into cash by finding someone whose trade or other financial affairs left him in the position of having a surplus of coin in the country which he needed to transfer to London or persuade his creditors to take bills that he drew on his factor. By the late eighteenth or early nineteenth century, he could simply draw bills on his factor or customer and discount them with a local banker for bank notes which anyone would accept as currency. From the perspective of the role of the bill, however, the difference is not all that great. Rather than passing through the hands of various merchants, storekeepers, and travellers on its way to London, the bill passed through the hands of various bankers and bill brokers. The end result, though, was the same. The country merchant or manufacturer was using the credits due to him to settle the obligations he owed. Thus, the economic transformation that made bills of exchange a matter of everyday financial life, and hence a subject that would require special attention by the legal system, was not so much the development of the banking institutions that facilitated the use of trading credits, but the developments in the system of domestic manufacture and trade that created those trading credits in the first place.

6

THE CUSTOM OF MERCHANTS AND THE
DEVELOPMENT OF THE LAW OF BILLS

The preceding chapter examined the changes in commercial and financial practice in the seventeenth and eighteenth centuries associated with the transformation of bills of exchange into instruments having economic significance independent of the older form of exchange dealings. This chapter examines the corresponding legal changes.

ACTIONS ON BILLS VERSUS
ACTIONS ON EXCHANGE CONTRACTS

In chapter 3 it was shown that in the period up to the beginning of the early seventeenth century, courts of all kinds in England enforced monetary obligations arising out of exchange transactions, but none had developed any special body of law governing bills. By the seventeenth century, the situation was very different. Execution of a bill of exchange gave rise to enforceable legal obligations, regardless of whether the bill was issued in connection with an exchange transaction. The new analysis of bills is well illustrated by one of the earliest reported decisions in the central courts of an action on a bill of exchange, *Edgar* v. *Chut* (1663).[1]

In *Edgar*, a butcher who had bought cattle from a Norfolk grazier persuaded a parson who had funds in London to draw a bill on his London correspondent and give it to the butcher to use in paying the grazier. The parson had instructed his London correspondent not to pay the bill until the butcher paid him the money, but the butcher went bankrupt before reimbursing the parson. The parson was held liable to pay the bill as drawer after the

---

[1] 1 Keb. 592, 636.

drawee in London dishonoured it. The case is a good illustration of
the newer form of bill dealings examined in the previous chapter.
The drawer of the bill, the parson, had funds in London and
thereby was in a position to provide remittance services to the
butcher who needed to make a payment for cattle. The parson gave
the butcher the bill before receiving payment from him. Whether
he realized it at the time, or only after he had to pay the bill to the
grazier, the parson had, in effect, loaned his London funds to the
butcher. Indeed, the transaction was quite similar to those in
which country clothiers made local loans by giving bills on London
to persons who were to reimburse them later.

If bill dealings had still been analysed from the standpoint of the
exchange contract, it would be hard to see how the parson could
have been held liable to the grazier. This was not a case where
someone took up money and drew a bill on his correspondent as a
means of directing repayment of the advance. The parson was not a
party to any exchange contract, and he had received no value for
the bill. Yet as bills were used in the payment system that
developed in the seventeenth century, it is easy to see why someone
in the parson's position should be held liable. For a bill on London
to function as a payment medium, those who took it, such as the
Norfolk grazier, had to be assured that someone would be legally
bound to pay the bill. If all went well, the bill would have been
accepted and paid by the drawee in London, but at the time that he
took the bill the grazier had no way of knowing whether that would
happen. Thus, if bills were to be acceptable as media of payment,
it was essential that those who took bills be assured that execution
of the bill in itself bound the drawer to pay if the drawee did not.

The conception of the obligations of parties to bills that developed in the seventeenth century was of particular significance
given that bills were frequently transferred from person to person
by indorsement. The older view that the obligations in exchange
contracts were based on the delivery of money in exchange transactions would have been very ill-suited to the bill circulation
practices of the eighteenth century, even in those cases where the
bill was originally issued in an exchange transaction of the older
form. Suppose, for example, that a Lancashire clothier received
money from a tax collector, giving a bill on his London factor in
return. If the tax collector sent the bill directly to London for
collection and it was dishonoured, the tax collector, as original

deliverer of the money in the exchange transaction, might have sued the clothier for return of the money. If, however, the bill had passed through many hands on its way toward the drawee in London, the ultimate holder would have been in a very difficult position if the legal obligation had been grounded on the original delivery of the money. The problem was not, as is commonly supposed, whether causes of action were legally assignable or whether transferees took free from defences. Rather, the important point was how the cause of action was defined. The deliverer's cause of action for refund of the money given in an unperformed exchange contract might have been fully assignable, and might even have been assignable free from defences, yet the various parties through whose hands the bill passed would have had no way of knowing the facts of the exchange transaction and thus might have been unable to prove the elements of a cause of action on the exchange contract. Bills were usable as transferable media of exchange only once the execution of a bill itself created a legal obligation binding the drawer, independent of any obligation that may have arisen in the underlying exchange transaction.

DEVELOPMENT OF PLEADINGS FOR ACTIONS ON BILLS

In chapter 3, we saw that in the late sixteenth and early seventeenth centuries the common law courts enforced obligations arising out of exchange transactions through actions in *assumpsit*. In that period, the pleadings set forth in detail the facts of the underlying exchange transactions, and the basis of legal obligation was the receipt of money in the exchange transaction rather than the execution of a bill of exchange. Indeed the pleadings for actions on exchange contracts sometimes did not even mention the bill. During the seventeenth century, different forms of pleading came into use. By careful examination of the changes in the form of pleadings, one can trace the emergence of the principle that execution of a bill of exchange creates enforceable legal obligations.

The first change in the form of pleading occurred in the early part of the seventeenth century. The declarations set out the facts of the underlying exchange transactions, in much the same form as the earlier pleadings, but then added an allegation about the 'custom of merchants' concerning bills. A seventeenth-century form book gives two examples of this form of pleading from actions against persons who had accepted bills, *Matthew Reuse* v. *Charles H.* (1605) and *Peter de Prill* v. *Philip Barnardi* (1616).[2] Both pleadings begin, in the same fashion as the late-sixteenth- and early-seventeenth-century declarations, by alleging that a merchant abroad had delivered money to another merchant in an exchange transaction, and that the taker had drawn a bill of exchange for the sum on his representative in England. Unlike the earlier pleadings, however, these two declarations then allege that there is, and has been from time immemorial, a custom observed by English and foreign merchants that if any merchant or his factor delivers a sum of money abroad to another merchant to be paid by a bill of exchange, and if the person to whom the bill was directed accepts the bill, then the person who accepted the bill is liable to pay the sum mentioned in the bill to the person named in the bill. Similar pleadings can be found for actions against drawers in the early part of the seventeenth century.[3]

By the middle years of the seventeenth century, another change in the form of pleading had occurred. A good example of the newer form of pleading is found in the declaration in *R. G.* v. *J. T.* (1636).[4] The declaration begins by alleging that London and Lisbon are each ancient cities and that there is, and has been from

---

[2] Brownlow, *Declarations and Pleadings in English*, 1: 267, 2: 58. The accuracy of Brownlow is, however, subject to some doubt, as it is apparent from the printed text that various errors or omissions were made in the translation from the original Latin to English. The dates of 1605 and 1616 are the dates given in the factual allegation of the declarations, though for the 1616 case Brownlow gives a citation to the rolls for Hilary, 4 Jac., roll 155, which would place the case in January 1607. Perhaps the citation for the rolls should have been 14 Jac.

[3] *Mounsey* v. *Traves* (1620), in Vidian, *Exact Pleader*, 66; *Aswel* v. *Osborn* (1627), ibid., 67; *Whitmore* v. *Hunt* (n.d., c. 1620–40), Brownlow, *Declarations*, 1: 269. *Whitmore* v. *Hunt* can be roughly dated by virtue of the description of the plaintiff George Whitmore as 'Citizen and Alderman of London'. The *Dictionary of National Biography* shows a George Whitmore as an alderman of London from 1621 to 1643. There is also one obscurely reported decision in that period, *Barnaby* v. *Rigalt* (1632), Cro. Car. 301, which seems to have involved a similar form of declaration in an action against a drawer.

[4] Brown, *Vade Mecum*, 22, citing rolls of Hil. 11 Car. I. The declaration also appears in a much later form book, Bohun, *Declarations* (1733), 53, with the dates changed to the 1730s. There are many similar declarations dating from the mid- and late seventeenth century in the form books. *Bucknam* v. *Carr* (n.d.), Vidian, *Exact Pleader*, 17; *Aboas* v. *Raworth* (1666), ibid., 30; *Colville* v. *Cutler* (1666), ibid., 31; *Ashurst* v. *Thomas* (1666), ibid., 33; *H. S.* v. *R. W.* (1678), in Brownlow, *Brownlow Latine Redivivus*, 74; *S.* v. *J. W.* (n.d.), ibid., 77.

time immemorial, a custom used and approved among merchants and others, that if any merchant or other person to whom a bill of exchange was directed subscribed and accepted the bill with his hand according to the laws and customs of merchants, then he is liable according to the laws and customs of merchants to pay the sum named in the bill to the person named in the bill. The declaration then sets out the facts of the case corresponding to the custom. On 11 September 1635, Thomas Kendal, a merchant at Lisbon, had by his bill of exchange directed the defendant J. T. to pay to the plaintiff R. G. the sum of £115 17s 6d at thirty days' sight of the bill. On 10 October 1635, the defendant, knowing the bill to be so directed and acknowledging that he had received it, had accepted the bill according to the use of merchants. The declaration then concludes with the stylized allegation of non-performance in *assumpsit* actions, alleging that the defendant, notwithstanding his acceptance but contriving to deceive and defraud the plaintiff, had not paid the sum of £115 17s 6d to the plaintiff.[5]

The difference between the pleading in *R. G.* v. *J. T.* (1636) and the earlier forms is subtle but significant. All of the previous pleadings against drawees or acceptors contained detailed allegations of the delivery of money in the exchange transaction in which the bill was issued. In the sixteenth-century form,[6] the essential allegations were that money had been delivered in an exchange transaction between agents of the parties and that the money had not been repaid. Even in the early-seventeenth-century pleadings, where the allegation that acceptors are bound under the custom of merchants first appeared, the declarations still alleged that the deliverer handed over money to the drawer to be paid abroad.[7] By contrast, the declaration in *R. G.* v. *J. T.* (1636) neither says anything about any delivery of money to the drawer, nor gives any

---

[5] The same transformation is found in pleadings in actions against drawers. By the mid- to late seventeenth century there are declarations in *assumpsit* against drawers based on the custom of merchants, in which the only facts alleged are that the defendant drew a bill of exchange that was not paid. *Oades* v. *Potter* (1683), in Clift, *Declarations*, 893.

[6] E.g., *C. W.* v. *J. B.* (1595), Rastell, *Entrees*, 3rd edn, 338r.; *Hampton* v. *Calthrope* (1584), Brown, *Vade Mecum*, 23; and *Williamson* v. *Holiday* (1611), Brown, *Vade Mecum*, 26, discussed in chapter 3.

[7] E.g., *Matthew Reuse* v. *Charles H.* (1605); *Peter de Prill* v. *Philip Barnardi* (1616).

other information about why he drew the bill. Nothing is said about the relationship between the drawer Kendal and the defendant J. T. who had accepted the bill, nor is there any information about why the plaintiff R. G. was named in the bill as the person to receive the money. The only facts stated are that Kendal drew a bill on the defendant payable to the plaintiff and that the defendant accepted the bill.

Examples of this newer form of pleading can also be found in reported decisions. A pleading of this form seems to have been used for an action against an acceptor in *Oaste* v. *Taylor* (1612).[8] According to the very brief report, David Oaste, 'a merchant stranger', brought an action in *assumpsit* against William Taylor, merchant, alleging that 'by the custom of London, between merchants trafficking from London into the parts beyond the seas, if any merchant ... direct his bill of exchange ... to another merchant ... upon such a merchant's accepting a bill and subscribing it according to the use of merchants, it hath the force of a promise, to compel him to pay it at the day appointed in the bill'. Oaste alleged that one William Kenton, a London merchant, drew a bill of exchange on the defendant Taylor at Middleburgh, directing him to pay £355 Flemish to the plaintiff, and that the defendant had accepted the bill but did not pay it. Oaste obtained a verdict, and the defendant moved in arrest of judgment that the declaration had not specifically averred that the defendant was a merchant at the time the bill was accepted. The report, however, does not show how the court ruled on the motion. The question whether this form of declaration on bills was allowed only in actions among merchants will be considered later; for present purposes the significance of *Oaste* v. *Taylor* is that no other objection is reported to have been taken to the declaration. Thus, if the report accurately describes the declaration, the case suggests that as early as 1612 it may have been possible to recover in an action in *assumpsit* alleging no facts other than that the defendant had accepted a bill payable to the plaintiff.

At the end of the seventeenth century, yet another change in the form of pleading occurred. The lengthy and detailed recital of mercantile custom disappeared, leaving only the specific facts concerning the drawing, accepting, and non-payment of a par-

[8] Cro. Jac. 306.

ticular bill. The only vestige of the allegation of the custom of merchants was in the stylized phrase that the bill had been drawn, accepted, or whatever, 'according to the custom of merchants'. In several cases in the 1690s, the judges rejected arguments that pleadings had not sufficiently or correctly set out the customs on which the actions were based. In *Mogadara* v. *Holt* (1691),[9] Mr Justice Eyre observed that, 'though the plaintiff hath alleged custom contrary to his fact, yet that is but surplusage, for it is no more than the law of merchants, and that is *jus gentium*, and we are bound to take notice of it'. Similarly, in *Williams* v. *Williams* (1693),[10] it was said that 'this custom of merchants, concerning bills of exchange, is part of the common law, of which the Judges will take notice *ex officio*, . . . and therefore 'tis needless to set forth the custom specially in the declaration, for 'tis sufficient to say that such a person, *secundum usum et consuetudinem mercatorum*, drew the bill; therefore all the matter in the declaration concerning the special custom was merely surplusage, and the declaration good without it'. Eventually, pleaders seem to have adopted the practice suggested by the judges. In *Soper* v. *Dible* (1697),[11] the plaintiff's declaration did not set out the custom in detail, but simply stated that '*secundum consuetudinem et usum mercatorum* the acceptor is bound to pay'. The court applauded the practice, noting 'that it is a better way than to show the whole at large'. Innumerable examples of such pleadings can be found in eighteenth-century form books.

THE SIGNIFICANCE OF THE CHANGES IN PLEADING

To understand the significance of these changes in pleading style, it is important to identify precisely what facts had to be pleaded in order to establish a cause of action. From this perspective, the early-seventeenth-century cases in which the allegation of mercantile custom first appears are the most puzzling, for aside from the allegation of custom they seem to be virtually identical to the declarations of the earlier era. For example, except for the allegation of custom, the declarations in *Matthew Reuse* v. *Charles H.* (1605) and *Peter de Prill* v. *Philip Barnardi* (1616) are essentially

---

[9] 1 Show. 317, Holt 113, 12 Mod. 15.   [10] Carth. 269.
[11] 1 Ld Raym. 175.

the same as in the late-sixteenth- and early-seventeenth-century actions against merchants for money taken up by their foreign factors.[12] Thus, one is left with some puzzlement about why pleaders of the early seventeenth century thought it necessary or useful to add the allegation of custom to declarations in *assumpsit* that would seem to have been sufficient without it.[13]

An examination of the cases in which the custom of merchants first appears may provide some clues. The earliest-known explicit mention of the 'custom of merchants' is in *Sheppard* v. *Beecher*, which dates from 1600.[14] The declaration was in essentially the same form as in other late-sixteenth- and early-seventeenth-century actions by deliverers against takers, making no mention of any custom of merchants. The record shows that the case went to trial and that the jury returned a special verdict finding that the facts were as alleged in the declaration and that there was a certain 'custom and usage of merchants (*consuetudo et usus mercatorum*)' used from time immemorial that if any factor or party to whom any bill of exchange is directed shall not pay the sum of money directed to be paid according to the tenor of the bill, then he who sub- scribed or directed the bill ought to pay the sum delivered to him whenever he that received such sum should be by the deliverer thereof required. The jurors left it to the judgment of the court whether on the facts and custom it found the defendant was bound in *assumpsit*. According to Baker, the court took the matter under advisement for two terms, but no judgment was recorded.[15]

---

[12] E.g., *C. W.* v. *J. B.* (1595), *Hampton* v. *Calthrope* (1584), and *Williamson* v. *Holiday* (1611), discussed in chapter 3. The same phenomenon appears in cases against drawers. The declarations in cases such as *Mounsey* v. *Traves* (1620), Vidian, *Exact Pleader*, 66, include all of the allegations of the earlier style of declarations for actions against deliverers, e.g., *Anon* (c. 1560s), Rastell, *Entrees*, 10r.; *J. L.* v. *E.* (1594), Rastell, *Entrees*, 3rd edn, 338r.; and *Toft* v. *Garraway* (1613), Brown, *Vade Mecum*, 27, but add the allegation of mercantile custom.

[13] As Baker has pointed out, the addition of the allegation of custom was not a simplification of pleading, as Holden and others have suggested, but a compli- cation which demands explanation, for 'plaintiffs are not wont to introduce complexities, with the concomitant risk of being tripped up *in banc*, unless they feel compelled to do so'. Baker, 'Law Merchant and Common Law', 356–57.

[14] Baker describes the case as it appears in the King's Bench rolls, K.B. 27/1361, m. 507d, for 1600. Baker, 'Law Merchant and Common Law', 358. The full text of the declaration and other entries from the rolls is printed in Brown, *Vade Mecum*, 29. The declaration and entries from *Sheppard* v. *Beecher* are also found, in an English translation with some modifications, in Bohun, *Declarations*, 59.

[15] Baker, 'Law Merchant and Common Law', 358. The special verdict also included a finding on the meaning of the term 'usance' in mercantile custom, which was

Since there seem to have been many instances of successful actions by deliverers against takers without any mention of the custom of merchants,[16] the special verdict and inconclusive result in *Sheppard* v. *Beecher* is explicable only if the facts differed, in some significant respect, from the earlier cases. One may speculate, but can hardly be sure, that the problem may have been that the drawer was not acting as the principal in the transaction. If the transactions were conducted for the account of the takers, actions against takers on unperformed exchange contracts required no more sophisticated legal principle than that one who borrows money must repay it. Many of the earlier actions by takers against drawers, both in the mercantile courts and in the common law courts, seem to have arisen out of such transactions. For example, in *J. L.* v. *E.* (1594),[17] the declaration states that the defendant took up £150 in England and engaged that the money would be repaid by his factor at Hamborough. The cases would not be so simple if the position of the parties were reversed. Suppose that in *Sheppard* v. *Beecher* the defendant had taken up money from the plaintiff for some mercantile venture that the defendant was conducting not for his own account, but for the account of the person on whom he drew the bill. If the drawee refused to pay the bill, a simple action might be brought against him, particularly if the money had in fact been devoted to his use. On the other hand, an action against the drawer could not be based on underlying debt; rather the drawer's liability would have to be based on a rule that an agent who contracts a debt on his principal's account stands as guarantor of the principal's credit. From the facts and custom found in *Sheppard* v. *Beecher*, one simply cannot tell whether Beecher was the principal or the agent. Unlike some of the earlier cases against takers, such as *J. L.* v. *E.* (1594), the declaration in *Sheppard* does not specifically describe the drawee as the factor of Beecher, but neither does it indicate the contrary. So too, the special verdict of custom is ambiguous on the point, stating that the custom is that if a factor or party ('factor vel pars') to whom a bill is directed does not pay it, then the drawer is liable.

presumably only a matter of specifying the meaning of commercial jargon that might not have been familiar to jurors or judges.

[16] E.g., *Anon* (c. 1560s), Rastell, *Entrees*, 10r.; *J. L.* v. *E.* (1594), Rastell, *Entrees*, 3rd edn, 338r.; and *Toft* v. *Garraway* (1613), Brown, *Vade Mecum*, 27.

[17] Rastell, *Entrees*, 3rd edn, 338r.

Some support for these speculations can be found in another case, *Knappe* v. *Hedley*, which also dates from 1600.[18] The case seems to have arisen out of a *foenus nauticum* transaction similar to those that are found in the sixteenth-century Admiralty Court records. The declaration alleged that the defendant's factors abroad had received money from the plaintiff's factor and drew bills for the sum on the defendant, payable within six weeks after the arrival of a certain ship in England. The defendant accepted the bills but paid only part of the sum, and the plaintiff sued for the balance. The custom of merchants figures in the declaration in a somewhat peculiar fashion. The declaration alleges that the custom of merchants is that masters have always accepted bills drawn on them by their factors, and that if they failed to do so, the bills were protested, and the factors were bound to pay. Then, in asserting the defendant's liability as acceptor, the declaration states that in consideration of the premises and in consideration of the plaintiff's agreement not to protest the bills, the defendant had accepted and assumed to pay. If the defendant's factors had taken up the money for the necessary expenses of the voyage or for other authorized purposes, it is hard to see what the problem might have been in holding the defendant liable either for the underlying debt or on his promise as acceptor. On the other hand, perhaps some dispute had arisen about the agent's authority or the defendant's liability on the debt, yet the defendant decided to accept the bills anyway. In that case, one could not say that the defendant was liable on his promise because he was liable on the debt, and the plaintiff would want to show some other consideration for the defendant's promise to pay the bill. The allegations of the custom of drawer's liability on protested bills and the plaintiff's agreement to forego pursuit of the drawers might have been added as additional grounds for holding the defendant liable on his promise to pay the bills.

The first declarations against acceptors that mention the custom of merchants are also consistent with the surmise that the practice of pleading the custom may have arisen in cases in which the defendant was acting as agent rather than principal. Payees of bills apparently succeeded in *assumpsit* actions against the drawees as

---

18 Baker describes the case briefly, giving a citation to the rolls of K.B. 27/1359, m. 621. Baker, 'Law Merchant and Common Law', 358–59. A declaration which appears to be from the same case is included in *Brownlow Latine Redivivus*, 76.

early as the late sixteenth century, without any allegations of
custom, so long as they alleged that a sum of money had in fact
been delivered in the exchange transaction in which the bill was
given. In most of these cases, however, the actions were brought
between the principals, seeking to recover money advanced in
exchange transactions conducted by their agents or factors
abroad.[19] By contrast, in the slightly later declarations in *Matthew
Reuse v. Charles H.* (1605) and *Peter de Prill v. Philip Barnardi*
(1616), it appears that the merchants had taken up money for their
own account, drawing bills on their factors for repayment. The
factors had accepted the bills but refused to pay. The obligation of
the acceptor in such cases cannot be explained quite as simply as in
the earlier cases. The obligation of the principal to repay a loan
contracted by his agent can readily be grounded on the underlying
debt; the obligation of the agent to repay a loan contracted by his
principal can only be grounded on the promise.[20]

Hence, although it is very difficult to reach any confident
conclusions on the basis of the sketchy evidence, it is at least
possible that the allegation of custom may have first been used in
situations where the defendant's role was such that his liability
could not easily be based on the obligation to repay value advanced
in the underlying exchange transaction. The way that the custom
was described in the declarations of the transitional period is
consistent with this surmise, for the allegation of custom usually
refers not simply to execution of a bill, but to the giving of value
followed by execution of a bill. Thus, in the actions against acceptors, *Matthew Reuse v. Charles H.* and *Peter de Prill v. Philip
Barnardi*, the custom was said to be that if someone had delivered
money to another and the recipient of the money had drawn a bill
which was accepted, then the acceptor of the bill was liable.
Similarly, in actions against drawers, the custom was said to be

---

[19] E.g., *C. W. v. J. B.* (1595), *Hampton v. Calthrope* (1584), and *Williamson v.
Holiday* (1611). But see *W. S. v. R. H.*, in Herne, *Pleader*, 136 (action against
Hamburg factor of English merchant who had taken up money by exchange and
drawn bill on the defendant). The date of *W. S. v. R. H.* is uncertain. Herne
gives a citation to the rolls of Trinity 13 Eliz., which would be 1571, but the facts
are alleged to have occurred in September of 28 Eliz., which would be 1582.

[20] There is, however, an undated declaration, *John Bate v. J. Luce*, in Vidian,
Exact Pleader, 70, of an action against the acceptor of a bill in essentially the
same form as in *Matthew Reuse v. Charles H.* and *Peter de Prill v. Philip
Barnardi*, where it is hard to tell whether the acceptor was acting as principal or
factor in the transaction.

that if one drew a bill for the value received, then on nonpayment one was liable for the value received. The function of the custom in these declarations does not seem to have been to explain why those who have received value in the transaction are bound, for no custom would be needed as the basis for such a simple point. Rather, the point seems to have been to expand the liability for the underlying debt to those who had not actually received the benefit of the advance of money or goods, but had agreed to repay it.[21]

The most significant step in the seventeenth-century development, however, was not the mention of the custom of merchants in these early-seventeenth-century pleadings, but the evolution of the mid-seventeenth-century form of declaration, such as was used in *R. G.* v. *J. T.* (1636)[22] and *Oaste* v. *Taylor* (1612).[23] The striking point about these pleadings is not what they say, but what they do not say. All of the pleadings of the earlier era alleged that money had been delivered in an exchange transaction. By contrast, in the mid-seventeenth-century form, the only facts alleged were that the defendant had either drawn or accepted a bill of exchange and that the bill was not paid. Thus, the evolution of this form of pleading was the manifestation in legal procedure of the separation of the bill of exchange from the exchange contract. It is, then, not at all an overstatement to say that the appearance of this form of pleading marks the birth of a body of law that can properly be called the law of bills of exchange.[24] Various courts in England had long enforced the obligations incurred in exchange transactions by

---

[21] Professor Baker has pointed out to me that inasmuch as the earliest bills cases using the custom of merchants device date from the period just before *Slade's Case* (1602), another possible explanation of the allegation of custom was to avoid objection that a debt was not recoverable in *assumpsit* without pleading some extra element.

[22] Brown, *Vade Mecum*, 22.   [23] Cro. Jac. 306.

[24] Accordingly, *Oaste* v. *Taylor* (1612) can properly be described as the first reported decision of an action on a bill of exchange. A slightly earlier case, *Martin* v. *Boure* (1603), Cro. Jac. 6, is usually cited as the first reported case on a bill, but the case is so obscurely reported that it is hard to tell what the facts were or what legal issues were involved. It is probably best interpreted as an ordinary action in special *assumpsit* on a promise that happened to be made in connection with exchange dealings, rather than as an action to enforce either an exchange contract or a bill of exchange. In the first half of the seventeenth century, there are only a handful of other reports of decisions in cases involving bills, and these shed relatively little light on the development of the law. See *Vanheath* v. *Turner* (1621), Winch. 24; *Woodford* v. *Wyatt* (1626), ms. report printed in Baker and Milsom, *Sources of English Legal History*, 458; *Eaglechild's Case* (1631), Het. 167; *Barnaby* v. *Rigalt* (1632), Cro. Car. 301.

means of generic principles and procedures for the enforcement of monetary obligations, yet it is only with the appearance of the pleadings on the custom of merchants in the early-seventeenth-century actions in the common law courts that the bill of exchange came to have legal effect independent of the transaction in which it was issued.

THE ROLE OF THE CUSTOM OF MERCHANTS

The pleadings on the custom of merchants used in the seventeenth century are commonly interpreted as the device by which the common law courts incorporated the special body of substantive law governing bills of exchange that had developed as part of the law merchant applied in the mercantile courts. We have seen, however, that the assumptions underlying this account are inaccurate. The common law courts had been handling litigation arising out of exchange transactions for at least a century before the appearance of the pleadings on the custom of merchants, and had been treating those cases in essentially the same fashion as the so-called mercantile courts. It is true that there was a significant change in the law relating to bills in the seventeenth century, and that change occurred through the device of pleadings on the custom of merchants. The concept of the custom of merchants is, however, far more ambiguous than it first appears. Indeed, when one examines carefully how the concept of the custom of merchants was used in the seventeenth century, one reaches almost the opposite conclusion from the usual view that this was a device by which the judges of the common law courts deferred to mercantile practice.

There is, of course, nothing unusual about the idea that legal rights can be based on custom. From earliest times, the common law courts recognized and enforced local customs that differed from the ordinary rules of the common law. Local customs might, for example, give rights or immunities concerning the use of land, as in the cases of local customs permitting one to turn one's plough upon adjoining land or to dry fishing nets upon another's land.[25] It

---

[25] Y.B. Pasch. 21 Edw. IV, f. 28, pl. 23 (1482); Y.B. Pasch. 22 Edw. IV, f. 8, pl. 24 (1483); Y.B. Mich. 8 Edw. IV, f. 18, pl. 30 (1465); Viner's *Abridgment*, Customs F 1 & 2. As Coke put it, '*Consuetudo* is one of the maine triangles of the lawes of

seems only natural to suppose that the concept of 'custom of merchants' was used in the early pleadings on bills in the same sense as in other actions to enforce obligations based on special customs. If so, the binding force of the rules would have derived not from the general principles of the common law as articulated by the judges, but from the customary rules of mercantile practice.

On their face, the pleadings in the mid-seventeenth-century bills cases do appear to be based on the concepts of special custom. The declarations set out the specific practices or rules concerning bills in detail, describing them as customary practice of merchants observed from time immemorial. Moreover, the custom was often alleged as a special custom observed by merchants trading between two specific cities. Given the usual view that one of the distinctive traits of the law merchant was its universal, trans-national character, it seems odd to speak of rules governing obligations on bills as special customs of specific cities. On the other hand, if the pleaders who devised this technique were thinking of declarations on special customs, the peculiar manner of describing the custom is entirely understandable, for the typical special customs of English law were practices growing out of particular circumstances of some specific location.[26]

A more careful examination of the seventeenth-century cases, however, belies the appearance that the custom of merchants was treated as a species of special custom. Claims of special custom were subject to well-settled rules. To be legally binding, a special custom had to have existed and been followed from time immemorial, and had to have been limited to some specific location. The custom had to be specifically alleged in the pleadings, and the facts of the specific case had to be proven to fall within the specific

England; those lawes being divided into common law, statute law, and custome'. Coke, *First Part of the Institutes of the Laws of England*, 110b.

[26] Coke, *First Part of the Institutes of the Laws of England*, 110b, 113b; Blackstone, *Commentaries*, 1: 67–79. The quintessential, though perhaps apocryphal, example of a special custom based upon particular local conditions is the custom supposedly observed on the Isle of Man that taking another's horse was not a felony. The theory was that since there was no way to get a horse off the island undetected, the thief probably only intended to borrow it. By contrast those who stole chickens were to be hanged, since they probably intended to eat the birds. Y.B. Mich. 35 Hen. VI, f. 25, pl. 33 (1456), noted in Viner's *Abridgment*, Customs H 10.

custom alleged.[27] None of these principles seem to have been seriously applied to actions on the custom of merchants.

Although the pleadings commonly referred to the customs of merchants concerning bills as having been used and approved from time immemorial, no one could seriously have regarded those allegations as literally true, yet the point seems never to have been raised in any of the reported decisions. So too, although many of the mid-seventeenth-century actions on bills spoke of the customs observed in specific cities, or by merchants trading between specific cities, that practice was by no means universal. Baker has pointed out that in the earliest pleadings of this form, dating from the beginning of the seventeenth century, the custom was described as a custom used among merchants throughout England; the practice of laying the custom as a custom of specific cities seems to have developed only in the mid-seventeenth century.[28] Even in the mid- to late seventeenth century, pleaders sometimes framed their declarations as based on the custom of merchants throughout the realm of England, yet there seem to be no reported cases in which objection to this form of pleading was sustained. The point seems to have been raised in *Woodward* v. *Rowe* (1666)[29] and *Milton's Case* (1668),[30] but both decisions went off on other grounds. In *Pinkney* v. *Hall* (1697)[31] the issue was squarely addressed, and the court ruled that it was permissible to lay the custom of merchants as a custom extending throughout the realm.

It is often suggested that although the customs of merchants were not confined to specific locales, they were still treated as limited special customs in that they applied only to a particular class of persons, merchants.[32] Although it has generally been assumed that actions on the custom were initially permitted only

---

[27] Coke, *First Part of the Institutes of the Laws of England*, 110b, 113b; Blackstone, *Commentaries*, 1: 67–79; *Le Case de Tanistry* (1608), Davis 28; *Beresford* v. *Bacon* (1604), 2 Lutw. 1317; *Yates Case* (1655), Style 477, 2 Rolle 471.
[28] Baker, 'Law Merchant and Common Law', 364–66.   [29] 2 Keb. 105, 132.
[30] Hardr. 485, reported as *Anon.*, identified as *Milton's Case* in *Browne* v. *London* (1670), 1 Mod. 285.
[31] 1 Ld Raym. 175, 1 Salk. 126.
[32] Blackstone, for example, mentions the custom of merchants in his passage on special customs, noting that 'to this head may most properly be referred a particular system of customs used only among one set of the king's subjects, called the custom of merchants or *lex mercatoria*'. Blackstone, *Commentaries*, 1: 75.

between merchants, and that this limitation was applied rigorously in the early stages of the development of the law of bills, the evidence is somewhat more ambiguous. There is a one sentence note in *Hetley's Reports* stating that in 1630 one of the serjeants remarked in the Common Pleas that the King's Bench had ruled that an action on the custom could not be maintained between non-merchants;[33] and in a late-seventeenth-century case Chief Justice Treby remarked that actions on bills of exchange at first extended only to foreign merchants trading with English merchants, then to English merchants trading among themselves, and finally to all persons.[34] The cases, however, suggest that the limitation to merchants may never have been taken all that seriously. Defendants regularly raised the objection, but with little success. In cases where it appeared that the parties actually were merchants, the courts regularly rejected arguments that the failure specifically to allege that fact in the pleadings was fatal.[35] Even where the parties were clearly not merchants, the judges found some way around the problem. For example, in *Edgar* v. *Chut* (1663),[36] where the drawer of the bill was a parson, the court accepted the plaintiff's imaginative argument that 'such merchant is to be referred only to him to whom the bill is directed, and to the procurers of such bill, and not the drawers, or they for whose use the money is to be paid'. In *Sarsfield* v. *Witherly* (1689),[37] a different but equally disingenuous tack was taken. A young gentleman had borrowed money while travelling in Paris and drawn a bill for repayment on his father, a London doctor. The court dismissed the objection that none of the parties were merchants on the grounds that 'drawing a bill must surely make him a trader for that purpose'.[38]

33 *Eaglechild's Case* (1630), Het. 167.
34 *Bromwich* v. *Loyd* (1697), 2 Lutw. 1582, 1585. In the first reported decision in an action on a bill, *Oaste* v. *Taylor* (1612), Cro. Jac. 306, the defendant objected that the declaration did not aver him to be a merchant at the time the bill was accepted, but no ruling on the objection is reported.
35 *Barnaby* v. *Rigalt* (1632), Cro. Car. 301; *Frederick* v. *Cotton* (1678), 2 Show. 8.
36 1 Keb. 592, 636.
37 1 Show. 125, 2 Vent. 292, Holt 112, Carth. 82, Comb. 45, 152. The declaration is printed in the report in *Ventris*.
38 Even before *Sarsfield* v. *Witherly* there are some indications that the limitation to merchants might not be enforced. In *Woodward* v. *Rowe* (1666), 2 Keb. 105, 132, the judges of King's Bench are reported to have stated that 'the law of

Although the mid-seventeenth-century pleadings treated the customs as matters of fact that were alleged in detail, it is open to question whether proof of these allegations was required. Hale, who served as a judge from the 1650s to the 1670s, is reported to have treated a defendant's contention that the plaintiff had to prove the custom as somewhat risible.[39] Variance between the statement of the custom and the specific factual averments, which would have been fatal on the ordinary theory of special custom, was treated as inconsequential.[40] By the end of the seventeenth century, any pretence that the custom of merchants was to be treated as special custom had been dropped, for the judges had ruled that the custom need not even be set out in the pleadings.

Perhaps the best explanation of the fact that the usual rules governing special customs were not enforced in seventeenth-century bills cases is that – at least by the late seventeenth century – actions on bills based on the 'custom of merchants' were regarded as analogous to the peculiar, but well-established, family of actions in English law based upon the concept of the 'custom of the realm'. There were at least three varieties of such actions, dating from as early as the fourteenth century: actions for damages resulting from negligent failure to keep fire safely, actions against innkeepers for loss or theft of guests' goods, and actions against common carriers for loss of goods.[41] The form and wording of the pleadings used in these actions was very similar to the declarations in actions on bills. For example, a pleading in an action against an innkeeper would typically begin with an allegation that 'according to the law and custom of our realm of England, innkeepers, who keep common inns to entertain persons passing by the places where such inns are, and lodging in the same, are bound to keep the goods of such persons deposited therein without subtraction night and day, so that by the default of the innkeepers no damage may

---

merchants is the law of the land, and the custome is good enough generally for any man, without naming him merchant'.

[39] In *Buller* v. *Crips* (1703), 6 Mod. 29, Chief Justice Holt is reported to have remarked that he remembered that years before in an action on an inland bill, the defendant's counsel argued that the plaintiff had to prove the custom, 'at which Hale, Chief Justice, who tried it, laughed, and said, they had a hopeful case of it'. See also *Carter* v. *Palmer* (1700), 12 Mod. 380.

[40] E.g., *Mogadara* v. *Holt* (1691), 1 Show. 317, Holt 113, 12 Mod. 15.

[41] Baker, *Reports of Sir John Spelman*, 2: 227–28; Fifoot, *History and Sources of the Common Law*, 154–59; Baker and Milsom, *Sources of English Legal History*, 552–63.

come in any manner to the guests'. The declaration would then allege that the defendant was a common innkeeper, that the plaintiff was a guest who had lodged his goods with the defendant, and that the goods had been lost or stolen.[42]

Although these actions were, in form, based upon a custom set out in the pleadings, it was made clear as early as the beginning of the fifteenth century that this was not to be taken literally, in the sense of local customs. In *Beaulieu* v. *Finglam* (1401),[43] an action for damage resulting from the spread of fire was brought on a writ reciting that by the law and custom of the realm every man is bound to keep his fire safely. The defendant's lawyer argued that the action should be dismissed because it was not alleged that the custom had been observed from time immemorial. The court rejected the argument out of hand: 'Answer over; for the common custom of the realm is the common law of the realm'. In other words, although the pleadings purported to base liability upon a 'custom', the rule in question was actually treated as a rule of law, to which the principles governing pleading and proof of special customs were not applicable.

Indeed, there is very strong evidence that lawyers and judges of the time thought of the custom of merchants as the custom of the realm in this sense. In *Carter* v. *Downish* (1688),[44] one of the pleadings stated simply that a bill had been indorsed '*secundum legem mercatoriam*', without going through a lengthy recital that there was a custom of merchants that a bill could be indorsed and if so indorsed was payable to the indorsee. Opposing counsel seized upon the point as grounds for demurrer to the plea, arguing that the plea 'had not set forth the custom of merchants, without which all these assignments are void, of which custom the Court cannot take any judicial notice, but it must be pleaded'.[45] The lawyer arguing for the sufficiency of the plea responded with as clear an argument as one could make that the custom of merchants was custom of the realm, not special custom:

It was argued that the custom of merchants is not a particular custom and local, but it is of an universal extent, and is a general law of the land. The pleading it as it is here is good; for if an action be brought against an

---

[42] Fitzherbert, *New Natura Brevium*, 94; *Registrum Brevium*, 4th edn (1687), 105.

[43] Y.B. 2 Hen. IV, f. 18, pl. 6, reprinted in Fifoot, *History and Sources of the Common Law*, 166–67, and Baker and Milsom, *Sources of English Legal History*, 557–58.

[44] 1 Show. 127, Carth. 83, 3 Mod. 226.   [45] 3 Mod. at 227.

inn-keeper or common carrier, it is usual to declare *secundum legem et consuetudinem Anglie*, for it is not a custom confined to a particular place, but it is such which is extensive to all the King's people. The word *'consuetudo'* might have been added, but it imports no more than *'lex'*, for *custom* itself is *law*.[46]

The judges in the Court of Exchequer Chamber agreed, stating 'that they ought *ex officio* to take notice of the law of merchants, because 'tis part of the law of the land; and especially they ought to take notice of this custom concerning bills of exchange, because 'tis the most general amongst all their customs'.[47]

The cases dealing with whether the custom of merchants had to be limited, either to specific locales or to a specific class of persons, also support this interpretation. If actions on bills had truly been based on special custom, then they must necessarily have been limited in some fashion. The allegation of mercantile custom would be needed only if the legal rule was not recognized by general common law; yet if the custom had been universal, then it was part of the common law, and there would have been no need to plead it as a special custom. The argument was made quite clearly in *Cramlington* v. *Evans* (1690),[48] where the declaration had been framed as based on a custom observed 'in the realm of England . . . among merchants and other persons'. The defendant's lawyer pointed out the logical inconsistency, noting that 'the custom is laid generally, not confined to place, or persons, and so is the common law, and therefore ill as a custom, and also ill, because a thing laid as the common law, which is against the common law, is certainly ill'.[49] The objection, however, was dismissed on the grounds that in *Sarsfield* v. *Witherly* (1689) it had been held persons other than merchants were also bound according to the custom of merchants. The issue was finally settled in *Pinkney* v. *Hall* (1697)[50] where the court dismissed an objection to a declaration that had referred to the custom of merchants as a custom observed throughout the realm, noting that 'though heretofore this [objection] has been allowed, yet of late time it has always been overruled, and in an action against a carrier it is always laid *per consuetudinem Anglie*, &c.'. This was by no means an isolated remark. The analogy to the innkeepers, carriers, and fire cases was

[46] Ibid.   [47] Carth. 83.
[48] Skin. 264, 1 Show. 4, 2 Show. 509, Carth. 5, Holt 108, 2 Vent. 296, 307.
[49] Skin. at 265.   [50] 1 Ld Raym. 175, 1 Salk. 126.

mentioned by counsel and judges in a number of other seventeenth-century bills cases.[51] Conversely, the remarks made in bills cases to the effect that the custom of merchants is the common law were often cited in discussions of the concept of the custom of the realm as used in the innkeepers, carriers, and fire cases.[52]

The possibility that the concept of the custom of merchants is to be interpreted as custom of the realm has major consequences for the jurisprudential analysis of the development of the law of bills. If the custom of merchants was special custom, then the statements in the late-seventeenth-century cases to the effect that the custom or law of merchants is part of the common law can plausibly be interpreted as showing that the common law courts were willing to accept mercantile custom and practice as the basis of rules of law. If, however, the custom of merchants was custom of the realm in the sense used in the innkeepers, carriers, and fire cases, then such statements mean exactly the opposite – the rules governing bills are and always have been rules of law whose jurisprudential status is no different from any other rule of the common law.

Perhaps the best way of studying the role of mercantile practice in the development of the law of bills is to consider the procedural setting of the cases in which the rules concerning bills were articulated. If it were true that the common law courts looked to mercantile practice as the source of the law of bills, then one would expect that the procedures used would have permitted and facilitated the creation of a factual record concerning the relevant mercantile practices. In fact, at least by the later part of the seventeenth century, when cases involving bills became relatively common and the details of the rules governing bills began to be worked out, cases presenting important questions about the law of bills were routinely decided on the pleadings.

Consider the procedure in *Cramlington v. Evans* (1690),[53] where the issue was whether a bill payable to A to the use of B could be negotiated by A free from B's claim to the funds. The plaintiff's

51 *Milton's Case* (1668), Hardr. 485, reported as *Anon.*, identified as *Milton's Case* in *Browne* v. *London* (1670), 1 Mod. 285; *Williamson* v. *Harrison* (1690), Carth. 160, Holt 359, Salk. 197.

52 In Bacon's *Abridgment*, *Milton's Case* is cited in the passage on carriers' liability, and *Carter* v. *Downish* is cited in the passages on carriers' liability and innkeepers' liability.

53 Skin. 264, 1 Show. 4, 2 Show. 509, Carth. 5, Holt 108, 2 Vent. 296, 307.

declaration alleged that the custom of merchants was that even if a bill had been made payable to A or his order to the use of B, if it was indorsed by A to another, then upon dishonour the drawer was bound to pay the amount of the bill to the indorsee. If the question had been regarded as an issue to be decided on the basis of mercantile custom, then one would have expected the defendant to put in a general denial, so that at trial he could dispute the existence of the alleged custom. Instead, the defendant chose a tactic that seems to have been specifically designed to get a ruling on the issue as a matter of law. The defendant put in a special plea, beginning with a *'protestando*, that there was no such custom as set forth in the declaration', and then setting out the specific matter of his plea, to wit, that the debt for which the bill had been drawn had been paid to the use of B. The plaintiff demurred to the defendant's special plea, thus joining issue on the legal question it raised.

To understand the procedural setting of the case, one must note that the effect of the *'protestando'* clause in a plea was to concede the matter in question for purposes of the specific case, but reserve the right to dispute it in other litigation.[54] Thus, the defendant's plea asserted that even if it were conceded that the custom of merchants was as alleged in the declaration, payment of underlying debt to the use of B gave the drawer of the bill a full defence to the indorsee's action. If the allegation of the custom of merchants had been treated as an allegation of fact, the defendant would certainly not have put in such a plea. Since the defendant's plea admitted the custom as pleaded by the plaintiff, judgment could have been given for the plaintiff on the grounds that the defendant had admitted all of the essential allegations of the complaint. No one, however, seems to have thought that the case was so simple. The issue was argued several times in the King's Bench over a two-year period, and after the King's Bench finally gave judgment for the plaintiff, the case was brought before the Court of Exchequer Chamber by writ of error.

From the general tenor of the arguments, it is clear that the question was treated as an issue of law to be decided by the judges in the same fashion as any other common law question. Counsel disputed whether B had a legal or only equitable interest, they cited decisions from the common law courts as far back as a mid-fifteenth-century yearbook case, they argued about the application of cases on whether debt or account would lie against one who had agreed to pay money to the use of another, and even cited as an analogy the proposition that in 'a feoffment to uses by feoffees before the Statute of Uses, as to one having notice of the use, he shall be seized to the first use'.[55] Thus, despite the allegation of mercantile custom in the declaration, the question of the legal significance of a particular way of drawing a bill of exchange was resolved in *Cramlington* on a demurrer that was argued and decided on grounds of common law arguments and analogies.

The procedure in *Cramlington* was not at all atypical. There are many other cases in the late seventeenth century in which significant questions about the law of bills were resolved on the pleadings, without any opportunity for a trial at which evidence of the mercantile customs alleged could have been introduced.[56] The full implications of the proposition that allegations of the custom of merchants were not treated as raising issues of fact are made clear in two cases, *Bank of England* v. *Newman* (1698),[57] and *Lambert* v. *Oakes* (1699),[58] dealing with the liabilities of parties who discounted bills or notes. In the first of these cases, Newman had a bill made payable to him or bearer. The Bank of England agreed to discount it, and took it without indorsement. When the

[55] One of the reports of the decision in Exchequer Chamber does note as an additional ground of decision that the custom concerning indorsement of such bills had been alleged in the declaration and was confessed. 2 Vent. at 310. Cf. *Anon.* (1652), Style 366. It is, however, doubtful that the court in *Cramlington* regarded this as anything more than a make-weight argument since none of the issues that had been disputed throughout the litigation would have been relevant if that had been a sufficient ground of decision.

[56] *Sarsfield* v. *Witherly* (1689), 1 Show. 125, 2 Vent. 292, Holt 112, Carth. 82, Comb. 45, 152 (bills binding on persons other than merchants); *Claxton* v. *Swift* (1686), 2 Show. 441, 494, Comb. 4, 3 Mod. 86, 1 Lutw. 878, Skin. 255 (obtaining judgment against drawer does not amount to an election not to sue indorsers in the event judgment against drawer is uncollectible); *Williamson* v. *Harrison* (1690), Carth. 160, Holt 359, Salk. 197 (defence of infancy available in actions on bills); *Mogadara* v. *Holt* (1691), 1 Show. 317, Holt 113, 12 Mod. 15 (whether a bill payable at a specific date had to be presented for acceptance within that time, or whether a presentment and protest after the date of payment sufficed to charge the drawer); *Hawkins* v. *Cardy* (1698), 1 Ld Raym. 360, Carth. 466, 1 Salk. 65, 12 Mod. 213 (partial indorsement ineffective).

[57] 12 Mod. 241, 1 Ld Raym. 442, 1 Com. 57.

[58] 1 Ld Raym. 443, 12 Mod. 244, Holt 117, 118, 1 Salk. 127. The instrument is referred to as a note in Lord Raymond's report, but the other reports describe it as a bill. Lord Mansfield pointed out in *Heylyn* v. *Adamson* (1758), 2 Burr. 669, 677–78, that the case almost certainly involved a note rather than a bill.

bill was dishonoured, the Bank sought to recover the money from Newman on the theory that the transaction should be treated as a loan from the Bank to Newman. At trial, the jury ruled for the Bank, but the court set aside the verdict and granted a new trial, 'the verdict being against the law; for whatsoever may be the practice among the bankers, the law is, that if a bill or a note be payable to one "or bearer", and he negotiate the bill, and deliver it for ready money paid to him, without any indorsement on the bill, this is a plain buying of the bill; as of tallies, bank-bills, &c.; but if it be indorsed, there is a remedy against the indorser'.[59] In the second case, the note had been made payable to Oakes or his order, so that when he discounted it he had to indorse it in order to transfer title. The note was dishonoured, and the holder sued Oakes on his indorsement. Oakes sought to escape liability by contending that he had intended merely to transfer it, without adding his credit, arguing 'that this was a plain sale of the bill, and the indorsement shall not subject the indorser to an action, because the bill cannot be sold, to entitle the vendee to take the benefit of it, without indorsement; and the practice among merchants is so'.[60] The court, however, rejected the argument, and reaffirmed the principle of law laid down in *Bank of England* v. *Newman*, that whether one who discounted a bill was liable or not turned on whether he had indorsed it. Chief Justice Holt responded specifically to the defendant's argument that the practice among merchants was that one who discounted a bill did not incur liability on it. 'Their practice cannot alter the law ... the indorsement, though upon discount will subject the indorser to an action'.[61] It would be hard to imagine an issue more central to the law of bills, or more significant to commercial practice involving bills, than this question of the obligations of those who transfer bills. The striking point about *Bank of England* v. *Newman* and *Lambert* v. *Oakes* is that they show that the common law courts adhered firmly to the view that these issues were to be resolved by the courts as matters of law, and should not be left to depend on evidence of mercantile practice.

In light of these cases, the statements that we find in the cases to the effect that the custom of merchants is part of the common law, or that the judges will take notice of the custom of merchants, take

---

[59] 12 Mod. 241.   [60] 1 Ld Raym. 443   [61] Ibid.

on quite a different meaning than has usually been supposed. Such comments have conventionally been interpreted as conclusive evidence that the judges of the common law courts based the rules of commercial law on the customary rules of the law merchant.[62] In fact, when we examine the late-seventeenth-century cases carefully, rather than simply quoting phrases out of context, we find that the real meaning of the proposition that the custom of merchants was part of the law of England is the exact opposite of the usual interpretation. The judges invoked this proposition to justify their rejection of arguments based on the view that the legal rules depended on mercantile practice.[63] The case of *Hawkins* v. *Cardy* (1698),[64] makes this particularly clear. The issue in *Hawkins* was whether the holder of a bill could make a partial indorsement, that is, direct that only a portion of the sum be paid to the indorsee. The plaintiff's declaration alleged that the custom of merchants was that if 'the person to whom the bill was made payable indorses the said bill, for the payment of the whole sum therein contained, or any part thereof, to another man, the first drawer is obliged to pay the sum so indorsed to the person to whom it is indorsed payable'. The plaintiff, however, never had the opportunity to prove that this was the custom of merchants, for the case was heard on a demurrer. The court ruled that the partial indorsement was ineffective on the basis of the common law principle that a cause of action cannot be split because that would expose the obligor to two different suits.[65] The court specifically responded to the plaintiff's contention that the declaration was sufficient because it alleged that the custom of merchants permitted partial indorsements. 'Holt, C. J. answered, that this is not a particular local custom, but the common custom of merchants, of which the law takes notice; and therefore the Court cannot take the custom to be so.' Saying that the custom of merchants is part of the common law, or that the

[62] Street, *Foundations of Legal Liability*, 2: 343–53; Holden, *History of Negotiable Instruments*, 30–36.
[63] *Williamson* v. *Harrison* (1690), Carth. 160, Holt 359, Salk. 197; *Mogadara* v. *Holt* (1691), 1 Show. 317, Holt 113, 12 Mod. 15; *Hussey* v. *Jacob* (1696), 1 Ld Raym. 87, Carth. 356, 1 Com. 4, Holt 328, 5 Mod. 170, 175, 12 Mod. 96, 1 Salk. 344; *Vanheath* v. *Turner* (1621), Winch 24.
[64] 1 Ld Raym. 360, Carth. 466, 1 Salk. 65, 12 Mod. 213.
[65] That the issue was treated as a matter of common law is clear from the fact that the court justified its ruling on the basis of cases dealing with attempts to apportion rent-charges or warranties in deeds of land.

judges will take notice of the custom of merchants, was not an acknowledgment that the judges would defer to the merchants, it was a way of explaining why the judges were not necessarily bound to look to mercantile practice in order to resolve a dispute about the law governing bills.

If the device of pleadings on the custom of merchants was not a mechanism for adoption of customary rules of mercantile practice, we are left to wonder why the device was used. Part of the answer may simply be that it *was* used. As Milsom has pointed out,[66] practising lawyers do not devise grand jurisprudential strategies for changing the law; they deal with the immediate cases before them. If the solution they hit upon works, other lawyers are likely to follow suit. In retrospect we may trace the development of evolving legal principles, though those who participated in the development had no conscious plan for changing the law. One can, however, note certain respects in which the device of pleadings on the custom of merchants offered certain distinct advantages as a device for the development of the basic principles of the law of bills.

At the most fundamental level, the utility of the concept of the custom of merchants was that it provided a convenient vocabulary within which the idea of specialized mercantile obligations could be discussed. The basic principle of the law of bills that developed in the seventeenth century was that people incur enforceable legal obligations merely by signing bills. The common law of private obligations provided little basis for such rules. Obligations acknowledged in formal sealed bonds were enforceable by actions in debt, but bills of exchange were not sealed bonds. Informal promises were enforceable in *assumpsit*, but only if the consideration for the promise was proven. What was needed was a way of saying that people who sign a certain type of informal writing, used in a certain type of transaction, are bound notwithstanding the usual rules of private obligations. The concept of the custom of merchants provided an avenue for development of the special principles governing bills that was consonant with the principles and methods of the common law. Even the general principles of the common law were, at least in theory, ultimately based on

---

[66] Milsom, 'Reason in the Development of the Common Law', 152; Milsom, *Historical Foundations of the Common Law*, 6–7.

custom. Moreover, the idea of special rules of private rights and obligations tailored to specific circumstances or callings was familiar both in the special customs founded on immemorial local usages and in the 'custom of the realm' in the innkeepers, carriers, and fire actions. Finally, the notion that merchants' affairs require special treatment was familiar from the medieval notion of the law merchant as an exemption from the usual rules of procedure in the interests of speedy adjudication.

Ironically, the ambiguity of the concept of the custom of merchants may have been one of its principal virtues. Inasmuch as the allegations of the custom of merchants in the declarations could be interpreted as assertions of fact, evidence of mercantile practice could be introduced at trial. The judges of the central courts who were called upon to resolve issues of law at argument before the full bench in Westminster were, of course, the same judges who tried cases at *nisi prius*. The seventeenth-century reports show that it was quite common for evidence of business practice to be introduced at trials in actions on bills.[67] When merchants, notaries, and bankers gave testimony about how transactions involving bills were conducted, their testimony would enable the judges to gain the practical knowledge that they would need when called upon to settle issues of law concerning bills of exchange. At the same time, when disputes arose that seemed best treated purely as matters of law, the judges could always invoke the principle that the custom of merchants was part of the common law. Thus, the concept of the custom of merchants provided a mechanism for the judges to educate themselves about business practices concerning bills of exchange without forcing them to yield control over the development of the law of bills.

---

[67] See, e.g., *Dehers* v. *Harriot* (1691), 1 Show. 163, 164 (counsel pointed out that 'twenty merchants attested their customs to be' as he contended); *Tassel* v. *Lewis* (1695), 1 Ld Raym. 743 ('Merchants in evidence at a trial . . . swore the custom of merchants to be such.').

7

THE CIVILIANS AND THE LAW OF BILLS IN
THE SEVENTEENTH CENTURY

One of the meanings that is sometimes given to the notion that the law of bills developed by incorporation of the law merchant is that the judges of the common law courts looked to the writings of continental jurists and their English followers as the basis of the law of bills. It is certainly true that by the seventeenth century a substantial literature had developed outside the sphere of the common law on the subject of mercantile affairs and mercantile law. This chapter considers whether it is really the case that this body of literature had any significant influence on the development of the English law of bills of exchange in the seventeenth century.

CIVILIAN LITERATURE ON THE LAW MERCHANT
AND EXCHANGE

In the sixteenth and seventeenth centuries, continental jurists began to regard the affairs of merchants as matters of sufficient interest to warrant special attention and separate treatment in legal writing. Beginning with Benvenuto Straccha's *De Mercatura, seu Mercatore Tractatus* published in Venice in 1553, a substantial literature on commercial law developed. From the time of Sigismundo Scaccia's *Tractatus Commerciis et Cambio* (1619), exchange transactions were an important topic in this literature. As Sutherland has pointed out,[1] one consequence of the continental jurists' interest in merchants' affairs was that the phrase 'law merchant' took on a new meaning. In medieval times the term had little more content than the notion that cases involving travelling merchants should be resolved expeditiously. Once the continental

---

[1] Sutherland, 'Law Merchant in England'.

jurists began to integrate commercial matters into the intellectual system of civil law, the law merchant began to be treated as a coherent body of substantive law. Inasmuch as the notion of international law and the law of nations was one of the prime subjects of intellectual interest among continental jurists of the period, it was only natural that the law merchant would be described as a branch of the *jus gentium* or the law of nations.

At least by the mid-seventeenth century, the concept of the law merchant as a body of private international law was current in England as well as on the continent. The more specific notion that the law governing exchange and bills of exchange was a part of the cosmopolitan law merchant was also well known in seventeenth-century England. Discussion of exchange and bills of exchange can be found in various British books on mercantile practice and commercial policy,[2] many of which were based at least in part on earlier continental books. Not surprisingly, the English books often echoed the view that exchange law was based on trans-national mercantile custom and the law of nations. Malynes, for example, said that 'the Law-Merchant hath always been found ... constant and permanent ... according to the most Ancient Customs, concurring with the Law of Nations in all Countreys',[3] and he stated that matters involving bills are 'not subject to any prescription by Law or otherwise', but are governed by 'a revered custom, used and solemnized concerning the same'.[4] Molloy remarked that 'the right measure of judging on Bills of Exchange, is purely by the laudable Custom often reiterated over and over'.[5] So too, the judges of the common law courts sometimes spoke of the law governing bills as part of the *jus gentium* or law of nations.[6]

---

[2] Malynes, *Lex Mercatoria* (1622); Roberts, *Merchants Map of Commerce* (1638); Marius, *Bills of Exchange* (1651); Molloy, *De Jure Maritimo* (1676); Scarlett, *Stile of Exchanges* (1682); Forbes, *Bills of Exchange* (1703); Justice, *General Treatise of Monies and Exchanges* (1707); Postlethwayt, *Dictionary of Trade and Commerce* (1751); Beawes, *Lex Mercatoria Rediviva* (1752); Rolt, *New Dictionary of Trade and Commerce* (1756).

[3] Malynes, *Lex Mercatoria*, Epistle Dedicatory, 2.

[4] Malynes, *Lex Mercatoria*, 269.

[5] Molloy, *De Jure Maritimo*, 278.

[6] "The law of merchants is *jus gentium*, and part of the common law'. *Mogadara* v. *Holt* (1691), 12 Mod 15, s.c. 1 Show. 317, Holt 113. 'The custome of merchants is part of the common law of this kingdome, of which the Judges ought to take notice; and if any doubt arise to them about their custome, they may send for the merchants to know their custome, as they may send for the civilians to know their law'. *Vanheath* v. *Turner* (1621), Winch 24.

While the concept of the law merchant as a cosmopolitan body of substantive law was certainly part of the rhetoric of seventeenth-century English discussion of mercantile affairs, it is far more difficult to tell exactly what difference this made in the development of the law of bills of exchange. English lawyers certainly made some use of works on mercantile practice, such as Malynes, Marius, and Molloy, that were in part based on continental sources. Yet the reports of the decisions in the seventeenth and eighteenth centuries certainly do not suggest that these works were the principal source of law in cases on bills. In fact, there are relatively few references to books on the law merchant in the cases on bills. The first explicit reference to any such work is in *Ward* v. *Evans* (1703),[7] where one of the counsel cited Malynes and Marius and Chief Justice Holt remarked that these were good books.[8] Yet by that time, the common law courts had already worked out most of the basic principles of the law of bills of exchange, and the reports of the decisions of the common law courts contained nearly 100 cases on bills. In the eighteenth century, one finds somewhat more frequent references to such works,[9] but the number of instances is still very small in comparison to the volume of litigation.

THE POLITICAL CONTEXT OF THE
SEVENTEENTH-CENTURY ENGLISH LITERATURE
ON THE LAW MERCHANT

It is certainly true that various seventeenth-century writers described the law merchant as an ancient body of substantive law distinct from the English common law. Gerard Malynes stated that

the Law-Merchant ... doth properly consist of the custom of Merchants, in the course of Traffick, and is approved by all Nations, according to the definition of Cicero, *Vera Lex est recta Ratio, Natura congruens, diffusa in*

[7] 2 Ld Raym. 928, 1 Com. 138, 6 Mod. 36, 12 Mod. 521, Holt 120, 2 Salk. 442, 3 Salk. 118.
[8] A marginal note at 2 Ld Raym. 929 (not included in the version printed in *English Reports*) says, 'Note, Holt Chief Justice said *Marius*'s book was a very good book'. The report in 6 Mod. 799 says that Holt described '*Lex. Mercat.* . . . [as] an excellent book concerning these matters'.
[9] *Thorold* v. *Smith* (1706), Holt 462, 463, s.c. 11 Mod. 71, 87; *Wegersloffe* v. *Keene* (1719), 1 Str. 214, 217, 220; *Lumley* v. *Palmer* (1734), Cas. t. Hard. 74, 75, s.c. 7 Mod. 216, 2 Str. 1000; *Colehan* v. *Cooke* (1743), Willes 393, 396, 2 Str. 1217; *Simmonds* v. *Parminter* (1747), 1 Wils. K.B. 185; *Blesard* v. *Hirst* (1770), 5 Burr.

omnes, Constans sempiterna: True Law is a right Reason of Nature, agreeing therein in all points, diffused and spread in all Nations ... I have been moved, by long observation, to put the worthiness of the *Customary Law of Merchants*, in plain and compendious writing, by undoubted principles, familiar examples and demonstrative reasons, without affectation of curious words, more than the gravity of them in some places did require.

I have entitled the Book according to the Ancient name of *Lex Mercatoria*, and not *Jus Mercatorum*; because it is a customary Law, approved by the Authority of all Kingdoms and Commonwealths, and not a Law established by the Sovereignty of any Prince, either in the first foundation, or by continuation of Time.[10]

Similarly, in a work written in the early seventeenth century, Sir John Davies remarked that the

Common-wealth of Merchants hath always had a peculiar and proper Law to rule and govern it; this Law is called the Law Merchant, whereof the Laws of all Nations do take special knowledge ... Until I understood this difference between Merchandizes & other goods, and between the Law Merchant and the Common Law of England, I confess I did not a little marvel, England being so rich, and entertaining Traffic with all Nations of the World, having so many fair Ports, and so good Shipping ... What should be the cause that in our books of the Common Law of England, there are to be found so few cases concerning ships or merchants ... But now the reason thereof is apparent, for the Common Law of the Land doth leave these cases to be ruled by another Law, namely, the Law Merchant, which is a branch of the Law of Nations.[11]

While such statements seem to support the theory, for which we have found so little other evidence, that from medieval times commercial cases had been heard by specialized mercantile courts applying a special body of substantive law known as the law merchant, one must be very wary of taking them at face value. It is virtually impossible to find anyone who wrote on commercial law in the seventeenth century from the perspective of a disinterested observer of the development of the legal system. Rather, most such statements appear in works written to advance some particular political objective.

Malynes' remarks are a mild example of the influence of partisanship on statements about the jurisprudence of the law merchant.

2670; *Dawkes* v. *De Lorane* (1771), 3 Wils. K.B. 207, 212, s.c. 2 Bl. W. 782; *Salomons* v. *Staveley* (1783), 3 Doug. 298; *White* v. *Ledwick* (1785), 4 Doug. 247.

[10] Malynes, *Lex Mercatoria*, preface.
[11] Davies, *The Question Concerning Impositions*, 10, 16–17.

As was noted in chapter 4, Malynes was not simply a compiler of mercantile custom but a polemicist on economic policy and law. As one of the first of the generation of writers who began the modern discipline of economics, Malynes fervently maintained that the economic well-being of the nation required that trade be promoted through all institutions of state policy, including law. Malynes' remarks, quoted above, to the effect that the law merchant has always been adopted and approved by all nations were made in the context of a passage arguing that mercantile affairs were honourable and should be encouraged. Given that for Malynes the concept of law merchant probably referred not simply to private law, but to all aspects of state policy toward trade and economic development, his statement about the jurisprudential nature of mercantile law might be more plausibly regarded as exhortation than description. Whether or not it was true that all countries had adopted laws to facilitate trade, Malynes certainly thought that they ought to do so. Similarly, Malynes' remarks about the antiquity of the law merchant probably say more about his own approach to economic policy than about historical reality. Malynes stands as a transitional figure between medieval scholasticism and the emerging secular economics of the mercantilists.[12] As one of the last in the tradition of scholastic writing on economic affairs, Malynes continued to look to inherent natural lodestars as the foundations of economic morality and policy. Given his views on these matters, it is hardly surprising that he would wish to portray the law merchant as an ancient body of customary law approved by all nations in all times. The idea that mercantile law was based on age-old simple principles of natural justice must have seemed particularly appealing to one whose views on exchange were still grounded in the notion that money had an inherent natural use and value which was being perverted by the emerging practices of the money market.

A more extreme version of the problem of separating description from advocacy is presented by Davies' comment to the effect that until he understood the difference between the law merchant and the common law he could not understand why there were no commercial cases in the common law courts. It is probably not an exaggeration to say that this passage from Davies' book has had a

---

[12] de Roover, 'Gerard de Malynes as an Economic Writer'.

greater impact on the received traditions of the history of commercial law than any other single datum. Davies' comment was quoted at length in Richard Zouch's *The Jurisdiction of the Admiralty of England Asserted*, which acquired considerable renown when published in 1663 as a rejoinder to Sir Edward Coke's attack on the Admiralty jurisdiction and remained known long thereafter by virtue of having been bound together with a widely used edition of Malynes' *Lex Mercatoria*. Davies' remarks were passed on to modern lawyers by two of the most influential late-nineteenth-century writers on the history of commercial law, Sir John Macdonell and Sir Thomas Scrutton, both of whom began their discussions of the subject with quotations from Davies.[13]

Sir John Davies (1569–1626) was a rather intriguing figure. He was a lawyer and held various public offices in Ireland in the era in which Ireland was brought under English rule, though he is best known to history as a poet.[14] The work in which Davies' remarks on the law merchant appeared was a book entitled *The Question Concerning Impositions, Tonnage, Poundage, Prizage, Customs, and c.*, which was published posthumously in 1656 but apparently written in the early part of the seventeenth century.[15] One cannot help but wonder why a discussion of the nature of the law merchant appears in a book devoted to the seemingly unrelated topic of customs duties. The puzzle is easily resolved if one examines the book as a whole rather than merely quoting the remarks on the law merchant out of context.

The issue addressed in Davies' book was an aspect of one of the most hotly debated political issues of the first Stuart monarchies, the extent of royal prerogative to levy taxes without the consent of Parliament. Both James I and Charles I vigorously pressed the strategy of transforming the king's inherent regulatory powers over various topics into lucrative sources of revenue not subject to parliamentary control. The efforts to impose and collect such levies led to a series of controversies in Parliament and the

---

[13] Macdonell, Introduction to Smith's *Compendium of Mercantile Law*, lxiii; Scrutton, *Elements of Mercantile Law*, 5.

[14] Davies was called to the bar in 1595, but expelled two years later after he burst into the barrister's dining room at Middle Temple and broke a cudgel over the head of a fellow barrister who had apparently been overly witty in his criticism of Davies' poetry. *Dictionary of National Biography*, 5:591.

[15] The title page notes that the work was dedicated 'to King James in the latter end of his reign'.

courts.[16] One of the early episodes in the long controversy was prompted by the effort of James I to levy special charges or 'impositions' on imports and exports, in excess of the customs duties established by Parliament. In *Bate's Case* (1606),[17] the court had ruled that the king's prerogative power extended to the regulation of foreign trade and that impositions levied in order to regulate such trade were lawful. The issue, though, remained a matter of controversy long thereafter, if only because of the inherent difficulty of drawing the line between charges imposed to regulate trade and charges imposed to raise revenues.

Davies' book on impositions was a polemic produced by a loyal supporter of James I in favour of royal prerogative to levy impositions. The well-known passage on the law merchant appears as part of a make-weight argument added as an embellishment to the main contentions. The point of the argument was that the challenge to royal prerogative was based on the principle that by the common law of England the king cannot levy taxes on his subjects without consent of Parliament. Davies noted, however, that foreign trade was not governed by the common law, but by the law merchant. Thus, he concluded, the king's power over foreign trade was not limited by the common law. The argument was obviously fallacious because it confused various meanings of the term 'common law'. Even if it were true that foreign commerce was governed by a body of law separate from the 'common law', in the sense of the rules of private law developed by the king's courts, it would not follow that matters of foreign commerce are not subject to the 'common law', in the sense of the fundamental principles of English constitutional law. The important point for present purposes, however, is not the weakness of the argument on its own terms, but the realization that Davies' remarks on the law merchant came in the context of a work dealing with matters wholly unrelated to either the substance or the jurisprudential nature of commercial law, and were influenced if not wholly determined by the writer's desire to advance a particular political cause. Davies' remarks may be the most extreme and peculiar example of the

[16] The best-known incident was the *Ship Money Case* (1637), 3 Howell's State Trials 825, in which the court upheld the royal prerogative to raise money for purposes that the king deemed essential to the defence of the realm, a position later repudiated by the Long Parliament and the Bill of Rights. Holdsworth, *History of English Law*, 6:40–49.

[17] 2 Howell's State Trials 371.

impact of partisan bias on statements about the law merchant. The problem, however, is quite widespread. Seventeenth-century discussions of the concept of the law merchant can only be understood in their particular political context.

The controversy that most pervasively affected seventeenth-century discussions of the concept of the law merchant was the struggle between the common lawyers and the English adherents of the civil law tradition. As Coquillette's book on the English civilians, published in 1988, has shown, the rhetoric of jurisprudential theory played a major role in this battle of practical politics.[18] Although the English civilians were always a small group in comparison to the common lawyers, they had important professional strongholds. The study of law in the universities was exclusively within the control of the civilians, as were a number of significant specialities of legal practice, including practice before the ecclesiastical courts and the Admiralty Court. During the sixteenth century, it seemed possible that the civilians might expand beyond these fields of speciality and achieve a position of significant influence over the development of English law, but by the end of the sixteenth century the common lawyers waged an increasingly successful battle against the civilians' influence. By the early seventeenth century, the English civilians abandoned their expansive goals and focused on preserving their existing jurisdictions. As the dispute between the civilians and the common lawyers came increasingly to centre on the jurisdiction of the Admiralty Court, the concept of the law merchant became a central focus of the rhetorical battle.

The English civilians were intellectually dedicated to the continental movements that had given rise to sophisticated theories of international law, so they were naturally inclined to describe the law merchant in terms of the *jus gentium* and related concepts. By the same token, their very survival had come to rest primarily on their claim to special competence in matters of foreign commerce. Thus, the seventeenth-century civilian writers who sought to protect the Admiralty Court from the encroachments of the common law courts were led to stress that their law was not only different from the common law but superior within its special preserves.

[18] Coquillette, *Civilian Writers of Doctors' Commons.*

The civilian position was well represented by Richard Zouch's *The Jurisdiction of the Admiralty of England Asserted*. In defending the jurisdiction of the Admiralty Court against the encroachments of the common law courts, it was important for the civilians to insist that mercantile matters were governed by a body of law wholly distinct from the common law. Thus, Zouch insisted that 'it is manifest, that the Causes concerning Merchants are not now to be decided by the peculiar and ordinary Laws of every Country, but by the general Laws of Nature and Nations'.[19] He and other English civilians frequently cited and quoted Davies' remarks to the effect that there were no mercantile cases in the common law courts because these matters were governed by the law merchant.

When one turns from rhetoric to substance, however, one finds little evidence to suggest that the English civilians had developed a specialized body of law governing bills of exchange. Coquillette has concluded that the English civilians 'had no better doctrines ... to accommodate bills of exchange' than the common lawyers; 'bills simply did not fit into the Corpus Juris any better than into the Register of Writs'.[20] The extensive body of literature produced by the English civilians in the late seventeenth century in defense of the Admiralty jurisdiction confirms the view that bills of exchange were not regarded as an Admiralty speciality. The principal defenders of the Admiralty jurisdiction, such as Richard Zouch, John Godolphin, John Exton, and Sir Leoline Jenkins, all argued that certain subjects were inherently within the jurisdiction of the Admiralty Court.[21] There was, to be sure, some variation in detail and expression among the various authors' lists of Admiralty subjects, but the core was fairly constant, comprising charter-parties, bills of lading, bottomry and other forms of sea loans, freight obligations, seamen's wages, and other contracts and disputes involving ships and shipping. Bills of exchange were conspicuously absent.

Indeed, the civilians seem to have been quite willing to concede that the subject of bills of exchange was not within their speciality.

---

[19] Zouch, *Jurisdiction of the Admiralty*, 7, 9.
[20] Coquillette, *Civilian Writers of Doctors' Commons*, 255.
[21] Zouch, *Jurisdiction of the Admiralty*, 30–34; Godolphin, *View of the Admiralty Jurisdiction*, 91–118; Exton, *Sea-Jurisdiction of England*; Jenkins, 'Argument, in Behalf of a Bill to ascertain the Jurisdiction of the Admiralty', in Wynne, *Sir Leoline Jenkins*, 1: lxxvii.

One of the points of contention in the jurisdictional controversy between the common law courts and the Admiralty Court in the sixteenth and seventeenth centuries was whether the Admiralty Court should have exclusive jurisdiction over contracts made or to be performed abroad.[22] Exchange transactions would seem to have been a perfect example of the kind of contracts that fell within the disputed region, for by definition an exchange contract was made in one place and performed in another. Yet jurisdiction over exchange contracts seems not to have been a point of contention. In 1648 the advocates of the Admiralty succeeded in having an act passed in the Long Parliament confirming the jurisdiction of the Admiralty Court over maritime affairs. If ever there would have been a time for the advocates of the Admiralty to lay claim to exchange contracts, this would have been it. Yet quite the contrary, exchange transactions were specifically excluded; a proviso following the long list of Admiralty causes states 'that the said Court of Admiralty shall not hold pleas, or admit actions upon any bills of exchange, or accounts betwixt merchant and merchant, or their factors'.[23] Thus, even at a moment of victory, the advocates of the Admiralty jurisdiction seem to have been willing to disclaim special expertise in matters of exchange.

A GENUINE BUT UNSUCCESSFUL EFFORT
TO INCORPORATE CIVILIAN LAW

A further basis for scepticism about the notion that civilian sources were the basis for the development of the English law of bills in the seventeenth century emerges from an examination of the efforts of someone who genuinely tried to 'incorporate' civilian law, the Scots professor, William Forbes. Forbes' *A Methodical Treatise concerning Bills of Exchange*, published in Edinburgh in 1703, is one of the most interesting, but least known, works in the English language on the law of bills of exchange. Scots law had long been based on Roman and civilian law sources. From the citations in Forbes' book, it is quite clear that he was familiar with all of the

---

[22] Coquillette, *Civilian Writers of Doctors' Commons*, 106–15; Holdsworth, *History of English Law*, 1: 553–59; Mears, 'History of the Admiralty Jurisdiction'; Prichard and Yale, *Hale and Fleetwood on Admiralty Jurisdiction*.
[23] Act of 12 April 1648.

continental literature on the subject of exchange and bills of exchange. Yet despite his obvious desire to base the Scots law of bills of exchange on a continental civilian foundation, his book shows that he found the continental literature to be of little use in his effort to create a modern but systematic body of law for bills of exchange as used in his time.

The preface to Forbes' book consists of an unusually strongly worded version of the customary prefatory comments to the effect that the author was prompted to undertake the work by the deficiencies of the existing literature on the topic. In part, his comments on the literature suggest that he was simply a curmudgeon who had a rather low opinion of nearly everyone.[24] Yet there does seem to be a common thread running through Forbes' deprecatory comments about the literature. The civilian literature on exchange seems to have struck Forbes as recondite disputation on matters of no conceivable significance. As he put it, 'Many great Men, both Lawyers and Divines have indeed discoursed it; but . . . with their useless Niceties, and unintelligible different Notions about the Nature and Lawfulness of it; and their fanciful Divisions and Subdivisions; instead of clearing up the Matter, they've unhappily perplexed and confounded It more and more.'[25] Forbes'

---

[24] The works of the Italians Sigismund Scaccia and Raphael de Turri 'speak much Subtlety and Learning: But then they're prolix to a Degree, stuft with a Many of Superfluities, nauseous and idle Questions, and defective in Things more material'. The French fare no better. Mareschal's work is 'cramm'd with Citations of Laws and Doctors; but then he slubbers over bills so slightly, and disorderly, that it's more than likely, he understood them but so so'; Cleirac's work was 'printed . . . to as little purpose'; and Savary 'manages the Argument so superficially and imperfectly, that he appears not to have thought to the Bottom on't'. As for the English writers, Malynes' and Marius' books 'are mighty fat, and heavily writ, Withal such as one may pore upon long enough, without being in Hazard of reaping from the former a competent or satisfactory Insight into the Matter of Bills; or any tolerable Notion of it from the latter', while Scarlett's book 'is but an undigested Collection of incoherent Rules or Aphorisms, blended with inconsistencies, whereof some are very indistinct, others again as useless'. Forbes, *Bills of Exchange*, iii–viii.

[25] Forbes, *Bills of Exchange*, iii. The same attitude toward the continental literature is displayed in the preface to Scarlett's *Stile of Exchanges* (1682), 'The greatest Doctors of Divinity . . . and . . . the greatest Doctors of the Law . . . can[not] . . . agree among themselves about the nature thereof; some will have exchanging to be properly a Bartering, others a Borrowing and Lending; some will have it to be Depositing; and others not knowing what to term it, call it, Contractus Innominatus; some will have it to be a Changing of Moneys for Moneys; others, Contractus Locations; and some will have it to be a Buying and Selling properly; while others again will assert, that All these are included in it

reference to the civilian writers' discussions of the 'lawfulness' of exchange suggests that the reason he found the civilian sources so bewildering and unhelpful was that the continental sources approached the law of exchange from the perspective of the usury controversy.

The continental literature on exchange was the product of a particular cultural and temporal context, in which the development of exchange dealings coincided with heightened tensions between the usury proscription and the development of modern credit institutions. Forbes and the English writers dealt with the law of exchange and bills of exchange in a very different cultural and temporal milieu. First, there was the simple problem of chronology. By the time Forbes wrote, the earliest of the continental works on exchange were nearly a century old, and a century and a half to two centuries had passed since the time that the usury analysis of exchange first became a matter of debate in Genoa, Antwerp, and other cities on the continent. Once the underlying social and ethical problems had passed beyond memory, it is not surprising that their legal manifestations, such as the disputes over the classification of exchange contracts, seemed like arid arcana. British writers may well have faced an additional hurdle in comprehending the continental literature. By the late seventeenth century, the usury issues might have seemed archaic even to continental writers on commercial law,[26] yet at least they were working within the same analytical and historical tradition. By contrast, the problem of the usury analysis of exchange transactions never seems to have been a major issue in English or Scots law or policy. Thus to the British writers, the forces that had formed the continental literature were not only issues of an earlier age, they were issues that never were important in their own legal culture.

and applicable to it; and indeed, it's not a pin matter whether it be all or any of these, if commutative Justice be but observed, nor shall I further trouble the Reader or myself with these Controversies'. Similarly, Alexander Justice began his 1707 work, *General Treatise of Monies and Exchanges*, by noting that although his work was based on a translation of Ricard's *Traité Général du Commerce* (1702), he would not follow the example of 'some Authors, [who] in treating of exchange, have needlessly consumed a great deal of paper, and more time, in telling us confusedly what it is not; ... as I don't so well comprehend the necessity of negation in discourses of this nature'.

26 Dr Siegbert Lammel of Frankfurt, Germany, has told me that the preface of a book on the law of bills of exchange written by an anonymous Frankfurt notary public in 1676 contains remarks on the earlier literature quite similar to those in Forbes.

Despite Forbes' obvious perplexity with the continental literature on exchange, he did attempt to use it as the basis for a
systematic treatment of the legal problems of late-seventeenth-
century British commercial practice. Forbes' analysis of the law of
bills of exchange began with a basic definition, followed by careful
exegesis of the elements of the definition. Yet the defined term was
not 'bill of exchange', as would be the case in all later legal
treatises. Rather, Forbes based his entire work on a definition of an
'exchange contract', which he viewed as a contract between the
person who drew the bill and the person to whom it was given.[27]
Indeed, Forbes explicitly stated that the other parties, that is, the
holder and the drawee, were simply the means by which the
contract between the drawer and the remitter was performed.[28]
Forbes' conception of exchange as a contract between the deliverer
and the taker, which was to be carried out by means of a payment
directed by a bill of exchange, would undoubtedly have seemed
entirely sensible and familiar to English lawyers of the fifteenth or
sixteenth century. His analysis, however, took no account of the
fundamental transformation in the conception of exchange and
bills of exchange which occurred in the seventeenth century. By
the end of the seventeenth century, the key point in the legal
analysis of bills was the principle that the holder of a bill had the
right to enforce it against the acceptor or drawer – a right in no way
dependent upon the obligations that may have been incurred in the
underlying exchange transaction. Yet for Forbes, exchange was
still a contract between the deliverer and the taker; the bill of
exchange was nothing more than a piece of paper commonly used
in the implementation of the contract. Thus, the principal consequence of Forbes' dedication to an intellectual project that could
genuinely be called 'incorporation' was that he was led to adopt a
conceptual structure that had become obsolete during the century
before he wrote.[29]

---

[27] Forbes, *Bills of Exchange*, 19–20.   [28] Ibid., 27–28.

[29] It is ironic, but hardly surprising, that succeeding generations of Scottish
writers on bills of exchange looked upon Forbes with a sense of bemusement not
unlike his own attitude toward the continental literature of the preceding
century. The preface of the next Scottish legal treatise on bills, Glen, *Law of
Bills of Exchange* (1807), notes that although there are many English treatises on
bills, in Scotland 'the only work on the subject is that of Mr. Forbes, Professor of
Law in the University of Glasgow, which was written and published about a
hundred years ago; a performance unquestionably of merit in its day, and
displaying considerable erudition, but which is now rather obsolete, both in
matter and style'.

THE IMPOSSIBILITY OF INCORPORATION

When one considers carefully the task that the English judges faced in the seventeenth and eighteenth centuries, it becomes apparent that they could not have simply lifted a pre-existing body of law from some other source and dropped it into the common law to serve as the English law of bills. The task that they faced was not to engraft an addition on to English law but to rework the common law system itself to accommodate the major changes in economic conditions and commercial practice that were occurring in the seventeenth and eighteenth centuries. In many countries on the continent, where special commercial courts were established and thrived, substantive commercial law could and did develop as an independent system of law. In England, however, commercial law developed as a part of the ordinary domestic legal system. As Holdsworth pointed out, 'in England alone among the nations of Europe commercial and maritime law became simply a branch of the ordinary law, founded indeed on those principles and rules of the cosmopolitan Law Merchant which were introduced into England during this period, but developed by the machinery and in the technical atmosphere of the courts of law and equity'.[30] Even so, Holdsworth probably overstates the influence of these 'principles and rules of the cosmopolitan Law Merchant.' The hardest part of the task was not deciding what the rules on bills should be, but integrating these rules into the categories and procedures of the common law.

In chapter 6, it was shown that the changes in pleading practice in actions involving bills in the seventeenth century were the procedural manifestation of changes in the economic and legal analysis of bills. It would, though, be just as accurate to state the same thing in the converse. The changes in the substantive principles concerning the obligations of parties to bills were the consequence of the changes in pleading rules. Many, if not most, of the reported decisions involving bills in the seventeenth century were disputes about the application of the rules of pleading and procedure to cases involving bills. Those questions can only be answered on the basis of authorities and arguments within the common law system. Consider, for example, any of the late-

[30] Holdsworth, *History of English Law*, 5: 153.

seventeenth-century cases in which it was argued that a pleading in an action on a bill was deficient because the specific factual averments did not correspond to the allegation of the custom. The general principle involved was the rule that no pleading can be 'repugnant', that is, all of the allegations must be internally consistent. That is a technical principle of English law that can only be discussed in the technical argot of the profession.[31] It is hard to see how the judges or lawyers of the time could possibly have found any guidance on these questions in the 'law merchant', whatever one might mean by that term. Neither the most experienced merchant nor the most learned doctor of civil law would be able to provide any assistance in answering the questions, if indeed, either would have understood them.

One of the best examples of this phenomenon is *Milton's Case* (1668).[32] The case was an action against the acceptor of a bill, and would have been entirely unproblematic as an action in *assumpsit* on the custom of merchants. The plaintiff, however, had framed the suit as an action in debt.[33] The defendant argued that this form of action was improper, analogizing the position of an acceptor to

---

[31] For example, in *Mogadara* v. *Holt* (1691), 1 Show. 317, Holt 113, 12 Mod. 15, the argument was phrased as follows, 'that here the custom was part of the case: that they had set it forth specially; that they had declared of all the facts, *secundum consuetudinem pred.* and that *virtute consuetud' pred.* the defendant became chargeable, and in consideration thereof *assumpsit* ... yet here they fail, because they have declared of a custom to which they apply all their facts, which does not quadrate'. 1 Show. at 317–18. Opposing counsel could respond with equally technical legal arguments, such as analogizing to a different concept of custom in English law. For example, in *Carter* v. *Downish* (1688), 3 Mod. 226, s.c. 1 Show. 127, Carth. 83, counsel responded that 'the pleading it, as here, is good, for if an action be brought against an innkeeper or common carrier, it is usual to declare *secundum legem et consuetudinem Anglie*, for it is not a custom confined to a particular place, but it is such which is extensive to all the king's people'.

[32] Hardr. 485, reported as *Anon.*, identified as *Milton's Case* in *Browne* v. *London* (1670), 1 Mod. 285.

[33] Hale's opinion suggests that the reason may have been to seek a simpler form of pleading in which the lengthy recital of mercantile custom would not be necessary. 'If an action of debt will lie, it will be a short cut, and pare off a long recital. For if debt lies, a man may declare upon a bill of exchange accepted in debt, or in an *indebitatus assumpsit* for so much money'. Hardr. at 486. The implication of *Milton's Case*, that the payee of a bill could not bring an *indebitatus assumpsit* against the acceptor, was confirmed in *Browne* v. *London* (1670), 1 Mod. 285, printed with record entry in Baker and Milsom, *Sources of English Legal History*, 459, though later writers expressed some doubt as to the soundness of this decision: see Chitty, *Bills of Exchange*, 220–21.

that of someone who had agreed to pay for goods delivered to another, against whom neither debt nor its offspring *indebitatus assumpsit* would lie. In response, the plaintiff pointed to various instances in which debt or *indebitatus assumpsit* had been held to lie for customary obligations. Sir Matthew Hale, then Chief Baron of the Exchequer, noted that 'the acceptance of the bill amounts clearly to a promise to pay the money; but it may be a question, whether it amounts to a debt or not'.[34] Being unsure on the matter, Hale suggested that perhaps it would be 'worth while to enquire what the course has been among merchants; or to direct an issue for trial of the custom amongst merchants in this case. For although we must take notice in general of the law of merchants; yet all their customs we cannot know but by information.' It is hard to imagine that the court could really have obtained any useful information from merchants on so technical a legal question. Not surprisingly, Hale's suggestion was not followed. Instead, the question was answered in the only way that it could have been. 'Precedents were ordered to be searched; and afterwards ... all of the clerks in Guild Hall certified, that they had no precedent in London of debt in such case.'[35] After receiving the report of the clerks, the court ruled against the action. The case well illustrates the necessary limits of the guidance that the judges could draw from mercantile custom. Mercantile custom could tell the judges that the acceptor of a bill should be required to pay it, but could not tell them how to characterize the obligation. For this norm of commercial behaviour to become a rule of law, someone had to decide how it was to be fitted into the conceptual and procedural structure of the common law system. That is a task that the judges and participants in any legal system necessarily have to undertake themselves.

The problems presented by the task of integrating the law of bills into the common law system were by no means limited to questions of pleading and procedure. The courts were presented with a host of technical legal problems about the relationship between the law of bills and more general rules of English law. Does the exemption from the statute of limitations for 'such accounts as concern the trade of merchandise between merchant and merchant' apply to actions on bills, or do they fall within the

[34] Hardr. at 486.   [35] Ibid., 487.

general provision governing actions of trespass, account and case?[36] Are actions on bills exempt from the statute of limitations altogether, as akin to debts represented by sealed bonds?[37] Is the only proper venue for an action against the drawer of a bill the county where the drawer lives, or can it be brought in the county where the drawee lives on the theory that the case will require evidence of dishonour as well as drawing?[38] When the payee of a dishonoured bill dies intestate, does the right to appoint an administrator lie with the bishop of the place where the bill was located as if it were a sealed bond, or the place where the intestate died as in the case of a simple contract claim?[39] Does taking a bill of exchange in satisfaction of a debt represented by a sealed bond extinguish the obligation on the bond?[40] Does taking a sealed bond in satisfaction of a debt represented by a bill of exchange extinguish the obligation on the bill?[41] Is the defence of infancy available to the acceptor of a bill?[42] If someone draws a bill to pay a gambling debt, can the acceptor plead that his obligation is unenforceable by virtue of the statutory provision rendering gambling debt void, or should the acceptor's obligation be treated differently from the gambling debt for which the drawer issued it?[43] To develop an English law of bills, the judges had to resolve questions of this sort day in and day out. Nothing in sources external to English law could possibly provide any guidance on them.

Thus, while it is certainly true that English lawyers in the seventeenth and eighteenth centuries sometimes described the law merchant as *jus gentium*, there is little evidence to suggest that the substantive rules of the law of bills and notes were drawn from the continental literature on mercantile law or the law of bills. Rather, the English judges and lawyers necessarily built the law of bills from native materials.

[36] *Chievly* v. *Bond* (1691), 4 Mod. 105, Carth. 226, 1 Show. 341, Holt 427. See 21 Jac. I, c. 16 (1623).
[37] *Renew* v. *Axton* (1687), Carth. 3.   [38] *Anon.* (1698), 2 Salk. 669.
[39] *Yeoman* v. *Bradshaw* (1696), Carth. 373, Comb. 392, Holt 42, 12 Mod. 107, 3 Salk. 70, 164.
[40] *Hilliard* v. *Smith* (1686), Comb. 19.
[41] *Hackshaw* v. *Clerke* (1696), 5 Mod. 314.
[42] *Williamson* v. *Harrison* (1690), Carth. 160, Holt 359, Salk. 197.
[43] *Hussey* v. *Jacob* (1696), 1 Ld Raym. 87, Carth. 356, 1 Com. 4, Holt 328, 5 Mod. 170, 175, 12 Mod. 96, 1 Salk. 344.

A good deal of the confusion on this score in the traditional accounts of the history of the law of bills and notes is probably attributable to the failure to distinguish among the various subjects that might be included within the broad term mercantile law. In particular, one must be careful to observe the difference between maritime law and other branches of mercantile law. It is undoubtedly true that maritime law has always had a strong international aspect. In the battle over the jurisdiction of the Admiralty Court in the sixteenth century, the English civilians insisted that maritime law should be drawn from sources throughout the continental civilian tradition, and they were undoubtedly right in maintaining that there was such a body of transnational maritime law. For example, the ancient codes of sea laws, such as the Laws of Rhodes, Oleron, Wisby, and the Hanse towns, were readily available in England in collections published in the seventeenth and early eighteenth centuries.[44] In maritime cases, the English courts did at times explicitly refer to these sources of law. For example, Lord Mansfield's well-known opinion in *Luke* v. *Lyde* (1759)[45] cited these sources as well as Malynes, Molloy, and continental treatises on maritime law. It is, however, a non sequitur to conclude from such evidence that the law of bills, or other branches of commercial law, had the same international flavour.[46]

Another source of confusion about the role of international law and the continental literature in the development of the English law of bills is a misunderstanding of the concepts and terminology of seventeenth- and eighteenth-century jurisprudence. Remarks by lawyers and judges of that era to the effect that 'the law of merchants is *jus gentium*', are often interpreted as statements of historical fact – that the law of merchants *came from* a body of transnational substantive law. In the seventeenth and eighteenth centuries, however, the statement that 'the law of merchants is *jus*

---

[44] E.g., Justice, *A General Treatise of the Dominion and Laws of the Sea*; Miege, *The Ancient Sea-Laws of Oleron, Wisby, and the Hanse-Towns*; Welwood, *Collection of all Sea-Laws*.

[45] 2 Burr. 882.

[46] A striking example of this confusion can be found in Scrutton's account of the history of English commercial law where he misquotes Mansfield as having stated in *Luke* v. *Lyde* that 'Mercantile Law is not the law of a particular country, but the law of all nations.' Scrutton, *Elements of Mercantile Law*, 6. What Mansfield actually said was that 'the maritime law is not the law of a particular country, but the general law of nations'. 2 Burr. at 887.

gentium' probably had more to do with jurisprudential classification than with the origins or sources of the rules. The view that
mercantile law was *jus gentium* expressed a belief that the rules
developed within all legal systems on commercial matters should
be and could be at least generally consistent. That aspiration,
however, is entirely consistent with the historical fact that most of
the work that had to be done within each legal system to accomplish that goal was a matter of adapting the rules and concepts of
the particular legal system to the needs of commerce. Thus, in the
development of the law of bills, the principal role played by the *jus
gentium* concept may have only been to reinforce the view that
transactions involving bills should be governed by special rules
rather than by the ordinary law of private obligations.

8

TRANSFERABILITY AND NEGOTIABILITY

In the previous chapters, little attention has been devoted to a subject that is commonly taken to be the main point of interest in the history of the law of bills and notes, the development of the principle of negotiability. This omission is quite intentional. One of the premises of this book is that a major flaw in the traditional accounts of the development of the law of bills and notes is the preoccupation with the concept of negotiability. This chapter attempts to place this issue in proper perspective by examining the issues concerning the transfer of bills and notes that were and were not matters of real concern in the seventeenth and eighteenth centuries.

TRANSFERABILITY

Indorsement

Precisely how and when the practice of indorsing bills developed is not entirely clear, even though the point has probably attracted far greater attention from legal and economic historians than it truly warrants. Historians of continental business practice have found isolated instances of indorsed bills dating from the early sixteenth century, but it is generally thought that the practice did not become common on the continent until after 1600.[1] Evidence on English practice suggests a similar date.[2]

[1] de Roover, 'New Interpretations of the History of Banking', 219–20; de Roover, *Medici Bank*, 137–40; van der Wee, 'Anvers et les innovations de la technique financière', 1081–82; Usher, *Early History of Deposit Banking*, 98–101.
[2] As has often been noted, Malynes' *Lex Mercatoria* (1st edn 1622) contains no mention of indorsement, while Marius' *Bills of Exchange* (1st edn 1651) does discuss assignment and gives forms of indorsed bills.

Contrary to the usual view that the main theme of the early history of the law of bills was the struggle against the common law principle that choses in action are not assignable, the practice of transferring bills seems to have been accommodated by the common law courts with relatively little difficulty. Form books contain precedents of declarations in actions on bills by indorsees dating from as early as the 1660s,[3] and there are a number of reported decisions of actions on indorsed bills in the 1660s to the 1680s where indorsement is discussed in a way that suggests that it was a familiar practice.[4]

Once one understands the commercial practices that gave rise to bills, it is not at all surprising that indorsement did not present significant legal problems. Accounts of the history of the law of bills tend to assume that the typical transactions in which bills or notes were issued were credit sales of goods, in which either the buyer gave the seller a note for the purchase price or the seller drew a bill on the buyer which the buyer accepted. In such cases, indorsing the bill or note would be a way of assigning the cause of action for the price of the goods. In fact, however, the typical bill transaction was different, in a subtle but important way, from the assumed paradigm of a credit sale of goods. Bills were not simply credit instruments, they were means of making use of balances that one person held for the account of another. Even the inland bill of exchange was a bill *of exchange*, not simply a bill. A merchant who had shipped goods to a factor for sale would draw a bill on the factor when he had occasion to use the balances that he had built up in the factor's location. The bill did not serve merely as an evidence of the factor's obligation arising out of the underlying transaction, it served as the means by which the principal

---

[3] *Aboas* v. *Raworth* (1666), Vidian, *Exact Pleader*, 30; *Clarke* v. *Robinson* (1662), Vidian, *Exact Pleader*, 34; *Colville* v. *Cutler* (1666), Vidian, *Exact Pleader*, 31; *Oades* v. *Potter* (1683), Clift, *Declarations*, 893.

[4] *Dashwood* v. *Lee* (1667), 2 Keb. 303 (indorsee against acceptor); *Tercese* v. *Geray* (1677), Finch 301 (acceptor of bill ordered by equity court to pay amount of bill to second indorsee who had lost it, provided indorsee gives adequate indemnity); *Claxton* v. *Swift* (1686), 2 Show. 441, 494, Comb. 4, 3 Mod. 86, 1 Lutw. 878, Skin. 255 (indorsee against indorser; counsel remarked that 'the natural reason why the indorser is chargeable . . . is, because he is supposed to have received the value or other consideration from me, for assigning to me this bill; and it has been ruled often, that "value received" is implied in every bill and indorsement', 2 Show. at 497); *Death* v. *Serwonters* (1685), 1 Lutw. 885 (after third indorsee recovered from payee on his indorsement, payee can recover from acceptor).

instructed the factor how to disburse the funds that the factor had collected for the principal's account. When the factor accepted a bill that the principal drew on him, he was acknowledging that he had funds in his hands for the account of the drawer, or was willing to act as if he did. As it was commonly expressed in the eighteenth century, when a bill is accepted 'it is presumed that the bill is drawn on account of the drawee's having effects of the drawer in his hands'.[5]

Although a bill of exchange might be thought of as a means by which the drawer assigned to the payee his right to receive payment from the drawee, it implicated few of the concerns that gave rise to the ancient prohibition against assignment of choses in action.[6] It was not an assignment of an unliquidated, disputed right of recovery for breach of some obligation or duty, and hence did not pose problems of stirring up litigation. Moreover, the payee's right against the drawee depended upon acceptance, so that the drawee's obligation could not be assigned without his consent. Only if the drawee accepted would he incur obligations to the payee.

Indorsement raised no more problems with respect to assignment of choses in action than did the basic principle that an acceptor is liable merely by virtue of his acceptance. The effect of a bill was that the drawer, having funds to his credit in the hands of the drawee, instructed the drawee to pay the funds to the payee. Thus, after execution and acceptance of the bill, the payee was in the same position that the drawer formerly occupied, to wit, he had funds standing to his credit in the hands of the drawee. Indorsing the original bill was a means by which the payee could make use of those funds, just as if the payee had drawn a new bill on the acceptor. Indeed, the early reported cases commonly analysed the indorser's liability in that fashion. As Chief Justice Holt put it, 'the indorsement is quasi a new bill, and a warranty by the indorser, that the bill shall be paid; and the party may bring his action

---

[5] *Bickerdike* v. *Bollman* (1786), 1 T.R. 405, 410.
[6] Blackstone, *Commentaries*, 2: 442 ('no chose in action could be assigned or granted over, because it was thought to be a great encouragement to litigiousness, if a man were allowed to make over to a stranger his right of going to law'); Coke, *First Part of the Institutes of the Laws of England*, 214 ('the reason hereof is, for avoyding of maintenance, suppression of right, and stirring up of suites').

against any of the indorsers, if the bill be not paid by the acceptor'.[7]

Transfer of bearer instruments

Although the courts easily accommodated the practice of indorsing bills payable to order, transfer of bearer instruments presented a somewhat more complex situation. In a number of late-seventeenth-century cases, the courts ruled that someone other than the original payee could not maintain an action in his own name as bearer of an instrument payable to a specified person or bearer.[8] These cases are commonly portrayed as examples of the resistance of the English judges, particularly Chief Justice Holt, to the mercantile practice of transferring notes and bills.[9] Once the commercial context of the cases is understood, however, a rather different picture emerges.

At first blush it does seem odd that the transfer of bearer instruments was more troublesome than the transfer of order instruments. Today, the words 'pay to bearer' are the clearest possible indication of free transferability. These words have not, however, always had this connotation. There are examples as early as the thirteenth century of writings evidencing debts in which the debtor promised to make payment to the creditor or 'to his certain attorney bearing the writing'.[10] Such clauses seem to have been regarded as specifying the manner of designating representatives to collect the debts on behalf of the original creditors, rather than indicating that the debtor was attempting to create anything akin

---

[7] *Anon.* (1693), Holt 115, s.c. Skin. 343, query s.c. *Williams* v. *Field* (1693), 3 Salk. 68. See also *Claxton* v. *Swift* (1686), 2 Show. 441, 494, Comb. 4, 3 Mod. 86, 1 Lutw. 878, Skin. 255.

[8] *Horton* v. *Coggs* (1691), 3 Lev. 296, 299; *Hodges* v. *Steward* (1693), 12 Mod. 36, 1 Salk. 125, 3 Salk. 68, Skin. 332, 346, Holt 115, Comb. 204; *Nicholson* v. *Sedgwick* (1697), 1 Ld Raym. 180, s.c. sub nom. *Nicholson* v. *Seldnith,* 3 Salk. 67; *Carter* v. *Palmer* (1700), 12 Mod. 380; *Jordon* v. *Barloe* (1700), 3 Salk. 67. See also *Shelden* v. *Hentley* (1681), 2 Show. 160 (note under seal payable to bearer); *Hinton's Case* (1682), 2 Show. 235 (in action on bill of exchange payable to X or bearer, plaintiff must prove that he gave good consideration for the bill).

[9] Beutel, 'Development of Negotiable Instruments', 839–40; Fifoot, 'Development of the Law of Negotiable Instruments', 441; Fifoot, *Lord Mansfield*, 18; Street, *Foundations of Legal Liability*, 2: 363–72.

[10] *Brun de St Michel* v. *Troner* (1275), 2 SS 152; *Curteis* v. *Geoffrey de St Romain* (1287), 23 SS 26; *Abingdon* v. *Martin* (1293), 23 SS 65; *Hoppman* v. *Richard of Welborne* (1302), 23 SS 86.

to a circulating note.[11] For example, the bills involved in quite a few of the early English cases arising out of exchange contracts had been made payable to the deliverer's foreign representative 'or bearer', yet the actions were brought by the original payee, and the cases antedate both the practice of transferring bills by indorsement and the development of the independent legal significance of bills.[12] The late-seventeenth-century cases suggest that the phrase 'pay to X or bearer' may still have connoted a means of designation of a representative, rather than being an indication of free transferability. The cases indicate that the bearer could bring an action in the name of the original payee,[13] that possession of the instrument may have been sufficient proof of representative status,[14] and that payment to the bearer was a good defence.[15] The phrase that was used to make it clear that the parties contemplated that the instrument would circulate was not 'pay to bearer', but 'pay to X or his order'.[16]

---

[11] Beutel contended that the cases concerning these instruments showed that the fair courts fully recognized the modern concept of negotiability. Beutel, 'Development of Negotiable Instruments', 818–21. Beutel's contention, however, is extremely dubious. Only one of the fair court cases he cited, *Abingdon* v. *Martin* (1293), 23 SS 65, actually deals with the effect of the 'attorney bearing this writing' clause, and the meaning of that case is far from clear. The court seems to have allowed the plaintiff to sue without proof of representative capacity other than possession of the bond, but then allowed the defendant to deny liability on the basis of a release that he produced, without allowing the plaintiff to prove his contention that the release was forged. The case could hardly give comfort to someone who wished to rely on the 'bearer clause' as authorizing an action by the transferee of a bond. The other principal case on which Beutel relies is *Burton* v. *Davy*, 49 SS 117, the 1437 London Mayor's Court case involving a bill of exchange discussed in chapter 3.

[12] *Burton* v. *Davy* (1437), 49 SS 117; *W. S.* v. *R. H.* (1570s/1580s), Herne, *Pleader*, 136; *Hampton* v. *Calthrope* (1584), Brown, *Vade Mecum*, 23; *Williamson* v. *Holiday* (1611), Brown, *Vade Mecum*, 26; *Mounsey* v. *Traves* (1620), Vidian, *Exact Pleader*, 66; *Whitmore* v. *Hunt* (n.d., *c.* 1620–40), Brownlow, *Declarations*, 1: 269.

[13] *Nicholson* v. *Sedgwick* (1697), 1 Ld Raym. 180, s.c. sub nom. *Nicholson* v. *Seldnith*, 3 Salk. 67.

[14] The 1795 edition of *Salkeld's Reports*, reprinted in the *English Reports*, includes a note to the report of *Hodges* v. *Steward* indicating that a manuscript report of Judge Blencowe states that it was ruled in *Nicholson* v. *Sedgwick* that the bearer of a note payable to J. S. or bearer may bring an action 'in the name of the principal; and the bare possession of the note is, for that purpose, a sufficient authority'. 1 Salk. 125.

[15] *Hodges* v. *Steward* (1693), 12 Mod. 36, 1 Salk. 125, 3 Salk. 68, Skin. 332, 346, Holt 115, Comb. 204.

[16] The report of one of the hearings in *Hodges* v. *Steward* (1691), says that 'a difference was taken between a bill payable to J. S. or bearer, and J. S. or order;

In seeking to understand the courts' treatment of bearer instruments, it is worth noting that several of the principal cases involved goldsmiths' notes.[17] Thus, the cases must be considered in light of the variety of ways in which funds on deposit with a goldsmith could be assigned. In the early stages of deposit banking, there was considerable variation in banking practice on these matters.[18] For the most part, the courts seemed to have handled the practice of making payment by assigning balances on deposit at a goldsmith or banker without difficulty. Someone who maintained a running cash account at a goldsmith could write out 'drawn notes', as they were then called, instructing the goldsmith to make the payment. These writings, the ancestors of modern cheques, were in form essentially the same as inland bills and the courts seem to have treated them in the same fashion.[19] If the goldsmith had issued notes for the amount of the deposit, the depositor could make payment by indorsing such notes. Here too, the courts seem to have had no difficulty with the transfer, since the indorsement made it unambiguously clear that the depositor had intended that the note would be transferable.[20]

Only one form of goldsmith instrument seems to have given rise to difficulties. Goldsmith bankers sometimes gave their depositors a single note or receipt for the full amount of the deposit at the time the account was opened. Then, when the customer made withdrawals or directed the banker to make payments to others, the amount of the withdrawal or payment would be subtracted from the amount shown on the note, in somewhat the same fashion as

for a bill payable to J. S. or bearer is not assignable by the contract so as to enable the indorsee to bring an action, if the drawer refuse to pay, because there is no such authority given to the party by the first contract ... But when the bill is payable to J. S. or order, there an express power is given to the party to assign, and the indorsee may maintain an action'. 1 Salk. 125.

17 The instruments in *Horton* v. *Coggs* and *Nicholson* v. *Sedgwick* were goldsmiths' notes; the instruments in the other cases are not clearly identified in the reports.

18 Melton, *Sir Robert Clayton and the Origins of English Deposit Banking*, 95–125.

19 E.g., *Darrach* v. *Savage* (1691), 1 Show. 155, Holt 113 (payment made by 'a bill of exchange or note under the defendant's hand ... directed to a merchant in London, "Pray pay to Mr. Darrach or his order the sum of forty pounds, and place it to my account, value received, witness my hand"').

20 *Hill* v. *Lewis* (1694), 1 Salk. 132, Holt 116, Skin. 410, query s.c. *Tassel* v. *Lewis* (1695), 1 Ld Raym. 743 (goldsmith's note payable to one person and indorsed to another).

modern savings bank passbooks.[21] Sometimes the notes seem to
have been written in the form of a promise by the banker to pay the
amount of the deposit to the customer or to the bearer of the note.
These were the instruments that proved troublesome.

In *Horton* v. *Coggs* (1691)[22] the plaintiff alleged that one William
Barlow had paid a debt to him by delivering a goldsmith's note
payable to Barlow or bearer. The goldsmith, however, refused to
pay, and the court ruled against Horton's action, accepting the
argument that 'this custom to pay to the bearer was too general; for
perhaps the goldsmith before notice by the bearer had paid it to
Barlow himself (which at the Bar was said to be the truth of the
case)'.[23] The problem was not that the courts had any hostility to
the idea of transferable goldsmiths' notes, but that such notes in
bearer form were ambiguous, given the then prevailing ways of
conducting deposit banking business. If it was clear from the
instrument that transfers were contemplated, the courts had no
difficulty. In *Nicholson* v. *Sedgwick* (1697),[24] it was noted that 'the
difference is, where the note is made payable to the party or bearer,
and where it is payable to the party or order; in the latter case the
indorsee has been allowed to bring the action in his own name; for
there can be no great inconvenience, because the indorsement of
the party must appear on the back of the note, or some other thing,
sufficiently intimating his assent, but where it is payable to the
party or bearer, if the bearer be allowed to bring the action in his
own name, it may be very inconvenient; for then any one, who
finds the note by accident, may bring the action'.[25]

Given the variation in goldsmiths' deposit account practices in
the late seventeenth century, it is easy to see why actions by bearers
of goldsmiths' notes would have been thought problematic. A
writing in which a goldsmith promised to pay a certain sum of
money to a named person or bearer might have been intended
either as a circulating note or as a deposit receipt, akin to a bank
passbook. If it were the latter form, then allowing anyone who got

---

[21] Feavearyear, *Pound Sterling*, 107–08; Richards, *Early History of Banking in England*, 40. Examples of such transactions can be found in *Cooksey* v. *Boverie* (1683), 2 Show. 296, and *Ward* v. *Evans* (1703), 2 Ld Raym. 928, 1 Com. 138, 6 Mod. 36, 12 Mod. 521, Holt 120, 2 Salk. 442, 3 Salk. 118.
[22] 3 Lev. 296.   [23] 3 Lev. at 299.
[24] 1 Ld Raym. 180, s.c. sub nom. *Nicholson* v. *Seldnith*, 3 Salk. 67.
[25] 1 Ld Raym. at 181.

hold of it to sue the goldsmith for the amount of the deposit would have been problematic.

In the eighteenth century, engraved bank notes in bearer form became common. Inasmuch as these were obviously intended as circulating notes, the idea that the bearer clause was not adequate evidence of transferability must have come to seem odd. The issue was finally put to rest in *Grant* v. *Vaughan* (1764),[26] where a merchant drew a cash note upon his London banker and gave it to the master of one of his ships. The note was payable 'to ship Fortune or bearer'. The note was lost and afterwards came into the hands of a person who gave value for it without any notice that it had been lost. The Court of King's Bench, by then headed by Lord Mansfield, ruled that the action could be brought by the bearer of the note. Lord Mansfield remarked that the reasons given for the ruling in *Nicholson* v. *Sedgwick* 'were insufficient'; 'that "of the goldsmith's having perhaps paid the money to the original payee himself, before notice from the bearer", can never hold, it cannot happen in the course of business that the money should be paid to the nominee before notice from the bearer'.[27] As business was conducted in the late eighteenth century, that was certainly true. No banker who had given notes for a deposit would repay the deposit without asking for the notes.[28] By then bearer bank notes were common. As Mr Justice Wilmot remarked, the answer to the question whether such notes are in practice negotiated 'is as plain and notorious as that there is a Bank of England'.[29]

THE PROMISSORY NOTES CASES:
DRAWING THE BOUNDARY BETWEEN THE LAW OF BILLS AND THE GENERAL LAW OF OBLIGATIONS

Perhaps no chapter of the early history of the law of bills and notes has been more misunderstood than the story of Chief Justice Holt's decisions in the promissory notes cases, *Clerke* v. *Martin* (1702)[30] and *Buller* v. *Crips* (1703).[31]

---

[26] 3 Burr. 1516.   [27] 3 Burr. at 1522.
[28] When bank notes were lost, the practice seems to have been that the banker would pay them only if the claimant provided indemnity against the risk that the notes would later be presented. *Walmsley* v. *Child* (1749), 1 Ves. Sen. 341; *Glynn* v. *Bank of England* (1750), 2 Ves. Sen. 38.
[29] 3 Burr. at 1526.   [30] 2 Ld Raym. 757, 1 Salk. 129.   [31] 6 Mod. 29.

The cases are often loosely described as holding that promissory notes were not 'negotiable', and they are usually interpreted as showing that Holt held a reactionary and unthinking objection to mercantile innovations, such as the use of goldsmiths' notes as circulating media of exchange.[32] There is, to be sure, language in the cases that suggests this reading. In *Clerke* v. *Martin*, Holt complained that the attempts to sue on notes in the form of actions on the custom of merchants 'amounted to the setting up a new sort of specialty, unknown to the common law, and invented in Lombard Street, which attempted in these matters of bills of exchange to give laws to Westminster Hall',[33] and in *Buller* v. *Crips*, he remarked that 'the notes in question are only an invention of the goldsmiths in Lombard Street, who had a mind to make a law to bind all those that did deal with them'.[34]

The notion that Holt was expressing some reactionary objection to the practice of circulation of goldsmiths' notes is, however, difficult to square with his treatment of other cases involving goldsmiths' notes. Holt presided over the court that established some of the fundamental legal principles that formed the basis of the goldsmith banking system. Indeed, in another case concerning goldsmiths' notes, Holt remarked 'that goldsmiths' bills were governed by the same laws and customs as other bills of exchange'.[35]

To understand why Holt was troubled by the effort to treat promissory notes under the same rules as bills of exchange, one

---

[32] Holden, who takes a somewhat more charitable view of Holt than most, gives a nice compendium of the invective that has ever since been heaped upon Holt by writers on commercial law:

> Thus we are told that 'the case of *Clerke* v. *Martin* was a hasty, intemperate decision of Lord Holt, which was acquiesced in by the other judges, in consequence of his overbearing authority'; that his mind, at the time, 'was not in a proper state for calm deliberation and sound judgment'; that the decision was 'obvious error'; that Holt's attitude showed that he was 'narrow-minded', 'reactionary', 'peevish' and 'perverse'. An even more barbed and scathing comment was made by Mr. Fifoot in a paper read to the Institute of Bankers when he said that after the passing of the 1704 Act 'Lord Holt was left to comfort himself with the reflection that he had held up the course of trade for fifteen years'.

Holden, *History of Negotiable Instruments*, 80–81 (citations omitted).
[33] 2 Ld Raym. at 758.   [34] 6 Mod. at 29.
[35] *Hill* v. *Lewis* (1694), 1 Salk. 132, s.c. Holt 116, Skin. 410, query s.c. *Tassel* v. *Lewis* (1695), 1 Ld Raym. 743.

must start by identifying exactly what the issue was in these cases. In the first place, it appears that the cases did not involve gold-smiths' notes at all, but ordinary promissory notes.[36] The first of them, *Clerke* v. *Martin,* did not even involve a transfer of a note. The action was brought by the original payee of a note against the original maker; the only question was whether the suit could be maintained in the form of an action on the custom of merchants in the fashion of actions on bills of exchange. There was no doubt that the plaintiff could have brought an action to enforce the underlying obligation. Holt explicitly stated that the plaintiff could have brought a general *indebitatus assumpsit* action and that the note could have been admitted as evidence of the debt in that action. He objected only to the attempt to bring the action in the form used for bills of exchange. As Holt put it, 'the maintaining of these actions upon such notes, were innovations upon the rules of the common law; and . . . amounted to the setting up a new sort of specialty, unknown to the common law.'[37] In the second case, *Buller* v. *Crips,* the note had been transferred, but the issue was essentially the same as in *Clerke* v. *Martin.* The defendant gave a note for the price of wine that he purchased from the payee, and the payee indorsed the note to the plaintiff. The plaintiff declared on the custom of merchants as in actions on bills, but the court ruled against that procedure. The plaintiff's lawyer tried to distin-guish the case from *Clerke* v. *Martin* on the grounds that it was an action by an indorsee rather than the original payee, but Holt was of the opinion that the same principles controlled, noting that 'to allow such a note to carry any lien with it were to turn a piece of paper, which is in law but evidence of a parol contract, into a specialty'.[38]

Though the issue in these cases was described by counsel as

---

[36] It is not clear from the reports what sort of note was involved in *Clerke* v. *Martin,* but the note in *Buller* v. *Crips* was certainly an ordinary note rather than a goldsmith's note, for it was originally issued in payment for wine.

[37] 2 Ld Raym. at 758.

[38] 6 Mod. at 29. These remarks have provoked a good deal of discussion in the literature about whether Holt thought that bills were 'specialties'. It seems clear, however, that he was speaking in a somewhat loose or metaphoric sense. Neither Holt nor any other judge of his era thought that bills were to be treated as specialties in the technical sense of formal acknowledgments of obligations under seal. Rather, Holt's point was that notes were ordinary parol contracts, and should not be put in the same category as bills of exchange which had some, though not all, of the procedural advantages of specialties.

whether the notes were 'negotiable', it is obvious that they used that term in a different sense than do modern lawyers. The cases had nothing to do with the rule that a holder in due course takes an instrument free from claims and defences. No such claims or defences were raised, and the note in *Clerke* v. *Martin* had not even been transferred. Indeed, the cases were not even about whether promissory notes were assignable. In *Buller* v. *Crips,* Holt stated that the indorsement of a note was sufficient evidence of assignment to permit the indorsee to bring an action on the underlying obligation in the name of the original payee, and if he did so he could 'convert the money, when recovered, to his own use; for the indorsement amounts at least to an agreement that the indorsee should sue for the money in the name of the indorser, and receive it to his own use; and besides, it is a good authority to the original drawer to pay the money to the indorsee'.[39] Moreover, Holt also suggested that if the action had been brought against the indorser rather than the maker, it would have been permissible to bring it in the form of an action on the custom, on the theory that the payee's indorsement was equivalent to drawing a bill of exchange on the maker payable to the indorsee.

Thus, Holt's objection was only to suits on notes being brought against the original maker as actions founded on the custom of merchants. His comments about turning mere pieces of paper into a new form of specialty suggest that his concern was that permitting such actions would change the facts that the plaintiff had to prove in order to make out a prima facie case.[40] In an *indebitatus assumpsit*, the creditor would have to prove the facts that gave rise to the debt. By contrast, in an action on the custom of merchants, the plaintiff could obtain judgment merely by proving that the instrument had been signed by the defendant; if the defendant disputed the obligation, it would be up to him to prove the

---

[39] 6 Mod. at 30.
[40] In *Potter* v. *Pearson* (1703), 2 Ld Raym. 759, 1 Salk. 129, Holt 33, Holt rejected an attempt to get around *Clerke* v. *Martin* by pleading the custom as a special custom of London, ruling that 'it is a void custom, since it binds a man to pay money without any consideration. For the rule is, ex nudo pacto non oritur actio'. 2 Ld Raym. at 759. In *Cutting* v. *Williams* (1703), 7 Mod. 154, Holt stated that all of the judges had agreed 'that a declaration upon the *custom of merchants* upon a note, subscribed by the defendant to the plaintiff for so much money, or promising so much money, was void; for it tended to make *a note* amount to *a specialty*'. 7 Mod. at 155.

grounds of his defence. We have seen that this difference in the rules of pleading and procedure was precisely the point of the long process of evolution of the law of bills of exchange in the seventeenth century. The question to be answered, then, is why Holt felt that the conception of legal obligations that had developed for bills of exchange was not also appropriate for promissory notes.

The answer may well be that by the end of the seventeenth century it began to appear that the special body of rules for bills, which had developed to accommodate a particular class of mercantile transactions, might swallow up large portions of the common law of general obligations. It is important to remember that the common law had long included a general body of law governing monetary obligations. Monetary obligations had long been enforceable in actions of debt, and by the end of the sixteenth century the action of *assumpsit* had been expanded to cover most forms of debt obligations. In either form of action, however, the debtor had the benefit of significant procedural advantages. In debt on an informal obligation the defendant could wage his law, and in *assumpsit* the creditor had to plead and prove that the obligation was supported by a sufficient consideration. Creditors who wanted better security than mere parol promises could make use of formal sealed bonds or statutory recognizances. Since the only defence to an action in debt on an unconditional bond was a plea of *non est factum* denying its execution, or an acquittance under seal, a debtor who gave a bond for his debt was giving his creditor a formidable collection mechanism. Recognizances were even more severe. The debtor appeared before a public official and acknowledged the obligation in a formal sealed writing which was recorded in the public records. If the obligation was not paid, the creditor could obtain a judgment and proceed directly to execution without any lawsuit. These devices were certainly draconian; yet given the formalities involved in executing bonds and recognizances, it is unlikely that anyone would have done so without understanding the consequences of the act.

Though it had its flaws, the common law of monetary obligations was on the whole a rational and workable system, and one with which both lawyers and lay people were familiar. The common law of monetary obligations was, though, not well suited to the needs of the payment system based on bills of exchange that developed in the seventeenth century. It was to meet the special needs of that system that the judges of the common law courts developed the law of bills and the special procedures for actions on bills. By the end of the seventeenth century, however, the line of demarcation between the special commercial rules governing bills and the general principles of monetary obligations was becoming indistinct.

There are examples in form books of declarations dating from the 1680s and 1690s in which it was said to be the custom of merchants that if any merchant or other person engaged in commerce signs a note or bill in his own hand promising to pay a certain sum of money to another, then he is bound to do so.[41] Presumably many of these actions were successful, and there are at least a few reported decisions that seem to approve the practice, though without any indication that the courts had given careful consideration to the consequences of doing so.[42] By the end of the century, however, the judges began to be concerned that pleaders were pushing this device too far. In *Pearson* v. *Garrett* (1693),[43] the declaration was based on an alleged custom in London that if any merchant or other person signed a bill or note in his own hand promising to pay a certain sum of money at any time mentioned in the bill or note, then he was bound to do so. The instrument in question, however, turned out to be a note in which a young man promised to pay £60 if the payee succeeded in arranging a marriage for him. As the defendant's counsel pointed out, 'if such should be allowed to be within the *custom of merchants*, then every thing which is given without a consideration may as well be within the custom, which would quite change the law'.[44]

Though it seemed clear that a case like *Pearson* v. *Garrett* should be treated under ordinary contract law rather than the special law of bills, it was not clear how to draw the line. The older notion that actions on the custom might be limited to cases involving merchants was probably an effort to draw that line, but it had proven unsuccessful in such cases as *Edgar* v. *Chut* (1663)[45] and *Sarsfield* v. *Witherly* (1689),[46] where persons other than merchants became parties to genuine bills of exchange. What was needed was some

---

[41] Clift's *Entries* includes quite a number of such declarations.
[42] *Anon.* v. *Elborough* (1677), 3 Keb. 765; *Bromwich* v. *Loyd* (1697), 2 Lutw. 1582.
[43] 4 Mod. 242, Skin. 398, Comb. 227.   [44] 4 Mod. at 244.
[45] 1 Keb. 592, 636.
[46] 1 Show. 125, 2 Vent. 292, Holt 112, Carth. 82, Comb. 45, 152.

way of distinguishing commercial cases from non-commercial cases, rather than merchants from other persons. In *Pearson* v. *Garrett*, the contingent nature of the note provided a way out. The court ruled that 'if the note had been given by way of commerce it had been good, but to pay money upon such a contingency cannot be called trading, and therefore not within the custom of merchants'.[47] That solution, however, was of no help in cases of non-commercial, but non-contingent, promises to pay money. In *Woolvil* v. *Young* (1697),[48] the court directly confronted the problem of the practice of declaring on a general custom that if one signs a note or bill then he is bound to pay it. The court rejected the attempt, noting that 'this way of declaring so generally will exclude all considerations which must be averred'.[49] The plaintiff had argued that the declaration said that the defendants were '*residentes et negotiantes*' in the kingdom, but the court pointed out that 'every man is *negotians* in the kingdom; and if the plaintiff would have brought his case within the *custom of merchants*, he ought to have said *commercium habentes*, or have shown that the bill signed was *a bill of exchange*'.[50]

In light of these cases, Holt's position in *Clerke* v. *Martin* and *Buller* v. *Crips* is entirely understandable. Unless some way could be found to define the limits of the law of bills, a creditor might attempt to bring an action on the custom of merchants in any case where he could find some written evidence of the debt. The lawyer's natural sense of caution about radical change must have been aroused by the prospect that all of the law concerning the enforcement of monetary obligations in debt and *assumpsit* – a body of law that had been carefully developed over the past several centuries – might be swept aside as an unanticipated consequence of the development of the law of bills. Moreover, there were legitimate concerns about the fairness of this development to debtors. Since the law had long distinguished very sharply between formal bonds and parol promises, debtors might well have

---

[47] 4 Mod. at 244.   [48] 5 Mod. 367.

[49] Ibid. See also *Burman* v. *Buckle* (1686), Comb. 9, where the declaration alleged the custom as extending to merchants and other persons 'omitting the words commercio utenti', and the court rejected it, noting that 'all the precedents are, commercio utent', except one which passed sub silentio'.

[50] 5 Mod. at 367.

assumed that giving a simple unsealed writing as evidence of a monetary debt had relatively little practical significance. It is virtually impossible to execute a sealed bond unintentionally, and quite unlikely that one would sign a bill of exchange without realizing what it was. It is, however, quite possible to sign a writing without realizing that it might later be construed as a note. Distinguishing between promissory notes and bills of exchange may not have been the perfect solution to the problem of drawing the line between the general law of monetary obligations and the special commercial law of bills of exchange, but it may have seemed better than no solution at all.

Though Holt's decisions were entirely understandable, they obviously were not well received. Parliament overturned them with the statute of 3 & 4 Anne, c. 9 which provided that all 'notes in writing . . . made and signed by any person or persons . . . whereby such person or persons . . . promise to pay to any other person or persons . . . or their order, or unto bearer, any sum of money mentioned in such note shall be assignable or endorsable over, in the same manner as inland bills of exchange . . . according to the custom of merchants; and that the person or persons to whom such money is or shall be by such note made payable, shall and may maintain an action for the same, in the same manner as he, she, or they, might do upon any inland bill of exchange, made or drawn according to the custom of merchants'. It is hard to say exactly why Holt's decisions raised sufficient objection to prompt the enactment of the statute. One possibility – which would also explain Holt's remark that the notes involved in the cases were an 'invention of the goldsmiths in Lombard Street, who had a mind to make a law to bind all those that did deal with them' – is that the goldsmiths were concerned about the cases not from the perspective of their own note issues, but because they wished to be able to use the simplified procedure of actions on the custom to collect notes that they had discounted as part of the lending side of their business. It may, however, be a mistake to regard the statute of 3 & 4 Anne solely as a reaction to Holt's decisions in the promissory notes cases. Throughout the seventeenth century, economic writers had been advocating that English merchants adopt the Dutch practice of using transferable bills of debt in their trade and proposing that Parliament enact legislation to encourage or require the practice.[51] The dispute over Holt's decisions may simply have provided the occasion for enactment of measures that had long been urged for other reasons.

Though the statute overturned Holt's decisions, subsequent experience only confirmed his intuitions that there was a need for some way of distinguishing commercial from non-commercial instruments, and that including notes in the category of commercial instruments would be particularly problematic. Throughout the eighteenth century, the courts were confronted with cases in which actions were brought on the custom of merchants on writings that arose out of transactions far removed from the commercial settings for which the law of bills had been devised. Cases were brought under the statute on writings in which people had promised to pay money 'on account of [my] mother',[52] or 'if my brother doth not pay it within such a time',[53] or 'on the day of my marriage'.[54] Other cases involved notes payable to relatives found among the papers of deceased persons,[55] or payable a certain time after the death of the maker's father,[56] or payable on the death of a certain person 'provided he leaves [the makers] sufficient to pay the said sum, or if we shall be otherwise able to pay it'.[57] There

[51] Malynes, *Lex Mercatoria*, 71–73; Roberts, *Treasure of Traffike*, 31; Child, *Brief Observations concerning Trade*, 6; Child, *New Discourse of Trade*, 106–12. It is worth noting that the problem addressed in these tracts was not so much that English law was hostile to the transfer of debts, as that it was not the practice of English merchants to use written evidences of debts in their credit sales. Sir Josiah Child makes this point quite explicitly. 'The difficulty seems not to be so much in making of a Law to this purpose, as reducing it to practice, because we have been so long accustomed to buy and sell Goods by verbal Contracts only, that Rich and Great Men for some time will be apt to think it a Diminution of their Reputation, to have Bills under their Hands and Seals demanded of them for Goods bought; and meaner Men will fear the loosing of their Customers, by insisting upon having such Bills for what they sell'. Child, *New Discourse of Trade*, 106. Child proposed that a statute be enacted that would not simply permit the transfer of bills of debt, but would require merchants to begin using written bills of debts. Ibid., 107. The campaign of the seventeenth-century writers was not so much a plea for English law to accommodate the universal need of merchants for transfer of debts as it was an instance of the tendency of seventeenth-century English economic writers to assume that English commercial practice could be changed by enacting suitable legislation.
[52] *Garnet* v. *Clarke* (1709), 11 Mod. 226.
[53] *Appleby* v. *Biddle* (1717), cited in *Morice* v. *Lee* (1725), 8 Mod. 362.
[54] *Barnesley* v. *Baldwyn* (1741), 7 Mod. 417.
[55] *Disher* v. *Disher* (1712), 1 P. Wms. 204.
[56] *Colehan* v. *Cooke* (1743), Willes 393, 2 Str. 1217.
[57] *Roberts* v. *Peake* (1757), 1 Burr. 323.

were also cases where persons were sued on writings that could be construed as inland bills, but might well have been intended as nothing more than letters.[58]

The issues raised in such cases were matters routinely dealt with under various branches of the ordinary common law system, such as the rules on the consideration necessary to support an action in *assumpsit*, the formalities necessary for wills, or the enforceability of assignments of expected bequests. Yet if the actions could be brought on the custom of merchants, they would be treated under an entirely different set of rules. In most of these cases, it was argued that the statute of 3 & 4 Anne, like the law of bills in general, was only intended to apply to instruments given in commercial settings. The statute, however, was written in such broad and general terms it could not plausibly be interpreted as applying only to commercial cases. Instead, the courts were forced to devise complicated and not wholly satisfactory rules about whether notes or bills could be made payable upon contingencies, or at uncertain times, or out of particular funds; issues that are still with us in modern negotiable instruments law.

Whether Holt's proposal to limit the scope of commercial law by excluding promissory notes would have fared any better is hard to say. It is, however, a gross distortion to regard his decisions in *Clerke* v. *Martin* and *Buller* v. *Crips* as the raging of an intemperate reactionary against commercial and financial developments. Rather, they were an effort, albeit unsuccessful, to deal with the inherent problem of defining the limits of commercial law.

RIGHTS OF BONA FIDE HOLDERS

Although one of the themes of this book is that the concept of negotiability has been given undue emphasis in the orthodox accounts of the early history of the law of bills, it is certainly true that the rules protecting bona fide holders against claims and defences were well established by the late eighteenth century.

---

[58] *Josceline* v. *Lassere* (1713), Fort. 281, 10 Mod. 294, 316 (action brought on writing in which someone instructed monthly payments to be made 'out of his growing subsistence'); *Jenney* v. *Herle* (1724), 2 Ld Raym. 1361, 8 Mod. 265, 11 Mod. 384, 1 Str. 591 (action brought on writing in which someone instructed someone to pay a sum out of the money in his hands that belonged to the proprietors of a mine).

With respect to a bona fide holder's rights to a lost or stolen bill, as early as 1698 Chief Justice Holt ruled at *nisi prius* that an action in trover would not lie against a person who had given a valuable consideration for a bearer bank bill that the plaintiff had lost.[59] There were also several cases in the late seventeenth and early eighteenth centuries that implicitly recognized the special rights of bona fide holders, in that they indicated that a person who had lost a bill of exchange or bank note could recover the money only if sufficient indemnity was given to protect against the risk that someone else might present the instrument.[60] In a series of cases during Lord Mansfield's tenure as Chief Justice of the King's Bench, the rule that a bona fide holder of a lost or stolen instrument could obtain a good title was firmly established. The leading case, *Miller* v. *Race* (1758),[61] involved a Bank of England note that had been stolen from the mail and passed to an innkeeper. Displaying his characteristic concern that the rules of commercial law be settled and clear, Mansfield carefully articulated the rationale for the rule, noting that 'bank notes ... are not goods, nor securities, nor documents for debts, nor are so esteemed: but are treated as money, as cash, in the ordinary course and transaction of business, by the general consent of mankind, which gives them the credit and currency of money, to all intents and purposes'.[62] He also took pains to clarify prior reported decisions, particularly *Ford* v. *Hopkins* (1700),[63] in which Chief Justice Holt was reported to have said that since bank notes were identifiable they were to be treated like ordinary goods. Mansfield stated that the case must have been erroneously reported, both on the specific point that bank notes were to be treated like ordinary goods, and on the significance of identifiability. 'It is a pity that reporters sometimes catch at quaint expressions that may happen to be dropped at the Bar or Bench; and mistake their meaning. It has been quaintly said, "that the reason why money can not be followed is, because it has no ear-mark:" but this is not true. The true reason is, upon account of

---

[59] *Anon.* (1698), 1 Ld Raym. 738, 1 Salk. 126, 3 Salk. 71.
[60] *Tercese* v. *Geray* (1677), Finch 301; *Walmsley* v. *Child* (1749), 1 Ves. Sen. 341; *Glynn* v. *Bank of England* (1750), 2 Ves. Sen. 38.
[61] 1 Burr. 452.   [62] 1 Burr. at 457.
[63] Holt 119. *Ford* itself involved stolen lottery tickets, but the report states that Holt had distinguished money, which could not be recovered, from 'bank-notes, Exchequer notes, or lottery-tickets, &c.' which could be recovered because they 'are distinguishable, and they have distinct marks or numbers on them'.

the currency of it: it can not be recovered after it has passed in currency'.[64] Though much of the discussion in *Miller* v. *Race* was directed to the special nature of bank notes, subsequent decisions during Mansfield's tenure established that the same rule would apply to other instruments. *Grant* v. *Vaughan* (1764)[65] held that a bona fide holder of a stolen draft drawn on a banker payable 'to ship Fortune or bearer' was entitled to enforce it against the drawer, and *Peacock* v. *Rhodes* (1781)[66] applied the same rule to an inland bill of exchange payable to a specified person or order and indorsed in blank.[67]

Although the principles established in these cases provided considerable protection to persons who took instruments, it is worth noting that it was not the case that a bona fide holder of any bill or note took without risk that it had been lost or stolen. If an instrument was payable to a specified person or order, a subsequent holder had to prove that the signature of the first indorser was genuine.[68] A remote party might well have no way of knowing whether the payee's indorsement was genuine. The holder, however, would not be entirely without recourse if it turned out that the payee's indorsement was forged. The usual practice was that bills were indorsed upon each transfer, even though the indorsements were blank rather than special indorsements. Although only the first indorsement was necessary to establish the title of subsequent parties, the additional indorsement added security to the bill. As the saying went, the more indorsements, the better the bill.[69] Even if the holder was unable to prove the payee's indorsement, and therefore could not recover against the acceptor or drawer, the holder could still proceed against the person who

---

[64] 1 Burr. at 457. The difference between the 'identifiability' rationale and the 'currency' rationale for the rule in *Miller* v. *Race* is explored, primarily from the perspective of modern law, in Rogers, 'Negotiability, Property, and Identity', 501–05.

[65] 3 Burr. 1516.   [66] 2 Doug. 633.

[67] The instrument in *Peacock* was in fact a form of bank draft, for the drawee of the bill was Smith, Payne, and Smith, a well-known London banking firm. See Pressnell, *Country Banking in the Industrial Revolution*, 105–09. The report, however, refers to the instrument only as an inland bill of exchange, and nothing in the case seems to turn on the fact that it was drawn on a banking firm.

[68] *Smith* v. *Chester* (1787), 1 T.R. 654.

[69] *Claxton* v. *Swift* (1686), 2 Show. 494, 496, s.c. Comb. 4, 3 Mod. 86, 1 Lutw. 878, Skin. 255; *Bomley* v. *Frazier* (1721), 1 Str. 441; *Heylyn* v. *Adamson* (1758), 2 Burr. 669, 675.

indorsed the bill to him, or any prior indorser whose signature was genuine.[70] Thus, in taking an indorsed bill a person was necessarily relying to some extent on the credit of the person with whom he was dealing.

The aspect of negotiability that receives most attention in modern law is the rule that a bona fide holder takes free from most defences that the obligor might have raised against the original payee. Inasmuch as mercantile instruments were commonly circulated as a medium of payment in the seventeenth and eighteenth centuries, one would expect to find many cases in this era about whether defences such as breach of warranty, fraud, failure of consideration, and the like could be asserted against indorsees. Curiously, however, such cases seem to have been rather uncommon. By the end of Lord Mansfield's tenure as Chief Justice of the King's Bench in 1788, there were 300 or more reported cases on the law of bills, yet only a half dozen or so involved issues about whether a bona fide holder took free from or was subject to defences.

Although there are few cases in point, it seems fairly clear that the rule that a bona fide holder takes free from defences was recognized in the seventeenth and eighteenth centuries. In 1697, a person who had been sued on a bill of exchange sought relief in equity on the grounds that no consideration was given for the bill by the original payee. The Lord Chancellor denied the request, noting that to grant relief against 'an honest creditor [who came] by this bill fairly for the satisfaction of a just debt . . . would tend to destroy trade which is carried on every where by bills of exchange'.[71] By the late eighteenth century, one finds statements suggesting that the rules on defences were well settled. For example, in *Peacock* v. *Rhodes* (1781),[72] Lord Mansfield remarked that:

The holder of a bill of exchange, or promissory note, is not to be considered in the light of an assignee of the payee. An assignee must take the thing assigned, subject to all the equity to which the original party was

---

[70] *Critchlow* v. *Parry* (1809), 2 Camp. 182. Cf. *Lambert* v. *Oakes* (1699), 1 Ld Raym. 443, 12 Mod. 244, Holt 117, 118, 1 Salk. 127 (indorser of promissory note liable even though maker's signature was forged).

[71] *Anon.* (1697), 1 Com. 43. See also *Smith* v. *Haytwell* (1747), Amb. 66, 3 Atk. 566 (injunction granted to prevent payee of note given without legal consideration from transferring it, 'for the plaintiff will be otherwise without a remedy, if this note is disposed of for valuable consideration, and without notice').

[72] 2 Doug. 633.

subject. If this rule applied to bills and promissory notes, it would stop their currency. The law is settled, that a holder coming fairly by a bill or note, has nothing to do with the transaction between the original parties; unless perhaps in the single case, (which is a hard one, but has been determined,) of a note for money won at play.[73]

Most of the relatively few reported decisions involving defences dealt not with the general rule that bona fide holders take free from ordinary contractual defences, but with the exception to that rule for cases where the instruments were given in illegal transactions. In *Hussey* v. *Jacob* (1696)[74] it was ruled that the acceptor of a bill could defend an action by the payee on the grounds that the bill had been given for a gambling debt, but Chief Justice Holt stated obiter that the case would be different if the bill had been indorsed to a bona fide holder. However, when the issue was squarely presented in *Boyer* v. *Bampton* (1741),[75] the court ruled that the statutes making gambling contracts void necessarily implied that even a bona fide holder was precluded from recovering on a note that had been given for a gambling debt. During Mansfield's tenure as Chief Justice, a similar issue was presented in *Lowe* v. *Waller* (1781),[76] where the acceptor of a bill sought to raise the defence of usury when sued by indorsees who had taken the bill for fair value and without any notice of the defect in the original transaction. The court felt compelled to rule that the defence of usury could be asserted even against a bona fide holder, though Mansfield noted that he reached that conclusion with some reluctance: 'We have considered this case very attentively, and, I own, with a great leaning and wish on my part that the law should turn out to be in favour of the plaintiffs. But the words of the Act are too strong. Besides, we cannot get over the case on the statute against gaming, which stands on the same ground.'[77]

---

[73] 2 Doug. at 636. Similarly, *Thomas* v. *Bishop* (1733), 7 Mod. 180, Cas. t. Hard. 1, 2 Str. 955, 2 Barn. K.B. 320, 335, held that an acceptor who signed his own name was personally liable and could not introduce evidence that he was acting on behalf of a company. The court stated that 'if any evidence to destroy the bill itself should be allowed, it would be very dangerous for any one to take an indorsement, and would prevent the circulation of bills in a great measure'. 7 Mod. at 181–82. There are also several cases noted in treatises, but not included in the standard reports, recognizing the rule that bona fide holders take free from defences. *Snelling* v. *Briggs* (1741), cited in Buller, *Nisi Prius*, 274; *Morris* v. *Lee* (1786), cited in Bayley, *Law of Bills of Exchange*, 74.

[74] 1 Ld Raym. 87, Carth. 356, 1 Com. 4, Holt 328, 5 Mod. 170, 175, 12 Mod. 96, 1 Salk. 344.

[75] 7 Mod. 334, 2 Str. 1155.   [76] 2 Doug. 736.   [77] 2 Doug. at 744.

Though the rule that a bona fide holder takes free from ordinary contractual defences seems to have been settled, it is somewhat surprising that there are so few reported decisions dealing with such issues. One possible explanation is that the rule was so firmly established that no one even bothered to try to raise ordinary defences when sued by indorsees. That, however, seems unlikely. Parties who had such defences to raise could always have disputed whether the indorsee qualified as a bona fide holder, yet the requirements for bona fide holder protections do not seem to have been matters of significant dispute in the eighteenth century.[78] A more likely, though still partial, explanation may be that the form of many bill transactions in the eighteenth century was such that the defences familiar to twentieth-century lawyers would commonly not arise. Twentieth-century lawyers have assumed that in the typical bill transaction the person expected to pay the bill (the drawee-acceptor) incurred the obligation on it for the purchase price of goods sold. Accordingly, it would seem likely that the obligor would resist payment of the bill on the basis of defences arising out of the sale. Undoubtedly there were transactions of that form in the eighteenth century, and they may have even become the rule by the middle of the nineteenth century. Nonetheless, in the era in which the commission merchant system played a major role in the distribution of goods, many bills would arise out of a somewhat different form of transaction. A merchant might draw on his factor to make use of the funds in the factor's hands from the sale of the principal's goods, or on a banking house which had agreed to accept his bills as a form of finance. The obligation of the drawee-acceptor on the bill in such transactions was *not* an embodiment of a buyer's obligation to pay for goods purchased on credit. Rather, it was either a factor's obligation to remit collected funds to his principal, or a merchant banker's obligation to honour the commitment made when the banker accepted the bill. In such cases, it is hardly surprising that we do not see disputes about

[78] The opinions in *Miller* v. *Race*, *Grant* v. *Vaughan*, and *Peacock* v. *Rhodes*, indicate that the question whether the plaintiff truly took the instrument for value and without notice was inquired into at trial, but no disputes on that issue were raised when the cases were considered by the full bench. By the nineteenth century, however, there are a fair number of cases concerning the standards for bona fide holder protections. *Lawson* v. *Weston* (1801), 4 Esp. 56; *Gill* v. *Cubitt* (1824), 3 Barn. & Cress. 466; *Crook* v. *Jadis* (1834), 5 Barn. & Adol. 909; *Goodman* v. *Harvey* (1836), 4 Ad. & E. 870.

breach of warranty and other sales defences that the traditional legal history leads us to expect.

Although the circumstances of bill transactions in the classical era shed some light on the puzzling absence of discussion of the sale of goods defences that modern lawyers assume to be so significant, this cannot be a full explanation. Whether or not it was the archetypal bill transaction, it was certainly not unknown for a bill to be issued for the price of goods sold on credit.[79] Moreover, if a bill had been circulated as a medium of payment, an indorser might well incur his obligation on it in connection with the purchase of goods. The assumption that the principles of negotiability were essential to preclude the assertion of breach of warranty and other sales law defences against transferees is, however, somewhat anachronistic. In the eighteenth century, such defences generally could not be raised even against the original holder of a bill. As Lord Tenterden, Chief Justice of the King's Bench, put it in an 1830 decision,

> the cases ... have completely established the distinction between an action for the price of the goods, and an action on the security given for them. In the former, the value only may be recovered; in the latter ... the party holding bills given for the price of goods supplied can recover upon them, unless there has been a total failure of consideration. If the consideration fails partially, as by the inferiority of the article furnished to that ordered, the buyer must seek his remedy by a cross action.[80]

It was not until the procedural developments of the late nineteenth century concerning set-off and counterclaim[81] that one who had given a bill or note for goods was able to defend on grounds of breach of warranty or the like. Thus, the problem for which negotiability is usually assumed to be the solution did not develop until well after the period that the law of bills and notes became settled.

The best explanation of the seemingly surprising paucity of cases about breach of warranty and other sales law defences, however, lies in a problem of anachronism of a different sort. The usual view of the importance of negotiability is based on the

---

79 E.g., *Tye* v. *Gwynne* (1810), 2 Camp. 346.
80 *Obbard* v. *Betham* (1830), M. & M. 483. See also *Tye* v. *Gwynne* (1810), 2 Camp. 346; *Morgan* v. *Richardon* (n.d.), 1 Camp. 40n, 7 East 482n.
81 It was not until the Supreme Court of Judicature Act of 1873, 36 & 37 Vict., c. 66, that counterclaims became generally available in actions in the common law courts.

assumption that the major concern of the law of bills was whether the party expected to pay could raise defences. As we shall see in the next chapter, most of the difficult issues in the law of bills arose out of the different and more serious problems that arose when the person who was expected to pay became insolvent and thus would not have been worth suing whether or not he could have raised defences.

9

THE LAW OF BILLS AND NOTES IN THE EIGHTEENTH CENTURY

During the eighteenth century, the courts were confronted with so many cases and issues involving bills that a comprehensive survey of the history of the law in that period could easily occupy an entire volume itself. No effort will be made herein to examine all of the eighteenth-century developments in detail.[1] Rather, this chapter will discuss several of the principal legal issues raised by the structure of the eighteenth-century financial system. The chapter concludes with an assessment of the contribution of Lord Mansfield to the development of the law of bills.

Accustomed as we are today to our modern payment systems, it is hard for us fully to appreciate the practical and legal problems presented by the financial systems of earlier times. Indeed, the overemphasis of the concept of negotiability in most accounts of the history of the law of bills is probably attributable to anachronistic assumptions about commercial practice. The holder in due course rules are commonly assumed to have been essential in a world in which private instruments circulated as payment media because people would be unwilling to take an instrument if the original obligor could resist payment by raising defences arising out of the transaction in which it was issued. Implicit in that argument is the assumption that at the time instruments were passed in payment the transferee knew that the person who was expected to pay it was legally bound to do so, and was capable of paying.

In the seventeenth and eighteenth centuries, the law of bills had to deal with a different, and in many ways more difficult, kind of

---

[1] Holden's *History of Negotiable Instruments* remains useful as a survey of eighteenth- and nineteenth-century cases concerning bills and notes, though in many instances Holden's interpretation of the developments is at odds with the account presented herein.

case. Merchants and others would regularly have to take bills and notes as a form of payment, since there frequently was no other available payment medium. Yet at the time the instruments were taken, there would have been no way of knowing for sure whether they would be paid. A bill or note might have been transferred from hand to hand in a long chain of payment transactions on the assumption that it would be paid by the drawee or maker. In the case of bills, however, the drawee was not legally bound until acceptance. Thus bills would have been passed from person to person long before it was known whether the drawee would incur any legal obligation to pay. In the case of notes or bills circulated after acceptance, the maker or drawee was legally bound to pay, but a person taking the instrument had to confront another uncertainty. Would the obligor be capable of paying, or would he have become insolvent and be unable to pay regardless of whether he might have had defences? If the instrument was dishonoured, some or all of the transactions in which the instrument had been transferred might be unsettled as holders of the bill sought to shift the loss to prior parties. A very large part of the corpus of the law of bills and notes in the eighteenth century arose out of these problems.

ACCEPTANCE

The rules concerning acceptance of bills occupy a fairly minor role in present day commercial law. In early-twentieth-century treatises on the law of bills, one finds only brief treatment of acceptance, and it goes essentially unmentioned in most books of the late twentieth century.[2] By contrast, in a typical bills treatise of the late eighteenth or early nineteenth century, the chapter on acceptance was a major part of the book. In the first edition of Bayley, *Law of Bills of Exchange*, for example, the chapter on

---

[2] In Bigelow, *Law of Bills, Notes, and Cheques* (1893), acceptance accounts for only 10 pages of a 255 page work, about 4%. In Britton, *Law of Bills and Notes* (1943), acceptance is treated in only 24 pages of an 1,129 page book, about 2%. In the currently dominant treatise on American commercial law, acceptance is treated in one page, and the passage consists entirely of paraphrase and quotation of the Uniform Commercial Code sections with no case citations or discussion at all. White and Summers, *Uniform Commercial Code*, 558.

acceptance accounted for about a quarter of the discussion of the substantive law of bills and notes.[3]

Since the main function of bills was to make use of funds in another's hands as a medium of payment, a critical question for the holder of the bill was whether the drawee would agree to pay the bill. Thus, it is hardly surprising that issues about acceptance were matters of major concern in the seventeenth and eighteenth centuries. Many of the disputed issues about acceptance of bills grew out of the tension between the desirability of having simple and certain rules about liabilities on bills and the need to take account of the practical realities of the transactions in which bills were issued and transferred.

In order for an instrument to qualify as a bill or note, it had to include an unconditional promise or order for the payment of money. Accordingly, it seems somewhat surprising that it was well established that an acceptance could be conditional. When a bill was presented for acceptance, the drawee could respond that he would pay the bill if certain conditions were satisfied. If the holder was unsatisfied with that response, he could treat the bill as dishonoured and proceed against prior parties; yet if the holder was willing to do so, he could take the conditional acceptance, and the acceptor could be sued in an action on the bill provided that the condition was satisfied.[4] The anomaly is readily explained once it is recalled that bills commonly arose out of the relationship between a merchant and his factor or commission agent. Virtually all the conditional acceptance cases arose out of the same fact pattern. A merchant shipped goods to his factor or commission agent and drew a bill on him for the expected proceeds of the sale. The drawee was willing to accept only on condition that the goods in fact were received and sold. For example, in *Smith* v. *Abbott* (1741),[5] the drawee accepted a bill 'to pay it when the goods consigned to him, and for which the bill was drawn, were sold'.

---

[3] The first edition of Bayley was a small book, having only six chapters totalling seventy pages of text. Of this, the last two chapters, from pages 42 to 70, dealt with procedure and evidence in actions on bills. Thus only the first four chapters, pages 1 to 41, dealt with substantive questions, of which one chapter of ten pages covered acceptance.

[4] *Anon.* (1701), 12 Mod. 447; *Smith* v. *Abbott* (1741), 2 Str. 1152, 7 Mod. 426; *Julian* v. *Shobrooke* (1753), 2 Wils. K.B. 9; *Mason* v. *Hunt* (1779), 1 Doug. 297; *Sproat* v. *Matthews* (1786), 1 T.R. 182.

[5] 2 Str. 1152, 7 Mod. 426.

The goods were sold, but the drawee refused to pay. In the action against the drawee on his acceptance, it was argued that the uncertainty of such a conditional acceptance should prevent it from having the usual effect of binding the acceptor to an action on the bill. The argument, though, was rejected, on the grounds that 'it will affect trade, if factors are not allowed to use this caution, when bills are drawn before they have an opportunity to dispose of the goods'.[6]

A similar problem was presented by partial acceptances. In *Weggersloffe* v. *Keene* (1719),[7] a merchant residing in Norway drew a bill for £127 on an English merchant. Upon presentment, the drawee checked his accounts and found that he had only £100 due to the drawer. Accordingly, he wrote on the bill that he would accept it only for £100. Upon the drawee's failure to pay even the £100, the holder brought suit on the bill for the £100. The drawee argued that although the undertaking might have the effect of a simple contract, it should not be regarded as giving rise to liability on the bill itself because allowing partial acceptances would greatly confuse bill transactions and impair the circulation of bills.[8] As in the conditional acceptance cases, however, the need to adapt the rules on acceptances to the practical realities of the commission merchant system won out over the concern for facilitating the system of bill circulation. The court ruled that partial acceptances were permissible.[9]

One of the basic rules of twentieth-century negotiable instruments law is that a person is liable on a bill only if his signature appears on it.[10] In earlier times, however, a drawee could be bound as an acceptor of a bill even without a written acceptance on the bill. Though that seems anomalous from the perspective of the modern notion that the entire obligation represented by a negotiable instrument must be found within the four corners of the instrument, the rules on extrinsic and parol acceptances made good sense as bills were used in the seventeenth and eighteenth centuries.

A bill would commonly play a great deal of its role in the

---

[6] 2 Str. at 1152. [7] 1 Str. 214. [8] 1 Str. at 219.

[9] Drawees were also allowed to accept a bill on terms varying in other respects from the original tenor of the bill. *Petit* v. *Benson* (1697), Comb. 452; *Walker* v. *Atwood* (1708), 11 Mod. 190.

[10] Bills of Exchange Act §§ 17(2), 23; UCC §§ 3–401, 3–409.

payment system before it was presented to the drawee for acceptance or payment. The main point of bills was that they permitted a person in one location to make use of funds in the hands of his correspondent in another location. Frequently the bill would be passed from party to party in a series of payment transactions as it made its way from the drawer to the drawee. The facts of the well-known case of *Peacock* v. *Rhodes* (1781)[11] provide a good example. Rhodes, in Halifax in west Yorkshire, drew a bill on his correspondent in London payable to Ingham or order. The bill passed through several hands before being stolen from Joseph Fisher at York, about forty miles north-east of Halifax. We next find the bill forty miles further to the north-east at the coastal port of Scarborough where it was taken by a mercer in payment for cloth. From Scarborough the bill presumably was sent down to London by the regular coastal shipping routes, though it was dishonoured by the drawee in London. Thus, from the facts of the case one can trace the physical path of the bill through a series of transfers closer and closer to the drawee.[12]

If the drawee of a bill accepted and paid it, all of the transactions between prior parties would remain settled. If, however, the bill was not accepted or paid, some or all of the prior transactions would be unwound as actions were brought against prior parties to enforce their liability as drawer or indorser. Inasmuch as it promoted finality in the payment system to hold drawees liable as acceptors, it is not surprising that the requirements for acceptance were quite liberal. It was settled quite early that an acceptance need not be in writing. In *Anon.* (1698)[13] Chief Justice Holt noted that 'a bill of exchange might be accepted by parol, tho' the usual way be to do it by writing', and many other cases in the eighteenth century confirmed that rule.[14] Indeed, there seems to have been a

11 2 Doug. 633.
12 In *Goupy* v. *Harden* (1816), 7 Taunt. 159, we can follow the path of a bill in international commerce. The bill was drawn in London on a house in Lisbon. The payee indorsed it to a firm in Paris, who indorsed it to a firm in Genoa, who had it presented to the drawee in Lisbon.
13 Holt 296, s.c. 12 Mod. 345.
14 *Lumley* v. *Palmer* (1734), Cas. t. Hard. 74, 7 Mod. 216, 2 Str. 1000; *Clavey* v. *Dolbin* (1736), Cas. t. Hard. 278; *Powell* v. *Monnier* (1737), 1 Atk. 611; *Julian* v. *Shobrooke* (1753), 2 Wils. K.B. 9; *Sproat* v. *Matthews* (1786), 1 T.R. 182; Marius, *Bills of Exchange*, 16–17. *Lumley* v. *Palmer* upheld parol acceptances of inland bills despite the provision of the Promissory Notes Act of 1704 stating that 'no acceptance of any such inland bill of exchange shall be sufficient to charge

tendency to construe equivocal acts or words by the drawee as acceptance rather than dishonour. As Molloy put it, 'a small matter amounts to an acceptance'.[15] In *Sproat* v. *Matthews* (1786),[16] Judge Willes remarked that 'the Court has not of late been very nice with regard to what shall be construed to be an acceptance . . . indeed at present, almost any thing amounts to an acceptance'.[17]

As was noted in chapter 5, acceptance financing played an important role in the domestic and international credit system of the seventeenth and eighteenth centuries. The acceptance of a bill of exchange was a form of credit transaction even in the simplest bill transaction where a merchant shipped goods to his commission agent and drew a bill on the agent for the proceeds of the sale. To the extent that the drawer could obtain immediate value for the bill from someone before the drawee was called upon to pay it, the bill was being used as a credit device in addition to its role as a payment medium. The credit aspect of bills was even more prominent if the factor was willing to allow the merchant to draw a bill in advance of the factor's sale of the goods. If the factor's credit was good enough so that the merchant could discount the bill, then the factor, by lending his credit to the drawer, was effectively providing financing to the drawer.

This pattern of bill finance gave rise to one of the major issues in the law of bills in the eighteenth and early nineteenth centuries, the lengthy dispute over the issue of 'virtual' and 'extrinsic' acceptances.[18] In the bill finance transactions of the sort just described, the bill commonly played its principal credit role before it actually arrived at the drawee for acceptance. For example, if an American exporter was known to be a customer of a leading English merchant banking firm, such as the House of Baring, he would be able to obtain financing in America by discounting the bills he drew on Baring's. The critical point, however, was that others in the local community knew that the American merchant was entitled to draw

---

any person whatsoever, unless the same be under-written or indorsed in writing thereupon'. 3 & 4 Anne, c. 9, § 5. Chief Justice Hardwicke interpreted this provision as dealing only with liability for costs, damages, and interest, not with the liability of parties for the principal amount of the bills. Holden, *History of Negotiable Instruments*, 54–56, 103–05.

15 Molloy, *De Jure Maritimo*, 279.   16 1 T.R. 182.   17 1 T.R. at 185.

18 In the jargon of nineteenth-century bills law, 'extrinsic acceptance' referred to a collateral written undertaking to accept a bill already in existence, while 'virtual acceptance' referred to a promise to accept bills to be drawn in the future.

on Baring's. Thus, to facilitate the operations of the American merchant, Baring's might, in one form or another, have let it be known that he was entitled to draw on them, or, at the extreme, might have made a specific promise to accept specific bills that he drew.[19] Such undertakings seem to have been common in mercantile practice from an early date, for the seventeenth-century works on mercantile affairs include discussions of such letters of credit.[20] In the late eighteenth and early nineteenth centuries, precise specification of the effect of such undertakings became a major issue of controversy in English and American law.

In 1765, the issue came before the King's Bench in the famous case of *Pillans* v. *Van Mierop* (1765).[21] Pillans and Rose, a Rotterdam merchant banking firm, had agreed to accept bills for White, a merchant in Ireland, on the condition that White would arrange for Pillans to obtain reimbursement from a major London firm. White arranged for Van Mierop and Hopkins, in London, to reimburse Pillans by accepting bills drawn on them. Pillans paid White's bills and then wrote to Van Mierop for assurances that they would provide reimbursement. Van Mierop answered that they would accept bills drawn on them by Pillans. Van Mierop, however, refused to accept the bills drawn by Pillans, because White had become insolvent in the interim. The *Pillans* case has long attracted attention from scholars of contracts law, in large part because of the passages in Lord Mansfield's opinion suggesting that the doctrine of consideration should not be applied to preclude enforcement of promises made in mercantile transactions.[22] Some of the language in the opinions, however, suggests that rather than analysing the case as a contractual action for breach of the promise to accept, the letter from Van Mierop to Pillans could be treated as an acceptance, so that Van Mierop would be liable as acceptor of the bills that Pillans drew on them.

---

[19] Hidy, *House of Baring*, 136–37.   [20] E.g., Malynes, *Lex Mercatoria*, 76–77.
[21] 3 Burr. 1663.
[22] 'I take it, that the ancient notion about the want of consideration was for the sake of evidence only: for when it is reduced into writing, as in covenants, specialties, bonds, &c. there was no objection to the want of consideration. And the statute of frauds proceeded on the same principle. In commercial cases amongst merchants, the want of consideration is not an objection'. 3 Burr. at 1669. On that point, *Pillans* is generally said to have been overruled by *Rann* v. *Hughes* (1778), 4 Bro. P.C. 27, 7 T.R. 350.

Mr Justice Wilmot noted that 'whether this be an actual acceptance, or an agreement to accept, it ought equally to bind. An agreement to accept a bill "to be drawn in the future" would (as it seems to me) by connection and relation, bind on account of the antecedent relation. And I see no difference between its being before or after the bill was drawn'.[23]

English decisions in the early nineteenth century cut back considerably on the expansive view of acceptance taken in *Pillans*. The courts continued to hold that a separate promise to accept a bill that had already been drawn could operate as an acceptance,[24] but that rule was reversed by an 1821 statute which required that an acceptance be written on the bill itself.[25] Even before the statute, the courts had ruled that a promise to accept bills to be drawn in the future could not be treated as an acceptance itself.[26] American courts, however, generally held that a promise to accept bills not yet drawn could render the drawee liable as acceptor of bills later drawn under the promise.[27] The difference between the English and American rules became a matter of major import in the mid-nineteenth century. In 1837 the Bank of England decided to tighten up credit by, among other things, refusing financial accommodation to three major British merchant banking firms that had extensive dealings in the finance of American trade. The three firms promptly failed, with the result that some $8 million to $10 million worth of bills of exchange drawn by American merchants on the British houses were returned dishonoured, setting off a chain of bankruptcies among American cotton exporters and other merchants.[28] Many of the protested bills had been drawn under some form of letter of credit or other assurance of acceptance, giving rise to extensive litigation in the American courts about whether the British houses were bound either as acceptors or for breach of a promise to accept.[29]

---

[23] 3 Burr. at 1672–73.   [24] *Clarke* v. *Cock* (1803), 4 East 57.

[25] 1 & 2 Geo. IV, c. 78, § 2 (1821).

[26] *Johnson* v. *Collings* (1800), 1 East 98; *Bank of Ireland* v. *Archer & Daly* (1843), 11 M. & W. 383.

[27] *Coolidge* v. *Payson,* (1817) 15 U.S. (2 Wheat.) 66.

[28] The episode is described in Smith, *Second Bank of the United States*, 186–88; and Hammond, *Banks and Politics in America*, 457–62.

[29] *Russel* v. *Wiggin,* (1842) 21 F. Cas. 68 (C.C.D. Ma.) (No. 12,165) (Story J.); *Wildes* v. *Savage* (1839), 29 F. Cas. 1226 (C.C.D. Ma.) (No. 17,653) (Story J.).

DELAY IN PRESENTMENT AND NOTICE OF DISHONOUR

In the seventeenth and eighteenth centuries, a bill or note might have been transferred from hand to hand in a long chain of payment transactions on the assumption that it would be paid by the drawee or maker. If the instrument was dishonoured, some or all of these transactions might be unsettled as holders of the bill sought to shift the loss to prior parties. A very large part of the corpus of the law of bills and notes in the eighteenth century arose out of this phenomenon.

Suppose that a person had purchased goods or paid a debt by transferring a bank note. Ordinarily, the recipient of the note would either pass it on to another party or present it to the banker for redemption within a relatively brief time. Suppose, however, that the bank failed before the recipient of the note had passed it on or collected it. The first reaction of the recipient might be to lament the fortuitous twist of fate that saw the bank fail at the moment that the note happened to be in his hands. The second reaction was likely to be an effort to shift the consequences of the unfortunate fate to someone else.

Since bank notes were typically payable to bearer, they were transferred by delivery, without any indorsements. Thus the holder of the note would have no action on the note itself against anyone other than the failed bank. The holder might, however, try to proceed against the person who transferred the note to him. The cause of action would not be on the note itself, but on the underlying obligation for which the note was taken. For example, if the note had been taken for goods, the argument would be that the seller never received the money so the buyer was still liable for the price of the goods. A fundamental question that must be answered in any payment system based on the transfer of instruments is whether taking an instrument discharges the underlying debt.

In *Ward* v. *Evans* (1703),[30] Chief Justice Holt established the basic rules on this issue, ruling that if an instrument was taken at the time goods were sold, it would be presumed to have been taken as final payment; but where an instrument was taken for a pre-existing debt, the debt was not extinguished. Evidently this was a

---

[30] 2 Ld Raym. 928, 1 Com. 138, 6 Mod. 36, 12 Mod. 521, Holt 120, 2 Salk. 442, 3 Salk. 118.

controversial issue. Holt prefaced his ruling by noting that, 'I am of the opinion, and always was (notwithstanding the noise and cry, that it is the use of Lombard Street, as if the contrary opinion would blow up Lombard Street) that the acceptance of such a note is not actual payment'.[31] On one side it could be said that treating such notes as only conditional payment would hinder their use, because the debtor could not be certain that the affair was closed. Yet it could with equal force be said that the opposite rule would discourage use of bankers' notes, because creditors would be less willing to accept them if they lost all recourse against the debtor.

Ward v. *Evans* also established an important qualification to the rule that taking an instrument does not discharge a pre-existing debt. If the person who took the note delayed unreasonably in passing it on or presenting it for payment, the underlying debt would be discharged.[32] Thus, when a person who had paid a debt with a bank note or draft was sued on the underlying debt, he could defend by arguing that the loss was really the creditor's own fault. If the creditor had been more diligent in presenting the note or draft for payment, he would have been one of the lucky people who got paid just before the bank failed, rather than one of the unlucky ones left holding the notes of the failed bank.

In the late seventeenth century and throughout the eighteenth century, there were many cases dealing with this problem.[33] Indeed, the issue of what was a reasonable time for presentment seems to have accounted for a fairly large percentage of the bills

---

[31] 2 Ld Raym. at 930.

[32] 'When such a note is given in payment, it is always intended to be taken under this condition, to be payment if the money be paid thereon in convenient time. This note was demanded within convenient time, but if the party who takes the note, keep it by him for several days, without demanding it, and the person who ought to pay it becomes insolvent, he that received it must bear the loss; because he prevented the other person from receiving the money, by detaining the note in his custody'. 2 Ld Raym. at 930.

[33] *Cooksey* v. *Boverie* (1683), 2 Show. 296; *Vernon* v. *Boverie* (1683), 2 Show. 296; *Darrach* v. *Savage* (1691), 1 Show. 155, Holt 113; *Hill* v. *Lewis* (1694), 1 Salk. 132, Holt 116, Skin. 410; *Tassel* v. *Lewis* (1695), 1 Ld Raym. 743; *Anon.* (1700), Holt 298, 12 Mod. 408; *Phillips* v. *Phillips* (1700), 2 Freem. Chy. 247; *Ward* v. *Evans* (1703), 2 Ld Raym. 928, 1 Com. 138, 6 Mod. 36, 12 Mod. 521, Holt 120, 2 Salk. 442, 3 Salk. 118; *Crawley* v. *Crowther* (1702), 2 Freem. Chy. 257; *Turner* v. *Mead* (1720), 1 Str. 416; *Moore* v. *Warren* (1721), 1 Str. 415; *Holme* v. *Barry* (1721), 1 Str. 415; *Manwaring* v. *Harrison* (1722), 1 Str. 508; *Haward* v. *Bank of England* (1723), 1 Str. 550; *Mead* v. *Caswell* (1723), 9 Mod. 60; *Hoar* v. *Dacosta* (1732), 2 Str. 910; *Hankey* v. *Trotman* (1746), 1 Bl. W. 1.

and notes cases in this period. Until the latter part of the eighteenth century, the question whether the holder had acted within a reasonable time was entirely left to the jury. In the 1780s, however, the judges became dissatisfied with the unpredictable results of leaving the issue to juries and sought to take over the issue as a question of law. In *Medcalf* v. *Hall* (1782),[34] a debtor paid his creditor with a draft on his banker. The draft was given at one o'clock in the afternoon, and the bankers failed at five. The debtor was sued on the original debt, and defended on the grounds that the creditor had delayed unduly in not presenting the draft within the remaining four hours during that day before the bankers failed. At the trial, Lord Mansfield left the issue to the jury, but his instructions and summary of the evidence left them in no doubt about how he thought it should be decided. He suggested that it would be very desirable to have 'some certain rule to meet all cases of a like kind',[35] and commented favourably on the rule among many London bankers and merchants that presentment within twenty-four hours sufficed. He also admonished the jury that if they 'thought that a man taking a bill was to run to receive it, they must be aware of the inconvenience of taking drafts'.[36] The jury, though, did not take the hint and returned a verdict for the defendant. Mansfield directed a new trial, and the case came before the court *in banc* on the defendant's objection to the grant of a second trial. All of the judges agreed that the result reached by the jury was unreasonable. Mr Justice Buller contended that reasonableness of time should be treated as a question of law, and suggested that a general rule should be laid down that presentment the day after receipt sufficed. Mansfield and Ashhurst were willing to adopt Buller's suggestion, but Mr Justice Willes expressed some reluctance to lay down a general rule. The motion for a new trial was granted, but at the second trial the matter was again left to the jury, and the jury stuck to their position, returning a second verdict for the defendant, and 'delivering their reason in writing, that, according to the usage of the city, there was sufficient time for the plaintiff either to have received it himself or to have sent it to his bankers'.[37] A rule for a new trial was again obtained, and brought up for consideration by the full court, but before decision

---

[34] 3 Doug. 113.   [35] 3 Doug. at 113.   [36] 3 Doug. at 114.
[37] 3 Doug. at 116.

the plaintiff gave up and presented his claim in the bankruptcy proceedings against the bankers.[38]

In the dishonoured bank note cases, the only avenue of recovery was to sue on the obligation for which the note was taken. In many circumstances, however, the holder of a dishonoured instrument would have recourse on the instrument against various parties. If a bill was dishonoured by the drawee, the holder could sue the drawer. If a bill or note had been indorsed, the indorsers were also liable. Looking at the situation from the other side, the consequence of the rule that drawers and indorsers were liable on dishonoured bills and notes was that any person through whose hands the instrument had passed might find himself called upon to pay it months later as a result of the bankruptcy of some other person perhaps wholly unknown to him. An anecdote from the early years of President Andrew Jackson's life nicely illustrates the point. In 1795, having achieved considerable fortune in land dealings in Tennessee, Jackson travelled to Philadelphia where he sold some land to a wealthy Philadelphia merchant, David Allison, taking Allison's notes as payment. In turn, he bought goods, paying by indorsing over Allison's notes, and returned to Tennessee intending to set up business as a general merchant with the stock purchased in Philadelphia. Shortly after returning to Tennessee, Jackson learned that Allison had gone bankrupt. Jackson was forced to pay the notes as indorser, thereby losing the great bulk of his fortune.[39] In some respects, the surprising part of the story is that Jackson did pay on his indorsement. The more

---

[38] There was another case, *Appleton* v. *Sweetapple* (1782), 3 Doug. 137, involving a draft on the same bankers, Brown & Collinson, in which the creditor had received the draft at noon and deposited it for collection with his own bankers that afternoon. The collecting bank presented it to Brown & Collinson that evening, but following the practice among bankers it was not then paid, but was 'marked' to be paid at the clearings the next day. The draft was not paid before Brown & Collinson failed, and the creditor sued on the original debt. As in *Medcalf*, the jury gave a verdict for the defendant, and the case came before the King's Bench on a motion for new trial. Lord Mansfield backed off somewhat from the position taken in *Medcalf*, saying that although the general rule should be that presentment by the day after receipt sufficed, the time could be shortened by proof of a usage. He felt, however, that the usage had not been proved at trial. Judge Buller held to the position that the question was purely one of law, and if any usage were alleged it should be for the court to judge whether the usage was reasonable. A new trial was granted, but, as in *Medcalf*, the jury returned another verdict for the defendant at the second trial.

[39] James, *Andrew Jackson*, 74–78.

common reaction of drawers and indorsers seems to have been to grasp at any straw for an argument to avoid liability.

Reduced to simplest terms, the usual argument advanced by a person sued on a note or bill which had passed through his hands was that the holder should have sued someone else. More specifically, the argument was that if the holder had been more diligent in pursuing another party, he would have been able to collect. Thus, cases in which drawers or indorsers were sued on bills presented more or less the same issues as the bank note cases discussed above. For example, in the Andrew Jackson scenario, the usual argument for someone in Jackson's position would have been that if the holder of the notes had been more diligent he could have collected from Allison and so should be estopped from proceeding against Jackson.

Four years after the bank draft case of *Medcalf* v. *Hall,* the question of reasonableness of time for giving notice of dishonour in actions against a drawer or indorser came before the King's Bench in *Tindal* v. *Brown* (1786).[40] Tindal was the holder of a note made by Donaldson and indorsed by Brown. On the day the note became due, Tindal sent his clerk to Donaldson to demand payment. Donaldson was not home, so the clerk left word and returned the following morning. That day the clerk did find Donaldson home, and Donaldson said that he would pay the note that day when his bank was open. Donaldson, however, failed to do so, and when the clerk returned the following morning, Donaldson admitted that he could not pay it. The clerk then went to the indorser, Tindal, who refused to pay on the grounds that he was discharged by the holder's failure to notify him of dishonour on the first day that the note became due. The jury evidently felt that the holder had given notice within a reasonable time and gave a verdict against the indorser.

On the motion for a new trial, Mansfield stated that 'what is reasonable notice is partly a question of fact, and partly a question of law. It may depend in some measure on facts; such as the distance at which the parties live from each other, the course of the post, &c. But whenever a rule can be laid down with respect to reasonableness, that should be decided by the Court, and adhered to by every one for the sake of certainty'.[41] His brethren Ashhurst

[40] 1 T.R. 167.   [41] 1 T.R. at 168.

and Buller agreed that reasonableness of time should be regarded as a question of law. As Buller put it, 'the numerous cases on this subject reflect great discredit on the Courts of Westminster. They do infinite mischief in the mercantile world; and this evil can only be remedied by doing what the Court wished to do in the case of [*Medcalf* v. *Hall*], by considering the reasonableness of time as a question of law and not of fact'.[42] Although the judges left little doubt about their frustration with the inconsistent results of juries in these matters,[43] the case had come up on a motion for a new trial, so all the Court could do was grant a new trial. As in *Medcalf*, the jury stuck to their position and gave a second verdict for the holder. Counsel for the holder suggested that the judges should simply give up, rather than grant a third trial in a case involving only a small amount of money, but the judges held their ground and granted a third trial, at which the case was put to the jury only for a special verdict as to the facts and the court entered judgment for the indorser as a matter of law.[44]

Taking the issue from the jury was one thing; deciding what to do with it was another. Problems of specifying the precise obligations of a holder upon dishonour did not go away after *Tindal*. Rather, the problems came to occupy a larger and larger portion of the courts' time, for the judges had taken it upon themselves to resolve these matters by general rules rather than leaving them to the jury. From the end of the eighteenth century to the early

---

[42] 1 T.R. at 169.

[43] As Mansfield said, 'It was well observed by counsel that the juries were obstinate in the case of [*Medcalf* v. *Hall*], where they struggled so hard, in spite of the opinion of the Court, to narrow the rule, that they held that you must in certain cases demand payment on a banker's draft within an hour. Here the struggle is to give a greater latitude than is necessary'. 1 T.R. at 168–69.

[44] Although later decisions generally followed *Tindal's* ruling that reasonableness of time was partly a question of law and partly of fact, the procedure employed in the last trial in *Tindal* – having the jury return a special verdict as to the facts with the judge ruling on the reasonableness of the time – seems not to have been generally adopted. Rather, we find later cases coming before the full bench on motions for new trial after the question had been left to the jury. E.g., *Darbishire* v. *Parker* (1805), 6 East 3. Moreover, in cases involving bills payable a certain period after sight, there are decisions after *Tindal* explicitly holding that although the holder must either present the bill or put it into circulation within a reasonable time, the question of reasonableness must be left to the jury. *Goupy* v. *Harden* (1816), 7 Taunt. 159; *Fry* v. *Hill* (1817), 7 Taunt. 397. Treatise writers long after *Tindal* continued to note that it was unsettled whether the issue was for judge or jury. Chitty, *Bills of Exchange*, 4th edn (1811), 237–38; Bayley, *Bills of Exchange*, 5th edn (1830), ch. 7, § 1.

nineteenth century, innumerable cases posed fine points about the diligence required of the holder of a dishonoured bill.[45]

The difficulty of the task of specifying the rules on this subject is illustrated by the case of *Bickerdike* v. *Bollman* (1786),[46] where it was ruled that failure to give notice of dishonour might be excused in certain cases. In *Bickerdike*, a hard-pressed debtor tried to hold off one creditor by giving him a bill drawn on another firm. As it turned out, this was nothing but a crude stalling effort, for the firm on which the bill was drawn held no funds due to the drawer. Quite the contrary, the drawer actually owed a substantial sum to the drawee. The bill was, of course, dishonoured, and the disgusted holder did not bother with the formalities usually required in ordinary bill dealings. When the creditor sued, however, the debtor brazenly put in the defence that the debt was discharged because the creditor had not given him notice of dishonour of the bogus bill. That was too much even for judges who had so strongly urged the adoption of clear, certain rules in bill dealings. The court ruled that notice of dishonour was unnecessary in such a case. As Mr Justice Buller explained, 'the law requires notice to be given ... because it is presumed that the bill is drawn on account of the drawee's having effects of the drawer in the hands; and if the latter has notice that the bill is not accepted, or not paid, he may withdraw them immediately. But if he has no effects in the other's hands, then he cannot be injured for want of notice'.[47]

It is unlikely that the judges who decided the case had any idea how troublesome the *Bickerdike* rule would prove to be. Parties fighting over who should make good a dishonoured bill now had a vehicle for arguing that the loss should fall on another, even though they may have slipped in the attempt to follow the rigid rules. There turned out to be many cases where bills were drawn

---

[45] E.g., *Haynes* v. *Birks* (1804), 3 Bos. & Pul. 599 (if bill has been left with banker for collection, does this extend time for giving notice?); *Smith* v. *Mullett* (1809), 2 Camp. 208 (is it sufficient if holder puts notice in post at end of day following receipt but too late for last post?); *Williams* v. *Smith* (1819), 2 Barn. & Ald. 496 (if party to be notified is in different city, must notice be sent by the next practical post, or is it sufficient to send by post the following day?); *Geill* v. *Jeremy* (1827), M. & M. 61 (if no post goes out the next day, must holder give notice by the last post of day of receipt?).

[46] 1 T.R. 405. The case was decided in the period after Mansfield's failing health had prevented him from sitting, but before his formal retirement as Chief Justice.

[47] 1 T.R. at 410.

on someone who held no effects of the drawer in perfectly legitimate circumstances. For example, it was common for a merchant who shipped goods on commission to his agent to draw a bill for the expected sales proceeds in advance of the actual sale. In such cases, the drawer may have had no effects in the drawee's hands at the time the bill was drawn, yet the drawer had legitimate reason to assume that the drawee would honour the bill.[48] Also, there were the cases in which the accounts between drawer and drawee fluctuated between the time the bill was drawn and the time it was presented and dishonoured. Even though the drawer might, at some point, have had no effects in the drawee's hands, he could well have been prejudiced by want of notice.[49] Moreover, inasmuch as *Bickerdike* excused notice on the grounds that the drawer could not have been prejudiced where he had no effects in the drawee's hands, holders who failed to give notice in other circumstances could argue that they should be allowed to recover from prior parties if the want of notice did not cause any actual harm.[50]

The judges struggled to confine the *Bickerdike* exception narrowly, but the law on excuse of notice became exceedingly complex. As the author of a mid-nineteenth-century American treatise put it, 'It may be doubted whether any branch of commercial law, somewhat narrow in itself, exhibits so large a number of cases, and so boundless a variety in their facts and the conclusions from them . . . It is not easy to imagine any circumstance attending non-notice which in some form or other is not urged as an excuse for it. And the decisions of the courts permit authorities to be cited on both sides of almost every question'.[51] Indeed, by the early nineteenth century, many of the most prominent English judges noted their regret that the *Bickerdike* exception had ever been allowed.[52]

To modern lawyers, the rules on presentment, notice of

---

[48] *Rogers* v. *Stephens* (1788), 2 T.R. 713; *Rucker* v. *Hiller* (1812), 16 East 43.

[49] *Orr* v. *Maginnis* (1806), 7 East 359; *Blackhan* v. *Doren* (1810), 2 Camp. 503; *Thackray* v. *Blackett* (1812), 3 Camp. 164.

[50] *Staples* v. *Okines* (1795), 1 Esp. 332; *Dennis* v. *Morrice* (1800), 3 Esp. 158.

[51] Parsons, *Law of Promissory Notes and Bills of Exchange*, 1: 521. The chapter on excuse of notice runs over 110 pages.

[52] *Walwyn* v. *St Quintin* (1797), 1 Bos. & Pul. 652 (Eyre C.J.); *Dennis* v. *Morrice* (1800), 3 Esp. 158 (Kenyon C.J.); *Clegg* v. *Cotton* (1802), 3 Bos. & Pul. 239 (Alvanley C.J.); *Orr* v. *Maginnis* (1806), 7 East 359 (Ellenborough C.J.); *Ex parte Heath* (1813), 2 Ves. & Bea. 240 (Lord Eldon Ch.); *Cory* v. *Scott* (1820), 3 Barn. & Ald. 619 (Abbott C.J.).

dishonour, excuse of notice, and the like, seem inconsequential. For example, the currently dominant American treatise on commercial law devotes only a few pages to these topics, describing them as matters of 'boring and incessant detail'.[53] Because these subjects play so little role in modern law, they have rarely received much attention in accounts of the history of the law of bills and notes. Yet once one understands the business context, it becomes apparent that these issues were the very heart of the law of bills and notes in the eighteenth and early nineteenth centuries. The judges of this era frequently noted the importance of these matters. For example, in a case about the time for presentment of notes, Lord Kenyon remarked that 'this question is of ... infinite importance in every hour's transactions in the commercial world'.[54] Similarly, Chief Justice Abbott noted that 'it is of the greatest importance to commerce, that some plain and precise rule should be laid down, to guide persons in all cases, as to the time within which notices of the dishonour of bills must be given'.[55] And in 1841, Lord Denman remarked that 'perhaps Lord Mansfield never conferred so great a benefit on the commercial world, as by his decision of *Tindal* v. *Brown*, where his perseverance compelled them, in spite of themselves, to submit to the doctrine of requiring immediate notice as a matter of law'.[56]

LORD MANSFIELD AND THE LAW OF BILLS

No account of the history of the law of bills and notes can be complete without an evaluation of the contribution of Lord Mansfield. As we have seen in this chapter and the preceding one, many of the important principles of the law of bills were established or

---

[53] White and Summers, *Uniform Commercial Code*, 569. By contrast, in a typical treatise of the late eighteenth or early nineteenth century these issues take up a large part of the book. For example, in the fourth edition of Chitty, published in 1811, the chapters dealing with the steps that the holder must follow in dealing with the drawee and preserving rights against prior parties account for a bit over 30% of the book.

[54] *Brown* v. *Harraden* (1791), 4 T.R. 148.

[55] *Williams* v. *Smith* (1819), 2 Barn. & Ald. 496, 500.

[56] *Furze* v. *Sharwood* (1841), 2 Q.B. 388, 415.

settled during the period that Lord Mansfield served as Chief Justice of the Court of King's Bench from 1756 until 1788.[57] Mansfield provided a concise summary of his approach to commercial cases in a 1782 decision where he observed that 'in all mercantile cases there are two objects, convenience and certainty'.[58]

By 'convenience' Mansfield meant that the legal rules should facilitate trade and commerce. Accordingly, Mansfield was particularly concerned that the legal principles be established in the light of a sound understanding of commercial practices. The principal sources of the information necessary for this task were the testimony of merchants at trials and the findings of special juries of merchants. The reports show that merchants were commonly called as witnesses in commercial cases in Mansfield's era, and that he gave their evidence great weight.[59] Mansfield's use of merchant juries is well known. As Lord Campbell observed in his biographical account of Mansfield, 'he . . . did much for the improvement of commercial law in this country by rearing a body of special jurymen at Guildhall, who were generally returned on all commercial causes to be tried there. He was on terms of the most familiar intercourse with them; not only conversing freely with them in court, but inviting them to dine with him. From them he learned the usages of trade, and in return took great pains in explaining to them the principles of jurisprudence by which they were to be guided'.[60] Lord Mansfield's trial notebooks, which have only recently been discovered and studied, confirm that special juries of

---

57 A modern scholarly account of Mansfield's contribution to the development of English law in general is now available in Oldham, *Mansfield Manuscripts and the Growth of English Law*. See also Fifoot, *Lord Mansfield*; Heward, *Lord Mansfield*; Campbell, *Lives of the Chief Justices of England*.

58 *Medcalf* v. *Hall* (1782), 3 Doug. 113.

59 In *Lilly* v. *Ewer* (1779), 1 Doug. 72, Thomas Gorman, 'an eminent merchant', testified on the meaning of a certain provision in an insurance policy, and Mansfield remarked that he 'laid great stress on Mr. Gorman's testimony. I did not consider him as a common witness'. 1 Doug. at 74. Mansfield's notes from the trial are printed in Oldham, *Mansfield Manuscripts and the Growth of English Law*, 1: 551. Gorman also served as a special juror in cases tried by Mansfield, ibid., 1: 94, including at least one bills case, *Pierson* v. *Dunlop* (1777), 2 Cowp. 571.

60 Campbell, *Lives of the Chief Justices*, 2: 407. A more complete account of Mansfield's use of merchant juries and other special juries is given in Oldham, *Mansfield Manuscripts and the Growth of English Law*, 1: 93–99. See also Fifoot, *Lord Mansfield*, 82–117.

merchants were commonly used in commercial cases tried by Mansfield.[61]

Mansfield, however, was certainly not of the view that the role of judges in commercial cases was simply to adopt whatever rule the merchants thought should be followed. For example, in *Medcalf* v. *Hall* (1782), *Appleton* v. *Sweetapple* (1782), and *Tindal* v. *Brown* (1786), discussed earlier in this chapter, the courts repeatedly granted new trials when dissatisfied with jury findings on the issue of reasonableness of time for presenting bills or giving notice of dishonour. In *Edie* v. *East India Co.* (1761),[62] a bill payable to A or order had been indorsed by the payee to another, but the indorsement did not include the words 'to order'. The question presented was whether the indorsement in that form precluded further transfer. Mansfield noted that he 'thought, at the trial, that the defendants might be at liberty to go into the usage of merchants upon this occasion',[63] and a number of prominent merchants testified on the issue, with some conflict of views. By the time the case came before the court *in banc*, however, Mansfield had concluded that the issue should be settled as a matter of law. 'Since the trial, I have looked into the cases, and have considered the thing with a great deal of care and attention, and thought much about it: and I am very clearly of the opinion, that I ought not to have admitted any evidence of the particular usage of merchants in such a case. Of this, I say, I am now satisfied: for the law is already settled.'[64] Similarly, in *Grant* v. *Vaughan* (1764),[65] Mansfield submitted to the jury the question whether the practice in trade was to treat notes payable to a designated person or bearer as negotiable, but later concluded that

---

[61] Manuscript note books containing Lord Mansfield's records of the evidence at trials were discovered in 1967 at the home of his descendants. Brief synopses are given in Heward, 'Lord Mansfield's Note Books', and Rodgers, 'Continental Literature and the Development of the Common Law'. Extensive excerpts from the note books, along with commentary, are now available in Oldham, *Mansfield Manuscripts and the Growth of English Law*. On the subject of bills and notes, however, the materials in the note books do not significantly change or supplement the information in the reported decisions.

[62] 2 Burr. 1216.   [63] 2 Burr. at 1220.

[64] 2 Burr. at 1222. Although *Edie* held that a bill could be transferred despite the absence from an indorsement of the words 'to order', it was held in *Ancher* v. *Bank of England* (1781), 2 Doug. 637, that an explicit restrictive indorsement would preclude further transfer.

[65] 3 Burr. 1516.

'I ought not to have left the . . . point to them, for it is a question of law'.[66]

One may well wonder whether Mansfield literally meant what he said in *Edie* and *Grant*, that he should not have allowed the evidence of mercantile practice. It may be more likely that he was anxious to hear the evidence and see how the jury would rule, if only to make sure that he was fully informed about the commercial practices involved, even though the case might ultimately be resolved by the court as a matter of law. Indeed, Mansfield seems to have been relatively flexible in drawing the line between issues of law and fact. For example, in *Carvick* v. *Vickery* (1783),[67] the bill was payable to two persons, who were not partners, but only one had indorsed it. At the first trial Mansfield nonsuited the plaintiff because both parties had not indorsed. When the case came before the court *in banc*, it was argued that 'two persons, by joining in the same bill, hold themselves out to the world as partners, and, therefore, for that purpose are to be treated and dealt with as such'. The court was persuaded by that argument and so allowed the plaintiff a new trial. At a second trial before Mansfield and a special jury, the defendant 'offered to prove that, by the universal usage and understanding of all the bankers and merchants in London, the indorsement was bad, because not signed by both the payees'. The plaintiff objected that the evidence should not be allowed because the question was a matter of law that had just been resolved by the court. Mansfield, however, said that 'he did not think the question was so decided as to preclude the evidence offered'. The defendant 'called Mr. Gosling, an eminent banker, to prove the usage; but the jury, *una voce* declared they knew it perfectly to be as he had stated it; and, without hearing the witness, found a verdict for the defendant'.

The goal of certainty played a major role in Mansfield's approach to commercial law. The notion that commercial law should take account of mercantile practice could produce either confusion or certainty, depending on how the judges made use of the information about commercial practice that they obtained from merchants' testimony or the finding of special juries. Consider, for example, the case of *Banbury* v. *Lisset* (1744),[68] an action at *nisi prius* tried before Chief Justice Lee of the King's Bench, in which a

[66] 3 Burr. at 1523.   [67] 2 Doug. 653.   [68] 2 Str. 1211.

party sued on a bill defended on the grounds that the instrument
did not recite that it had been drawn 'for value received' and that
the acceptor had designated a specific fund as the source of
payment. The report indicates that at the trial Chief Justice Lee
suggested that issues about the proper form of bills ought to be
treated as matters of law, and that he thought that the objection to
payment from a particular fund was fatal. Nonetheless, the issue
was not resolved as a matter of law. Rather, Lee left the case to a
special jury of merchants, who found, on conflicting evidence of
mercantile practice, that a bill had to recite 'for value received'.[69]
Banbury was certainly a case where the judge deferred to evidence
of mercantile practice. The result, however, was not to advance the
development of commercial law, but to leave the matter
unresolved and to muddle the distinction between issues of law
and issues of fact.

Mansfield was never content with the approach taken in
Banbury, for he believed that certainty was at least as important in
commercial cases as conformity to commercial practice. As he
stated in *Medcalf* v. *Hall* (1782), 'Nothing is more mischievous
than uncertainty in commercial law. It would be terrible if every
question were to make a cause, and to be decided according to the
temper of a jury. If a rule is intended to apply to and govern a
number of like cases, that rule is a rule of law.'[70] In any case where
a significant issue of commercial law was raised, Mansfield made a
point of seeing to it that the issue was brought before the full court
at Westminster, rather than leaving it to the jury. Often he did so
even though he himself had no doubt on the issue. As he stated in a
1778 case dealing with an issue of bankruptcy law related to bills, 'I
had not a particle of doubt at the trial: but I desired a case to be
made for the opinion of the Court, for the sake of that, which is
perhaps more important than doing right: to bring all questions
upon mercantile transactions to a certainty. General verdicts do
not answer the purpose: but when a case is made, the profession
know the result, the merchants know the result.'[71] The insistence

---

[69] The confusion created by *Banbury* was cleared up during Mansfield's tenure,
when it was established as a matter of law that the words 'value received' were not
necessary in a bill. *White* v. *Ledwick* (1785), 4 Doug. 247.

[70] 3 Doug. at 115.

[71] *Hankey* v. *Jones* (1778), Cowp. 745, 750. See also *Peacock* v. *Rhodes* (1781), 2
Doug. 633, 636 ('I am glad this question was saved, not for any difficulty there is
in the case, but because it is important that general commercial points should be

that important issues in commercial cases be resolved on general principles was perhaps Mansfield's most important contribution to the development of commercial law. As his fellow judge and protégé Sir Francis Buller remarked in a case decided in the period after Mansfield's failing health had prevented him from sitting, but before his formal retirement as Chief Justice:

> Within these thirty years ... the commercial law of this country has taken a very different course from what it did before ... Before that period we find that in Courts of Law all the evidence in mercantile cases was thrown together; they were left to a jury, and they produced no general principle. From that time we all know, the great study has been to find some certain general principles, which shall be known to all mankind, not only to rule the particular case then under consideration, but to serve as a guide for the future. Most of us have heard these general principles stated, reasoned upon, enlarged, and explained, till we have been lost in admiration at the strength and stretch of the understanding. And I should be very sorry to find myself under a necessity of differing from any case on this subject which has been decided by Lord Mansfield, who may be truly said to be the founder of the commercial law of this country.[72]

The goal of certainty required not only that clear legal rules be enunciated, but also that they be integrated into a rational, systematic whole. An aspect of Mansfield's work that is often overlooked is that he displayed consummate skill at the ordinary tasks of legal analysis in the common law system, to wit, explaining and distinguishing prior decisions in a fashion that fitted them into a comprehensive and logical system. The bills and notes case that perhaps best exemplifies this characteristic is *Heylyn* v. *Adamson* (1758).[73]

The *Heylyn* case dealt with one part of the problem of settling rules on the diligence required of holders of dishonoured bills as a condition to their right of recovery from prior parties. Specifically, the issue was which party the holder must pursue before seeking recourse against those through whose hands a bill or note had passed. With respect to foreign bills of exchange, the issue was settled in *Bomley* v. *Frazier* (1721),[74] where it was ruled that if the drawee dishonours a bill, it was not necessary for the holder to

publicly decided'); *Tonkin* v. *Fuller* (1783), 3 Doug. 300, 302 ('I never had any doubt on this point, but as it is a very material one, I wished it to be considered here').
[72] *Lickabarrow* v. *Mason* (1787), 2 T.R. 63, 73.   [73] 2 Burr. 669.
[74] 1 Str. 441.

demand payment from the drawer before proceeding against indorsers. The court noted that people often take bills on the credit of their immediate indorser and that it could be very inconvenient if the holder were required to pursue the drawer, who might be located in a distant place.

There was, however, considerable disagreement about whether the holder of a promissory note was required to demand payment from the maker before proceeding against indorsers.[75] From the standpoint of modern law, it seems odd that there could have been doubt on this point. Indorsers are liable only if an instrument has been dishonoured. A note is dishonoured when demand is made on the maker and the maker refuses to pay. Thus it seems obvious that demand on the maker is a condition to an action against the indorser of a note. It is, however, not hard to see how this could have been a matter of legitimate dispute in the eighteenth century. The point was not simply whether the holder must demand payment from the maker, but whether the holder must use due diligence in seeking payment from the maker. If demand on the maker were not a condition to recovery from the indorser, then an indorser could not defend by arguing that if the holder had been more prompt in seeking payment, he could have collected from the maker. Good arguments could be made either way. On the one hand, an indorser could say that since a note first and foremost represents the promise of the maker, a person taking the note should first seek payment from the maker. On the other hand a person taking a note could argue that he had no idea who the maker was, but took it on the credit of the person who indorsed it to him.

The issue was resolved in *Heylyn*, which was one of Lord Mansfield's first major decisions on the law of bills and notes. *Heylyn* actually involved an inland bill of exchange, rather than a note. The payee had indorsed the bill to the plaintiff, and she was sued on her indorsement when the drawee dishonoured the bill. The defence raised was that the holder had not made demand on the drawer of the bill before proceeding against the indorser. The

---

[75] Cases indicating that demand on the maker of a note was required include: *Syderbottom* v. *Smith* (1725), 1 Str. 649; *Collins* v. *Butler* (1738), 2 Str. 1087; *Pardo* v. *Fuller* (1738), 2 Com. 579. Cases indicating that demand on the maker was not required include: *Harry* v. *Perrit* (1710), 1 Salk. 133; *Lawrence* v. *Jacob* (1722), 8 Mod. 43, 1 Str. 515; *Bilson* v. *Hill* (1734), 7 Mod. 198; *Cooper* v. *Le Blanc* (1736), Cas. t. Hard. 295, 2 Str. 1051; *Hamilton* v. *Mackrell* (1736), Cas. t. Hard. 322.

precise issue presented in *Heylyn* was fairly simple. It had been settled in *Bomley* v. *Frazier* (1721) that demand on the drawer of a foreign bill was not required. The only point that needed to be resolved to dispose of the *Heylyn* case was that the same rule should apply to inland bills. Mansfield's opinion carefully explained the reasons for the rule in *Bomley*, concluding that they applied equally to inland as to foreign bills. It is characteristic of Mansfield, however, that his opinion did not simply dispose of the issue on that basis, but also sought to set to rest all of the related issues in order to lay down simple and certain rules.

The main argument for the defendant in *Heylyn* rested on certain of the cases holding that demand on the maker of a promissory note was a condition to recovery from an indorser. Terminology was still somewhat unsettled in the seventeenth and eighteenth centuries, and the person who wrote a note was sometimes referred to as the drawer. Thus, the defendant in *Heylyn* could cite passages from earlier cases that literally said that demand on the 'drawer' was required before the holder of an instrument proceeded against an indorser. Mansfield went to some length to dispel the 'confusion [that] has . . . arisen from the maker of a promissory note being called the drawer'.[76] In particular, he carefully analysed the various somewhat garbled reports of a case from Chief Justice Holt's era, *Lambert* v. *Oakes* (1699),[77] which had been cited for the proposition 'that in actions upon bills of exchange, it is necessary to prove a demand upon the drawer'. Mansfield concluded that *Lambert* must have been a case on a note rather than a bill, dismissing as erroneous the reports that had described it as a bill. 'The report jumbles both together . . . misled, I dare say, by the equivocal sound of the term drawer, and by the Chief Justice's reasoning in the case of a promissory note, from the law upon bills of exchange.'[78]

Mansfield's opinion went still further, seeking not only to distinguish the earlier cases that could have been misconstrued as cases about bills but also to put to rest the dispute about whether the holder of a note was required to exercise diligence to recover from the maker before proceeding against an indorser. His opinion on this point was a *tour de force* of precise legal reasoning:

[76] 2 Burr. at 677.   [77] 1 Ld Raym. 443, 12 Mod. 244, Holt 117, 118, 1 Salk. 127.
[78] 2 Burr. at 679.

The law is exactly the same, and fully settled, upon the analogy of promissory notes to bills of exchange; which is very clear, when the point of resemblance is once fixed.

While a promissory note continues in its original shape of a promise from one man to pay another, it bears no similitude to a bill of exchange. When it is indorsed, the resemblance begins: for, then it is an order, by the indorser, upon the maker of the note, (his debtor, by the note,) to pay the indorsee. This is the very definition of a bill of exchange.

Therefore as soon as the note is indorsed by the payee, the indorser is the drawer; the maker of the note is the acceptor; and the indorsee is the person to whom it is made payable. The indorser only undertakes, in case the maker of the note does not pay. The indorsee is bound to apply to the maker of the note; he takes it upon that condition; and therefore must, in all cases, know who he is and where he lives; and if, after the note becomes payable, he is guilty of a neglect, and the maker becomes insolvent, he loses the money, and cannot come upon the indorser at all.[79]

As is often the case with great judges, Mansfield's description of the state of prior law was probably somewhat coloured by his own views. Contrary to his statement, the law on promissory notes was not 'fully settled' before *Heylyn* v. *Adamson;* it was in great disarray. It was only after Mansfield's masterful synthesis in *Heylyn* that the prior cases could be regarded as part of a consistent system of rules.

Though Mansfield's work in developing and articulating the law of bills warrants deep admiration, one must be careful not to lose sight of what he actually did as one celebrates how well he did it. A common form of the eulogistic view of Mansfield stresses the contrast between Mansfield and prior judges, particularly Chief Justice Holt. Indeed, one of the main reasons that the promissory notes cases, *Clerke* v. *Martin* (1702) and *Buller* v. *Crips* (1703), have attracted so much attention is that they serve as the vehicle for portraying Chief Justice Holt as a reactionary, anti-commercial figure to serve as a contrast to Mansfield.[80] The negative view of the common law prior to Mansfield that emerges from this portrayal plays directly into the incorporation theory. Holt and other judges before Mansfield are depicted as clinging to the technical rules of the common law, refusing to acknowledge the force of the rules of the law merchant that had developed outside the common law courts. Mansfield, then, is seen as the figure who

---

[79] 2 Burr. at 676.
[80] Fifoot's account is the prime example of this view. Fifoot, *Lord Mansfield*, 14–19.

broke down the barriers and allowed the law merchant to be recognized in the common law courts.[81]

The problems with the incorporation theory have already been discussed in detail. All that need be added on that score is to note that there is no more evidence from Mansfield's era than from earlier periods to suggest that the judges drew the law of bills from sources outside the common law system. To be sure, Mansfield was familiar with continental legal sources.[82] Moreover, he, like other judges and lawyers of his era, had considerable admiration for the jurisprudential theories of writers in the natural law, *jus gentium* tradition, such as Grotius and Pufendorf. Mansfield explicitly drew on these sources in some fields of mercantile law, such as maritime matters.[83] The law of bills and notes, however, was by Mansfield's time firmly established as a branch of the ordinary domestic law of England. In all of the bills cases decided during his tenure, Mansfield never seems to have cited any continental sources on mercantile law nor any of the English books on mercantile affairs derived from continental sources.[84] That is hardly surprising. The books of Malynes, Marius, and Molloy were a century or more old by Mansfield's time; the confused discussions of exchange transactions in these works were hopelessly outdated. By the late eighteenth century, the relevant sources of authority on the law of bills were the hundreds of decisions of the English courts spanning a period of nearly two centuries and the

---

[81] The most influential expression of this view is found in Scrutton, *Elements of Mercantile Law*, 13–16. The brief sketches of the history of the law merchant found in the introductory passages of treatises on the law of bills and notes often reflect this view. E.g., Ogden, *Law of Negotiable Instruments*, 6–8.

[82] Mansfield's library was destroyed when his house in Bloomsbury Square was burned by a mob in the Gordon Riots in 1780. Campbell, *Lives of the Chief Justices*, 2: 516–32. C. P. Rodgers, however, has located a manuscript inventory of books that Mansfield owned at the time of his death in 1793, which suggests that he had reacquired a substantial collection of continental legal works. Rodgers, 'Continental Literature and the Development of the Common Law', 169–72.

[83] E.g., *Luke* v. *Lyde* (1759), 2 Burr. 882. Mansfield's use of civilian sources is discussed in detail in Rodgers, 'Continental Literature and the Development of the Common Law'. Rodgers notes, however, that these sources played little role in the law of bills. Ibid., 169.

[84] Counsel cited Malynes and Molloy in a few cases during Mansfield's era, *Blesard* v. *Hirst* (1770), 5 Burr. 2670; *Salomons* v. *Staveley* (1783), 3 Doug. 298, as did one of Mansfield's fellow judges on at least one occasion, *Pillans* v. *Van Mierop* (1765), 3 Burr. 1663, 1674 (Yates J.).

emerging body of native English treatises in which the cases were digested and discussed.

The tendency to exaggerate the contrast between Mansfield and his predecessors obscures the real nature of his contribution to the development of the law of bills. The idea that judges needed to learn commercial practice in order to make good commercial law was certainly not new. Special juries of merchants had been used, albeit sporadically, as early as the fourteenth century.[85] There are numerous cases in the seventeenth century where merchants gave testimony on commercial practices concerning bills.[86] Judges long before Mansfield had expressed the view that convenience to trade and commerce was an important consideration in the law of bills.[87] So too, Mr Justice Buller's remark that before Mansfield's time no general principles had developed in commercial cases was an overstatement. We have seen that many of the fundamental rules of the law of bills were settled during Chief Justice Holt's era. To be sure, in the pre-Mansfield era there are cases, such as *Banbury* v. *Lisset* (1744),[88] where the courts left everything to the jury. Yet there are other cases in which the courts used evidence of commercial practice as skilfully as did Mansfield, recognizing that while mercantile custom could not make the law, the legal rules had to be adapted to the needs of commerce.[89]

---

[85] E.g., *Dederic* v. *Abbot of Ramsey* (1315), *Select Cases Law Merchant*, 46 SS 86, discussed in chapter 1.

[86] *Dehers* v. *Harriot* (1691), 1 Show. 163, 164 (counsel pointed out that 'twenty merchants attested their customs to be' as he contended); *Tassel* v. *Lewis* (1695), 1 Ld Raym. 743 ('Merchants in evidence at a trial ... swore the custom of merchants to be such').

[87] E.g., *Smith* v. *Abbott* (1741), 2 Str. 1152, 7 Mod. 426; *Bomley* v. *Frazier* (1721), 1 Str. 441; *Anon.* (1697), 1 Com. 43.

[88] 2 Str. 1211.

[89] For example, in *Stone* v. *Rawlinson* (1745), Willes 559, Barnes 164, 2 Str. 1260, 3 Wils. K.B. 1, the question was whether a note payable to the decedent could be indorsed by his administrator. The judges *sua sponte* made inquiries of merchants to learn what their practice was in such cases, but unlike the *Banbury* case where the issue was left to a jury, the court resolved the issue as a matter of law, taking pains to see to it that the law was settled in a fashion that took due account of mercantile practice. The court's explanation of the role of commercial practice in the development of commercial law could easily have been written by Mansfield: 'the Courts of Law have always in mercantile matters endeavoured to adapt the rules of law to the course and method of trade in order to promote trade and commerce instead of doing it any hurt, so we are determined in the present case to make this indorsement valid according to the practice, if we can by any means make it consistent with the words of the Act and agreeable to the rules of law'. Willes at 561.

Mansfield's view of the role of commercial practice in the development of commercial law was really very similar to the view implicit in the courts' use of the concept of the custom of merchants in the seventeenth century. As was shown in chapter 6, the notion that the law of bills was based on the custom of merchants did not mean that evidence of mercantile practice was conclusive. Rather, the judges used the principle that the custom of merchants was part of the common law as the basis for maintaining control over the development of the law, while the device of pleadings on the custom of merchants served as a mechanism by which the judges could obtain the information about commercial practices concerning bills that they needed in order to develop a sensible body of law. Mansfield used the findings of his merchant juries in very much the same fashion. As Fifoot put it,

A verdict was to be accepted as raw material brought to the court to be fashioned. The jury found a usage, the judge accepted or rejected it as furthering or impeding the convenience of trade. The jury solved the particular problem, the judge rationalized the solution for future use. The jury revealed a fresh facet of human experience, the judge framed it in the general policy of the law. By insisting upon these complementary functions, Lord Mansfield maintained an equilibrium between stability and expansion, and determined the axis about which the mercantile world could revolve.[90]

Mansfield even used some of the same techniques as the seventeenth-century judges to preserve some measure of flexibility in drawing the line between issues of law and issues of fact. Mansfield at times suggested that even on matters where a general rule had been established as a matter of law, the rule might be varied if it was proven that a particular 'usage' had developed within the trade, on the theory that if the parties were aware of the usage when they entered into the transaction it would bind them as if it had been an expressed term of their contract.[91] The same technique had been used in a 1697 decision, where the court ruled as a matter of law that if a bill is payable a certain number of days after sight the day of presentation would be counted as one of the days, but indicated that the result might have differed if a special custom

---

[90] Fifoot, *Lord Mansfield*, 114–15.
[91] *Appleton* v. *Sweetapple* (1782), 3 Doug. 137. Mansfield had proceeded on the same theory in allowing evidence of mercantile practice in the trial in *Edie* v. *East India Co.* (1761), 2 Burr. 1216.

among merchants on the issue had been pleaded and proved.[92] So too, just as the seventeenth-century judges used the notion that the law of merchants is part of the common law to ensure that they retained final say, Mansfield remarked on at least one occasion that 'the law of merchants and the law of the land is the same. A witness cannot be admitted to prove the law of merchants; we must consider it as a point of law.'[93]

The difference between Mansfield and his predecessors was a matter of degree, not of kind. Yet to recognize Mansfield's continuity with the past is by no means to denigrate his accomplishments. Campbell remarked that Mansfield 'cannot be considered a man of original genius. With great good sense, he adapted, he improved, – but he never invented',[94] and Holden suggested that his 'pre-eminent position in the history of commercial law was due primarily to the fact that he was able, over a long period of years, to redefine, with unusual clarity of expression, principles which had already been recognized'.[95] Such remarks miss the point. Mansfield's accomplishment was not that he invented the tools and materials used to develop commercial law but that he used them so skilfully. Other judges had sought out information on commercial practice; Mansfield did so in a routine and systematic fashion. Other judges had used that information to mould legal rules; Mansfield adopted procedures designed to ensure that every significant issue presented in commercial cases would reach the full bench and be resolved as a matter of general principle. Other judges had tried to integrate the rules of commercial law into the existing corpus of English law; Mansfield, in such cases as *Heylyn* v. *Adamson,* took the material that he found in the case-law of the preceding century and a half and reworked it into a coherent and logical system, explaining away the poorly reported or confused decisions and discarding those that could not be rationalized. For a judge in a legal system based on precedent, that is what constitutes greatness.

[92] *Bellasis* v. *Hester* (1697), 1 Ld Raym. 280. See also *Hawkins* v. *Cardy* (1698), 1 Ld Raym. 360, Carth. 466, 1 Salk. 65, 12 Mod. 213; *Buckley* v. *Cambell* (1706), 11 Mod. 92, 1 Salk. 131.
[93] *Pillans* v. *Van Mierop* (1765), 3 Burr. 1663, 1669.
[94] Campbell, *Lives of the Chief Justices*, 2: 576.
[95] Holden, *History of Negotiable Instruments*, 113.

10

THE PROBLEM OF ACCOMMODATION BILLS

Lord Mansfield and the other judges who participated in the development and systematization of the law of bills and notes in the eighteenth century did have one significant advantage. They were working in a period of great prosperity and expansion in trade, finance, and industry, when there seems to have been little disagreement over the general policies that the legal system should adopt toward commercial affairs. That is by no means the universal condition. We have seen that in the sixteenth and early seventeenth centuries, there was considerable controversy about the economic and moral issues posed by developments in financial techniques. At the end of the eighteenth and beginning of the nineteenth centuries, the English courts were faced with a somewhat similar problem. A financing device long considered legitimate and desirable was adapted – or perverted – to uses deemed improper under prevailing financial mores. This chapter explores the complex relationship between legal issues and controversies concerning economic policy and morality that lie beneath the surface of a body of seemingly dry, technical issues about 'accommodation bills'.

THE LIVESEY BANKRUPTCY AND ACCOMMODATION BILLS

In the year 1788, the firm of Livesey, Hargreaves & Co. of Lancashire went bankrupt. The firm was one of the largest cotton manufacturing enterprises that developed in the early stages of the Industrial Revolution in England. According to the English economic historians Alfred Wadsworth and Julia Mann, the firm 'employed between 700 and 1,000 printers . . . they were said to be "the means of giving bread to near 20,000 persons", and their cloth out at bleaching was reputed to occupy more than twelve miles'.[1] The outstanding debt of the firm at the time of its bankruptcy has been estimated at nearly £1.5 million.[2] To place those figures in perspective, one might note that in the 1780s the two largest cities in Lancashire, Liverpool and Manchester, each had populations of only 30,000 to 35,000,[3] and that the entire outstanding note issue of the Bank of England in 1788 was only about £10 million.[4]

In the aftermath of the Livesey failure, it was revealed that the firm had for some time been financing its operations by repeated issuance and circulation of accommodation bills. At the time, this revelation must have produced a reaction among the public of shock and outrage. To see why, one must attempt to understand late-eighteenth-century English views of financial propriety and monetary theory.

We may begin by examining the form of financial transaction involving bills of exchange that would have been considered legitimate in the late eighteenth century. Suppose that a manufacturer such as Livesey had shipped cotton to a distributor in London. If the shipment was either on consignment or a sale on credit terms, it would be some time before the manufacturer actually received cash for its goods. Unless the manufacturer was unusually well capitalized, it would wish to obtain cash in exchange for its right to receive payment from its customer several months hence, so that it could continue its manufacturing enterprise. The typical mechanism for obtaining such financing would have been for the manufacturer to draw a bill of exchange on the London distributor for the amount of the sale, payable at the end of the agreed credit period. The London distributor would accept the bill, thereby engaging to pay it when due. The manufacturer might take the bill to a bank or other financial entity and discount it for cash, or might make the bill payable directly to one of its suppliers or other creditors and use it to make payment of its obligations. Even if the bill was initially used by the manufacturer to pay one of its suppliers, the end result would probably be the same, for the payee of the bill would probably discount it for cash. Bills of exchange, then, were the commercial instruments used in the system by

---

[1] Wadsworth and Mann, *Cotton Trade and Industrial Lancashire*, 307.
[2] Ibid.
[3] Ibid., 311.   [4] Clapham, *Bank of England*, 1: 297.

which manufacturers and merchants obtained what we would now call 'working capital' financing.

Accommodation bill finance was, in essence, a device by which firms could raise funds in the market developed for working capital financing even though they had not actually engaged in sales transactions.[5] Suppose that a firm's sales had fallen off, that it wished to expand rapidly and lacked capital to construct facilities or machinery, that its owners were siphoning off large sums for personal consumption, or that for any other reason the firm was desperate for cash. The firm's ability to raise money for other purposes would be greatly enhanced if the firm could make it appear to the participants in the money market that it was simply engaging in routine working capital financing via the discount of bills arising out of the sales of its output. The trick was to create bills that looked like the kind of bills that arose out of the actual sale of goods in commerce. In one common scheme, a firm wishing to engage in such practices would find another firm or individual willing to assist – or 'accommodate' – it by accepting bills even though no goods had been sold or shipped nor any other actual transaction had occurred between the firms. Firm A would draw a bill on Firm B in some odd amount that looked as though it might have been the amount due for goods shipped from Firm A to Firm B. Firm B would accept the bill, and Firm A could then use it to pay creditors or could discount it for cash. When the bill came due, Firm B would raise the funds to do so by repeating the process with the parties switched. Firm B would draw a bill on Firm A, Firm A would accept, and Firm B would discount the bill to get the money needed to pay off the first bill. Some version of this scheme has probably been practised as long as bills of exchange have been in

---

[5] One of the difficulties in understanding the problem of accommodation bills is that the word 'accommodation' is still used in modern negotiable instruments law, but in a different sense. In modern law, the term accommodation is used to distinguish those who signed instruments as guarantors from those who signed as principals. By contrast, in the eighteenth and nineteenth centuries, the classification turned on the economic nature of the transaction out of which the bill arose. If the bill arose out of an actual mercantile transaction, it would not have been called an accommodation bill, regardless of whether some of the parties to the bill had signed as guarantors. Syntax reflects the difference in meaning. In the eighteenth and nineteenth centuries, the word 'accommodation' usually modified *bill*; one spoke of accommodation bills versus real bills. By contrast, today the term 'accommodation' modifies *party*; one speaks of accommodation parties to bills versus non-accommodation parties.

use. For example, in *The Wealth of Nations*, Adam Smith
described and decried the 'well-known shift of drawing and re-
drawing . . . to which unfortunate traders have sometimes recourse
when they are upon the brink of bankruptcy'.[6] It was, however, the
Americans who devised the most colourful slang for the practice.
Nineteenth-century American writers lamented the use of 'race
horse bills' that chased each other back and forth as swiftly as prize
horses.[7]

One difficulty with carrying on a practice of repeated issuance of
accommodation bills was that if the same names kept appearing on
all of the bills, the scheme might become apparent. That problem,
however, could easily be solved. The firms simply made up names
for parties to the bills. This was precisely what Livesey, Hargreaves & Co. had been doing for some time prior to their bankruptcy.[8]

The reports of the various lawsuits arising out of the Livesey
failure give a good picture of Livesey's bill finance practices.[9] A
typical transaction is depicted in *Collis* v. *Emett*. Livesey owed
£1,500 to Thomas Jeffrey in London for goods. Being unable to
pay when the debt came due, Livesey persuaded Jeffrey to take a
bill which he could then get discounted. Livesey, of course, would
not have wanted it generally known that they could meet their

---

[6] Smith, *Wealth of Nations*, 328. More simply still, the borrower might just issue
bills, persuading friends to indorse for him, get them discounted, and then repeat
the practice as money was needed to pay the maturing bills. The second edition of
Defoe's *Complete English Tradesman* included an Appendix cautioning the
traders against various dangerous financing practices, including a chapter
entitled 'Of Discounting and Endorsing Bills, and of the scandalous Practice of
passing Promissory Notes, on purpose to borrow money by Discount'.

[7] Catterall, *Second Bank of the United States*, 158–59.

[8] As was said in one of the Livesey cases, 'the obvious reason of inserting the name
of a fictitious payee is, that too many bills should not appear in circulation in the
same name at the same time'. *Gibson* v. *Minet* (1791), 1 Bl. H. 569, 624–25 (Heath
J.). In a similar case in 1769, Lord Mansfield had remarked that 'the intent of the
bill was only to enable Cox to raise money, and the reason why it was not made
payable to the order of Cox was, that there were other bills at the same time made
payable to his order; if this had also been payable to the same order, too many
would have been in circulation at the same time, in the same name, which would
have had the appearance of a fictitious credit'. *Stone* v. *Freeland* (1769), reported
in a note to *Collis* v. *Emett* (1790), 1 Bl. H. 313, 316.

[9] *Collis* v. *Emett* (1790), 1 Bl. H. 313; *Minet* v. *Gibson* (1789), 3 T.R. 481, aff'd 1 Bl.
H. 569 (1791); *Gibson* v. *Hunter* (1794), 2 Bl. H. 288.

obligations only by repeated issues of short-term paper, and so would have wanted it to appear that the bill was a 'real bill' that had arisen out of an actual mercantile transaction. The bill that Livesey gave Jeffrey had this appearance. It was drawn by John Emett, one of the partners at the Lancashire works, on the Livesey branch in London, payable to one George Chapman, accepted by Livesey, and indorsed by Chapman to Jeffrey. In fact, however, there was no such person as George Chapman. Livesey had simply made up the name, drawn the bill to his order, and then indorsed it to Jeffrey in the name of Chapman. Indeed, the London branch of the Livesey firm seems to have kept on hand a stock of bills drawn in blank which were filled in with fictitious names and amounts and discounted whenever cash was needed. Evidence was given in one of the other cases that Livesey regularly sent blank bill forms to an associate in Falmouth who signed them and returned them to Livesey in London where they were filled in, usually with the name of fictitious payees, and indorsed to creditors. The Livesey clerks who took the bills around to creditors in London had to take some care in handling the bills to avoid smearing the still wet ink on the bills that purportedly had been drawn days before in Falmouth.[10]

The fictitious payee cases arising out of the Livesey bankruptcy were the first, and perhaps most spectacular, episode of a controversy that would dominate the law of bills from the last decade of the eighteenth century to the early decades of the nineteenth century. From the perspective of the late twentieth century, however, it is easy to dismiss the accommodation bills cases as nothing more than instances in which people made foolish loans to uncreditworthy or untrustworthy borrowers and had to suffer the consequences. To approach the accommodation bills cases from that perspective, however, is to miss precisely what is most interesting about the episode, for the underlying tension in these cases was whether the legal system should regard the problems in that light or should take a more active role in the effort to control economic abuses. In order to gain some understanding of how contemporary lawyers and judges might have perceived the problems presented by the accommodation bills cases, one must place them in the context of contemporary economic thought.

[10] *Gibson* v. *Hunter* (1794), 2 Bl. H. 288, 292.

THE ECONOMIC CONTEXT
OF THE ACCOMMODATION BILLS CASES

From the earliest stages of the development of banking, it was perceived that banks could provide a medium of exchange to supplement or take the place of specie,[11] and by the eighteenth century it was apparent that increases in the money supply were not an unmixed blessing. The influx of vast stores of silver from the Americas in the sixteenth and seventeenth centuries had not brought wealth and prosperity, but long-term inflation. After the experiences of the collapse of John Law's system in France and the South Sea Bubble in England in the early part of the eighteenth century,[12] the possibility that undue expansion of paper money could have the same adverse effects as expansion of the specie supply could hardly have been regarded as a mere theoretical point. By the end of the eighteenth century, however, a theoretical account had developed that seemed to provide an elegant and simple solution to the potential problems posed by banks' ability to create paper money. Although elements of the theory can be found in earlier writings,[13] the most articulate and influential statement of the 'real bills' theory, as the doctrine has come to be known, was set out by Adam Smith in 1776.

According to Smith, if bankers confined their lending to the discount of real bills, the aggregate volume of circulating paper would automatically be held to an appropriate level. As Smith put it:

What a bank can with propriety advance to a merchant or undertaker of any kind, is not either the whole capital with which he trades, or even any considerable part of that capital; but that part of it only, which he would otherwise be obliged to keep by him unemployed, in ready money for answering occasional demands. If the paper money which the bank advances never exceeds this value, it can never exceed the value of the gold and silver, which would necessarily circulate in the country if there was no paper money; it can never exceed the quantity which the circulation of the country can easily absorb and employ.

When a bank discounts to a merchant a real bill of exchange drawn by a real creditor upon a real debtor, and which, as soon as it becomes due, is

---

[11] Usher, *Early History of Deposit Banking*, 180–82; de Roover, *Money, Banking and Credit in Mediaeval Bruges*, 202–05.

[12] Carswell, *South Sea Bubble*.

[13] See Mints, *History of Banking Theory*, 13–25; Horsefield, 'Duties of a Banker', 1–5.

really paid by that debtor; it only advances to him a part of the value which he would otherwise be obliged to keep by him unemployed in ready money for answering occasional demands.[14]

Thus, the key element of Smith's theory of money and banking was that the only instruments that should circulate, either directly or in the form of bank notes issued on discount of the instruments, were 'real bills'. It is, therefore, easy to see why financing practices of the sort Livesey engaged in would have been regarded as abusive.

The problem of preventing excessive circulation of bills became particularly significant in 1797. Rumours of a French invasion caused a run on London banks, leading to an order that the Bank of England cease payment of its notes in specie.[15] Since Bank of England notes were the single largest component of the money supply, and since the notes of the country banks were, in practice if not law, redeemable in Bank of England notes rather than specie, the effect of the order was that the English economy was placed, for the first time in history, on an inconvertible paper money standard. Though the suspension order was initially intended as a temporary measure, the Bank was not to resume specie payment until nearly a quarter of a century later, in 1821. Somewhat surprisingly, economic conditions immediately after the suspension order remained relatively calm. However, with the long continuance of the suspension, the public became concerned about whether the Bank of England, or the banking system in general, could be conducted on a sound basis in these unprecedented circumstances.

One consequence of the suspension was that the early decades of the nineteenth century were one of the most active and creative periods in the history of banking and monetary theory in England.[16] The suspension controversy brought to the forefront of

[14] Smith, *Wealth of Nations*, 322–23.
[15] Cannan, Introduction to *The Paper Pound of 1797–1821: A Reprint of the Bullion Report*, vii–xvii.
[16] The literature on the monetary theory of this period is enormous. The account herein is based principally upon the following sources: Cannan, ed., *The Paper Pound of 1797–1821: A Reprint of the Bullion Report* [hereinafter cited as *Bullion Report*]; Thornton, *Paper Credit of Great Britain*; Fetter, *British Monetary Orthodoxy*; Horsefield, 'Duties of a Banker'; Mints, *History of Banking Theory*; O'Brien, *Classical Economists*; Santiago-Valiente, 'Historical Background of Classical Monetary Theory'; Viner, *Theory of International Trade*; *New Palgrave Dictionary of Economics* (1987), s.v. 'Banking School, Currency School,

public discussion and debate the concerns about the distinction between real and accommodation bills that had been raised in eighteenth-century banking theory. When Adam Smith articulated the 'real bills theory', he was discussing a banking system based on convertible notes. Accordingly, the occasion did not arise for him to consider in any detail whether confining bank discounts to real bills really was sufficient in itself to prevent excessive issuance of paper money. The requirement that bank notes be paid in specie placed an independent limit on overissue. A banker who issued notes to excess, whether by discount of accommodation paper or in any other fashion, was subject to the restraint that he had always to keep on hand sufficient specie reserves to pay his outstanding notes. During the period of suspension, however, the limiting force of convertibility was removed. Unless some other restraint was operating, there seemed to be nothing to prevent a banker, and particularly the Bank of England, from issuing notes without limit, thereby setting off a spiral of inflation.

By the end of the first decade of the nineteenth century, suspicion began to grow that the Bank of England was in fact overissuing. The price of gold bullion rose to a considerable premium over the mint rate, and the foreign exchange value of the pound fell dramatically. A school of monetary writers, who have become known as the 'Bullionists', contended that the rise in the price of gold and fall in the exchanges were caused by an overissue of bank notes by the Bank of England. The matter became of sufficient public concern that a special commission was appointed by Parliament to study the problem.

The representatives of the Bank of England who testified before the Bullion Committee maintained strenuously that the Bank had not overissued, and that the rise in the price of bullion and fall in the exchanges were due to the extraordinary circumstances of the wars, requiring massive payments abroad for the maintenance of the troops. Of more significance for present purposes, the Bank witnesses maintained that excessive issuance of bank notes was simply not possible, as long as notes were issued only on discount of real bills of exchange. The *Bullion Report* (1810) summarized the Bank's position as follows:

Free Banking School', 'Bullionist Controversy', 'Classical Theory of Money', and 'Real Bills Doctrine'.

The Bank Directors, as well as some Merchants who have been examined, shewed a great anxiety to state to Your Committee a doctrine, of the truth of which they professed themselves to be most thoroughly convinced, that there can be no possible excess in the issue of Bank of England paper, so long as the advances in which it is issued are made upon the principles which at present guide the conduct of the Directors, that is, so long as the discount of mercantile Bills is confined to paper of undoubted solidity, arising out of real commercial transactions, and payable at short and fixed periods.[17]

For a number of reasons, the Bullionists rejected the Bank's position.[18] First, as one of the authors of the Bullion Report had pointed out in earlier writing, tying note issues to real bills would not necessarily result in an automatic regulation of the volume of the currency, because the distribution of a given shipment of goods might result in one or dozens of bills, depending on the number of hands through which the goods passed and the credit terms of the sales.[19] More importantly, the Bank's position rested on the notion that the demand for loans was completely independent of the cost of credit. The Bank directors contended that since no sane merchant would pay interest for a loan he did not need, no matter what the interest rate might be, no one would borrow unless the funds were truly needed to settle the transactions that had occurred in the regular course of economic activity.[20] The Bullionists, by contrast, pointed out that whether firms borrowed depended on whether they expected to be able to earn a greater return than they had to pay for the funds borrowed. If the expected returns in trade or manufacture exceeded the interest rate charged by the Bank, there would be essentially no limit to the demand for loans, even those obtained on discount of bills arising out of real commercial transactions.[21] As Ricardo put it, 'whilst the Bank is willing to lend, borrowers will always exist, so that there can be no limit to their overissues'.[22]

Although modern writers on monetary theory have generally not thought much of the real bills doctrine, the matter of importance to the present inquiry is not whether it was sound, but that it was

---

[17] *Bullion Report*, 46.
[18] 'That this doctrine is a very fallacious one, Your Committee cannot entertain a doubt'. *Bullion Report*, 50.
[19] Thornton, *Paper Credit of Great Britain*, 85–87.   [20] *Bullion Report*, 46–48.
[21] *Bullion Report*, 51–52; Thornton, *Paper Credit of Great Britain*, 252–59.
[22] Ricardo, 'The Price of Gold', quoted in Fetter, *British Monetary Orthodoxy*, 43.

held so strongly by as knowledgeable and influential a segment of English society as the Directors of the Bank of England. Nor did the theory soon die under the pressure of the Bullion Report's trenchant criticism. In the first place, the Bullion Committee's recommendation that convertibility should be restored forthwith was not accepted by Parliament; resumption of specie payment did not come until a decade after the Committee's Report. Moreover, as Lloyd Mints has shown, versions of the real bills doctrine continued to play an important role in debates on monetary theory throughout the nineteenth and into the twentieth century.[23]

It is also important to bear in mind that the debate at the time of the Bullion Report was not about whether it was safe to lend on accommodation paper. No one was so bold as to suggest openly that circulating or discounting accommodation bills was proper or safe. Quite the contrary, the Bullion Report explicitly accepted the conventional view that loans should be limited to the discount of real bills.[24] The point of dispute was not whether it was necessary to avoid accommodation bills, but whether doing so was sufficient to prevent overissue of bank notes. The Bullionists thought not, while the Directors of the Bank of England fervently maintained that adherence to the real bills doctrine provided complete assurance of a safe and stable banking and monetary system.

THE JUDICIAL RESPONSE TO ACCOMMODATION BILLS

The conventional wisdom at the time of the Livesey bankruptcy was that the issuance and circulation of fictitious or accommodation bills not only endangered the solvency of the banks or firms who took the bills, but threatened the stability of the monetary system as a whole. It is this aspect of the public concern with the circulation of accommodation bills that provides the perspective essential to understanding the accommodation bills cases arising

---

[23] Mints, *History of Banking Theory*. Among the more significant manifestations of the real bills doctrine as a general monetary theory were the Banking School writers' theory of 'reflux' advocated by them in opposition to the Currency School theory adopted in Peel's Act in 1844, which strictly tied the note issue of the Bank of England to its specie reserves, and the effort of the framers of the American Federal Reserve System in 1913 to limit central bank lending operations to the discount of 'eligible paper'.

[24] *Bullion Report*, 46.

out of the Livesey bankruptcy and the similar cases that troubled the English courts from the 1790s to the 1830s. Seen only in the light of private losses, a spectacular failure such as Livesey's might be regarded only as a warning to those who might be tempted to engage in similar practices. Given a system where the entire banking and monetary system stood on a foundation of bills of exchange, and given an economic theory that taught that the foundation was sound only in so far as it was built of real bills, those having responsibility for the formulation of policy could hardly fail to see a calamity such as the Livesey failure as posing the challenge of devising some means of preventing the circulation of accommodation paper.

The Livesey fictitious payee cases

The courts' first major encounter with the problem of accommodation bills came in the series of cases in which holders of fictitious bills circulated by the Livesey firm sought to recover on the bills from Livesey and its associates, or, at least, to share in the distribution of their assets in bankruptcy. As was described above, the Livesey firm had been circulating bills which had been drawn payable to fictitious names in order to obscure the realities of their financial practices. For example, the bill of exchange involved in *Gibson* v. *Minet* (1791),[25] which became the test case for resolution of the problems presented by the Livesey paper, had originally been made payable to the order of one 'John White'. The bill bore an indorsement purporting to be that of John White, and eventually ended up in the hands of Hughes Minet and James Fector. By the time the bill was presented for payment, Livesey had gone bankrupt, leaving Minet and Fector in the position of attempting to collect the bill by legal process.

Under the by then well-settled rules governing procedure in actions on bills, one suing on a bill had to prove his title in order to establish a prima facie case. If the bill was payable to bearer, title was established merely by possession. On the other hand, if the bill was originally payable to the order of a specified person, the holder had to prove the authenticity of the first indorser's signature.[26] In

[25] 1 Bl. H. 569.   [26] *Smith* v. *Chester* (1787), 1 T.R. 654.

the Livesey cases, the bills had all been made payable to the order of named persons – John White in the example above. The problem was that there were no such persons. The plaintiffs, then, found themselves in the peculiar position that in order to establish their claims, they had to accomplish the impossible task of proving the authenticity of the signature of non-existent people. The judges of both the King's Bench and the Common Pleas managed to evade the obstacle by permitting the holders of the bills to resort to the pleading fiction of declaring on the bills as if they had been made payable to bearer.[27] The issue, though, was sufficiently difficult and controversial that the test case of *Gibson* v. *Minet* was taken up to the House of Lords.[28]

The fictitious payee cases arising out of the Livesey failure presented the courts with a classic legal dilemma. Although the cases turned on very narrow and technical rules of pleading and evidence, major issues of justice and economic policy were implicated. From the perspective of the holders of the bills, the argument against them seemed outrageous. Having resorted to the sham of issuing the bills in the name of fictitious payees, the perpetrators of the scheme sought to escape liability on the grounds that the holders were unable to prove the handwriting of the non-existent payees. That view of the cases clearly influenced many of the judges.[29] The matter, however, was not really that simple. Since Livesey had gone bankrupt, the real fight was not between the holders of the fictitious bills and the partners of Livesey, but between the holders of such paper and other creditors of the firm. If the holders of the fictitious paper could not recover, the other creditors would receive a larger dividend in the Livesey

---

[27] *Tatlock* v. *Harris* (1789), 3 T.R. 174; *Minet* v. *Gibson* (1789), 3 T.R. 481; *Collis* v. *Emett* (1790), 1 Bl. H. 313.

[28] 1 Bl. H. 569, 584, (1791). Kyd's treatise on bills includes a report of the case, including the opinions of Lords Kenyon, Loughborough, and Bathurst, and Lord Chancellor Thurlow, which are not included in Blackstone's report of the case. Kyd, *Law of Bills of Exchange*, 2nd Amer. edn (1800), 214–68.

[29] 'It is ... impossible not to feel that the Plaintiffs in error avow themselves to be in this situation, namely, of palpably endeavouring to avail themselves of their own fraud; an attempt, which the law will in no case endure, much less assist'. 1 Bl. H. at 584 (Baron Hotham). 'It is contrary to justice, and not to be endured, that fraudulent drawers and acceptors should receive benefit by their own acts, and their estates be exonerated from the demands of their just creditors'. 1 Bl. H. at 589 (Baron Perryn).

bankruptcy.[30] Thus, even as a matter of private rights, the case was a hard one.

The cases were made even more difficult by the public concerns they raised. These cases were the first real test of how the law of bills should respond to the economic problems posed by use of accommodation paper. One of the striking things about the cases is that the judges quite openly discussed the possible economic and social consequences of the decisions that they were called upon to make. As Mr Justice Heath said in his opinion in the House of Lords,

It is agreed on all hands, that the circulation of these bills is extremely mischievous, and ought to be restrained. It is the great commercial evil of these days, which has grown to a gigantic height. It has enabled needy adventurers to engage in desperate undertakings, relying on the money which they raise on this fictitious credit. On the present question, a million of property now depends. No wonder that this traffic has spread poverty, distress, and bankruptcy, through large districts which it has pervaded.[31]

There was, however, no agreement on the proper response of the legal system. Mr Baron Hotham observed that 'the great ends of circulation, the support of credit, and the extension of commerce, would be in constant danger of fatal checks, if bills were permitted to be made so as to enable confederate acceptors to set up their own fraud, as a justification for refusing payment'.[32] The opposing view was expressed most forcefully by Chief Baron Eyre:

I take the interests of commerce to be deeply concerned to support fair, and to discountenance false credit. I take it that the interests of gentlemen who trade in the discount of paper money, and the interests of commerce are not exactly the same. I apprehend that the commerce of the kingdom may receive a deep wound from the failure of a capital house for half a million, when the persons who have been discounting the paper of such a house shall receive not less than twenty shillings in the pound, by proving their debts under twenty commissions of bankrupt. That gentlemen of this description should loudly complain of any check or interruption given to the circulation of fictitious bills of exchange, I can conceive ... That the merchant should join in the complaint, is to me incomprehensible. He

---

[30] Although the opinions in *Minet* v. *Gibson* and the other cases make no mention of this aspect, it must have been obvious to all. Stewart Kyd's treatise begins its discussion of the cases by noting that when Livesey went bankrupt 'the other creditors felt it their interest to resist the claims of the holders of these bills'. Kyd, *Law of Bills of Exchange*, 2nd Amer. edn (1800), 210.

[31] 1 Bl. H. at 624.   [32] 1 Bl. H. at 587.

ought not to forget the original and true use of bills of exchange; that they
are bottomed in real mercantile transactions, that they are then the signs
of valuable property and equivalent to specie, enlarging the capital stock
of wealth in circulation, and thereby facilitating and increasing the trade
and commerce of the country. Such are the bills of exchange which the
usage and custom of merchants originally introduced into the commercial
world, and intended to protect. Let the merchant contrast such bills of
exchange with that false coinage of base paper money which has been of
late forced into circulation; the use of which is to encourage a spirit of rash
adventure, a spirit of monopoly, a spirit of gaming in commerce, luxury,
extravagance and fraud of every kind, to the ruin and destruction of those
whose credulity can be practised upon by a false appearance of regular
trade, carried on upon a solid bottom; and then let him say whether he
dreads the reversal of this judgment.

I confess I thought that a fortunate occasion did now present itself, for
interposing a most salutary check to a growing evil; an evil already swollen
to a most enormous bulk, the weight of which must necessarily cramp and
depress every man who trades upon his own capital, and which threatens
to overwhelm the fair trader. Let us not deceive ourselves. There is but
one remedy for the evil. If such bills may be recovered upon, if they may
be proved under commissions of bankrupts, there are persons enough
interested to give them circulation, let the hindmost fare as he may. To
check them, and oblige men to deal fairly, as far as real names go to
constitute fairness, the recovery must be stopped. If the real parties can
keep back their own names by using fictitious names, they can cover this
false credit in impenetrable darkness.[33]

In the end, the Lords were unpersuaded by Chief Baron Eyre's
arguments; they upheld the ruling of the King's Bench allowing
the holders to declare on the bills as if they had been made payable
to bearer, thereby dispensing with the need for proof of the payee's
indorsement.

Contemporary sources show that the issues in the fictitious
payee cases were considered of utmost importance. The first
edition of Stewart Kyd's treatise on bills, which appeared when
Gibson v. *Minet* was under consideration in the House of Lords,
described the cases and arguments at considerable length, noting
that the fictitious payee issue 'has long agitated the commercial
world'.[34] By the time the second edition appeared, the House of
Lords had decided the case, and Kyd included very full reports of
the opinions of all of the Lords; indeed, the discussion accounts
for more than one-fifth of the entire book.[35] Other contemporary

---

[33] 1 Bl. H. at 618–19.   [34] Kyd, *Law of Bills of Exchange*, 137–50.
[35] Kyd, *Law of Bills of Exchange*, 2nd Amer. edn (1800), 214–68.

authors were, with some regret, somewhat more restrained. Evans, for example, outlined the issues and then remarked that 'the several opinions in support of these opposite positions, are stated in Mr. Henry Blackstone's Reports and Mr. Kyd's Treatise on Bills. I reluctantly forbear swelling this essay to a disproportionate extent by inserting them, but cannot too strongly recommend their perusal to all who are engaged in judicial studies.'[36] Other treatises of that era also reflect the impact of the cases. Chitty, for example, added a passage in the introductory sections of the fifth edition of his treatise noting the dire economic consequences of accommodation bills.[37]

The continuing struggle with accommodation bills

Although the fictitious payee cases growing out of the collapse of Livesey, Hargreaves & Co. may have been the most spectacular legal manifestation of the economic problem of accommodation paper, they were by no means the only setting in which the courts were confronted with thorny legal issues growing out of the use of accommodation bills. Over and again in the late eighteenth and early nineteenth centuries, courts struggled with the question whether accommodation paper should be treated differently from real bills.[38] Underlying many of these seemingly technical disputes

---

[36] Evans, *Essays on the Law of Bills of Exchange*, 204.

[37] 'The pernicious effects of a fabricated credit, by the undue use of accommodation bills of exchange ... have been too much felt to require any observation; the use of them ... is injurious to the public as well as to the parties concerned in the negotiation ... The use of fictitious names to bills has not been infrequent, but this practice is not only censurable but in some cases punishable criminally'. Chitty, *Treatise on Bills of Exchange*, 5th edn (1818), 5–6.

[38] The most basic rules on accommodation paper were relatively easily settled. The acceptor of an accommodation bill was liable to a holder who gave value for the bill, even if the holder took with knowledge that the acceptor signed only for accommodation. *Smith* v. *Knox* (1799), 3 Esp. 47; *Charles* v. *Marsden* (1808), 1 Taunt. 224. Between the immediate parties, however, obligations would be determined by the usual rules of suretyship, regardless of the liabilities that might otherwise follow from the capacity in which they signed the bill. Thus, although a drawee who accepted a bill would ordinarily be liable on it to the drawer if the drawer were forced to pay, *Simmonds* v. *Parminter* (1747), 1 Wils. K.B. 185, an accommodation payee would not be liable to the person he accommodated. Rather, the drawer or other principal debtor was bound to indemnify an accommodation acceptor who paid the bill. *Jones* v. *Brooke* (1812), 4 Taunt. 464; *Young* v. *Hockley* (1772), 3 Wils. 346. Beyond such simple points, however, agreement disappeared, and the fundamental conflicts over the proper

was the fundamental conflict that faced the judges in cases on accommodation bills. Should the legal system attempt to check the use of accommodation bills, or should the courts proceed in a fashion neutral to the economic problems that were widely felt to flow from the extensive use of accommodation paper?

A good illustration was the dispute over the availability of suretyship defences to an accommodation acceptor. The conventional legal parsing of the relationship of the parties to an ordinary 'real bill' transaction was that once the drawee had accepted the bill he was the person primarily liable, and the drawer was a surety for the acceptor.[39] Thus, although the drawer would be discharged if the holder agreed to extend the time for the acceptor to pay, or if the holder failed to give proper notice of dishonour, the acceptor would rarely be discharged by anything other than payment of the bill.[40] With accommodation bills, however, the reality of the underlying transaction was usually just the opposite. The acceptor was lending his credit to assist the principal debtor, usually the drawer, to raise money. Should an accommodation acceptor be able to raise suretyship defences, or should he be bound by the form of the instrument?

In 1809, the question came before Lord Ellenborough at *nisi prius* in *Laxton* v. *Peat*.[41] So far as appears from the report, Lord Ellenborough seems to have thought it a very simple case. 'This being an accommodation bill within the knowledge of all the parties, the acceptor can only be considered a surety for the drawer; and in the case of simple contracts the surety is discharged by time being given, without his concurrence, to the principal.'[42] To other judges, however, the issue seemed far less clear. In an 1813 ruling at *nisi prius*, Mr Justice Gibbs of the Common Pleas noted that 'grave doubts have been entertained' about Ellenborough's decision in *Laxton*.[43] In the particular case, Gibbs was able

function of bills emerged as a significant influence on the development of the law of bills.
[39] *Rowe* v. *Young* (1820), 2 Br. & B. 165, 237.
[40] *Dingwall* v. *Dunster* (1779), 1 Doug. 247.
[41] 2 Camp. 185.
[42] 2 Camp. at 186. A few years later, the flip side issue came before Ellenborough at *nisi prius*, and he ruled, consistently with *Laxton*, that in an accommodation bill the drawer would not be discharged by time being given to the acceptor. *Collot* v. *Haigh* (1812), 3 Camp. 281.
[43] *Kerrison* v. *Cooke* (1813), 3 Camp. 362.

to distinguish *Laxton*, though he remarked that he was 'sorry the term accommodation bill ever found its way into the law, or that parties were allowed to get rid of the obligations they profess to contract by putting their names to negotiable securities'.[44] When the issue came before the full Court of Common Pleas later that year in *Fentum* v. *Pocock* (1813),[45] the judges virtually recoiled in horror at the suggestion that the acceptor should be able to raise suretyship defences. As Chief Justice James Mansfield[46] put it, 'No doubt, if the defendant can succeed in establishing the principle that we must so subvert and pervert the situation of the parties as to make the acceptor merely a surety, and the drawer a principal, the consequence contended for must follow.'[47] The court declined to follow *Laxton*, noting that 'certainly the paying respect to accommodation bills is not what one would wish to do, seeing the mischiefs arising from them'.[48] Later decisions in the King's Bench seemed to follow *Fentum*,[49] though it was generally said that in equity the tendency was to allow the acceptor to prove his suretyship defences.[50]

In *Fentum*, the judges faced the question of the treatment of accommodation bills in the easiest procedural setting. The accommodation party was arguing for an exception to the usual rules of the law of bills, so that both economic policy and technical legal rules weighed in favour of the same result. The problems were considerably more difficult in circumstances where these concerns were not congruent. In a number of settings, the tendency to react with aversion to accommodation bills gave rise to legal rules that proved difficult to apply and justify.

[44] 3 Camp. at 363.   [45] 5 Taunt. 192.

[46] James Mansfield, Chief Justice of the Common Pleas from 1804 to 1814, had the misfortune of sharing his surname with the name taken by William Murray upon his being raised to peerage at the time of his appointment as Chief Justice of the King's Bench in 1756. Were it not for the inevitable comparison with his more renowned namesake, James Mansfield might well have escaped such left-handed praise as Foss' description of him as 'a good average lawyer'. Foss, *Biographical Dictionary of the Judges of England*, 429.

[47] 5 Taunt. at 195.

[48] 5 Taunt. at 196. Similarly, Mr Justice Heath observed in *Fentum* that 'whoever draws an accommodation bill, procures another to accept it, and negotiates it without letting the person to whom he passes it know it is an accommodation bill, is, as I think, guilty of a gross fraud'. 5 Taunt. at 197.

[49] *Price* v. *Edmunds* (1830), 10 Barn. & Cress. 578; *Nichols* v. *Norris* (1831), 3 Barn. & Adol. 41; *Harrison* v. *Courtauld* (1832), 3 Barn. & Adol. 36.

[50] Byles, *Law of Bills of Exchange*, 8th edn (1862), 226.

As was noted in the previous chapter, the rules on notice of dishonour had become quite complex by the end of the eighteenth century. Cases involving accommodation bills further complicated the issue. In *Walwyn* v. *St Quintin* (1797),[51] the problem came before the court of Common Pleas, then headed by Chief Justice Eyre, who had argued so strongly against accommodation bills in the House of Lords deliberations in the fictitious payee cases. Thomas had prevailed upon Deane and St Quintin to assist him in raising money, the specific mechanism being that St Quintin drew a bill on Deane payable to Thomas, which was indorsed to Walwyn for value after acceptance by Deane. Thus, the reality of the transaction was that the payee was the principal debtor, and both the drawer and acceptor were acting for his accommodation. Walwyn sued the drawer, St Quintin, who sought to defend on the grounds that Walwyn had unduly delayed in giving him notice of dishonour. Walwyn contended that since the acceptor held no effects of the drawer, notice of dishonour was excused under the rule of *Bickerdike* v. *Bollman* (1786).[52] Although it was a bit difficult to apply the *Bickerdike* rule in this case where the principal debtor was the payee rather than the drawer, Chief Justice Eyre left no doubt about how he felt about such transactions.

In a regular bill transaction the drawing by A. payable to B., or payable to A'.s own order, and indorsing the bill to B., is a mode by which the drawer pays a sum of money to his payee or indorsee through an acceptor. The transaction in this case, as far as it had any pretensions to be deemed a real transaction, was a mode by which the acceptor advanced a sum of money to the payee, and the drawer was a mere instrument of the acceptor. This is reversing the order of things. As far as concerns the drawer, it is what has been called a mere accommodation; and all consideration of effects of the drawer in the hands of the acceptor may be laid aside ... If there be any case in which notice should be dispensed with, surely it is this ... Where the drawer has no effects, and has no fair pretence for drawing, or where he draws without having effects intended to be applied in payment, and only for the purpose of raising money by discount for himself, and a fortiori for the acceptor, which is this case, it is fairly deducible from the cases which have been resolved, that notice need not be given.[53]

In *Walwyn*, the aversion to accommodation bills was manifested in an exception to the usual rule requiring notice, but the result was to preclude the accommodation party from escaping liability. The

<hr>

[51] 1 Bos. & Pul. 652.   [52] 1 T.R. 405, discussed in chapter 9.
[53] 1 Bos. & Pul. at 654–55.

sense that there was something improper about accommodation paper might, however, lead to the opposite result.

In actions on ordinary bills, consideration was presumed. In cases tainted by fraud or other suspicious circumstances, however, the holder was required to show that he had no connection with the impropriety and had taken the bill for a good consideration.[54] Should such proof be required if the defendant showed that he signed only for accommodation, or should the usual presumption of consideration apply? There seem to have been no clear holdings on the matter in the early decades of the nineteenth century,[55] but the practice seems to have been to require the holder of an accommodation bill to prove that he gave consideration.[56] That requirement would, at the least, make actions on accommodation bills somewhat more difficult, and could easily preclude a holder from recovering simply because he was unable to recall precisely how he came by the bill. Thus, in this setting, putting accommodation bills on the same footing as transactions tainted by fraud led to a result favourable to the parties who had issued the bill.

It was hard enough for the judges to decide what to do in cases where the desire to discourage circulation of accommodation bills pointed in one direction and the desire to punish those who had already circulated the bills pointed in the opposite direction. Worse still, they were confronted with cases where it was virtually impossible to figure out who would be benefited or harmed by one approach or the other. The best examples are the cases that arose when two firms had been accepting accommodation bills for each other, and then both firms went bankrupt.[57] The holders of the

---

[54] *Duncan* v. *Scott* (1807), 1 Camp. 100 (bill issued under duress – drawer imprisoned and threatened with guillotine if he did not draw it); *De la Chaumette* v. *Bank of England* (1829), 9 Barn. & Cress. 208 (stolen note); *King* v. *Milsom* (1809), 2 Camp. 5 (same); *Heath* v. *Sansom* (1831), 2 Barn. & Adol. 291 (bill issued by partner for personal debt).

[55] There was, however, broad language in several opinions that was taken to imply that the holder must prove consideration whenever the defendant showed that he did not receive anything for the bill, *Thomas* v. *Newton* (1827), 2 Car. & P. 606, or if the bill for any other reason would not have been enforceable among the initial parties, *Heath* v. *Sansom* (1831), 2 Barn. & Adol. 291, 296.

[56] In an 1835 case in the Court of Exchequer, Lord Abinger stated that in his long experience at the bar, the practice had universally been to require such proof. *Simpson* v. *Clarke*, 2 Cr. M. & R. 342.

[57] E.g., *Cowley* v. *Dunlop* (1798), 7 T.R. 565; *Ex parte Walker* (1798), 4 Ves. Jun. 373; *Ex parte Earle* (1801), 5 Ves. Jun. 833; *Ex parte Metcalfe* (1805), 11 Ves. Jun. 404; *Ex parte Rawson* (1821), Jac. 274.

accommodation bills would have commonly had a cause of action against each of the firms, for on any given bill one of the firms would usually have been liable as acceptor while the other was secondarily liable as drawer. If the holders of the accommodation bills were allowed to prove their claims, it would become necessary to sort out the rights between the two firms. Applying the ordinary bills rules, if one of the firms was called upon to pay as drawer, it would in turn have an action against the other firm as acceptor. If suretyship law applied, the accommodation acceptor would have a right of recourse against the drawer. If the holders of the accommodation paper were precluded from proving their claims, that might increase the dividend that could be paid to the other creditors by reducing the total amount of claims, or it might have the opposite effect by excluding the firm's claims for reimbursement in the bankruptcy of the other firm, thereby reducing the assets available for distribution.

These mutual accommodation cases totally bewildered the courts, as Lord Eldon candidly admitted in an 1821 case. Counsel for one of the parties had cited a previous case, *Ex parte Walker*, in support of his view of the problem, prompting the following reminiscence by Lord Eldon:

I think I argued that case of *Ex parte Walker*, and I must say that the speculations about paper certainly outran the grasp of the wits of courts of justice. When I first came into Westminster Hall, there was no such thing as an acceptor saying that he had no effects: his acceptance was an acknowledgment that he had. That, however, was overruled, and it was decided that when the acceptor had no effects, it was not necessary to give notice; for before it was the constant rule to give notice, even if the acceptor was a bankrupt, and, therefore, every one knew that he could not pay a farthing.

This new sort of circulating medium puzzled as able a man as ever sat here, Lord Thurlow. I remember the first case of it. It was then small in amount, one bill and another. He then considered the acceptance of the one as a consideration for the other, and allowed both to prove, but then there was this difficulty, that it lessened the fund for paying the holder of the bill, and thus by proving, they prejudiced their own creditors. It was found this would not do, and then it was said, if you will prove, you must first take up your acceptance, which got rid of the objection of the party proving in competition with his own creditor.

Then came the case of those houses at Liverpool and Manchester drawing on one another to the amount of £500,000. What was to be done then? The Courts were puzzled and distressed. At last, however, we came to a sort of anchorage in that case, *Ex parte Walker*; I have no difficulty in saying that I never understood it. I am satisfied that though, no doubt, the Court understood that judgment, yet none of the counsel did.[58]

The denouement: reaching an accommodation with accommodation bills

By the 1820s and 1830s the idea that legal rules should reflect economic policy discouraging accommodation bills began to hold less and less appeal. In part, this shift in attitude may simply have been a reaction against the complexities of the rules that developed in the effort to distinguish between accommodation and real bills. It does, though, seem that more was involved than practical problems, and that the old attitudes toward accommodation bills were withering. For example, on the issue of excuse of notice, a case all but indistinguishable from *Walwyn* came before the King's Bench in 1820 in *Cory* v. *Scott*.[59] Lough & Co. had borrowed some £200 from Cory, giving a bill for the debt on which Scott and Gordon appeared as accommodation parties. The bill was drawn by Scott on Gordon, payable to Scott, and was indorsed to Lough & Co. after acceptance by Gordon. Cory sued Scott on the bill, and Scott objected that he had not been given timely notice of dishonour. Cory contended that since neither Scott nor Lough & Co. had any effects in Gordon's hands, notice was not required under *Bickerdike* and *Walwyn*. The opinions in *Cory*, however, show that the *Bickerdike* rule had been significantly reinterpreted. *Bickerdike* and *Walwyn* had gone on the grounds that drawing a bill on one who held no effects was an act so far beyond the realm of legitimate dealing that the drawer could not demand the usual protection of the rules on notice of dishonour. By the time of *Cory*, however, the critical question was not whether the drawer had effects, but whether the party who did not receive notice would have had a right of recourse against someone else.[60] Since the drawer, Scott, could have sought indemnity from the principal debtor, Lough & Co., and perhaps from the acceptor, the lack of timely notice might have prejudiced his ability to seek recourse. Accordingly, the court ruled that notice was required. Mr Justice Holroyd's opinion is

---

[58] *Ex parte Rawson* (1821), Jac. 274, 277–78. The author has not positively identified the 'case of those houses at Liverpool and Manchester' referred to by Lord Eldon, but does not think that it was one of the Livesey cases.
[59] 3 Barn. & Ald. 619.   [60] 3 Barn. & Ald. at 622.

ample evidence of the shift in attitude toward accommodation paper. After noting that the *Bickerdike* case was often thought to rest on fraud, he remarked that 'here the party who has only lent his name as surety is guilty of no fraud'.[61] Twenty-five years earlier, the attitude had been exactly the opposite. For Chief Justice Eyre in *Walwyn*, the fact that the bill was mere accommodation paper was enough to take it out of the usual rules for regular bill transactions. For the judges of the King's Bench at the time of *Cory*, the task was to be sure that the rules were properly tailored to meet the circumstances of accommodation bill dealings.

A similar shift in attitude can be seen in the cases dealing with the question whether one suing on an accommodation bill had to prove that he gave consideration. In several cases in the early 1830s Sir James Parke had suggested that proof of consideration should not necessarily be required in actions on accommodation bills.[62] The issue came to a head in the 1830s in several decisions in the Court of Exchequer. In *Simpson* v. *Clarke* (1835),[63] the Chief Baron, Lord Abinger, expressed some surprise that the rule requiring proof of consideration in actions on accommodation bills had been questioned. Responding to the distinction made in argument between accommodation bills and bills obtained by fraud, Abinger remarked 'is it so clear that an accommodation bill has nothing of fraud in it? . . . At all events, they do not deserve much encouragement. A bill of exchange purports on the face of it to be a transaction between the parties for value; it imports prima facie payment of a debt, or an acceptance by way of security for goods delivered. But in what case is the public, if bills of exchange which are taken to be great indications of the flourishing state of commerce, and evidences of bona fide mercantile transactions, turn out to be mere nullities, indicative of no value whatsoever?'[64] Lord Abinger was, however, struggling against the tide; when the issue returned a year later in *Mills* v. *Barber* (1836),[65] he relented. The barons consulted with the judges of the King's Bench, and the consensus was that proof of consideration should no longer be required merely because the bill was accommodation paper.

[61] 3 Barn. & Ald. at 625.
[62] *Heath* v. *Sansom* (1831), 2 Barn. & Adol. 291, 297; *Percival* v. *Frampton* (1835), 2 Cr. M. & R. 180, 183.
[63] 2 Cr. M. & R. 342.   [64] 2 Cr. M. & R. at 347.   [65] 1 M. & W. 426.

Perhaps the most revealing evidence of the shift in attitude toward accommodation bills is the tone of Lord Abinger's opinion in *Simpson* v. *Clarke*. Referring to Chief Justice Mansfield's remarks about accommodation paper in the *Fentum* case some twenty years before, Abinger observed that 'it was the opinion at that time, more indeed as a question of political economy than of law, that to use a mercantile instrument, which may have a very extensive circulation, and be supposed to represent a real trans-action, but which had in fact no reality at all, was hardly moral, and bore with it something of actual fraud'.[66] Abinger recalled how decades before 'Lord Kenyon used to alarm the juries at Guildhall by the vigour with which he poured out his eloquence against the toleration of accommodation bills at all'.[67] The wistful mood is apt, for Abinger's opinion may have been the last hurrah of the abhor-rence toward accommodation paper that had been so forcefully expressed in the Livesey cases.

Although real bills theory would continue to influence economic thought until well into the twentieth century, the effort to enforce that economic policy through the law of bills and notes seems to have been all but abandoned by the 1830s. If one examines treatises on the law of bills published in the mid-nineteenth century, one finds that a great deal of the work is devoted to questions of suretyship law arising out of the flourishing of what previously would have been condemned as mere accommodation paper.[68] Sir Mackenzie Chalmers, the author of the British Bills of Exchange Act of 1882, aptly summed up the attitude of nineteenth-century English law in a remark contrasting the paths taken by English and French law on bills, 'In England bills have developed into a perfectly flexible paper currency. In France a bill represents a trade transaction; in England it is merely an instrument of credit. English law gives full play to the system of accommodation paper; French law endeavours to stamp it out'.[69]

---

[66] 2 Cr. M. & R. at 348.   [67] 2 Cr. M. & R. at 347.

[68] For example, a separate chapter on issues of suretyship defences, under the title 'Indulgence', was added to Byles' treatise on the law of bills, beginning with the second edition. Beginning with the fourth edition, the chapter was entitled 'Of the law of Principal and Surety in its Relation to Bills and Notes'.

[69] Chalmers, *Digest of the Law of Bills of Exchange*, xii.

THE ACCOMMODATION BILLS CONTROVERSY
AS AN ILLUSTRATION OF THE ROLE OF LAW
IN ECONOMIC CONTROVERSIES

It is often suggested that the task of those who formulate commercial law is simply to facilitate commercial transactions.[70] The relationship between private law and social forces is far more complex than that. We have seen that the early history of exchange is intimately connected with the controversies over usury and economic policy that were presented by the development of exchange as a significant means of finance in the seventeenth century. In the controversy over accommodation bills, 200 years later, we find very much the same story. It would be difficult to find any less accurate way of describing the relationship between law and social policy manifested in the early accommodation bills cases than to say that law merely follows business. In the hundreds of pages of opinions and treatise discussions of the Livesey fictitious payee cases, one cannot find a single word suggesting that anyone thought that the proper response to the problem was to say that since businessmen were using fictitious bills, law should simply accept that practice. Quite the contrary, the judges who decided the Livesey cases uniformly agreed that the financing practices involved were pernicious and should be stopped; they disagreed only on how legal rules should implement the relevant principles of social and economic morality. That is not to say that the history of the law of bills teaches that private law can or should attempt to influence the outcome of social or economic conflicts. Legal history cannot resolve that perennial problem; it can only show that it is indeed a perennial problem.

Although the accommodation bills cases show clearly that legal rules cannot be divorced from their economic and social context, there is ample room for disagreement on the interpretation of the episode from the perspective of the relationship between law and social conflict. One interpretation would be that the accommodation bills cases show the futility of attempting to use the rules of private law to force business practice to conform to the dictates of

---

[70] The late-nineteenth-century judge Lord Bowen is reported to have remarked that 'law should follow business; it should not divert or anticipate the course of business, except for the most urgent reasons'. Bigelow, *Law of Bills, Notes, and Cheques*, 2nd edn (1900), 7.

economic or ethical policy. The judges in the early accommodation bills cases explicitly sought to express in legal rules the conventional abhorrence of accommodation bills, but they found the task beyond their abilities. The cases involving the *Bickerdike* excuse of notice rule, and the cases involving the bankruptcy of firms that had been accepting accommodation bills for each other, show that the effort to establish special rules for accommodation bills became hopelessly complex. Moreover, when the courts did seek to implement special rules for accommodation bills, they faced the dilemma of conflict between the desire to do justice in the immediate case, by ensuring that those who had circulated the bills did not escape liability, and the desire to curtail future uses of such bills, by enunciating rules that would render precarious the legal position of those who took the bills. Eventually, they simply gave up in frustration.

One might, on the other hand, cast the episode in a different light by focusing on possible economic explanations for the change in attitude toward accommodation paper that one sees between the 1790s and the 1830s. There is quite a close correlation between the shift in attitude toward accommodation bills evidenced in the opinions and significant changes in economic conditions. In 1810, the Bullion Committee's recommendation that the Bank of England resume specie payment forthwith may not have seemed feasible given the continuance of hostilities with the French. However, with the final defeat of Napoleon in 1815, the original cause and continuing justification for the suspension was removed, and demands for resumption increased. After many years of debate, the Resumption Act of 1819 was passed,[71] calling for a phased-in resumption of specie payment that would lead to a return to the old standard of the gold value of the pound by 1821. We have seen that in the 1820s and 1830s, the judicial decisions show far less concern with the potential problems of accommodation bills than in earlier decades. One explanation would be that with the resumption of specie payment the volume of money that could be created by banking operations was once more subjected to the check provided by the requirement of convertibility. In those circumstances, it may well have seemed less important to endeavour to stamp out accommodation paper than it had during the

---

[71] 59 Geo III, c. 49 (1819).

suspension period. Moreover, because the resumption plan took the form of a return to the old gold standard, essentially attempting to undo the previous decades' inflation, the economic effect of resumption was a significant curtailment of credit facilities and drop in price levels. Thus, in the period after resumption, demands for increased bank lending came to be at least as significant a force in public discussion of economic conditions as had concern with excessive lending in the suspension period.[72] Accordingly, legal rules designed with a view toward caution and restraint in banking and credit operations may well have lost a good deal of their appeal by the 1820s and 1830s.

Another possible interpretation of the change in the judicial attitude toward accommodation bills would focus not on specific circumstances concerning the banking and monetary system, but on general economic, social, and political changes in late-eighteenth- and early-nineteenth-century England. One might say that the approach to accommodation bills ultimately reached by the English courts in the 1830s was no less a reflection of social, ethical, and economic norms than was the position taken by Sir James Eyre in the Livesey cases. The difference was that the relevant norms had changed, or, to put the matter in harsher terms, that the power elite whose norms are reflected in law had changed. One need look no further than his own words to see Chief Baron Eyre's contemptuous attitude toward those 'gentlemen who trade in the discount of paper money' and whose newfangled financial practices 'encourage a spirit of rash adventure ... gaming in commerce, luxury, extravagance and fraud of every kind'. It is but a slight step to read these remarks as evidence of the hostility of entrenched power and wealth to the challenge of a new class of entrepreneurs. So too, one might read the remark in *Cory* v. *Scott* (1820) that 'one who has only lent his name as surety [to an accommodation bill] is guilty of no fraud', as the expression of the economic morality of that newer, and by 1820 nearly triumphant, class. It is worth noting that the period in which the shift in attitude toward accommodation bills was most pronounced, the 1820s and 1830s, was also the period of the struggles leading to the great Parliamentary Reform Bill of 1831, which by abolishing the 'rotten boroughs' and establishing new seats drawn largely from

[72] Viner, *Theory of International Trade*, 119.

the newly developed industrial and commercial centres such as Manchester and Liverpool effectively transferred a large measure of political power from the landed aristocracy to the middle classes.

One need not, however, conclude that the accommodation bills episode shows that any effort by law to influence or implement economic and social policy toward business practice is futile, or that law merely operates as a passive reflection of changing economic conditions, or that law's sometimes professed concern with normative values is nothing more than a guise for reflection of the interests of the currently dominant class. There may also be room for an interpretation that finds a valuable role for the legal system in the process of social change itself, regardless of the particular direction that change may have taken. The undeniable fact is that the economic and social issues presented by the use of accommodation bills did become legal issues. Lawyers and judges openly and explicitly discussed and debated the issues of economics and ethics that were presented by changing financial practices, and they did so in a public forum, which, by virtue of the implicit requirement that decisions be rationally justified, is particularly well suited to conferring moral authority on the outcome of the discussion. Whether one characterizes it as an expression of rigorous ethical propriety, conventional economic wisdom, or the class interest of the entrenched power elite, the views expressed by Chief Baron Eyre in the Livesey cases were expressed, and, at times, influenced the outcome of litigation and the formulation of legal rules. So too, the opposing position taken by the judges in the cases in the 1820s and 1830s, which is open to an equally broad range of characterization, was also expressed and had its influence. It may well be that it ultimately made little difference to the outcome of the social and economic conflict whether the courts took one view or the other. On the other hand, it may well have been very important, and, in any event, inevitable, that the issues were discussed in the courts.

CONCLUSION

Let us reconsider what is really meant by statements to the effect that 'the Law Merchant, or *Lex Mercatoria*, is part of the Common Law'. Much of the sense of mystery and jurisprudential complexity that surrounds that notion[1] is probably attributable to nothing more than the odd grammatical construction of the phrase 'Law Merchant'. In English, when a noun is made into an adjective, a suffix is usually added, and adjectives in English generally precede rather than follow nouns. Moreover, in the twentieth century, we no longer employ such stylistic flourishes as capitalizing nouns, or rendering them into Latin. If these ordinary conventions were followed, we would have the rather unremarkable sounding proposition that 'mercantile law is part of the common law', or, to say the same thing in different words, 'commercial law is part of English law'.

The proposition that 'commercial law is part of English law' is, however, not really as pedestrian as it may first seem. In chapter 1, it was shown that even in medieval times the common law courts regularly heard cases arising out of commercial transactions. On the other hand, it seems apparent that a medieval English lawyer would not have thought of describing these as *commercial law* cases, but as actions in account, debt, or whatever. That a case arose out of a commercial transaction was not a legally interesting point; that it raised an issue about resummons was. Indeed, the reason that it has so often been assumed that there were no commercial law cases in the common law courts before the seventeenth century is that the cases arising out of commerce are essentially invisible because that characteristic did not figure in any of

---

[1] 'No part of the History of English Law is more obscure than that connected with the maxim that the law merchant is part of the law of the land'. Blackburn, *Contract of Sale* (1845), 207, quoted in Baker, 'Law Merchant and Common Law', 341.

the classificatory schemes then used. By the early eighteenth century, it becomes easy to find commercial cases in the common law courts; not because they had newly appeared, but because the relevant categories begin to show up in the indices and tables of contents.

One will find no mention of bills of exchange or any other branch or topic of mercantile law in the topical headings of the fifteenth-, sixteenth-, and seventeenth-century abridgments. By contrast, Matthew Bacon's *New Abridgment of the Law* (1736–66), has a lengthy division under the title 'Merchant and Merchandize', with subheadings on such topics as principals and factors, partners, various maritime subjects, insurance, bottomry, and bills of exchange. In Viner's *General Abridgment of Law and Equity* (1741–53), commercial topics are even further integrated into the corpus of English law, for rather than being grouped together in a special heading on merchants' affairs, topics such as bills of exchange, factors, and partners were main entries in their own right. The treatment of bills in the eighteenth-century abridgments shows a remarkable advance over the earlier literature. In place of the jumble of half-understood remarks on the nature of exchange, dry exchange, and the like that one finds in seventeenth-century English works on exchange, Bacon and Viner give clear, logically organized presentations of the cases, discussing in turn the definition of bills and notes, the liabilities of the parties, methods of transfer, acceptance, and procedure in actions to enforce bills.

The difference between the law books of the sixteenth century and those of the eighteenth was not simply that a new category or categories covering commercial matters had been added. In itself that would have been a significant change. What is more remarkable still is that the appearance of the categories of commercial law represented a thoroughgoing recategorization of the materials of the law. One can see the change quite clearly in the section on factors in Bacon's *Abridgment*. This passage digests not only the contemporary cases dealing with the rights and duties of factors, but also various yearbook cases and other early authorities dealing with actions of account brought by merchants against their factors. In the earlier abridgments these were grouped together with cases involving manorial bailiffs and categorized only as actions in account. In Bacon's *Abridgment* they have been reclassified as actions involving factors. Thus, there is a sense in which the old canard about there being no commercial cases in the common law courts before the seventeenth century is true. Before the seventeenth century the only legally significant characteristic of these cases was that they had been brought in the procedural form of actions in account. They could be found only through the abridgments or other texts in which they were categorized only as such. They were account cases because that was the only way that they could have been described in the legal vocabulary of the time. By the eighteenth century, they had become commercial cases – not because anything about the cases themselves had changed, but because a new vocabulary had developed in which it was possible to describe them as such, and a new attitude toward trade and commerce had become prevalent which made it seem natural to think of them as cases about commercial factors.

This process of reconceptualization and systemization was, by its very nature, a task that the judges and lawyers of the common law system had to carry out themselves. A sound knowledge of mercantile practice was a prerequisite, but only that. The solutions to legal problems could not be found in mercantile practice. For much the same reason, the judges and lawyers of the common law system could find only the most limited guidance in the works of jurists from other legal systems. The common lawyers would have been no more assisted by discussions in the civilian literature about whether the obligations of parties to exchange contracts or bills of exchange should be classified as *mutuum, emptio-venditio,* or *permutatio*, than the civilians would have been by a common lawyer's explanation of the fine points of the distinction between *assumpsit* and debt.

The common metaphor of 'incorporation of the law merchant' is quite misleading as a description of the process by which the English law of bills developed. The difficult task that the judges and lawyers faced in the seventeenth and eighteenth centuries was not to adopt ready-made rules from some source outside the ordinary English law. Rather, new commercial transactions had to be fitted within the categories of the existing legal system; or perhaps more accurately, the categories of legal system had to be reworked so that they would accommodate new economic conditions. What the English judges 'incorporated' into the common law was not commercial *law* but commercial *practice*; by doing so they composed commercial law.

BIBLIOGRAPHY

Ames, James Barr. 'The History of Parol Contracts Prior to Assumpsit'. In *Select Essays in Anglo-American Legal History*, 3: 304–19. 3 vols. Boston: Little, Brown & Co., 1907–09. Reprinted from *Harvard Law Review* 8 (1895): 252–64.

Anderson, Adam. *Historical and Chronological Deduction of the Origin of Commerce*. Revised edn. 6 vols. Dublin, 1790 (1st edn 1762).

Anon. *The Mystery of the New Fashioned Goldsmiths or Bankers*. 1676. Reprinted in John Biddulph Martin. *'The Grasshopper' in Lombard Street*. London: Leadenhall Press, 1892.

Armstrong, Clement [attribution]. 'A Treatise concerninge the Staple and the Commodities of this Realme'. In *Tudor Economic Documents* 3: 90–114.

Ashley, W. J. *An Introduction to English Economic History and Theory*. 2nd edn. 2 vols. New York: G. P. Putnam's Sons, 1893.

Ashton, T. S. 'The Bill of Exchange and Private Banks in Lancashire, 1790–1830'. In *Papers in English Monetary History*, edited by T. S. Ashton and R. S. Sayers, 37–49. Oxford: Clarendon Press, 1953. Reprinted from *Economic History Review* 15 (1945): 25–35.

An Economic History of England: the Eighteenth Century. 1955. Reprint. London: Methuen and Company, 1959.

Atherton, Lewis E. *The Frontier Merchant in Mid-America*. Columbia, Mo.: University of Missouri Press, 1971.

The Southern Country Store 1800–1860. 1949. Reprint. New York: Greenwood Press, 1968.

Bacon, Matthew. *New Abridgment of the Law*. 5 vols. London, 1736–66.

Bagehot, Walter. *Lombard Street: A Description of the Money Market*. New York: Charles Scribner's Sons, 1895 (1st edn. London, 1873).

Baker, J. H. *An Introduction to English Legal History*. 3rd edn. London: Butterworths, 1990.

'The Law Merchant and the Common Law before 1700'. In *The Legal Profession and the Common Law: Historical Essays*, 341–68. London: Hambledon Press, 1986. Reprinted from *Cambridge Law Journal* 38 (1979): 295–322.

'New Light on Slade's Case'. In *The Legal Profession and the Common Law: Historical Essays*, 393–432. London: Hambledon Press, 1986. Reprinted from *Cambridge Law Journal* 29 (1971): 51–67, 213–36.

The Reports of Sir John Spelman. 2 vols. Selden Society, vols. 93, 94. London, 1977.

Baker, J. H. and Milsom, S. F. C. *Sources of English Legal History: Private Law to 1750.* London: Butterworth & Co., 1986.

Barbour, W. T. *The History of Contract in Early English Equity.* Oxford Studies in Social and Legal History, vol. 4. 1914.

Bayley, John. *A Short Treatise on the Law of Bills of Exchange, Cash Bills, and Promissory Notes.* London, 1789.

Summary of the Law of Bills of Exchange, Cash Bills, and Promissory Notes. 5th edn. London, 1830.

Beawes, Wyndham. *Lex Mercatoria Rediviva: or, The Merchant's Directory.* 4th edn. revised by Thomas Mortimer. London, 1783. Republished in 1970 by Gregg International Publishers Limited, Farnborough, Hants.

Belsheim, Edmund O. 'The Old Action of Account'. *Harvard Law Review* 45 (1932): 466–500.

Beutel, Frederick K. 'The Development of Negotiable Instruments in Early English Law'. *Harvard Law Review* 51 (1938): 813–45.

Bigelow, Melville M. *Elements of the Law of Bills, Notes, and Cheques, and the English Bills of Exchange Act.* Boston: Little, Brown, & Co., 1893.

The Law of Bills, Notes, and Cheques. 2nd edn. Boston: Little, Brown, & Co., 1900.

Bindoff, S. T. 'Clement Armstrong and his Treatise of the Commonweal'. *Economic History Review* 14 (1944): 64–73.

Blackstone, William. *Commentaries on the Laws of England.* 4 vols. Facsimile of the 1st edn of 1765–69. Chicago: University of Chicago Press, 1979.

Bland, A. E., Brown, P. A., and Tawney, R. H., eds., *English Economic History: Select Documents.* London: G. Bell and Sons, 1914.

Blomquist, Thomas W. 'The Dawn of Banking in an Italian Commune: Thirteenth Century Lucca'. In *The Dawn of Modern Banking,* 53–75. New Haven, Conn.: Yale University Press, 1979.

Bohun, W. *Declarations and Pleadings in the Most Usual Actions Brought in the Several Courts of King's-Bench and Common-Pleas at Westminster.* London, 1733.

Braudel, Fernand. *Civilization and Capitalism 15th–18th Century.* Translated by S. Reynolds. 3 vols. New York: Harper & Row, 1981–84.

Brevia Placitata, edited by G. J. Turner, completed with addition by T. F. T. Plucknett. Selden Society, vol. 66. London, 1951.

Britton, William Everett. *Handbook of the Law of Bills and Notes.* St Paul, Minn.: West Publishing Company, 1943.

Brown, William. *The Entring Clerk's Vade Mecum. Precedents for Declarations and Pleading in Most Actions.* London, 1678.

Brownlow, Richard. *Brownlow Latine Redivivus: A Book of Entries ...* London, 1693.

Declarations and Pleadings in English 2 pts. 1652, 1654.

Buck, Norman Sydney. *The Development of the Organization of Anglo-American Trade 1800–1850.* New Haven, Conn.: Yale University Press, 1925.

Buckley, H. 'Sir Thomas Gresham and the Foreign Exchanges'. *The Economic Journal* 34 (1924): 589–601.

Buller, Francis. *An Introduction to the Law relative to Trials at Nisi Prius.* 2nd edn. London, 1775.

Burgon, John William. *The Life and Times of Sir Thomas Gresham.* 2 vols. 1839. Reprint. New York: Burt Franklin, n.d.

Butterfield, H. *The Whig Interpretation of History.* London: G. Bell and Sons, 1931.

Byles, John Barnard. *A Practical Compendium of the Law of Bills of Exchange, Promissory Notes, Bankers' Cash-Notes, and Checks.* London, 1829.

A Treatise of the Law of Bills of Exchange, Promissory Notes, Bank-Notes and Checks. 8th edn. London: H. Sweet, 1862.

Calendar of Early Mayor's Court Rolls ... of the City of London, 1298–1307. Edited by A. H. Thomas. Cambridge: Cambridge University Press, 1924.

Calendar of Plea and Memoranda Rolls ... of the City of London, 1323–1482. Edited by A. H. Thomas and Philip E. Jones. 6 vols. Cambridge: Cambridge University Press, 1926–61.

Campbell, Lord John. *The Lives of the Chief Justices of England.* 2 vols. London: John Murray, 1849.

Cannan, Edwin, ed. *The Paper Pound of 1797–1821: A Reprint of the Bullion Report.* 2nd edn. London: P. S. King and Son, 1925. Reprint. London: Frank Cass and Company, 1969.

Carswell, John. *The South Sea Bubble.* London: Cresset Press, 1960.

Casus Placitorum and the Reports of Cases in the King's Court 1272–1278. Edited by W. H. Dunham, Jr. Selden Society, vol. 69. London, 1952.

Catterall, Ralph C. H. *The Second Bank of the United States.* Chicago: University of Chicago Press, 1903.

Chalmers, Sir Mackenzie. *A Digest of the Law of Bills of Exchange, Promissory Notes, and Cheques.* London, 1878.

Child, Sir Josiah. *Brief Observations concerning Trade and Interest of Money.* London, 1668. Reprinted in *Sir Josiah Child, Selected Works 1668–1697.* Gregg Press, Farnborough, Hants.

A New Discourse of Trade. London, 1693. Reprinted in *Sir Josiah Child, Selected Works 1668–1697.* Gregg Press, Farnborough, Hants.

Chitty, Joseph. *A Treatise on the Law of Bills of Exchange, Checks on Bankers, Promissory Notes, Bankers' Cash Notes, and Bank-Notes.* London, 1799.

A Practical Treatise on Bills of Exchange, Checks on Bankers, Promissory Notes, Bankers' Cash Notes, and Bank Notes. London: 4th edn 1811, 5th edn 1818.

Chitty, Joseph Jr. *A Practical Treatise on Bills of Exchange, Promissory Notes, and Bankers' Checks.* 2 vols. London: S. Sweet & Stevens and Sons, 1834.

Clapham, Sir John. *The Bank of England: A History.* 2 vols. Cambridge: Cambridge University Press, 1945.

Clark, Dorothy K. 'A Restoration Goldsmith-Banking House: The Vine on Lombard Street'. In *Essays in Modern English History in Honor of*

Wilbur Cortez Abbott. Cambridge, Mass.: Harvard University Press, 1941.

Clift, Henry. *A New Book of Declarations, Pleadings, Verdicts, Judgments and Judicial Writs; with the Entries thereupon.* 2nd edn. Digested by Charles Ingleby. London, 1719.

Coke, Edward. *The First Part of the Institutes of the Laws of England or, A Commentary upon Littleton.* 13th edn. London, 1788 (1st edn 1628).

The Fourth Part of the Institutes of the Laws of England. London, 1644. Reprint. Buffalo, N.Y.: William S. Hein Co., 1986.

Coleman, D. C. *The Economy of England 1450–1750.* London: Oxford University Press, 1977.

Coquillette, Daniel R. *The Civilian Writers of Doctors' Commons, London: Three Centuries of Juristic Innovation in Comparative, Commercial, and International Law.* Comparative Studies in Continental and Anglo-American Legal History, band 3. Berlin: Duncker & Humblot, 1988. Previously published in article form in *Boston University Law Review* 61 (1981): 1–89, 315–71; 67 (1987): 289–361, 877–970.

The Court Baron: Being Precedents for Use in Seignorial and Other Local Courts together with Select Pleas from the Bishops of Ely's Court of Littleport. Edited by F. W. Maitland and W. P. Baildon. Selden Society, vol. 4. London, 1891.

Cranch, William. Note appended to report of *Mandeville* v. *Riddle* (1803), 5 U.S. (1 Cranch) 367–466. Reprinted in part as 'Promissory Notes Before and After Lord Holt', in *Select Essays in Anglo-American Legal History*, 3: 72–97. 3 vols. Boston: Little, Brown & Co., 1907–09.

[Cunningham, Timothy.] *The Law of Bills of Exchange, Promissory Notes, Bank-Notes, and Insurances.* London, 1760.

Davies, Sir John. *The Question Concerning Impositions, Tonnage, Poundage, Prizage, Customs, and c.* London, 1656. Reprint. New York and London: Garland Publishing, 1979.

de Roover, Raymond. 'Cambium ad Venetias; Contribution to the History of Foreign Exchange'. In *Business, Banking, and Economic Thought in Late Medieval and Early Modern Europe: Selected Studies of Raymond de Roover* [hereinafter *BBET*], edited by J. Kirshner, 346–66. Chicago and London: University of Chicago Press, 1974.

'The Commercial Revolution of the Thirteenth Century'. *Bulletin of the Business History Society* 16 (1942): 34–39.

'Gerard de Malynes as an Economic Writer: From Scholasticism to Mercantilism'. In *BBET*, 346–66.

Gresham on Foreign Exchange: An Essay on Early English Mercantilism with the Text of Sir Thomas Gresham's Memorandum for the Understanding of the Exchange. Cambridge, Mass.: Harvard University Press, 1949.

Money, Banking and Credit in Mediaeval Bruges: Italian Merchant-Bankers, Lombards, and Money-Changers. Cambridge, Mass.: Mediaeval Academy of America, 1948.

'New Interpretations of the History of Banking'. In *BBET*, 200–38. Reprinted from *Journal of World History* 2 (1954): 38–76.

The Rise and Decline of the Medici Bank, 1397–1494. Cambridge, Mass.: Harvard University Press, 1963.

'What is Dry Exchange? A Contribution to the Study of English Mercantilism'. In *BBET*, 183–99. Reprinted from *The Journal of Political Economy* 52 (1944): 250–66.

Defoe, Daniel. *The Complete English Tradesman in Familiar Letters.* 2nd edn. 2 vols. London, 1727. Reprint. New York: Augustus M. Kelly, 1969 (1st edn 1726).

Dewar, M. 'The Memorandum "For the Understanding of the Exchange"': Its Authorship and Dating'. *Economic History Review*, 2nd ser. 17 (1965): 476–87.

Early Registers of Writs. Edited by Elsa de Haas and G. D. Hall. Selden Society, vol. 87. London, 1970.

Edwards, Michael M. *The Growth of the British Cotton Trade 1780–1815.* New York: Augustus M. Kelly, 1967; Manchester: Manchester University Press, 1967.

Ehrenberg, Richard. *Capital & Finance in the Age of the Renaissance; a Study of the Fuggers and their Connections.* Translated by H. M. Lucas. New York: Harcourt, Brace & Co., [1928].

Elder, Florence. 'The van der Molen, Commission Merchants of Antwerp: Trade with Italy, 1538–1544'. In *Medieval and Historiographical Essays in Honor of James Westfall Thompson*, edited by James. L. Cate and Eugene N. Anderson, 78–145. Chicago: University of Chicago Press, 1938.

Evans, William David. *Essays on the Action for Money Had and Received, on the Law of Insurances, and on the Law of Bills of Exchange and Promissory Notes.* Liverpool, 1802.

Ewart, John S. 'What is the Law Merchant?', *Columbia Law Review* 3 (1903): 135–54.

Exton, John. *The Maritime Dicaeologie, or Sea-Jurisdiction of England.* London, 1664

Feavearyear, Albert. *The Pound Sterling: A History of English Money.* 2nd edn. Revised by E. V. Morgan. Oxford: Clarendon Press, 1963.

Fenton, Roger. *A Treatise of Usurie.* London, 1611.

Fetter, Frank Whitson. *Development of British Monetary Orthodoxy, 1797–1875.* Cambridge, Mass.: Harvard University Press, 1965.

Fifoot, C. H. S. 'The Development of the Law of Negotiable Instruments and of the Law of Trusts'. *Journal of the Institute of Bankers* (1938): 433–56.

History and Sources of the Common Law: Tort and Contract. London: Stevens and Sons, 1949. Reprint. Westport, Conn.: Greenwood Press, 1970.

Lord Mansfield. Oxford: Clarendon Press, 1936.

Fitz-Herbert, A. *The New Natura Brevium.* 9th edn. 2 vols. London, 1794 (1st edn 1534).

Fleta. Edited by H. G. Richardson and G. O. Sayles. Selden Society, vols. 72, 89, 99. London, 1955, 1972, 1984.

Forbes, William. *A Methodical Treatise concerning Bills of Exchange.* 2nd edn. Edinburgh, 1718 (1st edn 1703).

Foss, Edward. *Biographia Juridica: A Biographical Dictionary of the Judges of England from the Conquest to the Present Time, 1066–1870.* London: John Murray, 1870.

Fusfeld, Daniel R. 'On the Authorship and Dating of "For the Understanding of the Exchange".' *The Economic History Review,* 2nd ser. 20 (1967): 145–52.

Glen, William. *A Treatise on the Law of Bills of Exchange, Promissory Notes, and Letters of Credit in Scotland.* Edinburgh, 1807.

Godolphin, John. *A View of the Admiralty Jurisdiction.* London, 1661.

Gras, N. S. B. *Business and Capitalism: An Introduction to Business History.* New York: F. S. Crofts and Co., 1939.

Grice-Hutchinson, Marjorie. *Early Economic Thought in Spain 1177–1740.* London: George Allen & Unwin, 1978.

The School of Salamanca: Readings in Spanish Monetary Theory 1544–1605. Oxford: Clarendon Press, 1952.

Hammond, Bray. *Banks and Politics in America from the Revolution to the Civil War.* Princeton, N.J.: Princeton University Press, 1957.

Hanham, Alison. *The Celys and Their World.* Cambridge: Cambridge University Press, 1985.

Harrington, Virginia D. *The New York Merchant on the Eve of the Revolution.* New York: Columbia University Press, 1935. Reprint. Gloucester, Mass.: Peter Smith, 1964.

Heckscher, Eli. 'Multilateralism, Baltic Trade, and the Mercantilists'. *Economic History Review,* 2nd ser. 3 (1951): 219–28.

Hening, Crawford Dawes. 'History of the Beneficiary's Action in Assumpsit'. In *Select Essays in Anglo-American Legal History,* 3: 339–67. 3 vols. Boston: Little, Brown & Co., 1907–09. Reprinted from *American Law Register,* o.s., 52 (1904): 764–79; 53 (1905): 112–27.

Herne, John. *The Pleader: Containing Perfect Presidents and Formes of Declarations, Pleadings, Issues, Judgments, and Proceedings.* London, 1657.

Heward, Edmund. *Lord Mansfield.* Chichester and London: Barry Rose, 1979.

'Lord Mansfield's Note Books'. *Law Quarterly Review* 92 (1976): 438–55.

Hidy, Ralph W. *The House of Baring in American Trade and Finance: English Merchant Bankers at Work 1763–1861.* Harvard Studies in Business History, no. 14. Cambridge, Mass.: Harvard University Press, 1949.

Hill, Christopher. *The Century of Revolution 1603–1714.* Edinburgh: Thomas Nelson and Sons, 1961.

Holden, J. Milnes. *The History of Negotiable Instruments in English Law.* London: University of London, The Athlone Press, 1955.

Holdsworth, W. S. *A History of English Law.* 16 vols. London, 1922–66.

Horsefield, J. Keith. *British Monetary Experiments 1650–1710.* London: G. Bell and Sons, 1960.

'The Duties of a Banker. I: The Eighteenth Century View'. In *Papers in*

English Monetary History, edited by T. S. Ashton and R. S. Sayers, 1–15. Oxford: Clarendon Press, 1953. Reprinted from *Economica* (February 1941).

Illingworth, William. *An Inquiry into the Laws, Antient and Modern, respecting Forestalling, Regrating, and Ingrossing.* London, 1800.

James, Marquis. *The Life of Andrew Jackson.* Indianapolis and New York: Bobbs-Merril Company, 1938.

Jenks, Edward. 'The Early History of Negotiable Instruments'. In *Select Essays in Anglo-American Legal History*, 3: 51–71. 3 vols. Boston: Little, Brown & Co., 1907–09. Reprinted from *Law Quarterly Review* 9 (1893): 70–85.

Johnson, E. A. J. *Predecessors of Adam Smith: The Growth of British Economic Thought.* New York: Prentice-Hall, 1937.

Jones, Norman. *God and the Moneylenders: Usury and Law in Early Modern England.* London: Basil Blackwell, 1989.

Joslin, D. M. 'London Private Bankers, 1720–1785'. *Economic History Review*, 2nd ser. 8 (1956): 167–86.

Justice, Alexander. *A General Treatise of the Dominion and Laws of the Sea.* London, 1705.

A General Treatise of Monies and Exchanges. London, 1707.

Kent, James. *Commentaries on American Law.* 4 vols. 1826–30. Reprint. New York: Da Capo Press, 1971.

Kerridge, Eric. *Trade and Banking in Early Modern England.* Manchester: Manchester University Press, 1988.

Kyd, Stewart. *A Treatise on the Law of Bills of Exchange and Promissory Notes.* London, 1790.

A Treatise on the Law of Bills of Exchange and Promissory Notes. 2nd American edn from 3rd London edn. Albany, N.Y., 1800.

Langdell, C. C. 'A Brief Survey of Equity Jurisprudence'. *Harvard Law Review* 2 (1889): 241–67.

Lex Mercatoria. In Bickley, Francis B., ed., *The Little Red Book of Bristol.* 2 vols. Bristol: Bristol Records Soc., 1900.

Lipson, E. *The Economic History of England.* Vol. 1, *The Middle Ages.* Rev. ed. London: Adam and Charles Black, 1937. Vols. 2 and 3, *The Age of Mercantilism.* London: Adam and Charles Black, 1931.

Lopez, Robert S., and Raymond, Irving W. *Medieval Trade in the Mediterranean World.* New York: Columbia University Press, 1955.

Lovelass, Peter. *A Full, Clear, and Familiar Explanation of the Law Concerning Bills of Exchange, Promissory Notes, and the Evidence on a Trial by Jury Relative thereto; A Description of Bank Notes and the Privilege of Attornies.* London, 1789.

Macaulay, Thomas Babington. *The History of England from the Accession of James II.* In *Macaulay's Complete Works.* 6 vols. People's Edition. Boston, Mass.: Estes and Lauriat, n.d.

Macdonell, Sir John. Introduction to *A Compendium of Mercantile Law*, by John W. Smith. 10th edn. London: Stevens and Sons, 1890.

Malynes, Gerard. *Consuetudo, vel, Lex Mercatoria: or, The Ancient Law-*

Merchant. 3rd edn. London, 1686. Reprint. Abingdon, England: Professional Books, 1981 (1st edn 1622).

A treatise of the Canker of England's Common wealth. London, 1601. Excerpted in *Tudor Economic Documents* 3: 386–404.

Mann, J. de L. *The Cloth Industry in the West of England from 1640 to 1880.* Oxford: Clarendon Press, 1971.

Manning, Edward Windham. *The Laws of Bills of Exchange, Promissory Notes, Bank-Notes, Bankers Notes, Drafts, and Checks.* London, 1801.

Marius, John. *Advice Concerning Bills of Exchange.* 4th edn. London, 1684 (1st edn 1651). Appended to Gerard Malynes, *Lex Mercatoria.* 3rd edn. London, 1686.

Maxwell, John I. *A Pocket Dictionary of the Law of Bills of Exchange, Promissory Notes, Bank Notes, Checks, and c.* London, 1802.

Mears, Thomas L. 'The History of the Admiralty Jurisdiction'. In *Select Essays in Anglo-American Legal History,* 2: 312–64. 3 vols. Boston: Little, Brown & Co., 1907–09.

Melton, Frank T. *Sir Robert Clayton and the Origins of English Deposit Banking, 1658–1685.* Cambridge: Cambridge University Press, 1986.

Miege, Guy. *The Ancient Sea-Laws of Oleron, Wisby, and the Hanse-Towns, Still in Force.* London, 1686. Appended to Gerard Malynes, *Lex Mercatoria.* 3rd edn. London, 1686.

Milsom, S. F. C. *Historical Foundations of the Common Law.* 2nd edn. Toronto: Butterworths, 1981.

'Reason in the Development of the Common Law'. In *Studies in the History of the Common Law,* 149–70. London: Hambleton Press, 1985. Reprinted from *Law Quarterly Review* 81 (1965): 496–517.

Mints, Lloyd W. *A History of Banking Theory in Great Britain and the United States.* Chicago: University of Chicago Press, 1945.

Molloy, Charles. *De Jure Maritimo et Navali: or, A Treatise of Affairs Maritime and of Commerce.* 4th edn. London, 1690 (1st edn 1676).

Muchmore, Lynn. 'Gerrard de Malynes and Mercantile Economics'. *History of Political Economy* 1 (1969): 336–58.

Mun, Thomas. *England's Treasure by Forraign Trade.* London, 1664. Reprint. Oxford: Basil Blackwell, 1949.

Munro, John H. 'Bullionism and the Bill of Exchange in England 1272–1663: A Study in Monetary Management and Popular Prejudice'. In *The Dawn of Modern Banking.* New Haven, Conn.: Yale University Press, 1979.

The New Palgrave: A Dictionary of Economics. Edited by John Eatwell, Murray Milgate, and Peter Newman. 4 vols. London: Macmillan Press, 1987; New York: Stockton Press, 1987.

Noonan, John T. *The Scholastic Analysis of Usury.* Cambridge, Mass.: Harvard University Press, 1957.

Novae Narrationes. Edited by Elsie Shanks, completed with introduction by S. F. C. Milsom. Selden Society, vol. 80. London, 1963.

O'Brien, D. P. *The Classical Economists.* Oxford: Clarendon Press, 1975.

Ogden, James Matlock. *The Law of Negotiable Instruments.* Chicago: Callaghan and Company, 1909.

Oldham, James. *The Mansfield Manuscripts and the Growth of English Law in the Eighteenth Century.* 2 vols. Chapel Hill and London: University of North Carolina Press, 1992.

Parsons, Theophilus. *A Treatise on the Law of Promissory Notes and Bills of Exchange.* 2 vols. Philadelphia: J. B. Lippincott and Company, 1863.

Plucknett, T. F. T. *A Concise History of the Common Law.* 5th edn. Boston: Little, Brown & Co., 1956.

Pollock, Frederick and Maitland, Frederic William. *The History of English Law before the Time of Edward I.* 2 vols. 2nd edn. London: Cambridge University Press, 1923.

Postan, M. M. 'Credit in Medieval Trade'. In *Medieval Trade and Finance.* Cambridge: Cambridge University Press, 1973. Reprinted from *Economic History Review* 1 (1928): 234–61.

'Private Financial Instruments in Medieval England'. In *Medieval Trade and Finance.* Cambridge: Cambridge University Press, 1973. Reprinted from *Vierteljahrschrift für Sozial- und Wirtschaftsgeschichte* 23 (1930): 26–75.

Postlethwayt, Malachy. *Universal Dictionary of Trade and Commerce.* 3rd edn. London, 1766 (1st edn 1751).

Power, E. E. 'The Wool Trade in the Fifteenth Century'. In *Studies in English Trade in the Fifteenth Century,* edited by Eileen Power and M. M. Postan, 39–90. London: George Routledge and Sons, 1933.

Pressnell, L. S. *Country Banking in the Industrial Revolution.* Oxford: Clarendon Press, 1956.

Prestwich, Michael. 'Italian Merchants in Late Thirteenth and Early Fourteenth Century England'. In *The Dawn of Modern Banking,* 77–104. New Haven, Conn.: Yale University Press, 1979.

Price, Jacob. 'Multilateralism and/or Bilateralism: the Settlement of British Trade Balances with "the North"', c. 1700'. *Economic History Review,* 2nd ser. 14 (1961): 254–74.

Prichard, M. J. and Yale, D. E. C. *Hale and Fleetwood on Admiralty Jurisdiction.* Selden Society, vol. 108. London, 1993.

Rastell, Wylliam. *Collecion of entrees, of declarations, barres, replicacions, rejoinders, issues ... and divers others matters.* London, 1566. (2nd edn. 1574, 3rd edn. 1596, 4th edn. 1670.)

Registrum Brevium tam Originalium, quam Judicialium. 4th edn. London, 1687.

Richards, R. D. *The Early History of Banking in England.* London: Frank Cass, 1958; New York: Kelly and Millman, 1958 (1st edn 1929).

Roberts, Lewes. *The Treasure of Traffike.* 1641. Reprinted in *Early English Tracts on Commerce,* edited by J. R. McCulloch. London, 1854. Reprint. Cambridge: Cambridge University Press, 1954.

The Merchants Map of Commerce wherein the Universal Manner and Matter of Trade is Compendiously Handled. 2nd edn. London, 1671. (1st edn 1638).

Rodgers, Christopher P. 'Continental Literature and the Development of the Common Law by the King's Bench: c. 1750–1800'. In *The Courts and the Development of Commercial Law*, edited by V. Piergiovanni, 161–93. Comparative Studies in Continental and Anglo-American Legal History, band 2. Berlin: Duncker & Humblot, 1987.

Rogers, James E. Thorold. *The First Nine Years of the Bank of England*. Oxford: Clarendon Press, 1887.

Rogers, James Steven. 'The Myth of Negotiability'. *Boston College Law Review* 31 (1990): 265–334.

 'Negotiability, Property, and Identity'. *Cardozo Law Review* 12 (1990): 471–508.

 'The Problem of Accommodation Bills: Banking Theory and The Law of Bills and Notes in the Early Nineteenth Century'. In *The Growth of the Bank as Institution and the Development of Money-Business Law*, edited by V. Piergiovanni, 119–55. Comparative Studies in Continental and Anglo-American Legal History, band 12. Berlin: Duncker & Humblot, 1993.

Rolle, John. *Pocket Companion to the Law of Bills of Exchange, Promissory Notes, Drafts, Checks and c.* 2nd edn. London, 1815.

Rolt, Richard. *A New Dictionary of Trade and Commerce*. London, 1756.

Salzman, L. F. *English Trade in the Middle Ages*. Oxford: Clarendon Press, 1931.

Santiago-Valiente, Wilfredo. 'Historical Background of the Classical Monetary Theory and the "Real-bills" Banking Tradition'. *History of Political Economy* 20 (1988): 43–63.

Savelli, Rudolfo. 'Between Law and Morals: Interest in the Dispute on Exchanges during the 16th Century'. In *The Courts and the Development of Commercial Law*, edited by V. Piergiovanni, 39–102. Comparative Studies in Continental and Anglo-American Legal History, band 2. Berlin: Duncker & Humblot, 1987.

Scarlett, John. *The Stile of Exchanges: Containing both their Law and Custom as Practised now in the most considerable places of Exchange in Europe*. London, 1682.

Schanz, Georg. *Englische Handelspolitik gegen ende des Mittelalters*. 2 vols. Leipzig: Verlag von Duncker & Humblot, 1881.

Scrutton, Sir Thomas Edward. *The Elements of Mercantile Law*. London: William Clowes and Sons, 1891.

Select Cases Concerning the Law Merchant. Edited by Charles Gross and Hubert Hall. Selden Society, vols. 23, 46, 49. London, 1908, 1930, 1932.

Select Pleas in the Court of Admiralty. Edited by R. G. Marsden. Selden Society, vols. 6, 11. London, 1894, 1897.

Select Cases in the Exchequer of Pleas. Edited by H. Jenkinson and B. Formoy. Selden Society, vol. 48. London, 1932.

Select Pleas in Manorial and other Seignorial Courts, Vol. 1, *Reigns of Henry III and Edward I*. Edited by F. W. Maitland. Selden Society, vol. 2. London, 1889.

Simpson, A. W. B. *A History of the Common Law of Contract: The Rise of the Action of Assumpsit*. Oxford: Clarendon Press, 1975.

Simpson, A. W. B., ed. *Biographical Dictionary of the Common Law.* London: Butterworths, 1984.

Smith, Adam. *An Inquiry into the Nature and Causes of the Wealth of Nations.* 2 vols. in 1. Chicago: University of Chicago Press, 1976 (1st edn 1776).

Smith, Walter Buckingham. *The Economic Aspects of the Second Bank of the United States.* 1953. Reprint. New York: Greenwood Press, 1969.

Sperling, J. 'The International Payments Mechanism in the Seventeenth and Eighteenth Centuries'. *Economic History Review,* 2nd ser. 14 (1961): 446–68.

Spufford, Peter. *Handbook of Medieval Exchange.* London: Royal Historical Society, 1986.

Statutes of the Realm. 11 vols. 1810. Reprint. London: Dawsons, 1963.

Stoljar, S. J. 'The Transformation of Account'. *Law Quarterly Review* 80 (1964): 203–24.

Street, Thomas Atkins. *The Foundations of Legal Liability: A Presentation of the Theory and Development of the Common Law.* 3 vols. Northport, N.Y.: Edward Thompson Company, 1906. Reprint. Littleton, Colo.: Fred B. Rothman and Company, 1980.

Supple, B. E. *Commercial Crisis and Change in England 1600–1642.* Cambridge: Cambridge University Press, 1959.

Sutherland, L. Stuart. 'The Law Merchant in England in the Seventeenth and Eighteenth Centuries'. *Transactions of the Royal Historical Society* 17 (1934): 149–76.

Tate, William. *The Modern Cambist; forming a manual of Foreign Exchanges.* 2nd edn. London, 1834.

Tawney, R. H. Historical Introduction to *A Discourse upon Usury* ... *[1572],* by Thomas Wilson. New York: Harcourt, Brace and Company, 1925.

Teetor, Paul R. 'England's Earliest Treatise on the Law Merchant'. *American Journal of Legal History* 6 (1962): 178–210.

Thornton, Henry. *An Enquiry into the Nature and Effects of the Paper Credit of Great Britain (1802).* Edited by F. A. v. Hayek. London: George Allen and Unwin, 1939. Reprint. New York: Augustus M. Kelly, 1965.

Tisdall, John. *Laws and Usages Respecting Bills of Exchange and Promissory Notes.* Philadelphia, 1795.

Tudor Economic Documents: Being Select Documents Illustrating the Economic and Social History of Tudor England, edited by R. H. Tawney and Eileen Power. 3 vols. London: Longmans, Green and Company, 1924.

Unwin, George. *Industrial Organization in the Sixteenth and Seventeenth Centuries.* Oxford: Clarendon Press, 1904.

Usher, A. P. *The Early History of Deposit Banking in Mediterranean Europe.* Harvard Economic Studies, vol. 75. Cambridge, Mass.: Harvard University Press, 1943.

van der Wee, Herman. 'Anvers et les innovations de la technique financière aux XVIe et XVIIe siècles'. *Annales Economies, Sociétés, Civilizations* 22 (1967): 1067–89.

Vidian, Andrew. *The Exact Pleader: A Book of Entries of Choice, Select and Special Pleadings in the Court of the King's-Bench in the Reign of His Present Majesty Charles II.* London, 1684.

Viner, Charles. *General Abridgment of Law and Equity.* 23 vols. London, 1741–53.

Viner, Jacob. *Studies in the Theory of International Trade.* New York and London: Harper & Brothers, 1937.

Wadsworth, Alfred P., and Mann, Julia de Lacy. *The Cotton Trade and Industrial Lancashire 1600–1780.* 1931. Reprint. Manchester: Manchester University Press, 1965.

[Welwood, W.] *A Collection of all Sea-Laws.* n.d. Appended to Gerard Malynes, *Lex Mercatoria.* 3rd edn. London, 1686.

Westerfield, Ray B. *Middlemen in English Business, Particularly between 1660 and 1700.* New Haven, Conn.: Yale University Press, 1915. Reprint. New York: Augustus M. Kelly, 1968.

White, James J. and Summers, Robert S. *Uniform Commercial Code,* 3rd edn. St Paul, Minn.: West Publishing Co., 1988.

Whitney, Frederick A. *Outline of Bills and Notes.* Brooklyn, New York: St John's University Press, 1948.

Willan, T. S. 'The Factor or Agent in Foreign Trade'. In *Studies in Elizabethan Foreign Trade,* 1–33. Manchester: Manchester University Press, 1959. Reprint. New York: Augustus M. Kelly, 1968.

The Inland Trade: Studies in English Internal Trade in the Sixteenth and Seventeenth Centuries. Manchester: Manchester University Press, 1976; Totowa, N. J.: Rowman and Littlefield, 1976.

Wilson, Charles. *Anglo-Dutch Commerce and Finance in the Eighteenth Century.* Cambridge: Cambridge University Press, 1941.

England's Apprenticeship 1603–1763. 2nd edn. London and New York: Longman, 1984.

'Treasure and Trade Balances'. *Economic History Review,* 2nd ser. 2 (1949): 152–61.

'Treasure and Trade Balances: Further Evidence'. *Economic History Review,* 2nd ser. 4 (1951): 231–42.

Wilson, Thomas. *A Discourse upon Usury . . . [1572].* Edited by R. H. Tawney. New York: Harcourt, Brace and Company, 1925.

Woodman, Harold D. *King Cotton and his Retainers; Financing and Marketing the Cotton Crop of the South, 1800–1925.* Lexington, Ky.: University of Kentucky Press, 1968.

Wynne, William. *The Life of Sir Leoline Jenkins.* 2 vols. London, 1724.

Zouch, Richard. *The Jurisdiction of the Admiralty of England Asserted.* London, 1663. A later printing, dated 1686, was appended to Gerard Malynes, *Lex Mercatoria.* 3rd edn. London, 1686.

recognizances 181
regrating 103
ricorsa bills 40
Roberts, Lewes 94–95, 96, 97

Scaccia, Sigismundo 151
Scarlett, John 98
Scots law 160–63
sea loan 52–53, 134
Smith, Adam 228–29
Soto, Dominic 72
specialty 179
storekeepers, payments through
   110–11

Straccha, Benvenuto 151

tally 29, 30–31
tax collectors, use of bills 105–6
Thornton, Henry 95, 99
Tower of London, mint 118

usance 38
usury 70–74, 89–90, 190

wager of law 23–24, 31
Wilson, Thomas 70, 72, 75, 91–92

Zouch, Richard 156, 159

Davies, Sir John 154, 155–58
de Roover, Raymond 36, 83
debt, action of 13–15, 181–82
Defoe, Daniel 106, 113, 226
discounting *see* bills of exchange
dry exchange *see* exchange transactions

Eldon, Lord 242–43
engrossing 103
exchange transactions
    actions on, in Admiralty Court
        51–54
    actions on, in Chancery Court 56
    actions on, in common law courts
        54–68
    actions on, in mercantile courts
        44–51
    balance of trade 86–88
    deliverer 34
    dry exchange 72–74, 79, 89
    fictitious exchange 72–74
    four parties 34, 94–95, 97–98, 106
    funds transfer by use of 32–36
    interest rate 37–40
    king's exchangers 76–77, 81, 84, 87
    lending by use of 36–40
    per viam excambii, meaning of 61
    profits speculative 71
    public policy concerning 75–88
    rechange 39
    ricorsa bills 40
    Royal Commissions on Exchanges
        37–40, 82–84
    taker 34
    usance 38
    usury 70–74, 89–93, 161–62
Eyre, Sir James 235–36, 240, 244, 248,
    249

factors 33–34, 102–8
fictitious exchange *see* exchange
    transactions
fictitious payees *see* accommodation
    bills
foenus nauticum see sea loan
Forbes, William 160–63
forestalling 103

goldsmiths 116–20, 175–77, 178
Gresham, Richard 81
Gresham, Sir Thomas 40, 83, 90

Holden, J. Milnes 46, 66, 194

Holt, John, Chief Justice King's Bench
    173, 177–86, 202–3, 218

indorsement *see* bills of exchange

Jackson, Andrew 205
Jenks, Edward 10

Kyd, Stewart 6–9, 236–37

law merchant
    civilian literature 151–53
    incorporation theory 1–4, 65–68,
        147–50, 160–63, 164–69, 219–20,
        250–52
    medieval, in common law courts
        27–31
    medieval, in mercantile courts 20–27
    partisan rhetoric 153–60
    Scots law 160–63
    see also custom of merchants
Livesey, Hargreaves & Co. 223–24,
    226–27, 233–37
London
    bills on 106–8, 111–12, 121–22
    growth of 107
    Mayor's Court 21, 41, 44–51

Malynes, Gerard 84–85
    economic theory 85–88, 90–91, 92
    Lex Mercatoria (1622) 84, 88–89,
        170
    on law merchant 153–54, 155
manorial courts 25–27
Mansfield, James, Chief Justice
    Common Pleas 239
Mansfield, Lord (William Murray),
    Chief Justice King's Bench 2,
    187–88, 189–90, 200, 204, 206–7,
    210–22
Marius, John 89, 98, 121, 170
mercantile courts *see* law merchant
merchant jury 26, 28, 29, 211–12
Merchants of the Staple 34
Misselden, Edward 85, 87
Mun, Thomas 85, 87

negotiability *see* bona fide holder

piedpowder courts 22
promissory notes 177–86, 215–18

real bills banking theory 228–32

INDEX

acceptance *see* bills of exchange
acceptance finance 112–14, 199–201
accommodation bills 223–27
    bankruptcy treatment of 241–43
    consideration, proof of 241, 244
    fictitious payee cases 233–37
    judicial attitude toward 232–45
    notice of dishonour 240, 243–44
    suretyship defences 238–39
account, action of 15–20, 30
Admiralty Court 51–54, 158–60
Armstrong, Clement 79–81, 83, 90
assumpsit, action of 56–68

Baker, J. H. 15, 21, 55, 132, 136
balance of trade *see* exchange
    transactions
bank notes 120, 175–77, 187–88, 202–5
Bank of England 120–21, 230–31,
    247–48
banking
    development of, seventeenth century
    116–24
    theory of, nineteenth century 228–32
    see also goldsmiths
Bayley, John 6–9
bearer, instruments payable to 46–47,
    173–77
Beutel, Frederick K. 46, 174
bills of debt, transfer of 184–85
bills of exchange
    acceptance 195–201
    consideration presumed 7, 241
    delay in presentment and notice of
        dishonour 202–10, 240, 243–44
    discounting 95, 121–22
    earliest action on 136
    financing by use of 112–16, 224–27
    illegality, defence of 190
    indorsement 112, 126–27, 170–73

inland bills 101–8
legal treatises on 6–9, 96–97
obligations of parties 125–37
payment by use of 109–12
pleadings in actions on 127–37
procedure in actions on 144–47
Scots law 160–63
see also acceptance finance,
    accommodation bills, bona fide
    holder, exchange transactions
Blackwell Hall 104–5
bona fida holder 2–11, 186–93, 194–95
bonds, sealed 14, 181
bottomry *see* sea loan
Braudel, Fernand 32, 33
bullion, export prohibited 75–79
Bullionists *see* banking
Byles, John Barnard 6–9

Champagne fairs 36
cheques 119, 175
Chitty, Joseph 6–9
Chitty, Joseph, Jr 5
chose in action, assignment 2–3, 172
civil law 151–53, 158–60
coinage 75–76, 118
commenda 19
commission merchants 33, 102–8, 191
consideration 181–82, 200
Coquillette, Daniel R. 158–59
covenant, action of 14–15
Cranch, Judge William 66
custom of merchants 1–2, 137–50,
    164–69
    allegation of in actions on bills 127–37
    custom of the realm, akin to 141–44
    not limited to merchants 139–40,
        143, 182
    special custom, distinguished from
        138–44

265